Stochastic Dominance

Stochastic Dominance

An Approach to Decision-Making Under Risk

Edited by
G.A. Whitmore
McGill University
M.C. Findlay
University of Southern California

Lexington Books
D.C. Heath and Company
Lexington, Massachusetts
Toronto

Library of Congress Cataloging in Publication Data

Main entry under title:

Stochastic dominance.

Bibliography: p.
Includes index.
1. Finance—Mathematical models. 2. Investments—Mathematical models. 3. Statistical decision. 4. Stochastic processes. I. Whitmore, G.A. II. Findlay, M. Chapman.
HG174.S76 332′.01′51 76-55111
ISBN 0-669-01310-2

Published simultaneously in Canada

Printed in the United States of America

International Standard Book Number: 0-669-01310-2

Library of Congress Catalog Card Number: 76-55111

Contents

List of Figures

List of Tables

Preface

This book has resulted from the writing efforts of several people and the research contributions of scores. As a theoretical concept in decision-making under risk, stochastic dominance (SD) is very old, but in terms of formal theoretical development and applications it is quite new.

The catalyst for this book was a Stochastic Dominance Symposium held during April 1974 under the auspices of the Faculty of Management, McGill University, Montreal. The coeditors organized the symposium with the intent of bringing together several of the key contributors to this field for a discussion of existing theory and applications of SD and potential future developments. The participants in the symposium were Roger P. Bey, Richard C. Burgess, M. Chapman Findlay, Peter C. Fishburn, Josef Hadar, R. Burr Porter, William R. Russell, Raymond G. Vickson, G.A. Whitmore, and W.T. Ziemba. The participants agreed that because SD was a new topic the symposium should not produce the usual published proceedings. Instead it was decided to draft collectively an integrated treatise on SD with sections contributed by and identified with specific participants. The coeditors' role, quite naturally, was to coordinate the individual efforts of participants, welding together their contributions and editing the full manuscript. The authors of the different sections of the book are identified in the chapter and section headings.

The book is intended to serve as a reference text on SD, although we know that it does not cover every topic published on the subject. To our knowledge, the bibliography is the most extensive one to be published as of the beginning of 1978. A number of topics presented in the book are published here for the first time; others are so new that many readers will be unfamiliar with them. The topical organization of the book is described in Chapter 1. In addition, editorial comments have been added at the beginning of each chapter to summarize that chapter's role in the overall plan of the book and to describe its scope and relationship to other work in the field. The last chapter section contains a discussion of the strengths and weaknesses of SD methodology as it presently exists, the areas of greatest need as far as future research is concerned, and the prospects for additional applications.

The book may be used in a variety of ways. All readers will want to read the introduction in the first section of Chapter 1, the discussion of theoretical foundations in Chapter 2 (the less mathematically inclined may want to omit the two appendixes in this chapter), and the concluding remarks in the last section of Chapter 8. Sections 1.2 and 1.3 present basic concepts in decision theory and portfolio theory for the reader who wishes a brief overview of one or both of these topics before proceeding to subsequent chapters. There is considerable independence among the remaining chapters, and each may be read or not as the reader's interests dictate. Chapters 3, 4, 5, and 6 are devoted to finance applications. Specifically, Chapters 3 and 4 describe empirical portfolio studies that employ SD methodology. Chapter 5 is concerned with computational aspects of optimal portfolio selection (and is not recommended to the nonmathematical reader). Chapter 6 is devoted to empirical and theoretical studies in financial management and capital markets that draw on SD analysis. Chapter 7 presents applications of SD in economic theory and analysis. Finally, the first two sections of Chapter 8 are devoted to additional topics, convex stochastic dominance, and statistical tests for SD, respectively.

Scholars and students in finance, economics, and other areas of the social sciences concerned with decision-theoretic methodology will find the book to be an invaluable research aid. Some instructors may wish to assign the book as supplemental reading for elective graduate courses and seminars. The organization and coverage of the book are ideally suited to the user who wants a cohesive and logical treatment of the subject without having to assemble and comb through the diverse published sources of the original works. An index has been provided to assist the reader in finding selected definitions, theorems, and other topics in the book. As mentioned already, researchers and students alike will find the extensive bibliography invaluable.

This book has been published with the help of a grant from the Social Science Federation of Canada, using funds provided by the Canada Council. We thank these organizations for their financial support.

The publication of this book also has required the assistance and encouragement of many other parties. D.C. Heath and Company are singled out for special thanks for seeing the manuscript through its various production stages. The reviewers are thanked for their valuable suggestions on the manuscript. We also thank Dean S. Shapiro of the Faculty of Management of McGill University, who made funds available to sponsor the symposium. The manuscript could not have been produced without the assistance of competent secretarial staff who helped each of the contributors. Katherine Ko and Teresa Moss, in particular, have the deep gratitude of all for providing so much help at various stages of the project. Khuzem Kaka has our thanks for his assistance in checking the bibliography. The coeditors extend their thanks to the individual contributors for their invaluable efforts and, seemingly, infinite patience with the editorial process. Last, and most important, thanks go to loved ones who had to stand aside for great lengths of time while attention was devoted to the book.

1 Introduction

G.A. Whitmore and *M.C. Findlay*

1.1 Introduction and Overview

1.1.1 Introductory Remarks

Decision-making is as old as the human race and, indeed, some might distinguish people from other creatures by their ability to introspect on their preferences and make choices in decision problems. The study of decision-making both as a phenomenon of empirical interest and as a deductive science is centuries, and perhaps, millennia, old. As is true in other subjects, however, this century has seen the systematization and axiomatization of the subject. This book is concerned with one methodological segment of decision theory: what we have chosen to call dominance criteria, or more precisely, stochastic dominance criteria. The advanced aspects of this concept are relatively new, and the purpose of the book is to expose both researchers and practitioners in different fields to the potential contributions of dominance methodology.

We recognize that readers come to this book with diverse backgrounds, which is why two review sections are included in this chapter. Section 1.2 reviews basic concepts in decision theory and Section 1.3 reviews the fundamentals of portfolio theory. Neither review was written as a comprehensive treatise on the subject matter, but each should be adequate to acquaint the unfamiliar reader with terminology and basic theoretic results. Readers familiar with decision and portfolio theory may want to omit both sections and proceed to Chapter 2 after reading the remainder of this introductory section.

1.1.2 Historical Notes and Comments on the Organization of the Book

In its simplest form, the concept of dominance has been part of decision theory so long that it is difficult to pinpoint its origin. The concept, although not always identified by the name "dominance," is found in diverse branches of the social and mathematical sciences. In classical economic theory, the concept is widely used in discussions of productive efficiency, consumption, and commodity exchange. A number of social welfare criteria such as Pareto optimality also have their roots in the notion of dominance. In statistical decision-making, hypothesis-testing, and estimation, the dominance principle arises in such properties as a uniformly most powerful test. In finance, almost all arbitrage and state preference arguments involve dominance principles.

Basic Theorems. The modern theoretical treatment of dominance begins with Masse (1962), Quirk and Saposnik (1962), and Fishburn (1964). Fishburn in particular set the subject on a solid conceptual foundation and derived numerous theoretical results, many of which are still being rediscovered. Since 1969, there has been a virtual explosion of developments. Chapter 2 summarizes the important theoretical advances in the subject since 1962, presenting the basic concepts, principal theorems, and other relevant theoretical discussion.

Portfolio Decision Problem. The major areas of application of dominance concepts have been finance and economics. In finance, the catalyst for the research has been the portfolio problem. A variety of approaches to the portfolio problem have been proposed in the finance and economic literature, the most famous being that of Markowitz (1959).

Dominance principles have an important role in understanding and solving the portfolio problem. Further, in spite of its specialized structure, decision problems of the portfolio type are pervasive in finance, insurance, economics, and related areas. For this reason, several chapters and chapter sections are devoted to dominance theory and applications related to the portfolio problem. Chapter 3 reviews a number of empirical studies that have employed dominance methodology. In Chapter 4, results of a simulation study, which draws on dominance concepts to compare mean-variance and mean-semivariance portfolio models, are presented. Chapter 5 deals with computational aspects of optimal portfolio construction; specifically, it is concerned with a comparison of mean-dispersion and dominance approaches to the portfolio problem. Finally, one section of Chapter 7 is concerned with portfolio diversification in the context of economic theory.

Other Applications in Finance and Economics. Dominance concepts have found and are continuing to find numerous applications in economics and finance in addition to their contribution to solving the portfolio problem. Chapters 6 and 7 contain a discussion of these applications. Specifically, Chapter 6 is concerned with financial management applications in areas such as capital budgeting and financial intermediation, and with applications in investigations of capital market efficiency. Chapter 7 looks at applications in economic theory and analysis.

Additional Topics. Although applications to date have been largely in economics and finance, this is more the result of uneven research interests than any inherent limitation of the methodology. Chapter 8 explores extensions of the dominance principle to other areas. The chapter also draws attention to a number of unexplored aspects of the methodology (of both a theoretical and applied nature) and to a number of inherent weaknesses of procedures based on dominance concepts.

Bibliography. The book ends with the presentation of a very complete list of references to the dominance literature. This book has drawn heavily, if not totally, on the works cited in the bibliography. References to the bibliography are given throughout the book in context, so no attempt will be made at this point to give summary comments about the literature.

1.2 Review of Decision Theory

1.2.1 The Traditional Decision Model

By definition, a decision involves a choice among alternative courses of action offering different consequences. To make a choice, the decision-maker must apply some criterion or valuation principle to the consequences to identify the alternative with the most desirable consequence. Having selected the best course of action, the decision-maker implements the action and the decision becomes historical.

Decision-making is an ongoing and virtually continuous activity. It determines the nature of our existence and is unavoidable. Even indecision is implicit decision-making, for choosing to do nothing is a choice to continue one's present course of action. Given the significance of decision-making, social scientists have built an abstract model of the decision problem so the phenomenon can be studied scientifically both from descriptive and normative viewpoints.

Decision Table. Figure 1-1 displays a decision problem in its simplest form, as a decision table. Each row of the table represents a feasible course of action or act for the decision-maker. A_i denotes the *i*th course of action. In all, there are m courses of action from which the decision-maker must choose one. The consequence of an act is generally uncertain. One useful way of viewing this uncertainty is to specify a set of outcome states or states of the world that may prevail after the decision-maker has selected the course of action for implementation. In Figure 1-1, S_j denotes the *j*th outcome state. It is assumed that one and only one of the n outcome states will ultimately prevail. Finally, each act entails some consequence that varies according to the outcome state that occurs. In Figure 1-1, C_{ij} denotes the consequence to the decision-maker of selecting act A_i when outcome state S_j eventually happens.

Examples. Although not all decision problems can be set in the framework of such a decision table, it is not difficult to imagine many

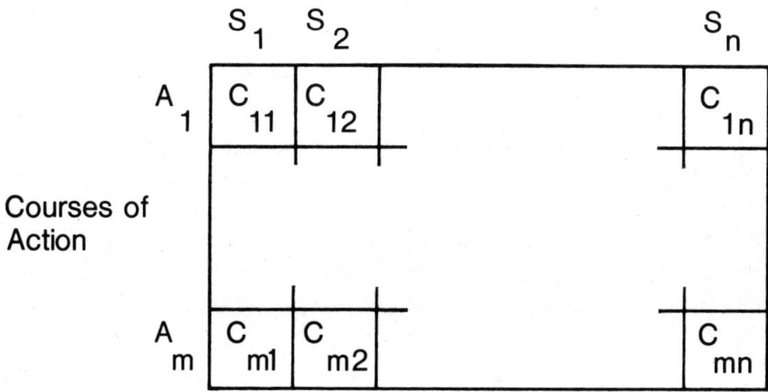

Figure 1-1. The Traditional Model of a Decision Problem

practical examples that can be described approximately by such a table. Several are presented here as illustrations.

Insurance. A decision-maker must choose among several insurance policies (including a policy of self-insurance). The outcome states correspond to different events that may happen to the insured's property or life over the term of the policy. The consequence C_{ij} represents his net financial position given he chooses policy i and event j occurs.

Security portfolio. An investor selects a given mix of securities for his personal portfolio. The outcome states describe the various investment climates that may prevail over the period during which this particular mix will be held. The consequence C_{ij} represents the terminal portfolio value of security mix i when investment climate j prevails.

Medical care. A patient must decide whether he will authorize his physician to perform an operation or not. The outcome states describe the degrees of success of the operation. The consequences represent the impact of the decision on the patient's health and economic circumstances.

Elements of a Decision. It would be naive to suggest that the decision table in Figure 1-1 provides an adequate framework for the study of all decision problems. It is simply a device used by decision theorists to highlight the basic elements of a decision problem. We now turn to a discussion of some practical considerations related to each of these elements.

Courses of action. Figure 1-1 presents the courses of action of a decision problem as an explicit, finite list of alternatives. In what ways is this formulation an abstraction of reality? In some decision problems, a very large number--or even an infinity--of alternatives is available to the decision-maker. In such problems, a description of the alternatives in a mathematical form may allow the numerous courses of action to be evaluated effectively. In other cases, though, the decision-maker may simply prepare a short list of alternatives from among all he might formulate and consider only these. The term bounded rationality is frequently used to describe the limited ability of a person to formulate decision problems in their totality. People have neither the time, the energy, nor the interest to search out all the possible courses of action in a decision problem. They consider the more obvious and potentially attractive alternatives and ignore the rest.

Outcome states. Like alternative courses of action, the outcome states of a decision problem are also frequently very large or infinite in number. Where a mathematical formulation allows one to consider the entire set of outcomes together, the decision problem may still be tractable. In many decision problems, however, bounded rationality limits attention to a few outcome states that are the most relevant to the decision problem.

Decision problems are frequently classified by the statistical character of the outcome states. If only a single outcome state can possibly prevail (at least for all practical purposes), the consequence of the decision problem is completely determined by the course of action selected. Thus this situation is often described as _decision-making under certainty_. If two or more outcome states are possible with differing consequences contingent on which outcome state prevails, the decision problem is said to involve risk or uncertainty. _Decision-making under risk_ is the term reserved for decision problems in which the decision-maker is prepared to associate a probability measure with the outcome states, i.e., he is willing to specify a probability of occurrence for each outcome state. _Decision-making under uncertainty_, on the other hand, is the term used when no probability measure is associated with the outcome states. There is some argument among researchers about whether a well-formulated decision problem ever would involve decision-making under uncertainty (as opposed to risk). Without taking a position on this argument, throughout this book we will devote attention only to decision problems that have probabilities assigned to the outcome states.

Thus far it has been assumed implicitly that the outcome states describe eventualities that for all practical purposes are outside the control of rational individuals, including the decision-maker. In some decision problems, though, the outcome states are partially or totally controlled by an individual or group of individuals pursuing their own interests. Decision problems of this type are often called _games_.

Consequences. To be totally accurate in formulating a decision problem, one would describe each consequence in great detail--perhaps going so far as to write a scenario. But again, bounded rationality dictates a more practical approach; consequences are usually described as simply as possible. The following simple rules might be used as guides in formulating consequences:

1. Any element that is found in every consequence of a decision problem will be irrelevant in deciding which act should be selected and therefore need not be considered explicitly.

2. Any element that neither contributes to nor subtracts from the desirability of a consequence can be omitted from consideration. Further, if an element has an insignificant effect on the

desirability of a consequence relative to other elements under consideration, for all practical purposes it can be ignored.

The consequences, even expressed in simple terms, may take diverse forms. They may involve quantitative factors, such as money or time, or qualitative factors, such as survival or taste. Since the decision problems with which we shall be concerned involve probabilistic outcome states, it is convenient to view the consequences of each course of action as a lottery or gamble that offers various objects or consequences with specified probabilities. For example, in the notation of Figure 1-1, course of action A_i is the equivalent of a lottery L_i where

$$L_i = \begin{bmatrix} C_{i1} & C_{i2} & \cdots & C_{in} \\ \\ p_{i1} & p_{i2} & \cdots & p_{in} \end{bmatrix} . \quad (1.1)$$

Here p_{ij} denotes the probability that outcome state S_j will prevail and, since course of action A_i has been selected, the consequence will be C_{ij} with this probability. By definition,

$$\sum_{j=1}^{n} p_{ij} = 1$$

for all i and $p_{ij} \geq 0$ for all (i,j). Each probability p_{ij} has two subscripts to show that it may depend not only on the outcome state j but also perhaps on the act i selected by the decision-maker. The term prospect is also used to describe the lottery associated with a course of action. A certain prospect or certain lottery is one that offers a single consequence with certainty, i.e., with probability one.

Decision-maker. The decision-maker is not always a single individual. In fact, much of decision theory has evolved as the result of the need to evaluate decisions faced by groups of individuals or organizations. If the preferences among different consequences are similar for all individuals in a group or organization, the group or organization can be viewed as a single decision-making entity. If, on the other hand, the preferences of group members are disparate, the decision analysis becomes more complicated. In fact, the simple decision structure of Figure 1-1 breaks down in this case, and it is meaningless to speak of a decision-maker as if the choice of an act is being made by a unitary entity. This latter case forms the basis of group decision theory.

Criterion of choice. The selection of a criterion of choice is perhaps the most difficult element of a decision problem. We turn to it now.

1.2.2 Preference Concepts and Utility Theory

As described in the previous section, in decision-making under risk, a lottery L_i is associated with each course of action A_i. The role of a criterion of choice is to identify the most desirable lottery and consequently the best act of the decision problem.

Utility. As a general approach to the criterion-of-choice problem, decision theorists have found it useful to quantify the desirability of a lottery. The measure they have chosen is called utility. The utility value of a lottery is a real number that represents the relative desirability of the lottery. For instance, consider two lotteries L_1 and L_2 with associated utility values $u(L_1)$ and $u(L_2)$. The relative magnitudes of $u(L_1)$ and $u(L_2)$ are interpreted as follows:

a. $u(L_1) > u(L_2)$ means L_1 is preferred to L_2,
b. $u(L_1) = u(L_2)$ means L_1 and L_2 are equally desirable. (1.2)
c. $u(L_1) < u(L_2)$ means L_2 is preferred to L_1.

Thus the concept of utility is nothing more than an association of lotteries (of whatever description) with real numbers in such a way that the larger the utility value of a lottery, the more desired is the lottery. Stated more formally, if $\mathcal{L}$ is a set of lotteries each defined over a fixed set of consequences and R is the set of real numbers, then u is a function mapping L into R. The assignment of utility values to lotteries is shown in Figure 1-2.

Utility maximization. If L_i is the lottery associated with act A_i in a decision problem, then the relative desirability of the act is measured by the utility value of its lottery, i.e., by $u(L_i)$. Since the best act is the one with the most desirable lottery, it follows from the definition of utility that the best act is the one for which $u(L_i)$ is a maximum. This is the most general criterion of choice in decision theory, and, by definition, it encompasses all others. It is called the criterion of utility maximization.

Complete ordering axiom. Certain conditions must hold before utility values can represent the relative desirabilities of different lotteries. Several of these are expressed in the following axiom, called the complete ordering axiom. This axiom must hold for the criterion of utility maximization to be valid.

> Complete Ordering Axiom: The preferences of the decision maker among the lotteries of L satisfy the following two conditions:
>
> a. For all pairs L_1, $L_2 \in L$, the decision-maker either prefers L_1 to L_2, L_2 to L_1, or is indifferent between them. Only one of these three possibilities is true for any pair of consequences. (1.3)
>
> b. If for any L_1, L_2, $L_3 \in L$, the decision-maker prefers L_1 as much as L_2 and L_2 as much as L_3, then he prefers L_1 as much as L_3.

The first condition of the axiom guarantees that the decision-maker's preferences for lotteries are not vague. He knows when one lottery is preferred to another or when two lotteries are equally desirable. The second condition in the axiom guarantees that preferences for more than two lotteries are consistent with preferences for pairs of lotteries. Preferences satisfying the second condition of the complete-ordering axiom are transitive. If

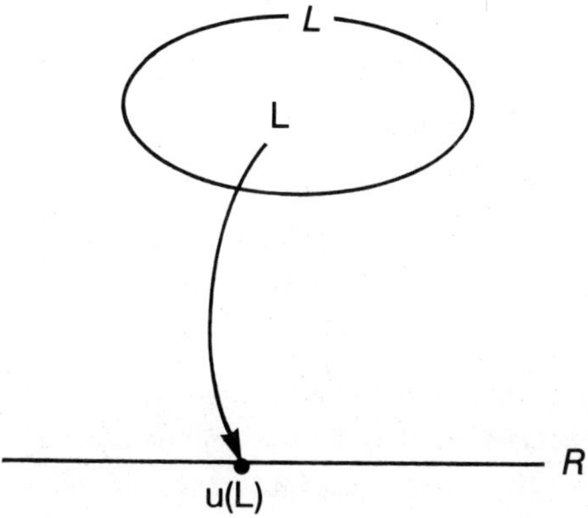

Figure 1-2. Mapping of Lotteries into Utility Values

preferences violate this condition, they are <u>intransitive</u>.

In precise mathematical terms, the complete ordering axiom requires that set L be totally ordered by the preference relation. Subsequently, the symbol $\geq_p$ will denote the preference relation ($>_p$ will denote strict preference and $=_p$ will denote indifference). From the way in which utility has been defined, we have the following equivalences:

$$\begin{aligned} &\text{a.}\quad u(L_1) \geq u(L_2) \text{ if and only if } L_1 \geq_p L_2,\\ &\text{b.}\quad u(L_1) > u(L_2) \text{ if and only if } L_1 >_p L_2,\\ &\text{c.}\quad u(L_1) = u(L_2) \text{ if and only if } L_1 =_p L_2. \end{aligned} \tag{1.4}$$

<u>Expected Utility Criterion</u>. The <u>maximum expected utility criterion</u> is one of the most significant contributions to utility theory to date. It was first proposed by Daniel Bernoulli about 1730, proved by Frank Ramsey in 1931, and independently proved again by John von Neumann and Oskar Morgenstern in 1947. More than any of the others, von Neumann and Morgenstern's published work introduced the expected utility concept to decision theory.

The maximum expected utility criterion is a rule that yields a utility value for a lottery in terms of (1) the utility values of the basic outcomes that constitute the lottery and (2) their associated probabilities. Specifically, consider any lottery L of the following general form:

$$L = \begin{bmatrix} O_1 & O_2 & \cdots & O_n \\ p_1 & p_2 & \cdots & p_n \end{bmatrix}.$$

Here $O_1, O_2, \ldots, O_n$ are n consequences, amounts, or objects, any one of which may be realized as the outcome of the lottery with probabilities $p_1, p_2, \ldots, p_n$, respectively. If $u(O_1), u(O_2), \ldots, u(O_n)$ are the utility values of the n objects, then the maximum expected utility criterion states that the utility value of lottery L, u(L), is given by

$$u(L) = p_1u(O_1) + p_2u(O_2) + \ldots + p_nu(O_n). \tag{1.5}$$

Formula (1.5) makes it clear why the criterion is called the "expected utility" criterion--the utility value of a lottery is equal to the expected utility value of the outcomes it comprises.

The maximum expected utility criterion is applicable to any decision problem involving consequences that are lotteries (i.e., the case of decision-making under risk) if the decision-maker is prepared to make decisions consistent with the expected utility axioms, which are discussed in the next section. Before that, a simple decision problem is used to illustrate criterion (1.5).

Illustration. A manufacturer is sending a shipment by sea to a foreign country. For simplicity, assume that the shipment either will arrive safely with probability .99 or will be a total loss with probability .01. The manufacturer will receive $20,000 if the shipment arrives safely. He can insure the shipment for its full value for $300, and he must now decide whether to purchase the insurance. The acts and consequences of this decision problem are shown in Table 1-1. Note that if he does purchase the insurance, he

Table 1-1
Insurance Purchase Decision

Acts	Outcome States and Probabilities	
	S_1 (shipment arrives safely)	S_2 (shipment is total loss)
	$P(S_1) = .99$	$P(S_2) = .01$
A_1: Don't purchase insurance	20,000	0
A_2: Purchase insurance	19,700	19,700

is certain to receive \$20,000, but he must pay the \$300 insurance premium. Thus his net financial position in this case is 20,000 - 300 = \$19,700, whether the shipment arrives safely or not.

The result of act A_1, "don't purchase insurance," is the following lottery:

$$L_1 = \begin{bmatrix} 20{,}000 & 0 \\ .99 & .01 \end{bmatrix}.$$

The result of act A_2, "purchase insurance," is the certain lottery:

$$L_2 = \begin{bmatrix} 19{,}700 & 19{,}700 \\ .99 & .01 \end{bmatrix} = \begin{bmatrix} 19{,}700 \\ 1 \end{bmatrix}.$$

To solve his decision problem, the manufacturer must decide whether lottery L_1 is preferred to lottery L_2, whether L_2 is preferred to L_1, or whether L_2 and L_1 are equally desirable. In terms of utility, if $u(L_1)$ and $u(L_2)$ are the utility values of lotteries L_1 and

L_2, respectively, he must decide if $u(L_1) > u(L_2)$, $u(L_1) < u(L_2)$, or $u(L_1) = u(L_2)$.

Lottery L_1 involves only two possible outcomes: \$20,000 and \$0, with probabilities of .99 and .01, respectively. Therefore, from the maximum expected utility criterion (1.5), the utility value of lottery L_1 is

$$u(L_1) = .99u(20{,}000) + .01u(0).$$

Lottery L_2 has only one possible outcome, \$19,700 (with probability 1), so its utility value is:

$$u(L_2) = .99u(19{,}700) + .01u(19{,}700) = u(19{,}700).$$

Of course, until the utility values u(20,000), u(19,700), and u(0) are known, the final evaluation of lotteries L_1 and L_2 cannot be made. Nevertheless, the maximum expected utility criterion has taken the evaluation some distance.

Expected Utility Axioms. The decision-maker must be prepared to accept four formal axioms if he is to use the maximum expected utility criterion in its usual form. One of these axioms is the complete-ordering axiom presented as (1.3). The other three axioms are the continuity, independence, and unequal probability axioms that are described below. Many decision-makers are prepared to accept that their preferences for lotteries should satisfy these axioms and therefore that the maximum expected utility criterion forms a reasonable basis for decision-making. The criterion has not gone unchallenged in the literature, although it is widely accepted as a normative basis for decision-making. The axioms are presented here in informal descriptive terms. A proof that the maximum expected utility criterion can be deduced from the axioms is not provided--the interested reader may wish to consult Marschak (1950), for instance, for a proof.

> Continuity Axiom: If lottery L_1 is preferred to lottery L_2, and lottery L_2 is preferred to lottery L_3, then a lottery L can be constructed, with lotteries L_1 and L_3 as outcomes, so that the individual is indifferent between L and L_2. (1.6)

To say that L is constructed with lotteries L_1 and L_3 as outcomes means the individual is offered lottery L_1 with some probability p and lottery L_3 with probability 1 - p. Symbolically, this can be written

$$L = \begin{bmatrix} L_1 & L_3 \\ p & 1 - p \end{bmatrix} .$$

> Independence Axiom: If an individual is indifferent between lotteries L_1 and L_2 and between lotteries L_3 and L_4, then he is indifferent between a lottery constructed from L_1 and L_3 and a lottery constructed from L_2 and L_4, provided the probabilities associated with L_1 and L_2, respectively, in these two lotteries are equal. (1.7)

> Unequal Probability Axiom: Assume that an individual prefers lottery L_1 to lottery L_2. If two new lotteries are constructed with lotteries L_1 and L_2 as outcomes, the new lottery with the larger probability for L_1 is preferred to the other. (1.8)

In formal terms, what the expected utility axioms provide is the following: If $\mathcal{C} \subseteq \mathcal{L}$ denotes the subset of $\mathcal{L}$ comprised of all certain lotteries (i.e., lotteries that offer a single object with probability one), then the expected utility axioms provide a basis for extending a utility mapping defined on $\mathcal{C}$ to a utility mapping defined on all of $\mathcal{L}$. In practical terms, this means that if the utility values of the objects offered by the lotteries are known, then the utility value of any lottery defined over these objects is readily obtained by the expected utility rule (1.5).

Thus far we have assumed implicitly that lotteries in $\mathcal{L}$ have only a finite number of possible outcomes. All the theory presented to this point readily extends to cases involving countably infinite or uncountably infinite sets of objects, provided the utility values of lotteries remain finite and hence defined. In subsequent discussion, unless we state to the contrary, we shall assume that utility values of lotteries under consideration are bounded.

Arbitrary Origin and Unit of Utility Measure. When the expected utility axioms apply, it follows mathematically that the utility scale for lotteries can be assigned an arbitrary origin and unit of measure. For instance, in the insurance purchase decision, the decision-maker is free to specify, say, u(0) as the origin of the utility scale and u(20,000) as one unit of utility. If he does so, then u(0) = 0 and u(20,000) = 1.

It is common to refer to the unit of utility measure as a *utile* in the same way that time has a unit of a minute or weight has a unit of a gram. In the insurance purchase decision, if u(0) and u(20,000) are selected as the origin and unit of the utility scale, respectively, then the lottery L_1 corresponding to the act, "don't purchase insurance," has a utility value equal to .99 utiles, i.e.:

$$u(L_1) = .99u(20{,}000) + .01u(0) = .99(1) + .01(0) = .99 \text{ utiles.}$$

To show that the utility scale can be given an arbitrary origin and unit of measure under the expected utility axioms, it suffices to show that if the utility values in any decision problem are subjected to a positive linear transformation, application of the expected utility rule (1.5) will still rank the acts of the decision problem in the same order with respect to preference. A positive linear transformation is a mathematical transformation of the following type--multiply the utility value u by some positive amount b and add some constant a to the product to obtain the new utility value u*, i.e.:

$$u^* = a + bu \qquad b > 0. \tag{1.9}$$

1.2.3 Monetary Lotteries

Decision problems involving monetary outcomes are so common that it is desirable to discuss the utility value of money as a special case. In decision-making under risk where the outcomes are monetary, the result of each act is a monetary lottery of the form

$$L = \begin{bmatrix} M_1 & M_2 & \cdots & M_n \\ p_1 & p_2 & \cdots & p_n \end{bmatrix} .$$

To determine the utility of a monetary lottery, it is necessary to know the utility values of the monetary amounts $M_1, M_2, \ldots, M_n$ provided by the lottery. In general, since the amount of money may be viewed as a continuous variable, it is necessary to know the utility value u(M) associated with each amount of money M--u(M) is called the utility function for money. Depending on the economic context of the problem, M may represent any one of several monetary variables such as wealth, income, present value, future value, cost saving, rate of return, etc.

The Shape of u(M). The shape of the utility function for money will be of considerable importance in the discussion in later chapters. Here we simply set out some preliminary observations about u(M). For the sake of keeping the discussion technically uncluttered, we assume that u(M) is a twice-differentiable function.

Positive marginal utility. In solving decision problems involving monetary lotteries, it is common to accept the axiom that decision-makers prefer more money to less, i.e., that money has positive marginal utility. In mathematical terms the axiom states that u(M) is an increasing function of M, or, equivalently, that $du(M)/dM > 0$.

A graph of a utility function for money that exhibits positive marginal utility is shown in Figure 1-3a.

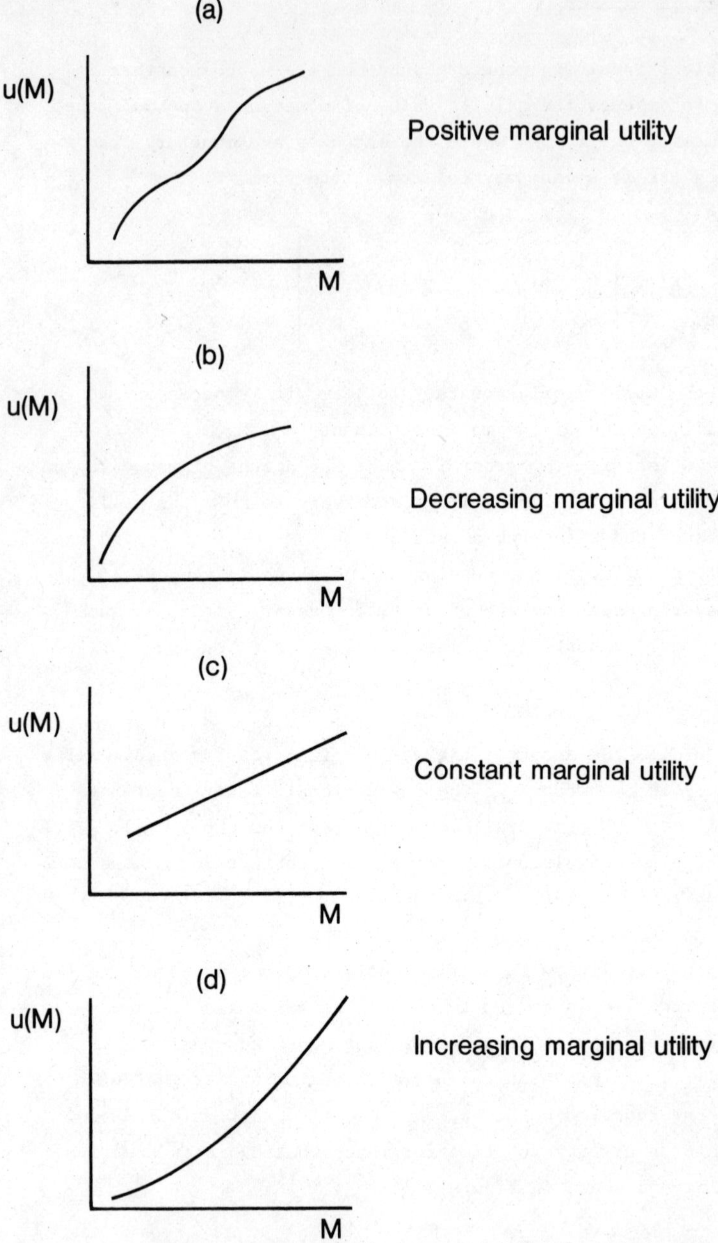

Figure 1-3. Utility Functions for Money Exhibiting Different Marginal Behavior

Decreasing marginal utility. To explain some economic behavior, it is necessary to go beyond the assumption of positive marginal utility to assumptions about the curvature of the utility function for money.

The desirability of money does not always increase in direct proportion to the amount involved. For instance, a business executive facing a loss of $50,000 may feel it is more than 50 times as serious as a loss of $1,000 because such a large loss will cause bankruptcy. This feeling is expressed in terms of utility by saying that the marginal utility of money decreases with increasing amounts. Decreasing marginal utility is exhibited by the utility function shown in Figure 1-3b. The function in Figure 1-3b is concave to the money axis. Mathematically, decreasing marginal utility is equivalent to the condition that $d^2u(M)/dM^2 < 0$. Thus decreasing marginal utility means the slope of the utility function decreases as M increases--each extra unit of money provides less additional utility than previous units. As we shall explain later, decreasing marginal utility for money is associated with risk-averse decision-making, a very common phenomenon in economic behavior.

Constant marginal utility. When the desirability of money increases in exactly direct proportion to the amount involved, the utility function is a straight line as it is in Figure 1-3c. Marginal utility in this case is a constant that is equal to the slope of the utility function. Since the utility function has no curvature in this case, constant marginal utility is equivalent to the condition that $d^2u(M)/dM^2 = 0$.

Since the utility function is a straight line in the case of constant marginal utility, it has the mathematical form $u(M) = a + bM$, where $b > 0$ because it has been assumed that more money is preferred to less. Under the expected utility axioms, it was established earlier [see (1.9)] that subjecting utility values to a positive linear transformation will not change the preference ranking of lotteries. Therefore the amount of money M can be used directly as a utility value in this case, i.e., $u(M) = M$. In other words, one dollar can be viewed as equivalent to one utile when marginal utility is constant.

Given that $u(M) = M$, it follows immediately from (1.5) that the maximum expected utility criterion is the same as the maximum expected value criterion. Specifically, if the monetary lottery is

$$L = \begin{bmatrix} M_1 & M_2 & \cdots & M_n \\ p_1 & p_2 & \cdots & p_n \end{bmatrix},$$

then the expected utility of L is

$$\begin{aligned} u(L) &= p_1 u(M_1) + p_2 u(M_2) + \ldots + p_n u(M_n) \\ &= p_1 M_1 + p_2 M_2 + \ldots + p_n M_n . \end{aligned} \tag{1.10}$$

Note that $u(M_i)$ has been replaced by M_i in each instance. The resulting value of $u(L)$ is none other than the expected monetary value of the lottery.

Although constant marginal utility is of interest in itself for explaining economic decision-making, it is important for the following additional reason: If the utility function for money has some curvature, it may be well approximated by a straight-line segment over a small range of monetary values. Thus the maximum expected value criterion may be applied in decision problems where monetary amounts vary over a small interval only, even though the exact utility function for money is not known.

Increasing marginal utility. A utility function for money that exhibits increasing marginal utility is shown in Figure 1-3d. This function is convex to the money axis, which is equivalent to the condition $d^2u(M)/dM^2 > 0$. The slope of the utility function increases with increasing monetary amounts, indicating that the individual obtains increasing increments of utility from each additional unit of money.

It is considered unusual for an individual to have a utility function for money exhibiting increasing marginal utility because it implies that his decision-making will be speculative and risk-seeking.

However, to explain some types of economic decision-making, such as the purchase of lottery tickets, decision theorists must resort to consideration of utility functions that are convex over some interval.

Other shapes. Decision theorists occasionally consider utility functions for money with shapes different from the three basic types discussed above. These other types of utility functions provide useful insights into and explanations of the economic decision-making behavior of individuals, but they are not considered in this book.

Certainty Equivalents and Risk Premiums

Certainty equivalent. Consider a decision-maker with a continuous utility function for money u(M). For any monetary lottery, there will exist a certain monetary amount that has the same utility value as the lottery. For instance, if the monetary lottery is

$$L = \begin{bmatrix} M_1 & M_2 & \cdots & M_n \\ \\ p_1 & p_2 & \cdots & p_n \end{bmatrix}$$

and the decision-maker adopts the expected utility axioms, then there exists an amount of money c such that

$$u(c) = p_1 u(M_1) + p_2 u(M_2) + \ldots + p_n u(M_n) \tag{1.11}$$

where c is called the <u>certainty equivalent</u> value of the monetary lottery.

To illustrate the concept of certainty equivalence, consider a decision-maker with a utility function u(M) = log M who faces the following lottery:

$$L = \begin{bmatrix} 100 & 200 & 300 \\ \\ .2 & .6 & .2 \end{bmatrix}.$$

From (1.11), it follows that the certainty equivalent value of this lottery is found by solving the following equation for c:

$$u(c) = (.2)u(100) + (.6)u(200) + (.2)u(300).$$

Since u(M) = log M, this equation has the form

$$\log c = (.2) \log 100 + (.6) \log 200 + (.2) \log 300.$$

Solving for c gives c = 189. Therefore from the definition of the certainty equivalent, it can be concluded that the decision-maker would be indifferent between having 189 with certainty and facing lottery L.

Risk premium. Consider any monetary lottery with a finite expected value μ. For instance, the lottery

$$L = \begin{bmatrix} M_1 & M_2 & \cdots & M_n \\ p_1 & p_2 & \cdots & p_n \end{bmatrix}$$

has an expected value of

$$\mu = p_1M_1 + p_2M_2 + \ldots + p_nM_n.$$

If c is the certainty equivalent value of lottery L, then the arithmetic difference between μ and c is called the decision-maker's <u>risk premium</u> for the lottery. Denoting the risk premium by π, the notational definition is

$$\pi = \mu - c \tag{1.12}$$

For instance, for the lottery shown below, c = 189, as was shown earlier, and μ = 200, as the reader may verify. Hence the decision-maker associates a risk premium of π = 200 - 189 = 11 with the lottery.

$$L = \begin{bmatrix} 100 & 200 & 300 \\ \\ .2 & .6 & .2 \end{bmatrix}.$$

Since the expected value of a lottery represents the average outcome that would be realized in repeated trials with the lottery and the certainty equivalent is that fixed amount that provides as much utility as the lottery itself, the risk premium measures the amount the decision-maker is prepared to lose relative to the lottery's expected value to avoid the riskiness of the lottery. Hence the term "risk premium."

As the reader may already suspect, the risk premium for any risky lottery will always be positive if the decision-maker's utility function exhibits decreasing marginal utility throughout the relevant range of monetary outcomes. The risk premium is zero if the utility function exhibits constant marginal utility, i.e., u(M) is linear in M. Finally, the risk premium is negative if the utility function exhibits increasing marginal utility. In the latter case the decision-maker is actually prepared to pay a premium over a lottery's expected value to have the risky lottery as opposed to its certainty equivalent. Decision-makers whose utility functions produce positive, zero, and negative risk premiums are said to exhibit <u>risk aversion</u>, <u>risk neutrality</u>, and <u>risk attraction</u>, respectively.

The concepts of risk premium and certainty equivalent play an important role in economic and financial decision-making under risk. As one example, consider the person facing lottery L given above. The lottery may be viewed as resulting from the person holding \$100 in cash and risky assets with the following payoff distribution:

$$\begin{bmatrix} \$0 & \$100 & \$200 \\ \\ .2 & .6 & .2 \end{bmatrix}.$$

Since the certainty equivalent of lottery L was calculated above to be c = \$189, it follows that this person would sell his risky assets if their market value exceeded \$89 (\$189 less the \$100 cash) and would hold them otherwise. Viewed differently, since the expected value of the risky assets based on the payoff distribution above is \$100, the person is receiving a premium (in expected value terms) of 100 - 89 = \$11 to bear the risk inherent to the assets.

As a second example, consider an insurance purchase decision. Suppose the person just considered has \$100 in cash and a \$200 house that may be partially or totally destroyed by fire with the following loss distribution:

$$\begin{bmatrix} \$0 & \$100 & \$200 \\ .2 & .6 & .2 \end{bmatrix}$$

Without insurance, the person faces a lottery with respect to his net financial position that is equivalent to lottery L. Since the certainty equivalent of lottery L is \$189, the value of the uninsured house to the owner is \$89 (\$189 less the \$100 cash). Consequently, for 100-percent fire insurance coverage, the owner would be prepared to pay as much as 200 - 89 = \$111. The expected fire loss (computed from the loss distribution above) is \$100. Thus if the insurance company can charge an insurance premium smaller than 111 percent of the expected loss, the owner would purchase the insurance.

In these two examples the risk premium π has played two different but related roles. In the first example it represents the extra amount that the decision maker must have in order to bear risk. In the second example it represents the extra amount that the decision-maker is prepared to forego in order to avoid risk.

1.2.4 Dominance

Methods for Determining Utility Values. There are two methods for determining the utility values of a decision-maker for the lotteries he faces in his decision problem.

Hypothetical choice method. With the hypothetical choice method, the decision-maker is asked to express his preferences in several simple and hypothetical decision situations posed to him in an experimental or laboratory setting. The assumption is then made that his preferences as expressed in the hypothetical choices will carry over to the more complex real-world decision problem and may be applied there to identify the most preferred lottery.

Revealed preference method. With the revealed preference method, a decision-maker's past decisions are analyzed to draw inferences about his current preferences among lotteries. These inferred or revealed preferences are then applied to the decision problem at hand to determine the best act. The assumption here is that the preferences revealed by past decisions have not changed and are relevant for present decision-making.

The methodological dichotomy described above clearly identifies the revealed preference method as an ex post measurement scheme and the hypothetical choice method as an ex ante measurement scheme. Although the hypothetical choice method is only a single method in principle, it has many formats in which it can be implemented.

Axiomatic structure. Whichever measurement method is chosen, it must be implemented within a formal axiomatic structure. In other words, the decision-maker must be prepared to accept some minimal set of conditions or rules as a basis for judging the relative desirability of lotteries. For instance, he might be asked to accept the axioms supporting the expected utility criterion. Once an axiom set has been adopted, preference data are gathered by means of either hypothetical choice experimentation or revealed preference methods. Finally, using both the axioms and the data, the utility values of the lotteries under consideration in the decision problem are assessed.

The Dominance Principle. The consideration of axiomatic structures in decision theory has produced an important decision principle that we shall call the dominance principle. The theoretical and practical aspects of the methodology derived from this principle occupy the rest of this book. In this section we shall simply introduce the basic elements of the dominance principle and postpone further work with it until subsequent chapters.

Dominance. For any specified set of lotteries L defined on a fixed set of objects, there is an infinity of mappings of the lotteries into utility values that a decision-maker might have. However, if a decision-maker is prepared to accept that his utility mapping for lotteries should satisfy certain axioms or conditions--say, the set of conditions C--then the mappings that are candidates for describing the decision-maker's preferences will form a smaller set. Specifically, let U_C denote the set of utility mappings that satisfy conditions C. If the conditions C are judiciously selected in the sense of being as stringent as possible without being unrealistic, then knowledge that the decision-maker's utility function for the lotteries in L lies in U_C can be used to reduce the number of acts that must be evaluated in a decision problem. More precisely, suppose a decision problem offers a choice from a set of acts denoted by A. If it can be shown that some act $A_1 \in A$ is more desirable than act $A_2 \in A$ for every utility function $u \in U_C$, then the decision-maker can eliminate A_2 from further consideration. We say in this case that A_1 _dominates_ A_2 for all $u \in U_C$ or, equivalently, that A_1 is more _efficient_ that A_2 for all $u \in U_C$. Subsequently, we shall denote the dominance relation based on conditions C as follows: $A_1 >_C A_2$. (If A_1 is not strictly preferred to A_2 by all $u \in U_C$, then we shall write $A_1 \geq_C A_2$.)

By eliminating all the dominated courses of action in A, one is left with some subset $A_C \subseteq A$, which we shall call the _efficient set_ of acts under conditions C. The decision-maker with $u \in U_C$ will find his best act for the decision problem in A_C. Of course, if A_C contains more than one course of action, the decision-maker must undertake further preference evaluation to make a final choice of an act. Nevertheless, the beauty of the dominance principle is that it isolates a smaller set of acts for explicit consideration. As will be shown in later chapters, this can represent a very significant gain. Further, knowledge of the contents of A_C can provide important insights into the nature of some decision problems.

Illustration. To illustrate the dominance principle by a very simple example, consider the decision problem in Table 1-2, which is concerned with the selection of a portfolio of securities. The five acts correspond to five security portfolios that represent alternative ways of investing $10 million for the coming year. The four outcome states correspond to four states of the economy that might prevail during the coming year. The consequences represent the changes in value of the portfolio (in millions of dollars) that will be experienced during the year under each possible state of the economy. Subjective probabilities for the possible states of the economy are also shown.

If the portfolio manager accepts the following condition, then an inspection of Table 1-2 shows that act A_2 dominates act A_5 so that act A_5 can be eliminated from further consideration.

> Condition C: One portfolio is preferred to another if in every possible outcome state it offers at least as large a gain as the other and if in some state it offers a larger gain.

The type of dominance produced by condition C is so conspicuous that one might wonder if the general principle isn't restating the obvious. For some applications of the principle this is true (although even in these cases the restatement of the "obvious" is sometimes beneficial). There are more subtle applications of the dominance principle, however, that produce nonobvious results. These applications and their theoretical basis are the subject of this book. To illustrate what can be accomplished by an application of the dominance principle, it turns out that all but one portfolio in the decision problem in Table 1-2 can be eliminated from consideration under certain reasonable assumptions about economic behavior. Act A_1 can be shown to dominate the other acts under these assumptions.

1.3 Review of Portfolio Theory

Because of the central role that the portfolio problem plays in the history and current interest in stochastic dominance methodology, some

Table 1-2
Portfolio Decision Problem Illustrating the Dominance Principle

		State of Economy and Their Probabilities			
		S_1	S_2	S_3	S_4
		$P(S_1) = .1$	$P(S_2) = .2$	$P(S_3) = .3$	$P(S_4) = .4$
Alternative Portfolios	A_1	2	1	0	1
	A_2	-1	2	1	0
	A_3	-1	2	0	1
	A_4	-1	1	1	1
	A_5	-1	2	0	0

familiarity with the terminology and basic theoretical results associated with this problem is essential. The review begins with a statement of the portfolio problem. [For a more extensive treatment of portfolio theory, see Sharpe (1970) for example.]

1.3.1 Portfolio Decision Problem

Consider a decision-maker who wishes to invest a fixed amount of wealth in a set of N financial securities, productive assets, or the like. If R_i denotes the return he will realize per dollar invested in security i over a fixed investment period and X_i is the proportion of his wealth invested in security i, the investor's return on his investment portfolio over the investment period is R, where

$$R = R_1X_1 + \dots + R_NX_N \tag{1.13}$$

The set of portfolio mixes $(X_1, X_2, \dots, X_N)$ from which the investor can select depends on operational constraints that apply in any given problem. Nevertheless, by definition, the mix must be such that $X_1 + X_2 + \ldots + X_N = 1$.

In general, the R_i's are random variables representing risky investment opportunities, so it follows that R is also a random variable (and hence a lottery) with a distribution function F(r) that depends on the portfolio mix $(X_1, X_2, \ldots, X_N)$. The investor must choose the portfolio mix with the distribution function yielding maximum expected utility.

The Markowitz Model. Markowitz (1952, 1959) described the portfolio problem as a quadratic programming problem of the following type:

$$\max \left[E = \sum_{i=1}^{N} E_i X_i \right] \tag{1.14}$$

subject to: (a) $\sum_{i=1}^{N} \sum_{j=1}^{N} \sigma_{ij} X_i X_j = V$

(b) $\sum_{i=1}^{N} X_i = 1$

(c) other relevant constraints on $(X_1, X_2, \ldots, X_N)$,

where the symbols denote the following:

E_i = expected value of R_i,
σ_{ij} = covariance of R_i and R_j,
X_i = proportion of wealth invested in security i,
E = mean portfolio return, i.e., expected value of R,
V = variance of portfolio return, i.e., variance of R.

Markowitz's rationale for model (1.14) was the following: The utility experienced by the investor faced with the portfolio problem will be a function of the mean portfolio return (E) and the variance of the portfolio return (V). Assuming the investor to be risk-averse, Markowitz argued that the portfolio mix should be selected to yield a maximum mean return for any fixed level of risk (as measured by variance) or, equivalently, to yield a minimum risk level for any fixed level of mean return. The portfolio mix that solves (1.14) for any specified level of V is called an efficient EV portfolio. The locus of all efficient EV portfolios is called the EV efficient frontier.

Figure 1-4 illustrates the Markowitz approach. The shaded region denotes all (E,V) combinations that correspond to feasible portfolios [i.e., feasible solutions of (1.14)]. The upper left boundary of the region of feasible portfolios is the efficient frontier and has been shown by a solid line. The scalloped appearance of the feasible region in the figure is the result of the quadratic relationships implicit in the constraint set of (1.14).

Riskless Borrowing and Lending. If the decision-maker is free to borrow or lend appropriately large amounts of capital at some riskless rate p, then a riskless investment is available to him. Let the first security denote this riskless investment so $E_1 = p$ and $\sigma_{1j} = 0$ for $j = 1, 2, \ldots, N$. Under this circumstance it can be shown that the EV efficient frontier is altered as shown in Figure 1-5. Note in this case that $\sigma = \sqrt{V}$, the portfolio standard deviation, is plotted on the horizontal axis. A portfolio consisting entirely of the riskless investment is labeled p in Figure 1-5. The shaded region again corresponds to the set of all feasible portfolios and extends as far to the right as borrowing will permit. In this case note that the efficient frontier is a straight line when its locus is plotted on an (E,σ) graph.

Index Model. Sharpe (1963) proposed a simplification of the Markowitz formulation that has come to be known as the index model (this review is restricted to the single index form of the model). Specifically, Sharpe noted that the covariance structure of the N investment returns, $R_1, R_2, \ldots, R_N$, is substantially simplified if all investment returns are linearly related to some common random variable I. The statistical model generally assumed in this case is the following:

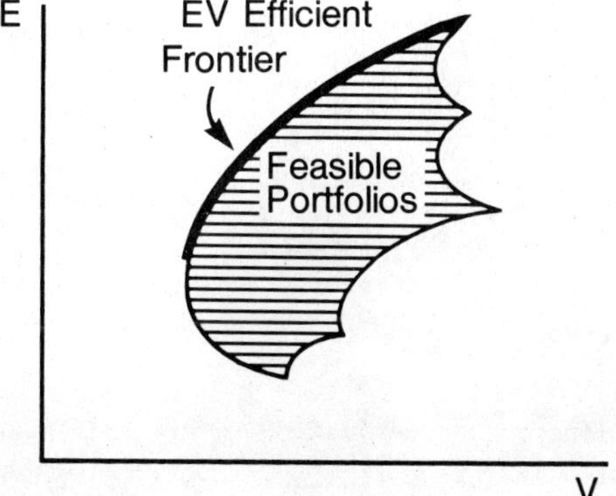

Figure 1-4. Graphical Representation of Markowitz Approach

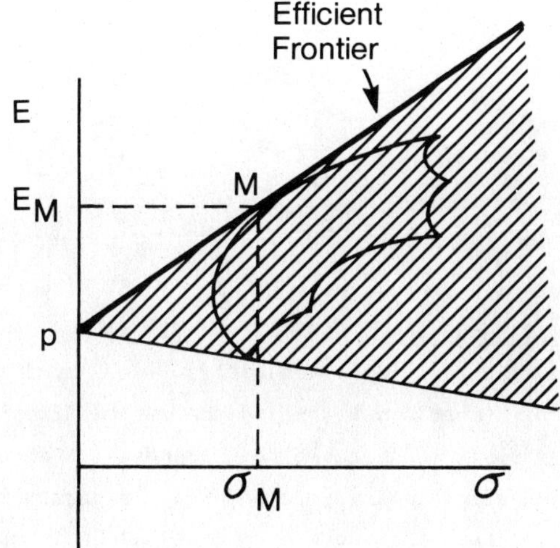

Figure 1-5. Efficient Frontier with Riskless Borrowing and Lending at Rate p

$$R_i = \alpha_i + \beta_i I + \varepsilon_i \quad i = 1, 2, \ldots, N. \tag{1.15}$$

Here α_i and β_i are constants associated with the ith security and ε_i is a random variable for which the following assumptions hold:

a. $E(\varepsilon_i) = 0$
b. $E(\varepsilon_i \varepsilon_j) = 0 \quad \text{for } i \neq j$
c. $E(\varepsilon_i^2) = \nu_i$
d. $E(\varepsilon_i I) = 0$

The mean and standard deviation of I are denoted by E_I and σ_I, respectively. I is usually interpreted as a market or other economic index that has a common influence on all security returns--hence the name "index" model.

Without dwelling on the derivation here, it is noteworthy that the mean and variance of the portfolio return simplify to the following expressions when the individual security returns are related to a single index as in (1.15):

$$E = \sum_{i=1}^{N} (\alpha_i + \beta_i E_I) X_i$$

$$V = \sum_{i=1}^{N} \nu_i X_i^2 + \left(\sum_{i=1}^{N} \beta_i X_i \right)^2 \sigma_I^2$$

The leftmost sum in the expression for V in (1.16) is usually called the <u>unsystematic risk component</u> of V because it is produced by factors that are unique to the individual securities, i.e., by the ε_i terms. In contrast, the rightmost sum is called the <u>systematic risk component</u> of V because it is risk attributable to the index I that exerts a common influence on all security returns. When a portfolio is diversified--in the sense that none of the X_i values is very large--it can be seen that the systematic risk component will tend to be the main determinant of V (under conditions that are likely to prevail in the real world).

1.3.2 Capital Market Equilibrium

The mathematical structure of the Markowitz formulation is sufficiently rich that under certain assumptions of capital market efficiency it yields a model of equilibrium security returns. The model is often called the Capital Asset Pricing Model (CAPM). Stated informally, the assumptions needed for the model are the following:

1. Investors hold identical expectations about mean security returns (E_i) and covariances (σ_{ij}).

2. There is a large population of securities available to all investors. The amount of wealth invested by each investor is fixed in value.

3. Each investor has unlimited ability to borrow or lend at the riskless rate p.

4. Each investor seeks an EV efficient portfolio (albeit with different desired levels of V).

5. Transaction costs and taxes either do not exist or have a neutral effect.

Capital Market Line. Under the foregoing assumptions, it turns out that the EV efficient frontier is the following linear function of σ when the capital market is in equilibrium:

$$E = p + \left(\frac{E_M - p}{\sigma_M}\right)\sigma. \tag{1.17}$$

Here E_M and σ_M denote the mean and standard deviation of a special portfolio called the market portfolio. The market portfolio is the portfolio consisting of all securities, each present in the proportion that its market value is of the total market value of all securities.

The straight line (1.17) is known as the capital market line. It is shown in Figure 1-5 as extended line p-M where M denotes the position of the market portfolio. Since investors are assumed to hold EV efficient portfolios in this capital market, it follows that all investors will hold portfolios lying on the capital market line. From (1.17) it can be seen that, in equilibrium, the differential between the mean return E of an efficient portfolio and the riskless rate p is proportional to the portfolio risk σ.

Security Market Line. In addition to the capital market line, when the capital market is in equilibrium (under the assumptions specified above), the expected returns E_i for individual securities bear the following relationship to one another:

$$E_i = p + \left(\frac{E_M - p}{\sigma_M^2}\right)\sigma_{iM} \tag{1.18}$$

where σ_{iM} denotes the covariance between R_i and the return on the market portfolio. Relation (1.18) indicates that in equilibrium a security will offer a differential in mean return over the riskless rate that is proportional to its covariance with the market portfolio. Because (1.18) expresses an equilibrium condition for all securities in the capital market, it is known as the security market line. Figure 1-6 presents a pictorial representation of the security market line.

1.3.3 Stochastic Dominance and the Mean-Variance Portfolio Model

As the previous two sections shown, the EV formulation not only allows an explicit solution of the portfolio problem but also provides a description of a capital market in equilibrium. With a model that provides this much, it may seem strange that researchers have sought out other approaches to the problem. Nevertheless, one aspect of the EV approach was nettlesome to some researchers, namely, that fairly strong restrictions had to be placed on the class of admissible utility functions for R, or on the class of admissible distribution functions for R, or on both of these, for EV efficiency to be consistent with the expected utility criterion. Stated roughly, the EV approach is valid in terms of expected utility only if a decision-maker who maximizes expected utility always selects a portfolio that is EV efficient. (The restrictions that are required to align the EV approach with the expected utility criterion are described in several sections of the book and therefore are not discussed here; see Chapter 2, Section 2.17, and Chapter 5, Section 5.2.)

As just stated, dissatisfaction with the restrictive assumptions that must hold for the EV approach to be appropriate has led

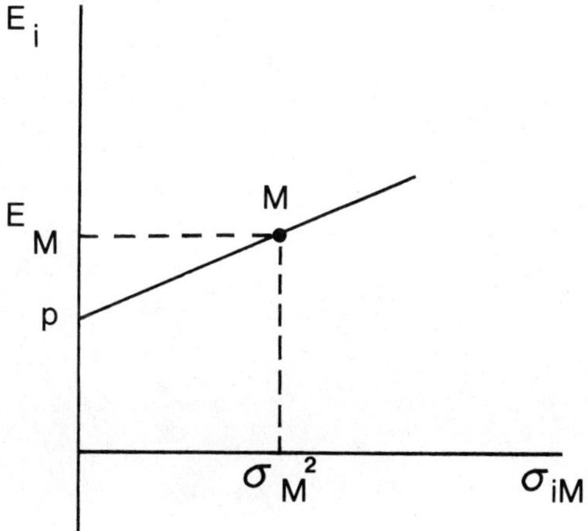

Figure 1-6. Security Market Line

researchers to consider alternative approaches to the portfolio problem. Among these alternative approaches are included consideration of different measures of portfolio risk and return such as semivariance, location and scale parameters, etc., and incorporation of higher-order parameters of portfolio return such as skewness and kurtosis. Stochastic dominance methodology has been developed and used by researchers to investigate these alternative formulations. It also has been used as a general criterion of efficiency in applications where consistency with the expected utility axioms is important and, consequently, the EV criterion would not have been satisfactory.

In this way, interest in the dominance principle has grown in parallel with interest in the portfolio problem. It should be noted at the outset, however, that stochastic dominance does not represent an operational alternative to an EV approach to portfolio construction --at least at this time, it doesn't. Nevertheless, it does represent a powerful concept for analysis and investigation, which is why it is receiving the attention of scholars and students alike. Additional commentary on the current strengths and weaknesses of stochastic dominance methodology and the role it may play in future research on portfolio and capital market theory is reserved for subsequent chapters.

Introduction to Chapter 2 Theoretical Foundations of Stochastic Dominance

Since stochastic dominance is a methodology that lies within decision theory, it is based necessarily on formal concepts and theorems that form part of this theory's fabric. In this chapter, Peter C. Fishburn and Raymond G. Vickson present a lucid and unified summary of the body of existing theoretical knowledge about stochastic dominance. Because the subject is extensive, the chapter is long.

The chapter is a technical prerequisite to the chapters that follow (with the possible exception of Chapter 5, which is largely self-contained). It sets out the terminology and theoretical results that are essential for understanding the applications of both a theoretical and empirical nature that are discussed in subsequent chapters. In addition to a unified treatment of material that heretofore has been available only in diverse and loosely connected published works, the authors have done a superb and unprecedented job of presenting definitions, theorems, proofs, and accompanying discussion with rigor and precision of language and without loss of clarity or readability. They have gone beyond a discussion of the more widely known and applied stochastic dominance results to consider topics on the frontiers of basic research in the field. Noteworthy in this regard are their presentation of a stochastic dominance rule for decision-makers exhibiting decreasing absolute risk aversion (an area of research to which Vickson has made a singularly large contribution), their summary of key results for multivariate stochastic dominance, and their discussion of nondimensional stochastic dominance (a topic that Fishburn treated thoroughly in his book Decision and Value Theory (1964) over a decade ago and which now is receiving renewed attention).

2 Theoretical Foundations of Stochastic Dominance

Peter C. Fishburn and
Raymond G. Vickson

2.1 Introduction

The concept of stochastic dominance (SD) or stochastic ordering of risky prospects was introduced in Chapter 1. For the decision-maker who is faced with a specific pair of risky prospects and who is armed with some general but limited information about his utility function, the existence or nonexistence of an SD relation between the prospects is a purely mathematical question. In this chapter we present the basic mathematical theory of various common types of SD. The theory is at present most highly developed for risky prospects having unidimensional outcomes and for utility functions characterized by a few simple properties. The chapter is concerned primarily with such cases, but we also present some limited results for multivariate stochastic dominance for completeness. In the main text, technical complications are held to a minimum. In particular, we shall assume that utility functions have continuous derivatives of first or higher order, depending on need. This permits a simple, orderly development of the main points of the theory. For readers with the necessary patience, a more demanding treatment of the theory under weaker assumptions is presented in Appendixes 2A and 2B. These can be skipped without seriously affecting the reader's understanding of most of the rest of the book.

Sections 2.2 through 2.4 review material about univariate random variables that is necessary for an understanding of stochastic dominance theory. They also set out the notation and definitions of terminology used throughout the book. Section 2.5 gives a brief introduction to the mean-variance ordering rule, for later reference.

Sections 2.6 and 2.7 review properties of multivariate distributions and conditional distributions. This material is needed only in the sections on multivariate stochastic dominance, and it can be skipped by readers who are not interested in such problems. Section 2.8 introduces the concept of a utility function for wealth as a vehicle for discussing financial decision problems of an individual investor. Sections 2.9 through 2.13 identify specific classes of utility for wealth functions that appear to be most relevant. These are the increasing functions, the increasing concave functions, the functions having decreasing absolute risk aversion, and the functions having positive third derivatives.

The remaining sections deal with stochastic dominance as such. Section 2.14 presents and illustrates the three basic stochastic dominance theorems that finance theorists have discussed; the theorems are proved in Section 2.15. Section 2.16 then examines miscellaneous consequences and special cases of the theorems, including results that hold for random variables having equal means and random variables in special families. In Section 2.17, the relation between the mean-variance dominance criterion and stochastic dominance ordering rules is summarized. Section 2.18 introduces stochastic dominance over the functions having decreasing absolute risk aversion and explores its relation to older work. An algorithmic procedure for testing this type of stochastic dominance is briefly outlined for special, discrete random variables.

The versions of stochastic dominance discussed in Sections 2.14 through 2.18 are concerned with probability distributions defined on the real line. Section 2.19 forms a bridge between the univariate and multivariate cases by establishing alternative forms of the stochastic dominance tests for increasing and increasing concave utility functions that are equivalent to, but more "abstract" than, those given in earlier sections. The generalization of these ideas to the multivariate situation is then examined briefly in Section 2.20. The main text of the chapter concludes in Section 2.21 with essentially nondimensional versions of stochastic dominance for distributions defined on a finite set of consequences in which the utility functions are based on the preferences of the decision-maker on the consequence set.

Appendix 2A treats classes of utility functions that are more general than those of Sections 2.9 through 2.13. Although the behavioral properties of these general utility functions are essentially identical to those in the main text, the mathematical properties are less stringent: boundedness of the domain or range is not assumed, and differentiability properties are significantly weakened. Appendix 2B presents the stochastic dominance theorems that are appropriate to these more general utility functions. The proofs, which are based solely on general properties of Lebesgue-Stieltjes integration, are valid for unbounded utility functions, unbounded random variables, and finite or infinite expected utility.

2.2 Univariate Distribution Functions

Throughout this book, P(A) denotes the probability of occurrence of an event A. There is insufficient space here to discuss either the mathematical foundations of probability theory or its philosophical conceptions. For the former, see, e.g., the books of Feller (1966, 1968), Loeve (1963), or Breiman (1968); for a bit of the latter, see, e.g., Fishburn (1964: Chapter 5). It is assumed throughout to be immaterial whether the probabilities are "objective" or "subjective," but they are assumed to obey the axioms of the mathematical theory of probability as set out in the books just cited.

A random variable is, intuitively speaking, a function whose values occur by chance. If X is a real-valued random variable, its distribution function F is defined as

$$F(x) = P(X \leq x) \quad \text{for all } x \in Re, \qquad (2.1)$$

where Re is the real line. F is also called a cumulative distribution function (cdf). Some texts, such as Loeve (1963) or Breiman (1968) define F as $P(X < x)$, but Eq. (2.1) is widely used. For notational simplicity, we shall often use different letters to denote distribution functions of different random variables. With F defined by Eq. (2.1), we require

$F(x) \to 0$ as $x \to -\infty$, $F(x) \to 1$ as $x \to \infty$;
F is nondecreasing: $F(x) \leq F(y)$ if $x \leq y$; (2.2)
F is right continuous: $F(x + h) \to F(x)$ as $h \to 0$ through positive values, or $h \downarrow 0$ for short.

Conversely, each F with these properties gives rise to a random variable X that satisfies Eq. (2.1). Knowledge of the function F suffices to compute many other probabilities of interest. Letting

$$F(x^-) = \lim F(x - h) \text{ as } h \downarrow 0, \tag{2.3}$$

we have $F(x^-) = P(X < x)$, $P(x < X \leq y) = F(y) - F(x)$, $P(x \leq X < y) = F(y^-) - F(x^-)$, and so forth. The probability that X assumes the particular value x is

$$P(\{x\}) = P(X = x) = P(x \leq X \leq x) = F(x) - F(x^-), \tag{2.4}$$

so that $P(\{x\})$ is positive if and only if F is discontinuous at x, or has a jump at x.

If the sum of all nonzero $P(\{x\})$ values equals 1, then X is a <u>discrete random variable</u> and F is essentially a step function; if $\Sigma P(\{x\}) = 0$, then X is a <u>continuous random variable</u> and F is continuous in the usual sense with $F(x^-) = F(x)$ for all $x \in \mathrm{Re}$; and if $0 < \Sigma P(\{x\}) < 1$ then X is a <u>mixed random variable</u>. Suppose X is a mixed random variable with $\lambda = \Sigma P(\{x\})$, $0 < \lambda < 1$. Then the distribution function F defined by Eq. (2.1) can be written as a convex combination, or weighted linear sum, of a discrete distribution function F_d and a continuous distribution function F_c. In particular,

$$F = \lambda F_d + (1 - \lambda)F_c$$

where

$$F_d(x) = \lambda^{-1}\Sigma\{P(\{y\}): y \leq x\},$$

$$F_c(x) = (1 - \lambda)^{-1}[F(x) - \Sigma\{P(\{y\}): y \leq x\}].$$

F_c is obtained by removing the jumps from F, which go into F_d. This is illustrated in Figure 2-1, where $F(x) = 0$ for $x < 0$.

The distribution function F has a <u>probability density function</u> f if $F(x) = \int_{-\infty}^{x} f(y)dy$ and $f(x) \geq 0$ for all $x \in Re$ and if $dF(x)/dx = F'(x) = f(x)$ for all x except on a set of probability zero. When F has a probability density function f and F' is not defined at point x, it is customary to take $f(x) = 0$. The density function f_c corresponding to F_c on Figure 2-1 is then $f_c(x) = 1/4$ for all $x \in (0,4)$ and $f_c(x) = 0$ elsewhere. All F that have probability density functions must be continuous, but not all continuous F have probability density functions. (In general, F must be "absolutely continuous" to have a probability density function.) We shall restrict our attention to distribution functions F having only finitely many jumps in any finite interval.

2.3 Expected Values

The <u>expectation</u> or <u>expected value</u> E(X) of X, also denoted by EX or by μ_X, is defined as

$$E(X) = \int_{-\infty}^{\infty} x \, dF(x) \tag{2.5}$$

whenever this quantity exists (it may be ∞ or $-\infty$). We shall restrict our attention to random variables that have finite expected values. E(X) is also called the <u>expected</u> or <u>mean value</u> (or simply, "mean") of the distribution F, and is denoted in this context by μ_F. If u is a real-valued function that is defined for all possible outcomes x of X, then under a mild restriction on u, $Z = u(X)$ is also a real-valued random variable. The expected value of Z is denoted as Eu(X), and is shown in the cited references to be given by

$$Eu(X) = \int_{-\infty}^{\infty} u(x)dF(x). \tag{2.6}$$

Again, we are usually interested only in functions u for which Eq. (2.6) gives a finite value for Eu(X). The alternative notation E(u,F) will be used to denote Eu(X) where convenient.

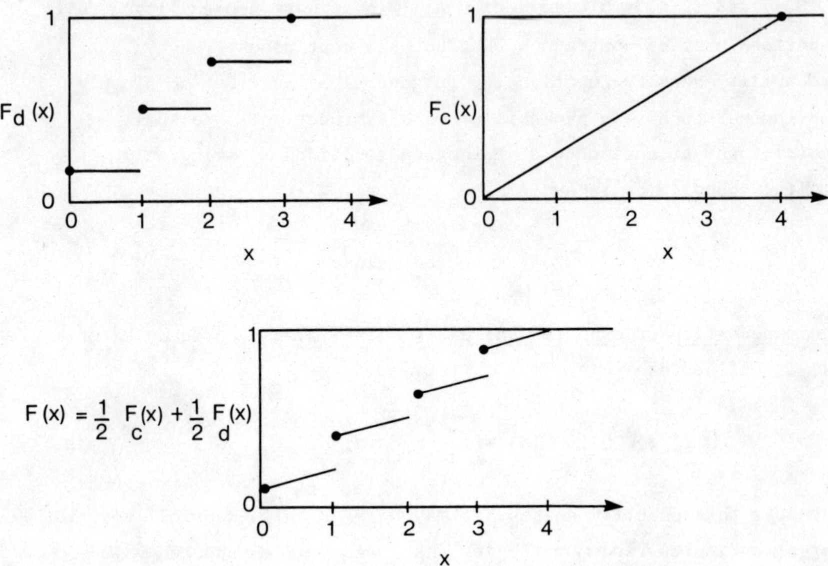

Figure 2-1. Decomposition of a Distribution Function F into Discrete (F_d) and Continuous (F_c) Parts

The expected-value operation has a number of properties needed in the sequel:

(a) If $Eu_i(X)$ is finite for $i = 1,2,...,n$, then

$$E \sum_{i=1}^{n} c_i u_i(X) = \sum_{i=1}^{n} c_i Eu_i(X) \quad \text{for any real constants } c_i. \tag{2.7}$$

(b) If $u(x) \geq 0$ for all x in the range of X, then

$$Eu(X) \geq 0. \tag{2.8}$$

(c) If F_1, F_2 are distribution functions, and if $E(u,F_1)$, $E(u,F_2)$ are finite, then

$$E(u,\lambda F_1 + (1 - \lambda)F_2) = \lambda E(u,F_1) + (1 - \lambda)E(u,F_2) \tag{2.9}$$
for all $0 \leq \lambda \leq 1$.

These properties follow immediately from Eq. (2.6).

2.4 Moments of Univariate Distribution Functions

In some problems, a detailed knowledge of the distribution function F is either unavailable, unenlightening, or unnecessary. In such cases a knowledge of a few general descriptive parameters may suffice. The mean μ_F is a simple and familiar measure of central tendency. To describe parametrically the distribution of X values about the mean, we must resort to expectations of nonlinear functions of X. The most familiar and most tractable parameters of this type are the <u>central moments</u>

$$\mu_F^{(n)} = E(X - \mu_F)^n = \int_{-\infty}^{\infty} (x - \mu_F)^n \, dF(x). \tag{2.10}$$

The second central moment, or <u>variance</u>, will be denoted by σ^2_F, and is given by

$$\sigma^2_F = E(X - \mu_F)^2 = E(X^2) - (EX)^2,$$

with <u>standard deviation</u> σ_F being the nonnegative square foot of σ^2_F. Occasionally the alternative notations σ^2_X and σ_X will also be used. Standard deviation has intuitive appeal as a measure of dispersion, and its importance is further enhanced by the Chebyshev inequality:

$$P(|X - \mu_F| \geq k) \leq \sigma^2_F/k^2 \quad \text{for } k > 0. \tag{2.11}$$

For a simple derivation of (2.11), see Feller (1968).

2.5 Mean-Variance Preference Ordering

The application of variance as a risk measure in portfolio analysis was promoted by Markowitz (1952), who suggested the famous <u>mean-variance</u>, or EV, ordering. In this theory the investor is assumed (or advised) to make portfolio decisions through a series of tradeoffs between mean return μ and "risk" or "variability" as embodied in the standard deviation measure σ. In a choice between distribution functions of return F and G, a risk-averse investor is presumed to prefer F to G, or to be indifferent between the two, if the mean of F is as large as the mean of G and the variance of F is not greater than the variance of G, i.e., if $\mu_F \geq \mu_G$ and $\sigma_F \leq \sigma_G$. Furthermore, if at least one of these inequalities is strict, then some investors prefer F to G in the strict sense and F is said to dominate G in the sense of EV. In this case G can be eliminated as a noncontender with no loss of optimality. If only one of the inequalities holds, the problem of choice depends on the individual's personal mean-variance tradeoffs, and neither F nor G can be eliminated under the criterion of EV dominance.

Using probability density functions f and g to represent the distributions F and G, Figure 2-2a illustrates a case in which F dominates G in the EV sense since F has larger mean and smaller variance. Neither F nor G is EV dominant in Figure 2-2b since F has the larger mean but G has the smaller variance.

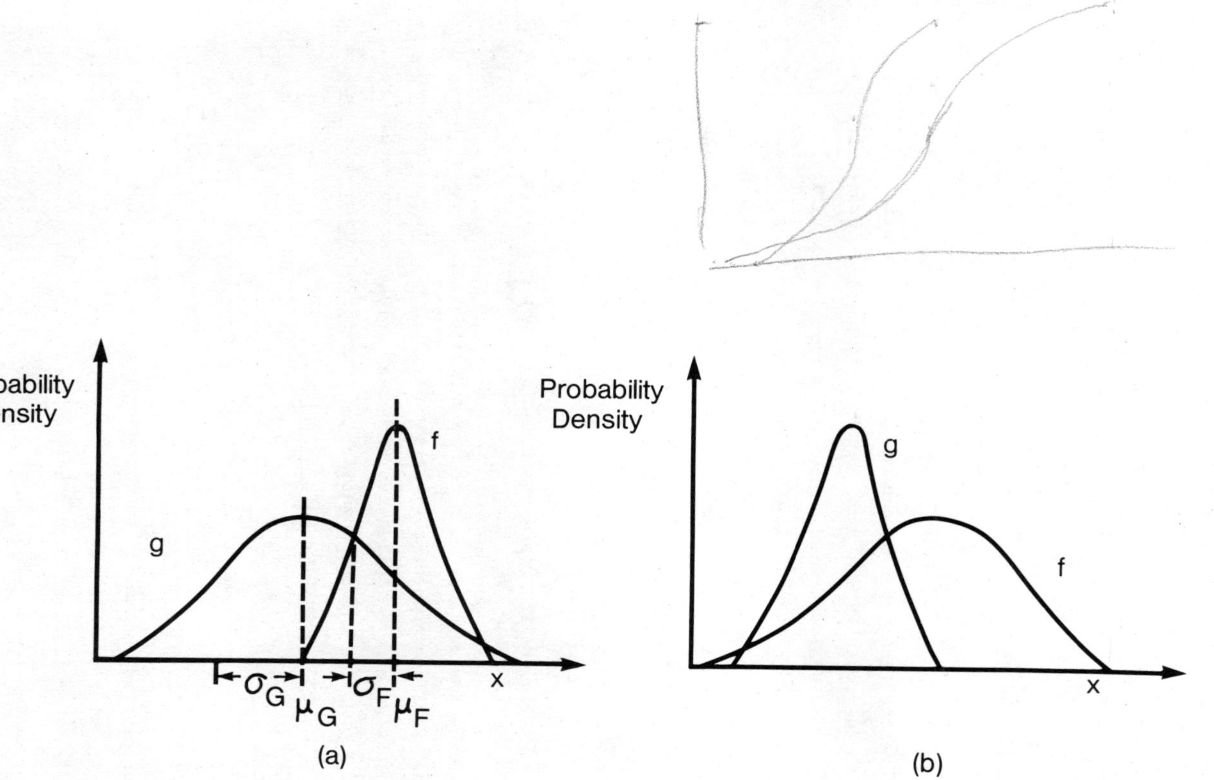

Figure 2-2. EV Dominance (a) and Nondominance (b)

Some of the implications of EV analysis for modern finance theory were reviewed in Chapter 1. Despite its simplicity and appeal, the EV dominance criterion, or EV rule, can fail to make a choice between two prospects even in obvious cases. As an example, consider outcomes X and Y, with distribution functions F and G respectively, for which $P(X = \$1) = P(X = \$2) = 1/2$, and $P(Y = \$1) = 1$. Then $\mu_F = \$3/2 > \mu_G = \$1$, and $\sigma_F = \$1/2 > \sigma_G = \$0$. The EV rule, blindly applied, is unable to choose F in preference to G even though F is obviously better than G for anyone who prefers a \$2 payoff to a \$1 payoff. Furthermore, EV analysis is generally not consistent with expected utility analysis in the presence of nonlinear utility functions, except in special cases. The relation between these two approaches is explored more fully in Section 2.17. A related criticism of the use of σ as a risk measure in financial decision problems concerns its symmetric treatment of high and low outcomes. Several "one-sided" risk measures that have been proposed recently will be discussed later in Chapters 3 and 4.

2.6 Multivariate Distribution Functions

An n-vector random variable is a random variable taking values in n-dimensional Euclidean space Re^n. Essentially, an n-vector random variable X is an ordered collection of n real-valued random variables $X_1, X_2, \ldots, X_n$, called the <u>components</u> of X. The <u>distribution function</u> of X, also called the <u>multivariate distribution</u> (or simply, <u>distribution</u>) of $X_1, \ldots, X_n$ is

$$F(x_1, \ldots, x_n) = P(X_1 \leq x_1, \ldots, X_n \leq x_n) \tag{2.12}$$

and has properties so similar to those of the univariate case that we refrain from stating them explicitly. Associated with the distribution F of $X_1, \ldots, X_n$ are n univariate distribution functions $F_1, \ldots, F_n$, called the <u>marginal distributions</u> of $X_1, \ldots, X_n$:

$$F_i(x_i) = F(X_1 < \infty, \ldots, X_{i-1} < \infty, X_i \leq x_i, X_{i+1} < \infty, \ldots, X_n < \infty) \tag{2.13}$$

for $i = 1,\ldots,n$. The X_i are said to be independent if $F(x_1,\ldots,x_n) = F_1(x_1)\ldots F_n(x_n)$ for all $(x_1,\ldots,x_n) \in Re^n$, and to be dependent otherwise. If $u(x_1,\ldots,x_n)$ is a real-valued function defined on the range of $X = (X_1,\ldots,X_n)$, then under restrictions similar to those of the univariate case, $u(X)$ is a real-valued random variable with expected value

$$Eu(X) = \int_{Re^n} u(x_1,\ldots,x_n)dF(x_1,\ldots,x_n). \tag{2.14}$$

Of particular importance are the means μ_i, defined as $\mu_i = E(X_i) \equiv \int_{-\infty}^{\infty} x_i \, dF_i(x_i)$, the variances $\sigma_i^2 \equiv \sigma_{ii} = E(X_i - \mu_i)^2 \equiv \int_{-\infty}^{\infty} (x_i - \mu_i)^2 \, dF_i(x_i)$, and the covariances $\sigma_{ij} = \sigma_{ji} = E[(X_i - \mu_i)(X_j - \mu_j)]$. The mean vector μ is the n-vector whose ith component is μ_i, and the variance-covariance matrix Σ is the matrix whose (i,j) element is σ_{ij}.

2.7 Conditional Distributions and Conditional Expected Values

Suppose X and Y are real-valued random variables with bivariate distribution function $H(x,y)$ and marginal distributions F and G, respectively. Suppose $a < b$ and $P(a \le Y \le b) = G(b) - G(a^-)$ is positive. Then the conditional distribution of X given $a \le Y \le b$ can be defined as

$$F^Y(x|a \le Y \le b) = P(X \le x, a \le Y \le b)/P(a \le Y \le b). \tag{2.15}$$

This is a univariate distribution function, and therefore it "corresponds" to a real-valued random variable that we might denote by the somewhat awkward symbol $[X|a \le Y \le b]$. Given a function u defined on the range of X, the conditional expectation $E[u(X)|a \le Y \le b]$ is defined as $\int_{-\infty}^{\infty} u(x) \, dF^Y(x|a \le Y \le b)$, and exists if $Eu(X)$ is finite. The concept of a conditional expectation of $u(X)$ given that Y assumes a specific value y, denoted by $E[u(X)|Y = y]$, is somewhat delicate to define properly. Essentially,

$$E[u(X)|Y = y] = \lim_{h \downarrow 0} E[u(X)|y - h \leq Y \leq y + h]$$

if this limit exists, which will be the case in most commonly encountered practical situations. For a proper treatment, see the books of Loeve (1963) or Breiman (1968). If Eu(X) exists, then $E[u(X)|Y = y]$ (when properly defined) exists except for a set of y of probability zero, and

$$Eu(X) = \int_{-\infty}^{\infty} E[u(X)|Y = y]\, dG(y). \tag{2.16}$$

Finally, the symbol $E[u(X)|Y]$ will be used to denote the random variable whose value on the event $(Y = y)$ is $E[u(X)|Y = y]$. In this notation, Eq. (2.16) reads as $Eu(X) = EE[u(X)|Y]$. Note in particular that if X and Y are independent, then $E[u(X)|Y] = Eu(X)$ with probability one.

2.8 Utility for Wealth Functions

From its very inception, the theory of portfolio choice has been based primarily on some form of mean-variance analysis. The reformulation of the theory in terms of expected utilities appears to be a recent innovation, with notable early works being those of Arrow (1965) and Samuelson (1967a). In these early writings, the portfolio problem is addressed in a static, or single-period, context. That is, the investor is assumed to possess a utility function for net wealth held at the end of the investment period, and the optimal portfolio decision is the one that maximizes the expected value of this function. In the case of the individual investor, it might be argued that a more fundamental approach should be based on the investor's utility function for consumption over time. Utility for wealth would be a secondary construct that summarizes the maximum expected utility of future consumption for the given wealth level. The most general treatment of the problem from this standpoint appears to be that of Fama (1970b). Fama shows, among other things, that the properties of nonsatiation and of risk aversion in the utility function for multiperiod consumption are propagated to all the static or single-period utility for net terminal wealth functions. Accordingly, we shall deal from now on with utility functions for net terminal wealth as though these were the fundamental entities of the theory.

The reader may note that the meaning of the term "wealth" has not been specified. This omission is intentional, since the appropriate definition of "wealth" depends on the problem context. If the investor's sole source of income is return on investment, then "wealth" means instantaneous net value of total asset holdings. If borrowing is permitted, wealth could be negative, and this may or may not correspond to "ruin," depending on borrowing constraints. If the investor receives income from sale of labor services but borrowing against future wages is not permitted, then wealth means single-period wage plus return on investment. On the other hand, if at least some borrowing against future wages is allowed, this can be included in wealth. In any case the stochastic dominance theorems themselves, as mathematical statements, are essentially independent of these details. What _does_ matter is that the utility function be well defined and finite over the entire range of possible random outcomes. That is, if I is the smallest interval such that all the random variables under consideration take values in I with probability one, then the utility function must be defined and finite on I. We shall further assume, unless otherwise stated, that the random variables are bounded from below and that I is a closed interval. Then, by a change in origin if necessary, we may take I to be either $[0,\infty)$ or a finite closed interval $[a,b]$, which for convenience will often be presumed to be $[0,1]$.

2.9 Increasing Utility Functions

The most general imaginable restriction on utility for wealth $u(x)$ is that it be nondecreasing in x, for all $x \in I$. In the present discussion we shall make the stronger assumptions that u is strictly increasing and bounded: $u(x) < u(y)$ if $x < y$, for $x,y \in I$, and there is some number M such that $u(x) \leq M$ for all $x \in I$. For simplicity we shall assume also that u is continuously once-differentiable with bounded derivative on I and positive derivative on the interior of I. The class of all such functions will be denoted by U_1. Formally:

$$U_1 = \{u{:}u,u' \text{ are continuous and bounded on I, and } u' > 0 \text{ on } I^0\}, \tag{2.17}$$

where I^0 is the interior of I with $I^0 = (0,\infty)$ if $I = [0,\infty)$, or (a,b) if $I = [a,b]$. The definition of U_1 allows u' to equal zero at an end-point of I.

Aside from nonsatiation, no clearly specified attitudes toward risk are apparent in this class; both risk-seeking and risk-avoiding behavior are possible. To see this, consider the gamble on total wealth X: $P(X = 0) = P(X = 4) = 1/2$. The actuarial or fair value of X is $\mu = E(X) = 2$. For $u_1(x) = x^{1/2}$ in U_1, we have $Eu_1(X) = 1 = u_1(1) < u_1(1.5)$. The function u_1 thus corresponds to risk-averse behavior, since a sure prospect of \$1.50 is strictly preferred to the gamble having the higher fair value \$2. On the other hand, for $u_2(x) = x^2$ in U_1, we have $Eu_2(X) = 8 = u_2(\sqrt{8}) > u_2(2.5)$. The function u_2 thus corresponds to risk-seeking behavior, since a sure prospect of \$2.50 is less preferred than the gamble whose fair value is only \$2. These examples can be generalized by introducing the concept of a certainty equivalent or a risk premium. If $u \in U_1$ and X is a gamble on wealth with distribution function F, the <u>certainty equivalent</u> is the unique value of c that satisfies

$$u(c) = E(u,F). \tag{2.18}$$

For example, c = 1 for u_1 and F above. Equation (2.18) and the theory of expected utility say that the individual is indifferent between a sure prospect of c and the option of "playing out" the risky prospect X with distribution function F. Thus he would exchange c for title to X, and conversely, but he would not give up title to X for any amount $x < c$. The difference between the fair value μ_F and the certainty equivalent c is called the <u>risk premium</u> π:

$$\pi = \mu_F - c \tag{2.19}$$

so that by Eq. (2.18), $u(\mu_F - \pi) = E(u,F)$. If $\pi > 0$, then the individual would accept a payment that is less than the fair value E(X) in exchange for X; if $\pi = 0$, then he values X at its fair value; and if $\pi < 0$, then he would not exchange X for its fair value. Generally speaking, these three possibilities are respectively associated with the notions of risk aversion, risk neutrality, and risk-seeking. As indicated, the class U_1 allows all three cases. It also allows all three types of risk associated behavior on different parts of I.

2.10 Increasing Concave Utility Functions

In an area of application like portfolio analysis, it appears to be reasonable to restrict attention to the subclass of U_1 that corresponds to risk-averse behavior. For special two-point gambles X of the form $P(X = x) = \alpha$, $P(X = y) = 1 - \alpha$, $0 \leq \alpha \leq 1$, risk aversion requires

$$\alpha u(x) + (1 - \alpha)u(y) \leq u[\alpha x + (1 - \alpha)y]. \qquad (2.20)$$

A function u that satisfies (2.20) for all $x,y \in I$ and all $\alpha \in [0,1]$ is said to be <u>concave</u> on I. If, in addition, the inequality is strict whenever $x \neq y$ and $0 < \alpha < 1$, the function is <u>strictly concave</u>. For simplicity, we will restrict attention to the class U_2 of strictly concave functions $u \in U_1$ having continuous and bounded second derivatives u'' in I. Since the strict concavity condition requires that the linear interpolation of u between any two points in I lie below the graph of u, as shown in Figure 2-3, it seems intuitively clear that the graph of u must continually "bend over" with increasing x, as indicated. Otherwise stated, strict concavity is equivalent to u' being strictly decreasing, or $u'' < 0$. For a proof of this equivalence, see, e.g., Hardy, et al. (1967), Mangasarian (1969), or Zangwill (1969). Our formal definition of the class U_2 is thus

$$U_2 = \{u : u \in U_1,\ u'' \text{ is continuous and bounded on } I, \text{ and } u'' < 0 \text{ on } I^0\}. \qquad (2.21)$$

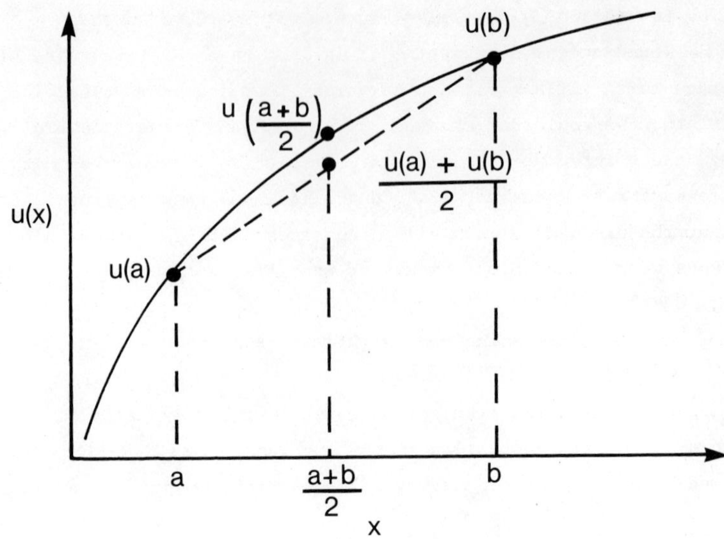

Figure 2-3. An Increasing, Strictly Concave Utility Function

If an investor's utility function is in U_2, then he is always strictly risk-averse and never risk-neutral to gambles in I. This follows immediately from Jensen's inequality:

$$E(u,F) < u(\mu_F) \text{ if } u \in U_2 \text{ and } F \text{ is nondegenerate on } I \text{ in the sense that } P(X \neq \mu_F) > 0. \tag{2.22}$$

Note that if u is concave but not strictly concave, (2.22) remains true with < replaced by ≤. For a simple proof of Jensen's inequality in the nonstrict case, see Feller (1966). The strict inequality case also follows almost immediately from Feller's method.

Of some potential interest in regard to U_2 is the fact that u $\in U_2$ if and only if u is in U_1, twice continuously differentiable with u'' bounded, and satisfies

$$\frac{1}{2}\,u(x) + \frac{1}{2}\,u(y) < u\left(\frac{x+y}{2}\right), \quad \text{for all distinct x and y in I.} \tag{2.23}$$

Hence the concavity property for U_2 can be expressed using only simple 50-50 or even-chance gambles.

There are a number of simple forms of utility functions in U_2 that are commonly used in "practice" because of their tractability. The power function $u(x) = -x^{-c}$ with $c > 0$ is in U_2 when $I = [a,b]$ or $I = [a,\infty)$ with $a > 0$, and the power function $u(x) = x^c$, $0 < c < 1$, and the logarithmic utility function $u(x) = \log x$ are in U_2 whenever I is a bounded closed interval included in $(0,\infty)$. The exponential utility function $u(x) = -e^{-cx}$, $c > 0$ is in U_2 for $I = [a,\infty)$ with a finite. The familiar quadratic utility function $u(x) = x - cx^2$, $c > 0$ is in U_2 for $I = [a,1/(2c)]$, $-\infty < a < 1/(2c)$. The quadratic function is strictly concave in the sense of (2.20) for all real x,y, but is increasing only for $x < 1/(2c)$. To verify these facts, one need only check the derivative conditions in definition (2.21).

To explore further the risk-aversion properties of functions in U_2, we follow Arrow (1965) and Pratt (1964) and define the _absolute risk aversion_ at x, $R_a(x)$, and the _relative_ (or proportional) _risk aversion_ at x, $R_r(x)$, by

$$R_a(x) = -u''(x)/u'(x) \tag{2.24}$$

$$R_r(x) = -xu''(x)/u'(x) = xR_a(x) \tag{2.25}$$

whenever u' and u'' exist and $u'(x) \neq 0$. For $u \in U_2$, $u'(x)$ can be zero only at the upper end-point of I if I is bounded. When u is in U_2 on I, $R_a(x)$ is positive for all x in I^0, and $R_r(x)$ is positive for all positive x in I^0. Since R_a and R_r involve second derivatives of u, they correspond to measures of the curvature of the graph of u. Note that the second derivative is also a curvature measure, but it is not a useful measure of risk aversion since it is not invariant under utility scale changes of the form $v(x) = au(x)$ with $a > 0$. R_a and R_r are, however, invariant under such scale transformations. All three of u'', R_a, and R_r are invariant under an origin change for u of the form $v(x) = u(x) + b$.

To interpret these measures, we follow Pratt (1964) in considering small fair gambles about a base wealth level x_0. Thus terminal wealth is $X = x_0 + \xi$, where ξ is a random variable with range $[-h,h]$, mean 0, and variance σ^2 that approaches zero as $h \downarrow 0$. If u is continuously differentiable three times in $[x_0 - h, x_0 + h]$, a Taylor series expansion of $u(x_0 + \xi)$ in powers of ξ up to order three is valid. This gives the following useful expression for the risk-premium π of the gamble:

$$\pi = \frac{1}{2}\sigma^2 R_a(x_0) + o(\sigma^2), \tag{2.26}$$

where $o(\sigma^2)$ stands for terms for which $o(\sigma^2)/\sigma^2$ approaches zero as σ^2 approaches zero. For gambles in which the random increment ξ (and hence also σ^2) is independent of x_0, π is essentially proportional to $R_a(x_0)$. For proportional gambles in which $\xi = x_0\eta$ for some fixed, small gamble η, the relative risk-premium $\pi_r = \pi/x_0$ is essentially proportional to $R_r(x_0)$.

2.11 Decreasing Absolute Risk Aversion

Let ξ denote a small favorable gamble, such as an even-chance gamble between winning \$10 and losing \$9, and consider a risk-averse individual who can accept or refuse ξ as he pleases. Inasmuch as his willingness to take the gamble may depend on his present net wealth, it does not seem unreasonable to suppose that if he would accept ξ when his present net wealth is x_0, then he would also accept ξ at any net wealth position that exceeds x_0.

If we accept the principle that a small gamble becomes more attractive (or at least does not become less attractive) to a risk-averse investor as his net wealth increases, then Eq. (2.26) implies that $R_a(x)$ is nonincreasing in x. We shall accordingly define a subclass U_d of U_2 such that R_a is bounded and continuously differentiable on I and $R'_a \leq 0$ on I. Formally,

$$U_d = \{u : u \in U_2,\ R'_a \text{ is continuous, bounded and nonpositive on } I\}. \tag{2.27}$$

Note that we are <u>not</u> requiring R_a to be strictly decreasing. Functions in U_d are said to exhibit decreasing absolute risk aversion, and we shall occasionally refer to them as DARA utility functions. A sufficient condition for the existence of R'_a on I^0 is the existence of the third derivative u''' of u. Then, $R'_a(x) = [-u'(x)u'''(x) + u''(x)^2]/[u'(x)]^2$, so $R'_a \leq 0$ only if $u'(x)u'''(x) \geq u''(x)^2$ for all $x \in I^0$. Since $u' > 0$ and $u'' < 0$ on I^0, this requires $u'''(x) > 0$ for all $x \in I^0$.

Under appropriate regularity conditions, Pratt (1964) proves that R_a is decreasing in wealth position x if and only if the risk premium π is a decreasing function of x for every nondegenerate X. And, according to Arrow (1965), whom we have paraphrased above, decreasing absolute risk aversion seems quite reasonable since it "amounts to saying that the willingness to engage in small bets of fixed size increases with wealth, in the sense that the odds demanded diminish. If absolute risk aversion increased with wealth, it would follow that as an individual became wealthier, he would actually decrease the amount of risky assets held" (p. 35). Arrow has also suggested that relative risk aversion $R_r(x)$ is likely to be an increasing function of wealth level x. Since the theoretical arguments in favor of this assumption are not very convincing, however, and since serious doubts about its empirical validity have been raised by Stiglitz (1969), we shall not impose this condition on the utility functions. The DARA hypothesis appears to be widely accepted, however. It is noteworthy that quadratic utility is not a member of the class U_d, since $u(x) = x - cx^2$ with $c > 0$ gives $R_a(x) = 2c/(1 - 2cx)$, and $R'_a(x) = 4c^2/(1 - 2cx)^2 > 0$. Although quadratic utility may seem to be entirely reasonable on other grounds, its use would force risky assets to be inferior goods, and such behavior would be difficult to justify.

2.12 Positive Third Derivatives

As noted above, if u''' exists and R_a is nonincreasing, then $u'''(x)$ must be positive for all $x \in I^0$. Thus a positive third derivative is a necessary condition for DARA utilities. It is not a sufficient condition, however, since it is possible to have $u''' > 0$ and not have decreasing absolute risk aversion. For example, the "almost quadratic" function $u(x) = x - cx^2 + \varepsilon x^3$ is in U_2 on $I = [0,1/(4c)]$ if $0 \leq \varepsilon < 4c^2/3$ and has positive third derivative if $\varepsilon > 0$. But if $\varepsilon < 4c^2/6$, then $R'_a(x) > 0$ for small values of x. Hence when we consider utility functions u with $u' > 0$, $u'' < 0$, and $u''' > 0$, we are viewing a situation that is intermediate between the U_2 and U_d contexts. The class of such utility functions will be denoted by U_3. Formally,

$$U_3 = \{u{:}u \in U_2,\ u''' \text{ is continuous and bounded on } I, \text{ and } u''' > 0 \text{ on } I^0\}. \tag{2.28}$$

In a manner of speaking, $\{u' > 0,\ u'' < 0,\ u''' > 0\}$ says that utility increases at a decreasing rate, the absolute value of which becomes smaller as x increases. If the effect of $u''' > 0$ is especially strong, then $|u''(x)|$ will approach zero as x gets large and u will be nearly linear. Insofar as $u' > 0$ and $u'' < 0$ tend to bend or curve the utility function from its initially rising trajectory back toward the horizontal, the effect of $u''' > 0$ is to slow the rate of this bending.

In conjunction with the simple inequality (2.23) for strict concavity in the increasing utility context, there are similar inequalities involving simple gambles for functions in U_3. For thrice-differentiable functions u, $u''' > 0$ on I^0 if and only if

$$\frac{1}{4}u(x) + \frac{3}{4}u(x + 2\delta) < \frac{1}{4}u(x + 3\delta) + \frac{3}{4}u(x + \delta) \tag{2.29}$$

for all $x \in I$ and all $\delta > 0$ such that $x + 3\delta \in I$. Since this result may be unfamiliar, we offer the following simple proof: Let

$$D(x,\delta) = \frac{1}{4}u(x + 3\delta) + \frac{3}{4}u(x + \delta) - \frac{1}{4}u(x) - \frac{3}{4}u(x + 2\delta).$$

By writing

$$u(x + \delta) = u(x) + \int_x^{x+\delta} u'(t)dt,$$

and so forth, we have

$$4D(x,\delta) = \int_x^{x+3\delta} u'(t)dt + 3\int_x^{x+\delta} u'(t)dt - 3\int_x^{x+2\delta} u'(t)dt$$

$$= \int_x^{x+\delta} u'(t)dt + \int_{x+2\delta}^{x+3\delta} u'(t)dt - 2\int_{x+\delta}^{x+2\delta} u'(t)dt$$

$$= \int_x^{x+\delta} [u'(t) + u'(t + 2\delta) - 2u'(t + \delta)]dt.$$

The condition $u''' > 0$ is equivalent to saying that the function $(-u')$ is strictly concave. Thus $u'(t) + u'(t + 2\delta) - 2u'(t + \delta) > 0$ for all t and all $\delta > 0$, and this implies $D(x,\delta) > 0$ as was to be shown. Viewed in a gambles format, as in the accompanying diagram with $x = \$1000$, $\delta = \$100$, option 1 for the left side of (2.29), and option 2 for the right side of

	Probability			
	1/4	1/4	1/4	1/4
Option 1	\$1000	\$1200	\$1200	\$1200
Option 2	\$1300	\$1100	\$1100	\$1100

(2.29), the inequality of (2.29) asserts that option 2 is preferred to option 1.

2.13 Examples of Utility Functions

The preceding sections identify the types of classes of utility functions that apply to the particular forms of stochastic dominance that will be discussed momentarily. Before going ahead with that, we shall summarize the previous discussion with some specific forms. It can be assumed that $I = [0,\infty)$ except in the quadratic case. However, because the logarithmic and power 1 functions are unbounded above, these will be in U_1 or U_2 as defined earlier only if I is bounded above.

	Linear	Quad.	Exponen.	Log.	Power 1	Power 2
u(x)	x	$x - cx^2$	$-e^{-cx}$	$\ln(x + d)$	$(x + d)^{1-c}$	$\frac{-1}{(x + d)^c}$
Subject to	*	$\left\{\begin{matrix} c > 0 \\ x < 1/(2c) \end{matrix}\right\}$	$c > 0$	$d > 0$	$\left\{\begin{matrix} d > 0 \\ 0 < c < 1 \end{matrix}\right\}$	$\{c > 0, d > 0\}$
u'(x)	1	$1 - 2cx$	ce^{-cx}	$\frac{1}{(x + d)}$	$\frac{(1 - c)}{(x + d)^c}$	$\frac{c}{(x + d)^{c+1}}$
u''(x)	0	$-2c$	$-c^2e^{-cx}$	$\frac{-1}{(x + d)^2}$	$\frac{-c(1 - c)}{(x + d)^{c+1}}$	$\frac{-(c + 1)c}{(x + d)^{c+2}}$
u'''(x)	0	0	c^3e^{-cx}	$\frac{2}{(x + d)^3}$	$\frac{(c + 1)(c)(1 - c)}{(x + d)^{c+2}}$	$\frac{(c + 2)(c + 1)c}{(x + d)^{c+3}}$
$R_a(x)$	*	$\frac{2c}{(1 - 2cx)}$	c	$\frac{1}{(x + d)}$	$\frac{c}{(x + d)}$	$\frac{(x + 1)}{(x + d)}$
$R'_a(x)$	*	$\frac{4c^2}{(1 - 2cx)^2}$	0	$\frac{-1}{(x + d)^2}$	$\frac{-c}{(x + d)^2}$	$\frac{-(c + 1)}{(x + d)^2}$
$R_r(x)$	*	$\frac{2cx}{(1 - 2cx)}$	cx	$\frac{x}{(x + d)}$	$\frac{cx}{(x + d)}$	$\frac{(c + 1)x}{(x + d)}$
$R'_r(x)$	*	$\frac{2c}{(1 - 2cx)^2}$	c	$\frac{d}{(x + d)^2}$	$\frac{cd}{(x + d)^2}$	$\frac{(c + 1)d}{(x + d)^2}$

The linear function (risk-neutral) requires no comment except to note that it is a limiting case of functions that satisfy concavity (2.23) along with (2.29). All other functions are risk-averse since $u' > 0$ and $u'' < 0$. Of these, the quadratic is the only one with increasing absolute risk aversion, and the exponential is the only one with constant absolute risk aversion. All the log and power functions, which together constitute a rather large family, have decreasing absolute risk aversion and increasing proportional or relative risk aversion. Relative risk aversion also increases for the quadratic and for the exponential. The log and power 1 functions have the occasionally important property that relative risk aversion is always less than unity. As seen by the u''' row, no third derivative is ever negative, and (2.29) holds except for the linear and quadratic forms.

2.14 Stochastic Dominance

The theorems for stochastic dominance in the ensuing sections have the common theme for unanimous preference between two risky prospects in the sense that all individuals whose utility functions are in U will regard one prospect as being at least as desirable as (or more desirable than) the other. The different types of SD correspond to the different U classes defined previously. Before embarking on the formal study, three simple examples are in order.

Example 1: Consider gambles X^1 and Y^1 with the following outcomes:

Outcome Probabilities

	1/6	1/6	1/6	1/6	1/6	1/6
X^1	1	4	1	4	4	4
Y^1	3	4	3	1	1	4

Because Y^1 is better for some outcomes and X^1 is better for others, it is not immediately obvious which gamble is better. Suppose the problem is to choose either X^1 or Y^1, portfolios not allowed. Then the correlations between the X^1 and Y^1 outcomes are irrelevant, and the gambles can be replaced by equivalent gambles X and Y with reordered outcomes:

	Probabilities					
	1/6	1/6	1/6	1/6	1/6	1/6
X	1	1	4	4	4	4
Y	1	1	3	3	4	4

Probabilistically speaking, gambles X^1 and X are the same in the sense that their distribution functions are equal, similarly for Y^1 and Y. The original problem is thus equivalent to choosing between X and Y. The solution is now clear, since X always returns at least as much as, and sometimes more than, Y. Any investor with an increasing utility function $u \in U_1$ will strictly prefer X to Y, hence also X^1 to Y^1. Note that neither X nor Y can be eliminated on the basis of the EV rule, since $\mu_X = 3 > \mu_Y = 8/3$ and $\sigma_X^2 = 2 > \sigma_Y^2 = 14/9$.

Example 2: Consider gambles X and Y as follows:

	Probabilities					
	1/6	1/6	1/6	1/6	1/6	1/6
X	1	1	4	4	4	4
Y	0	2	3	3	4	4

Since it is impossible to reorder the outcomes so that X is always at least as good as Y, X and Y are not ordered in the context of U_1. For if $u_1(x) = x$, then $Eu_1(X) = E(X) = 3 > Eu_1(Y) = E(Y) = 8/3$, and X is preferred; but if $u_2(x) = (x - 2)[(x - 2)^2 + .01]^{-1/2}$, which is in U_1, then $Eu_2(X) = 2.00492 < Eu_2(Y) = 2.98883$, and Y is preferred. If we impose the additional restriction of risk aversion, however, X becomes unambiguously preferred. To see this, let us decompose X and Y into mixtures of simpler gambles. X is equivalent to a 1/3 chance on a gamble X_1 and a 2/3 chance on a gamble X_2, where X_1 returns 1 with certainty and X_2 returns 4 with certainty. Y is equivalent to a 1/3 chance on a gamble Y_1 and a 2/3 chance on a gamble Y_2, where in turn Y_1 is an even-chance gamble on 0 and 2 and Y_2 is an even-chance gamble on 3 and 4. For every $u \in U_2$,

$$Eu(Y_1) = \frac{1}{2}u(0) + \frac{1}{2}u(2) < u(1) = Eu(X_1),$$

and

$$Eu(Y_2) = \frac{1}{2}u(3) + \frac{1}{2}u(4) < u(4) = Eu(X_2).$$

By Eq. (2.9),

$$Eu(Y) = \frac{1}{3}Eu(Y_1) + \frac{2}{3}Eu(Y_2) < \frac{1}{3}Eu(X_1) + \frac{2}{3}Eu(X_2) = Eu(X),$$

so X is strictly preferred to Y.

Example 3: Consider the example from Section 2.12:

	Probability			
	1/4	1/4	1/4	1/4
X	13	11	11	11
Y	10	12	12	12

We take I = [0,13] with outcomes in hundreds of dollars. Neither X nor Y is unambiguously preferred in U_2. For $u_1(x) = -4(13 - x)^3$ we have $Eu_1(Y) = -30 < Eu_1(X) = -24$, and X is preferred; for $u_2(x) = 4(x - 12) - 4[(x - 12)^2 + .01]^{1/2}$ we have $Eu_2(X) = -6.01996 < Eu_2(Y) = -4.30250$, and Y is preferred. However, as shown by (2.29), X is strictly preferred in U_3. Since the DARA utility functions U_d are a (strict) subclass of U_3, X is also strictly preferred to Y in U_d. It is also possible to construct examples that are unambiguously strictly ordered in U_d but not ordered in U_3. We shall return to this topic in Section 2.18 after the necessary tools have been developed.

We now generalize the preceding examples by introducing the concepts of first-, second-, and third-degree stochastic dominance. Higher-order degrees of stochastic dominance can be defined, but we shall not do so except for the case of DARA SD, which is treated in Section 2.18. On the theory that comparing a function with itself is an empty exercise, we shall assume in what follows that distribution functions denoted by different letters or subscripts are different functions. The interval I will be taken as $I = [0,\infty)$ or $I = [0,1]$ with no loss in generality, and all probability distributions assign total probability 1 to I.

DEFINITION. _For_ $i = 1, 2,$ _or_ 3 _we write_

$$F >_i G \text{ if and only if } E(u,F) > E(u,G) \text{ for all } u \in U_i. \tag{2.30}$$

We refer to $>_1$ as _first-degree stochastic dominance_, or _FSD_; to $>_2$ as _second-degree stochastic dominance_, or _SSD_; and $>_3$ as _third-degree dominance_, or _TSD_. The FSD, SSD, and TSD orderings have a number of properties that are extremely simple yet very important in practical applications. They are

(a) Asymmetry: if $F >_i G$, then it is false that $G >_i F$;
(b) Transitivity: if $F >_i G$ and $G >_i H$, then $F >_i H$.

Hence the dominance relations are partial orders on sets of risky prospects. It is clear that if one class of utility functions is a subset of another class, then dominance in the larger class necessarily implies dominance in the smaller class (but not conversely). Thus

(c) $F >_1 G$ implies $F >_2 G$ implies $F >_3 G$.

Recall that we defined the classes U_1, U_2, and U_3 via strict positivity or negativity conditions on various derivatives in the interior I^0 of I. If analogous classes of functions U are defined by weakening the derivative conditions to their nonstrict versions--or, more generally, by dispensing with derivatives entirely--then corresponding nonstrict stochastic dominance relations are obtained (see Appendix 2B). Therefore it might be more accurate to refer to the above as strict stochastic dominance definitions, but we shall not do so here.

Recall also that we have defined the U_i classes in such a way that utility and its relevant derivatives are continuous and bounded on I. Thus E(u,F) and E(u,G) are finite. The theorems given below under these assumptions hold also under more general conditions for utility functions, as we shall prove in Appendix 2B.

In Examples 1 through 3 above, we were able to verify the SD relations using ad hoc procedures. Theorems 2.1 through 2.3, which follow, enable us to prove or disprove the existence of an SD relation in terms of explicitly computable properties of the distribution functions. For any distribution F on I with $I = [0,\infty)$ or $I = [0,1]$, we define

$$\begin{aligned} F^1(x) &= F(x) \\ F^2(x) &= \int_0^x F^1(y)dy \\ F^3(x) &= \int_0^x F^2(y)dy. \end{aligned} \qquad (2.31)$$

Then $F^2(x)$ is the area under the graph of F(y) from y = 0 to y = x, and $F^3(x)$ is the area under $F^2(y)$ from y = 0 to y = x. The basic SD theorems are as follows, with $F \neq G$ and $I = [0,1]$ or $I = [0,\infty)$. Note that the theorems give conditions that are both necessary and sufficient for stochastic dominance.

THEOREM 2.1. $F >_1 G$ *if and only if* $G(x) \geq F(x)$ *for all* $x \in I$.

THEOREM 2.2. $F >_2 G$ *if and only if* $G^2(x) \geq F^2(x)$ *for all* $x \in I$.

THEOREM 2.3. $F >_3 G$ *if and only if*

(a) $\mu_F \geq \mu_G$, *and*

(b) $G^3(x) \geq F^3(x)$ *for all* $x \in I$.

For convenience in discussion and later proofs, we shall let

$$D^i(x) = G^i(x) - F^i(x)$$

so that $G^i(x) \geq F^i(x)$ is the same as $D^i(x) \geq 0$. Since we have assumed that F and G are not identical, it follows that if $D^i(x) \geq 0$ for all $x \in I$, then there exists a subinterval J of I such that $D^i(x) > 0$ for all $x \in J$. This fact is used in the theorems' proofs, which we shall give in Section 2.15.

It is important to note carefully the sense of the inequalities involved. Generally speaking, the stochastically larger random variable has the smaller distribution function. Intuitively, this corresponds to saying that a smaller distribution function describes outcomes that are distributed farther to the right. This is illustrated on Figure 2-4, where F starts out smaller than G but catches up to and crosses G as x gets larger. Therefore neither $F >_1 G$ nor $G >_1 F$. But as shown on the right part of the figure, $G^2(x)$ lies above $F^2(x)$ throughout (0,1] and therefore $F >_2 G$.

Theorems similar to Theorems 2.1 through 2.3 have a history in the literature of mathematics and mathematical statistics. The latter-day appearance of such theorems in the economics of risky decision-making is due to Blackwell and Girshick (1954), Quirk and Saposnik (1962), Fishburn (1964), Hadar and Russell (1969), Hanoch and Levy (1969), Rothschild and Stiglitz (1970), and Whitmore (1970). Theorem 2.1 has been applied extensively in probabilistic dynamic programming, especially in the optimal control of stopped random walks, where it is used to establish the form of the optimal policy. For examples of this type, see Breiman (1964), Ross (1970), or Pye (1966). Theorems analogous to Theorem 2.2 have been applied by Bessler and Veinott (1966) to optimization of multi-echelon inventory systems. An "abstract" version of Theorem 2.2, as outlined in Section 2.19, has been applied to the theory of information systems; for some of this material, see Butterworth (1972) and Ziemba and Butterworth (1975).

The theorems have an immediately obvious yet often very useful consequence. It is clear that if $F >_i G$ for any $i = 1,2,3$, then the first nonzero values of $G(x) - F(x)$ as x increases from the left of I

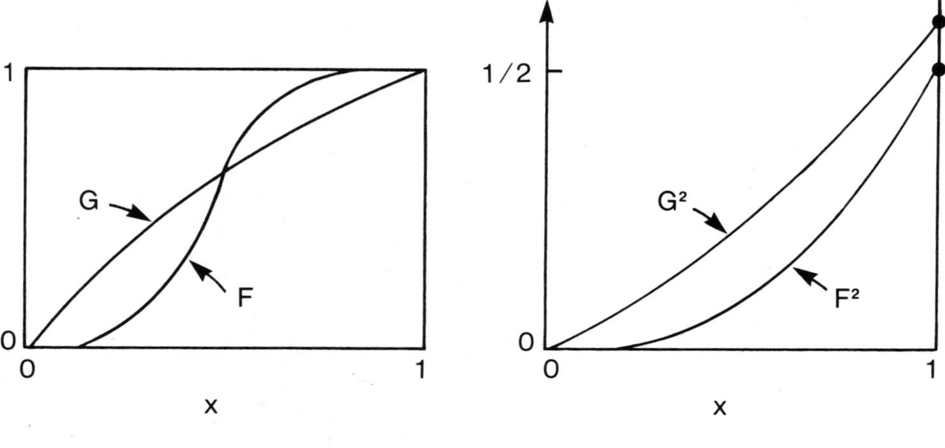

Figure 2-4. $F >_2 G$, or $G^2(x) \geq F^2(x)$ for All x

must be positive. Otherwise we would have $D^1(x) < 0$ for x close to the lower boundary of I, say, for all $x \in I_1$. Furthermore (as will be seen more clearly in the following sections) if $\mu_F > \mu_G$, then $G >_i F$ cannot hold. Therefore if $\mu_F > \mu_G$ and (G - F) "starts negative," neither $F >_i G$ nor $G >_i F$ is true. Note that this conclusion is true irrespective of the magnitudes of the probabilities attached to the "left tail" I_1. It thus can happen that G > F everywhere in I except for an extremely improbable left-hand region I_1 in which G < F. Nevertheless, F does not stochastically dominate G, for it is always possible to construct an appropriate utility function for which G is strictly preferred. We shall not explore this left-tail problem further, but we recognize it as being an important, if unfortunate, weakness in stochastic dominance methodology as it presently exists.

We now reexamine Examples 1 through 3 in the light of the theorems.

Example 1:

	Probability					
	1/6	1/6	1/6	1/6	1/6	1/6
X^1	1	4	1	4	4	4
Y^1	3	4	3	1	1	4

The graphs of the distribution functions F of X^1 and G of Y^1 are shown in Figure 2-5. Clearly, $D^1(x) = G(x) - F(x) \geq 0$ for all x, so $F >_1 G$ by Theorem 2.1.

Example 2:

	Probability					
	1/6	1/6	1/6	1/6	1/6	1/6
X	1	1	4	4	4	4
Y	0	2	3	3	4	4

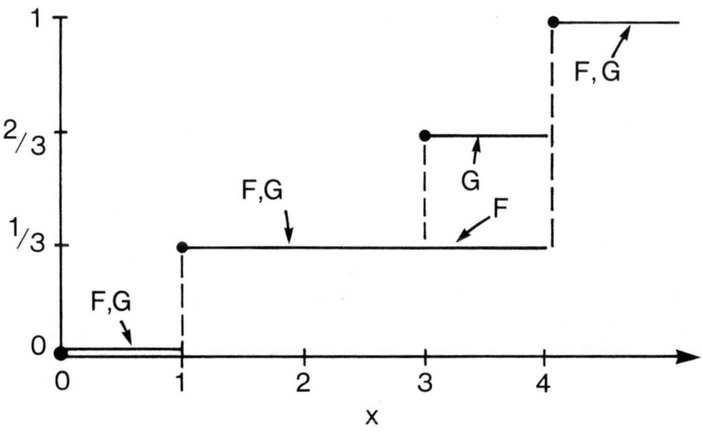

Figure 2-5. $F >_1 G$, or $G(x) \geq F(x)$ for All x

From the graphs of F for X and G for Y in Figure 2-6, we see that $D^1 = G - F$ assumes both positive and negative values. Theorem 2.1 thus implies that $F >_1 G$ and $G >_1 F$ are both false. This means that there must exist functions u_1 and u_2 in U_1 such that $E(u_1,F) > E(u_1,G)$ and $E(u_2,F) < E(u_2,G)$. The theorem allows us to draw this conclusion without having to construct specific examples. From Figure 2-6 it is clear that $D^2(x) \geq 0$ for all x. Thus $F >_2 G$, by Theorem 2.2.

Example 3:

	Probability			
	1/4	1/4	1/4	1/4
X	13	11	11	11
Y	10	12	12	12

The graphs of F^2 and F^3 for X and G^2 and G^3 for Y are shown in Figure 2-7. Since D^2 assumes both positive and negative values, SSD is not satisfied. It is not difficult, however, to verify that $D^3(x) \geq 0$ for all x as suggested by the figure. Since $\mu_F \geq \mu_G$, it follows that $F >_3 G$.

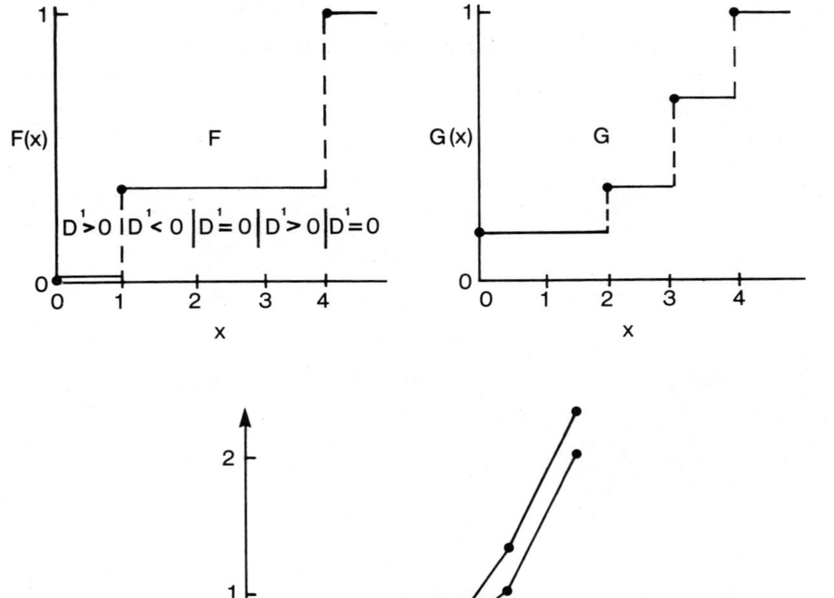

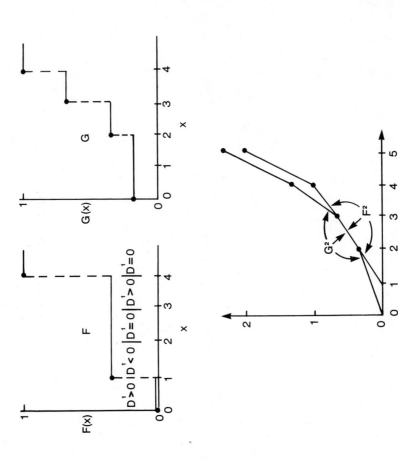

Figure 2-6. $F >_2 G$ When Neither $F >_1 G$ nor $G >_1 F$

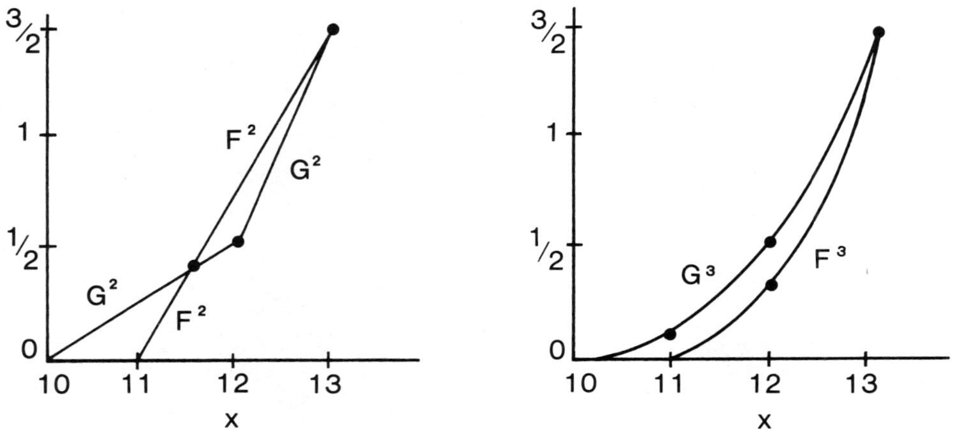

Figure 2-7. $F >_3 G$ When Neither $F >_2 G$ nor $G >_2 F$; $\mu_F = \mu_G$

2.15 Proofs of Stochastic Dominance Theorems

Theorems 2.1 through 2.3 give conditions that are both necessary and sufficient for stochastic dominance. We begin by proving the sufficiency parts. First, consider the case I = [0,1]. For u, u' continuous and bounded on I, we have

$$E(u,F) = \int_{-\infty}^{\infty} u(x)dF(x) = u(1) - \int_0^1 F(x)u'(x)dx. \tag{2.32}$$

To prove this, we note first that it follows immediately from integration by parts if F is continuous on Re [so that F(0) = 0, F(1) = 1]. If F is discrete with jumps at $x_0, x_1, \ldots x_n$ and 1, where $0 = x_0 < x_1 < \ldots < x_n < 1$, then:

$$E(u,F) = F(x_0)u(x_0) + \sum_{i=1}^{n} [F(x_i) - F(x_i^-)]u(x_i) + [1 - F(1^-)]u(1)$$

Since F is a right-continuous step function, we have

$$E(u,F) = F(x_0)u(x_0) + \sum_{i=1}^{n} [F(x_i) - F(x_{i-1})]u(x_i) + [1 - F(x_n)]u(1)$$

$$= - \sum_{i=1}^{n} F(x_{i-1})[u(x_i) - u(x_{i-1})] + u(1). \tag{2.33}$$

Since

$$u(x_i) - u(x_{i-1}) = \int_{x_{i-1}}^{x_i} u'(x)dx$$

Eq. (2.33) can be written as

$$E(u,F) = u(1) - \sum_{i=1}^{n} F(x_{i-1}) \int_{x_{i-1}}^{x_i} u'(x)dx$$

$$= u(1) - \int_0^1 F(x)u'(x)dx.$$

Finally, since a general distribution function is a mixture of a discrete and a continuous distribution, Eq. (2.32) follows from Eq. (2.9). From Eq. (2.32) and a similar expression for E(u,G), we have

$$E(u,F) - E(u,G) = \int_0^1 [G(x) - F(x)]u'(x)dx = \int_0^1 D^1(x)u'(x)dx. \quad (2.34)$$

Thus if $D^1(x) \geq 0$ for all $x \in I$ and $>$ holds for some subinterval of I, then $E(u,F) - E(u,G) > 0$ for all $u \in U_1$. This proves the sufficiency part of Theorem 2.1 for the case $I = [0,1]$. To examine the case of U_2, we integrate Eq. (2.34) by parts:

$$E(u,F) - E(u,G) = \int_0^1 u'(x)dD^2(x) = D^2(1)u'(1) - \int_0^1 D^2(x)u''(x)dx. \quad (2.35)$$

For $u \in U_2$, $u'(1) \geq 0$ and $u'' < 0$ on $I = (0,1)$, which proves sufficiency in Theorem 2.2.

Note that for the linear utility function $u(x) = x$, Eq. (2.35) gives $\mu_F - \mu_G = D^2(1) = \int_0^1 [G(x) - F(x)]dx$. Thus Eq. (2.35) can be rewritten as

$$E(u,F) - E(u,G) = (\mu_F - \mu_G)u'(1) - \int_0^1 D^2(x)u''(x)dx. \quad (2.36)$$

To examine U_3, integrate Eq. (2.36) by parts:

$$E(u,F) - E(u,G) = (\mu_F - \mu_G)u'(1) - D^3(1)u''(1) + \int_0^1 D^3(x)u'''(x)dx.$$

For $u \in U_3$ we have $u'(1) \geq 0$, $u''(1) \leq 0$ and $u''' > 0$ on I^0, which proves sufficiency in Theorem 2.3.

Next consider the unbounded case $I = [0,\infty)$. Defining

$$u(\infty) = \lim_{x\to\infty} u(x)$$

which is finite by assumption, we have

$$E(u,F) = u(\infty) - \int_0^\infty F(x)u'(x)dx. \tag{2.37}$$

To prove this, let $x_0 > 0$ be a continuity point of F, and assume without loss of generality that $u(0) = 0$, so that $u > 0$ on I^0. Then

$$E(u,F) = \int_0^{x_0} u(x)dF(x) + \int_{x_0}^\infty u(x)dF(x)$$

$$= u(x_0)F(x_0) - \int_0^{x_0} F(x)u'(x)dx + \int_{x_0}^\infty u(x)dF(x).$$

Now

$$0 \leq \int_{x_0}^\infty u(x)dF(x) \leq u(\infty) \int_{x_0}^\infty dF(x) = u(\infty)[1 - F(x_0)],$$

which approaches 0 as $x_0 \to \infty$. Similarly,

$$0 \leq \int_0^\infty F(x)u'(x)dx - \int_0^{x_0} F(x)u'(x)dx = \int_{x_0}^\infty F(x)u'(x)dx$$

$$\leq \int_{x_0}^\infty u'(x)dx = u(\infty) - u(x_0),$$

which approaches 0 as $x_0 \to \infty$. Thus as $x_0 \to \infty$, we get Eq. (2.37). Therefore

$$E(u,F) - E(u,G) = \int_0^\infty D^1(x)u'(x)dx \tag{2.38}$$

from which Theorem 2.1 follows if $D^1 \geq 0$ on I. To examine U_2 and U_3 we need only note that the boundedness of u on I implies that u', u'', and u''' all approach zero at ∞, so integration of Eq. (2.38) by parts, as in the finite case, is valid (by limiting arguments like the one above). Theorems 2.2 and 2.3 then follow in the same manner as in the finite case.

To prove the necessity parts of Theorems 2.1 through 2.3, we proceed by example. In the context of U_1, suppose that $D^1(x) < 0$ for some $x \in I$. Then there exists a point x_0, a continuity point of both

F and G and an interior point of I, such that $D^1(x_0) < 0$. Now

$$D^1(x_0) = [1 - F(x_0)] - [1 - G(x_0)] \qquad (2.39)$$

$$= E(f_{x_0},F) - E(f_{x_0},G),$$

where f_{x_0} is the step-function

$$f_{x_0}(x) = \begin{cases} 1, & x > x_0 \\ 1/2, & x = x_0 \\ 0, & x < x_0 \end{cases} . \qquad (2.40)$$

(Since x_0 is a continuity point of F, G, the value of $f_{x_0}(x_0)$ is immaterial; 1/2 is a convenient value.) Note that f_{x_0} is a non-decreasing function but is not in U_1. However, it is possible to approximate f_{x_0} arbitrarily closely by a function $u \in U_1$, so there exists $u \in U_1$ such that $E(u,F) < E(u,G)$. For example, take $u_n(x) = \frac{1}{2} + \frac{1}{2}(x - x_0)[(x - x_0)^2 + 1/n^2]^{-1/2}$. For $n > 0$, $u_n \in U_1$; and as $n \to \infty$, $u_n(x) \downarrow 0$ for $x < x_0$, $u_n(x) \uparrow 1$ for $x > x_0$, and $u_n(x_0) = 1/2$ for all n. Applying the Monotone or the Dominated Convergence Theorem [Loeve (1963), Breiman (1968)] on the intervals $I \cap \{x:x \leq x_0\}$ and $I \cap \{x:x \geq x_0\}$, we have:

$$E(u_n,F) \to E(f_{x_0},F) \text{ as } n \to \infty,$$

and a similar case for G. Thus $D^1(x_0) < 0$ implies $E(u_n,F) < E(u_n,G)$ for some n, so $F >_1 G$ is false.

In the context of U_2, suppose $D^2(x_0) < 0$ for x_0 in the interior of I, which is a continuity point of F and of G. Integrating by parts gives

$$D^2(x_0) = \int_0^{x_0} [G(x) - F(x)]dx = \int_0^{x_0} x[dF(x) - dG(x)]$$

$$+ x_0[G(x_0) - F(x_0)] \qquad (2.41)$$

$$= \int_0^{x_0} (x - x_0)[dF(x) - dG(x)] = E(g_{x_0},F) - E(g_{x_0},G),$$

where g_{x_0} is the piecewise-linear ramp function

$$g_{x_0}(x) = \begin{cases} x - x_0, \ x \leq x_0 \\ 0, \ x > x_0 \end{cases} \quad . \tag{2.42}$$

The function g_{x_0} is nondecreasing and concave, but it is not in U_2. However, the functions $v_n(x) = \frac{1}{2}(x - x_0) - \frac{1}{2}[(x - x_0)^2 + 1/n^2]^{1/2}$ are in U_2, and $v_n \to g_{x_0}$ as $n \to \infty$. By arguments like those above, $D^2(x_0) < 0$ implies $E(v_n,F) < E(v_n,G)$ for large n, so $F >_2 G$ is false.

To prove the necessity part of Theorem 2.3, we must establish two conditions: $\mu_F \geq \mu_G$ and $D^3 \geq 0$. Suppose first that $D^3(x_0) < 0$, with x_0 a continuity point of F, G, and an interior point of I. Integration by parts gives

$$\begin{aligned} D^3(x_0) &= \int_0^{x_0} D^2(x)dx = x_0 D^2(x_0) - \int_0^{x_0} D^1(x)x\,dx \\ &= -x_0 \int_0^{x_0} (x - x_0)dD^1(x) - \frac{1}{2}x_0^2 \int_0^{x_0} dD^1(x) + \frac{1}{2}\int_0^{x_0} x^2\,dD^1(x) \\ &= \frac{1}{2}\int_0^{x_0} (x - x_0)^2\,dD^1(x) = \frac{1}{2}\int_0^{x_0} [-(x - x_0)^2][dF(x) - dG(x)] \\ &= E(h_{x_0},F) - E(h_{x_0},G), \end{aligned} \tag{2.43}$$

where h_{x_0} is the piecewise-quadratic function

$$h_{x_0}(x) = \begin{cases} -\frac{1}{2}(x - x_0)^2, \ x \leq x_0 \\ 0, \ x > x_0 \end{cases} \quad . \tag{2.44}$$

Again, although $h_{x_0} \notin U_3$, the functions

$$w_n(x) = \frac{1}{2}\int_{x_0}^{x} \{[(y - x_0)^2 + 1/n^2]^{1/2} - (y - x_0)\}\,dy$$

are in U_3 for $n > 0$, and $w_n \to h_{x_0}$ as $n \to \infty$. Thus $D^3(x_0) < 0$ implies

$E(w_n,F) < E(w_n,G)$ for large n, and $F >_3 G$ is false.

Finally, suppose $\mu_F < \mu_G$. Consider the function $u(x) = -e^{-kx}$ $(k > 0)$, which is in U_3. Define $\phi_k(x) = kx - 1 + e^{-kx}$, and note that $0 \leq \phi_k(x)/k \leq x$ for all $x \geq 0$. Also, $\phi_k(x)/k \to 0$ as $k \to 0$, for all $x \geq 0$. The Dominated Convergence Theorem thus implies

$$\lim_{k \to 0} \int_I [\phi_k(x)/k] dF(x) = 0$$

so

$$\int_I \phi_k(x) dF(x) = o(k).$$

Thus $E(u,F) = -1 + k\mu_F + o(k)$ as $k \downarrow 0$, and similarly for $E(u,G)$. Then $E(u,F) < E(u,G)$ for sufficiently small k, and $F >_3 G$ is false.

2.16 Special Cases of the SD Theorems

This section examines special cases of the preceding SD theorems, including equal means, simple distribution functions, and single-crossing distributions.

Equal Means

The case of random variables having equal means yields a number of important generalizations and specializations of the stochastic dominance theorems. The first special property is simple, but noteworthy: if $\mu_F = \mu_G$, then $F >_1 G$ is impossible. This is obvious for our "strict" version of FSD by consideration of the linear utility function. More important, the result is true also for the "nonstrict" version of FSD treated in Appendix 2B.

The second special property is sufficiently important to be classed as a theorem.

THEOREM 2.4. *If* $I = [0,1]$ *and* $\mu_F = \mu_G$, *then* $E(u,F) > E(u,G)$ *for all strictly concave*, *strictly increasing* u *if and only if* $E(u,F) > E(u,G)$

for all strictly concave, strictly decreasing u *if and only if* E(u,F) > E(u,G) *for all strictly concave* u.

Proof: For $\mu_F = \mu_G$, Eq. (2.36) gives

$$E(u,F) - E(u,G) = - \int_0^1 D^2(x)u''(x)dx.$$

If $F >_2 G$ and u is strictly concave, i.e., $u'' < 0$, this gives E(u,F) > E(u,G). Thus the first statement implies the other two. Also, the third statement clearly implies the other two, so we need show only that the second implies the first. If the second statement holds, then $E(u_{x0},F) \geq E(u_{x0},G)$ for every $x_0 \in (0,1)$, where u_{x0} is the piece-wise-linear, concave nonincreasing ramp function $u_{x0}(x) = 0$ for $x < x_0$ and $u_{x0}(x) = x_0 - x$ for $x \geq x_0$. Although u_{x0} is not strictly decreasing and not strictly concave, $E(u_{x0},F) \geq E(u_{x0},G)$ follows by limiting considerations like those of the preceding section. It is easy to verify that $E(u_{x0},F) - E(u_{x0},G) = - \int_{x0}^1 [G(x) - F(x)]dx$. The statement that $\int_x^1 [G(y) - F(y)]dy \leq 0$ for all $x \in I$ combined with $\mu_F = \mu_G$ implies that $D^2(x) = \int_0^x [G(y) - F(y)]dy \geq 0$ for all $x \in I$. Thus the second statement in the theorem implies the first, as was to be shown.

A simple but important corollary of Theorem 2.4 follows from the strictly concave "utility function" $u(x) = - (x - \mu_F)^2$.

COROLLARY 2.1. *If* $\mu_F = \mu_G$ *and* $F >_2 G$ *then* $\sigma_F < \sigma_G$.

In the context of TSD and I = [0,1], a result similar to Corollary 2.1 also holds: if $\mu_F = \mu_G$ and $F >_3 G$, then $\sigma_F \leq \sigma_G$ (inequality not strict). To see this, consider $u_k(x) = - (x - 1)^2 + 1 - e^{-kx}$, which is in U_3 for $k > 0$. As $k \downarrow 0$, $u_k(x) \to - (x - 1)^2$ for all $x \in [0,1]$. Thus $E(u_k,F) > E(u_k,G)$ for all $k > 0$ implies $- E(X - 1)^2 \geq - E(Y - 1)^2$, and this in turn implies $\sigma_F^2 \leq \sigma_G^2$. Example 3 gives a case in which $\mu_F = \mu_G$, $\sigma_F = \sigma_G$, and $F >_3 G$.

Simple Probability Distributions

When the distribution functions F and G correspond to discrete, finite random variables, the stochastic dominance tests simplify greatly. Thus suppose that X,Y are concentrated on the finite point set $\Omega = \{x_1, x_2, \ldots, x_n\} \subset I$, with $x_1 < x_2 < \ldots < x_n$, and let $f_i = P(X = x_i) \geq 0$, $g_i = P(Y = x_i) \geq 0$, $\Sigma_{i=1}^n f_i = \Sigma_{i=1}^n g_i = 1$. Then

$$F(x) = P(X \leq x) = \sum_{x_i \leq x} f_i,$$

$$G(x) = P(Y \leq x) = \sum_{x_i \leq x} g_i,$$

and F and G are right-continuous step functions that are constant on the intervals $I_i = [x_i, x_{i+1})$, $i = 1, \ldots, n-1$, and $I_n = [x_n, \infty)$. To check for FSD, we need check only that $D^1(x) = G(x) - F(x)$ is non-negative for each x in the finite set Ω. Also $D^2(x) = \int_0^x D^1(y)dy$ is a continuous piecewise-linear function, so we need check only $D^2(x) \geq 0$ for $x \in \Omega$ to verify SSD.

Since D^3 is piecewise-quadratic, however, it is <u>not</u> sufficient to check $D^3(x) \geq 0$ only on Ω to verify TSD. In general, the sign of $D^3(x)$ also must be checked at the points x where $D^2(x) = 0$. For example, let X,Y be: $P(X = 1) = 4/5$, $P(X = 7) = 1/5$, $P(Y = 0) = 2/5$, $P(Y = 3) = 3/5$. The test functions $D^2(x)$ and $D^3(x)$ are plotted in Figure 2-8. We see that $D^3(x) \geq 0$ for $x = 0,1,3,7$, whereas $D^3(5) < 0$. Thus TSD is false. Because of a failure to take account of the piecewise-quadratic nature of $D^3(x)$, some published TSD algorithms [e.g., Porter, et al. (1973)] are incorrect.

Single-Crossing Distributions

The next special situation of some practical significance occurs when the distribution functions cross once, in the sense that $D^1 > 0$ for some interval $[0, x_0) \cap I$, $D^1 \leq 0$ on $[x_0, \infty) \cap I$, and D^1 is not identically zero on either of these intervals. An example of this is shown

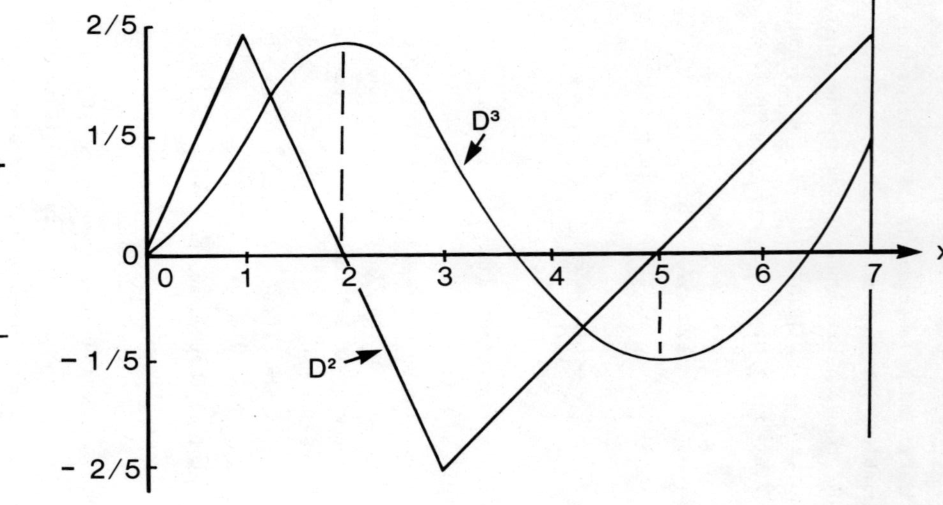

Figure 2-8. For TSD, $D^3(x)$ Needs Checked at x for Which $D^2(x) = 0$

in Figure 2-4. In this case, $F >_2 G$ if and only if $\mu_F \geq \mu_G$. The proof is immediate: $D^2(x) \geq 0$ for $x \leq x_0$; and for $x \geq x_0$, $D^2(x) \geq D^2(\infty) = \mu_F - \mu_G \geq 0$.

This result is particularly important for random variables restricted to a class of two-parameter distributions. Following Bawa (1975), we say that the distribution function F belongs to class F_0 if $F(x) = \psi[(x - e_F)/s_F]$ for all $x \in I$, where $s_F > 0$; and F belongs to class F_1 if $F(x) = \psi\{[t(x) - e_F]/s_F\}$ with $t'(x) \geq 0$ for all $x \in I$ and $s_F > 0$. Thus F_0 is the class of distribution functions characterized by a location parameter (e) and a scale parameter (s), while F_1 is the class of distribution functions for which a fixed monotonic transformation t of the random variables belongs to F_0. Suppose now that F and G belong to F_0 with $F(x) = \psi[(x - e_F)/s_F]$ and $G(x) = \psi[(x - e_G)/s_G]$ for all $x \in I$. If $\mu_F \geq \mu_G$ and $F(x_1) > G(x_1)$ for some $x_1 \in I$ (i.e., F and G cross), then $F >_2 G$ if and only if $s_F \leq s_G$. The same result holds if F, G belong to class F_1. These conclusions follow immediately by showing that F and G cross once. Noteworthy examples of distributions in class F_0 are the normal and stable Paretian distributions. Although normal or stable Paretian random variables require I = Re and hence are not bounded below, the general SSD theorem of Appendix 2B implies that the result stated above applies also in these cases. In particular, for the normal case, SSD reduces to the ordinary EV rule: $F >_2 G$ if and only if $\mu_F \geq \mu_G$ and $\sigma_F \leq \sigma_G$, since $s = \sigma$. (Recall that $F \neq G$ by prior convention.) An important example of a distribution in class F_1 is the log normal distribution. In this case SSD is equivalent to a mean/logarithmic-variance rule: $F >_2 G$ if and only if $\mu_F \geq \mu_G$ and Var (log X) $\leq$ Var (log Y).

2.17 Stochastic Dominance vs. EV Dominance

We can now give a brief summary of the relations between SD orderings and the classical EV ordering.

a. If $\mu_F = \mu_G$, a necessary (not sufficient) condition for either $F >_2 G$ or $F >_3 G$ is $\sigma_F \leq \sigma_G$ with strict inequality for the case of $>_2$.

b. If $\mu_F > \mu_G$, the condition $\sigma_F \leq \sigma_G$ is neither necessary nor sufficient for $F >_1 G$, $F >_2 G$ or $F >_3 G$. We have seen already in Examples 1 through 3 of Section 2.14 that the EV rule is not necessary for dominance. To see that it is also not sufficient, we consider the example of Hanoch and Levy (1969): $P(X = 1) = .8$, $P(X = 100) = .2$; $P(Y = 10) = .99$, $P(Y = 1000) = .01$. Then $\mu_X = 20.8 > \mu_Y = 19.9$, and $\sigma_X^2 = 1568.16 < \sigma_Y^2 = 9702.99$. However, for $u(x) = \log_{(10)} x$, which is in U_3 (hence also in U_2, U_1), $Eu(X) = 0.4 < Eu(Y) = 1.02$, so that Y is preferred.

c. For F, G in class F_0 (see Section 2.16), if the scale parameters s_F and s_G are monotone increasing functions of variance alone, then the EV rule is equivalent to SSD. In particular, the EV rule is the same as SSD for normally distributed random variables.

Tobin (1958) claimed that the EV rule is relevant in the sense of expected utility if the utility function is quadratic, or if all the distribution functions are members of a two-parameter family. Both statements are false. For quadratic utility, EV dominance is sufficient but not necessary for SSD; Example 1 of Section 2.14 violates the EV rule, but $E(u,F) > E(u,G)$ for all quadratic $u \in U_2$. For lognormal distributions, which are indeed members of a two-parameter family, the appropriate ordering rule involves logarithmic variance, not variance itself.

2.18 Stochastic Dominance for DARA Utility Functions

In Section 2.11 we introduced the class U_d of utility functions in U_2 having nonincreasing absolute risk aversion. Section 2.12 then introduced the class U_3 of utility functions having positive third derivatives in an attempt to capture some of the features of the smaller class U_d in a simple manner. We will now examine stochastic dominance within the class U_d itself. Since $U_d \subset U_3$, we can expect the U_d dominance relation to be stronger than TSD in the sense that it is able to order more pairs of random variables.

DEFINITION. *For* $F \neq G$, *write*

$$F >_d G \text{ \underline{if and only if} } E(u,F) \geq E(u,G) \text{ \underline{for all} } u \in U_d. \qquad (2.45)$$

We refer to $>_d$ as <u>DARA stochastic dominance</u>, or <u>DSD</u>. Because of non-increasing as opposed to decreasing absolute risk aversion, it is possible to have $E(u,F) = E(u,G)$ for some $u \in U_d$ when $F >_d G$, but in this case there will be other $u \in U_d$ for which $E(u,F) > E(u,G)$.

The first question of obvious importance is: What is the relation, if any, between TSD and DSD? The answer, as we will see, is that TSD and DSD are equivalent if and only if the random variables have equal means; otherwise, DSD is stronger. The next question is: What are the necessary and sufficient conditions for DSD in the unequal-means case? Here we are able to offer only a partial answer. For reasons outlined in Appendix 2A, it appears to be impossible to give a simple, general condition involving only a predetermined function of a single variable such as $D^i(x)$ of previous sections. Rather, we must resort to an algorithmic procedure to prove or disprove DSD in specific, given cases.

To begin, we establish the equivalence of DSD and TSD when means are equal.

THEOREM 2.5. <u>If</u> $\mu_F = \mu_G$, <u>then</u> $F >_d G$ <u>if and only if</u> $F >_3 G$.

<u>Proof</u>: Since $U_d \subset U_3$, $F >_3 G$ implies $F >_d G$. To prove the converse when $\mu_F = \mu_G$, let u_{k,x_0} $(k > 0,\ x_0 > 0)$ be the function whose derivative is

$$u'_{k,x_0}(x) = \begin{cases} e^{k(x_0-x)}/k, & x \leq x_0 \\ \\ 1/k, & x > x_0. \end{cases}$$

The absolute risk aversion $R_a(x)$ of $u_{k,x_0}(x)$ is a nonincreasing step function:

$$R_a(x) = \begin{cases} k, & x \leq x_0 \\ 0, & x > x_0. \end{cases}$$

Since R_a is not everywhere defined and differentiable, $u_{k,x_0} \notin U_d$. Arguments like those of Section 2.15, however, show that u_{k,x_0} can be approximated arbitrarily closely by a utility function in U_d. Thus $F >_d G$ necessarily implies $E(u_{k,x_0},F) \geq E(u_{k,x_0},G)$. [This holds for both cases $I = [0,1]$ or $I = [0,\infty)$, since the requisite Monotone or Dominated Convergence Theorems are true in either case.] Since $e^{k(x_0-x)} = 1 + k(x_0 - x) + o(k)$ for all $x \in [0,x_0]$, $u'_{k,x_0}(x) = (1/k) + h'_{x_0}(x) + o(k)/k$, where h_{x_0} is the piecewise-quadratic function defined in Eq. (2.44). Then

$$\begin{aligned} E(u_{k,x_0},F) - E(u_{k,x_0},G) &= \int_0^{x_0} D^1(x)u'_{k,x_0}(x)dx \\ &\quad + \int_{x_0}^{\infty} D^1(x)u'_{k,x_0}(x)dx \\ &= (\mu_F - \mu_G)/k + \int_0^{x_0} D^1(x)h'_{x_0}(x)dx \\ &\quad + o(k)/k \\ &= 0 + D^3(x_0) + o(k)/k \end{aligned} \qquad (2.46)$$

from Eq. (2.43). As $k \downarrow 0$ we get $D^3(x_0) \geq 0$ and, since this is true for all $x_0 > 0$, $F >_3 G$. This proves the theorem.

The equal-means assumption plays a crucial role in the proof. If $\mu_F > \mu_G$, then Eq. (2.46) becomes $(\mu_F - \mu_G)/k + D^3(x_0) + o(k)/k$, and no conclusion can be drawn about the sign of $D^3(x_0)$ as $k \downarrow 0$. In this case the result is actually false, as we will soon see by example.

To develop the partial DSD test, we will use an expression of the DARA property that is analogous to the "simple gambles" expression (2.29) for U_3. This is: $u \in U_d$ if and only if $u \in U_2$ and

$$\rho_\delta(x) = [u(x + \delta) - u(x)]/[u(x) - u(x - \delta)] \qquad (2.47)$$

is nondecreasing in x for all $x \in I$ and all $\delta > 0$ such that $x \pm \delta \in I$. To see this, we note first that as $\delta \downarrow 0$, $\rho_\delta(x) = 1 - \delta R_a(x) + o(\delta)$, so $\rho'_\delta(x) \geq 0$ implies $R'_a(x) \leq 0$ as $\delta \downarrow 0$. The converse follows from Theorem 1, part (e) on p. 128 of Pratt (1964).

We will now restrict our attention to random variables that are discrete and concentrated on finitely many points $x_0 < x_1 < \ldots < x_{n+1}$, and for which the spacings $x_1 - x_0$, $x_2 - x_1$, ..., $x_{n+1} - x_n$ are integer multiples of a common unit. Then by adding new points with zero probability if necessary, we can take the points $x_0, x_1, \ldots, x_{n+1}$ to be equally spaced: $\delta = x_1 - x_0 = x_2 - x_1 = \ldots = x_{n+1} - x_n$. If $P(X = x_i) = p_i \geq 0$ and $P(Y = x_i) = q_i \geq 0$, then

$$E(u,F) - E(u,G) = \sum_{i=0}^{n+1} (p_i - q_i)u(x_i). \qquad (2.48)$$

We now make use of an important algebraic identity, known as Abel's identity, or the formula for summation by parts: if a_j, b_j are real numbers for $j = 1,2,\ldots,N$, then

$$\sum_{j=1}^{N} a_j b_j = \sum_{k=1}^{N-1} (\sum_{j=1}^{k} a_j)(b_k - b_{k+1}) + (\sum_{j=1}^{N} a_j)b_N. \qquad (2.49)$$

Applying Eq. (2.49) to Eq. (2.48) we have

$$E(u,F) - E(u,G) = \sum_{i=1}^{n} D_i[u(x_{i+1}) - u(x_i)], \qquad (2.50)$$

where

$$D_i = \sum_{j=0}^{i} (q_j - p_j) \equiv D^1(x_i).$$

Now if $u \in U_d$, then $u(x_1) - u(x_0) > 0$ so that

$$[E(u,F) - E(u,G)]/[u(x_1) - u(x_0)] = D_0 + D_1 \frac{u(x_2) - u(x_1)}{u(x_1) - u(x_0)}$$

$$+ D_2 \frac{u(x_3) - u(x_2)}{u(x_2) - u(x_1)} \cdot \frac{u(x_2) - u(x_1)}{u(x_1) - u(x_0)} + \dots + D_n \frac{u(x_2) - u(x_1)}{u(x_1) - u(x_0)}$$

$$\cdot \frac{u(x_3) - u(x_2)}{u(x_2) - u(x_1)} \cdot \dots \cdot \frac{u(x_{n+1}) - u(x_n)}{u(x_n) - u(x_{n-1})}, \tag{2.51}$$

where we have inserted factors that cancel in the numerators and denominators. Next, define $\theta_1, \theta_2, \dots, \theta_n$ by

$$\theta_i = [u(x_{i+1}) - u(x_i)]/[u(x_i) - u(x_{i-1})], \quad i = 1,2,\dots,n. \tag{2.52}$$

Then

$$[E(u,F) - E(u,G)]/[u(x_1) - u(x_0)] = D_0 + D_1\theta_1 + D_2\theta_1\theta_2 \tag{2.53}$$

$$+ \dots + D_n\theta_1\theta_2\cdots\theta_n.$$

Defining $f(\theta_1, \theta_2, \dots, \theta_n)$ as the function on the right-hand side of Eq. (2.53), it follows that a necessary and sufficient condition for $F >_d G$ is that $f(\theta_1, \theta_2, \dots, \theta_n) \geq 0$ for all allowed values of the θ_i. Now increasing u implies $\theta_i > 0$ for all i; concave (strictly concave) u implies $\theta_i \leq 1$ ($\theta_i < 1$) for all i; and $u \in U_d$ implies, by definition (2.47), that $\theta_i \leq \theta_{i+1}$ for all i. Thus $u \in U_d$ implies the restriction

$$0 < \theta_1 \leq \theta_2 \leq \dots \leq \theta_n < 1, \tag{2.54}$$

and a <u>sufficient</u> condition for $F >_d G$ is that $f(\theta) \geq 0$ for all $\theta =$ $= (\theta_1, \theta_2, \dots, \theta_n)$ that satisfy (2.54). This condition is also <u>necessary</u>. For if $F >_d G$, then, necessarily, $E(u,F) \geq E(u,G)$ for all u such that $R_a = -u''/u'$ is a nonincreasing step function. (Recall our standard limiting arguments.) Given any θ satisfying (2.54), we can construct a u whose absolute risk aversion R_a is a nonincreasing step-function, and for which $\theta_i = [u(x_{i+1}) - u(x_i)]/[u(x_i) - u(x_{i-1})]$

for i = 1,2,...,n. (The construction is elementary, and we leave it to the reader.) Thus $F >_d G$ necessarily implies $f(\theta) \geq 0$ for all θ satisfying (2.54).

The preceding formulation reduces the test for DSD to an algebraic problem. Clearly, $f(\theta) \geq 0$ for all θ that satisfy (2.54) if and only if this is true also in the closure of the region defined by (2.54), i.e., including $\theta_1 = 0$ and $\theta_n = 1$. Let us call this region K:

$$K = \{\theta = (\theta_1,\ldots,\theta_n): \; 0 \leq \theta_1 \leq \theta_2 \leq \cdots \leq \theta_n \leq 1\}. \tag{2.55}$$

Then $f \geq 0$ on K if and only if the minimum of f on K is nonnegative. (Since f is continuous and K is compact, f has a finite minimum on K.) In this form, the DSD test involves the solution of a nonlinear programming problem. We shall omit a detailed discussion of solution techniques, except to note in passing that the problem's special structure allows a solution to the global minimization via a sequence of univariate polynomial minimizations in a dynamic programming form, so that practical solutions can actually be obtained with relative ease. See Vickson (1975a) for details and a description of a working algorithm.

We now present an example in which DSD, but not TSD, obtains. Let $P(X = 1) = .1$, $P(X = 2) = .5$, $P(X = 5) = .4$, and $P(Y = 0) = .1$, $P(Y = 3) = .9$. As is easily verified, TSD fails, since $D^3(2) > 0$ and $D^3(4) < 0$. To check for DSD, we set up the optimization problem outlined above:

$$f(\theta_1,\theta_2,\theta_3,\theta_4) = D_0 + D_1\theta_1 + D_2\theta_1\theta_2 + D_3\theta_1\theta_2\theta_3 + D_4\theta_1\theta_2\theta_3\theta_4$$

$$= .1 - .5\theta_1\theta_2 + .4\theta_1\theta_2\theta_3 + .4\theta_1\theta_2\theta_3\theta_4.$$

Multiplying by 10 for convenience,

$$10f(\theta) \equiv f_1(\theta) = 1 - 5\theta_1\theta_2 + 4\theta_1\theta_2\theta_3 + 4\theta_1\theta_2\theta_3\theta_4, \tag{2.56}$$

which is to be minimized over $0 \leq \theta_1 \leq \theta_2 \leq \theta_3 \leq \theta_4 \leq 1$. Regardless of the values of θ_1 and θ_2, θ_3 and θ_4 must be as small as possible to minimize f_1. Hence $\theta_4 = \theta_3 = \theta_2$, and $f_1*(\theta)$ (the minimum) is

$$f_1*(\theta) = 1 + \theta_1[- 5\theta_2 + 4\theta_2^2 + 4\theta_2^3]. \tag{2.57}$$

It is easy to check that the θ_2 term in brackets is negative over the interval $(0,(\sqrt{6} - 1)/2]) \simeq (0,.725)$. Then f_1* will be minimized by taking θ_2 somewhere in this interval, then letting θ_1 be as large as possible, namely, $\theta_1 = \theta_2$. We finally have

$$f_1*(\theta) = 1 - 5\theta_1^2 + 4\theta_1^3 + 4\theta_1^4, \; \theta_1 \in [0,1]. \tag{2.58}$$

The value that minimizes this is $\theta_1 = 1/2$, giving

$$\min \{f_1(\theta):0 \leq \theta_1 \leq \theta_2 \leq \theta_3 \leq \theta_4 \leq 1\} = f_1(.5,.5,.5,.5) = 1/2.$$

Thus $f > 0$ on K, so $E(u,F) > E(u,G)$ for all $u \in U_d$. Note that the means are unequal in this example: $\mu_X = 3.1 > \mu_Y = 2.7$.

2.19 Alternative Formulations of FSD and SSD Theorems

In Examples 1 and 2 of Section 2.14, we were able to verify FSD and SSD by apparently ad hoc methods: a reordering of outcomes in Example 1 instantly revealed the required FSD dominance; for SSD in Example 2, decompositions of the original distributions into mixtures also revealed the dominance relation. This section shows that these procedures generalize in the following sense: Suppose random variables X and Y have distribution functions F and G, respectively, with each of X and Y taking on a value in a finite interval I with probability one. Then we can construct new random variables X' and Y' on a sample space $\Omega = [0,1]$ so that X' and Y' also have distribution functions F and G, respectively, and such that

(a) if $F >_1 G$, then $X'(\omega) \geq Y'(\omega)$ for all $\omega \in \Omega$ and $X'(\omega) > Y'(\omega)$ for some $\omega \in \Omega$;

(b) if $F >_2 G$ then $E[Y'|X'] \leq X'$ with probability 1.

For FSD, (a) says that it is possible to represent X and Y by probabilistically equivalent gambles X' and Y' in which X' is as desirable as Y' for all "events." This is a generalization of the reordering argument used in Example 1 in Section 2.14. For SSD, (b) states that for each given value of X', the mean of the random variable $[Y'|X']$ does not exceed X', and thus it is a generalization of the mixture argument used in Example 2.

These alternative versions of the FSD and SSD results are computationally less useful than Theorems 2.1 and 2.2 for real-valued random variables. The new characterization of SSD generalizes to the multivariate case, however, where explicit distribution function tests are not available. In this context it serves as a basis for algorithms that in principle can be used to test for multivariate SSD for discrete, finite random variables. Extensions to the multivariate case are stated without proof in the next section.

Two random variables X and X' are <u>equal in distribution</u>, written $X \overset{d}{=} X'$, if the distribution functions of X and X' are identical. Random variables equal in distribution need not be identical, as when $\{a,b\}$ is the basic sample space, $P(a) = P(b) = 1/2$ (e.g., a is "heads" and b is "tails"), $X(a) = 1$, $X(b) = 2$, $X'(a) = 2$ and $X'(b) = 1$. The next theorem concerns FSD.

THEOREM 2.5. <u>Let</u> X <u>and</u> Y <u>be random variables on a finite real closed interval</u> I <u>with distribution functions</u> F <u>and</u> G <u>respectively</u>. <u>Then</u> $F >_1 G$ <u>if and only if there are random variables</u> X' <u>and</u> Y' <u>from</u> $\Omega = [0,1]$ <u>into</u> I <u>with distribution functions</u> F <u>and</u> G <u>respectively, such that</u> $X'(\omega) \geq Y'(\omega)$ <u>for all</u> $\omega \in \Omega$ <u>with</u> $X'(\omega) > Y'(\omega)$ <u>for some</u> $\omega \in \Omega$.

<u>Proof</u>: Suppose X' and Y' exist as asserted with $F(x) = P(X'(\omega) \leq x)$ and $G(x) = P(Y'(\omega) \leq x)$. Then clearly $F >_1 G$ since $G(x) \geq F(x)$ for all $x \in I$ and $G(x) > F(x)$ for some $x \in I$. Conversely, suppose X and Y are as described in the hypotheses of the theorem, with $F >_1 G$. Define

$$X'(\omega) = \inf \{x \in I : F(x) \geq \omega\},$$
$$Y'(\omega) = \inf \{x \in I : G(x) \geq \omega\} \qquad (2.59)$$

for all $\omega \in \Omega$. Since F and G are right-continuous and nondecreasing and I is bounded and closed, X' and Y' are everywhere defined on $\Omega = [0,1]$. Moreover, since $\{\omega : X'(\omega) \leq x\} = \{\omega : \omega \leq F(x)\}$ is implied by Eq. (2.59), the probability $P(X' \leq x)$ that X' takes on a value that does not exceed x is equal to the probability that X takes on a value y for which $F(y) \leq F(x)$. Because the latter probability is F(x), $P(X' \leq x) = F(x)$ for all $x \in I$ and hence $X' \overset{d}{=} X$. Similarly, $P(Y' \leq x) = G(x)$ and $Y' \overset{d}{=} Y$. Since $F >_1 G$, $G(x) \geq F(x)$ for all $x \in I$, hence $\{x : F(x) \geq \omega\} \subseteq \{x : G(x) \geq \omega\}$ for all $\omega \in \Omega$, and therefore $X'(\omega) = \inf \{x \in I : F(x) \geq \omega\} \geq \inf \{x : G(x) \geq \omega\} = Y'(\omega)$ for all $\omega \in \Omega$. Also, since $F \neq G$, $X'(\omega) > Y'(\omega)$ for some ω, and the proof is complete.

Expression (2.59) is illustrated for a mixed distribution function on the interval I = [a,b] in Figure 2-9. The value of $X'(\omega_1)$ for the point ω_1 in Ω that falls within a jump of F is the same as the value of $X'(\omega)$ for points above ω_1 but equal to or below $\omega' = F[X'(\omega_1)]$. Immediately above ω', the function $X'(\omega)$ has a discontinuity. In an interval of I where F is continuous and strictly increasing, $X'(\omega)$ equals the inverse of F at ω. Thus $X'(\omega_2) = F^{-1}(\omega_2)$.

An equivalent statement of Theorem 2.5 can be obtained by introducing another random variable Z, which is jointly distributed with X according to the bivariate distribution function H where

$$H(x,z) = P(X \leq x, Z \leq z) \qquad \text{for all } x,z \in I,$$

with the understanding that the marginal of H on its first component is F, so that $F(x) = H(x,b)$ if $I = [a,b]$ or $F(x) = H(x,\infty)$ if $I = [a,\infty)$. The marginal of H on its second component is the unconditional distribution function of Z. There is no presumption here that X and Z are independent random variables.

We are going to work with the sum of the random variables X and Z, and to avoid awkward formulations involving domains, we shall take

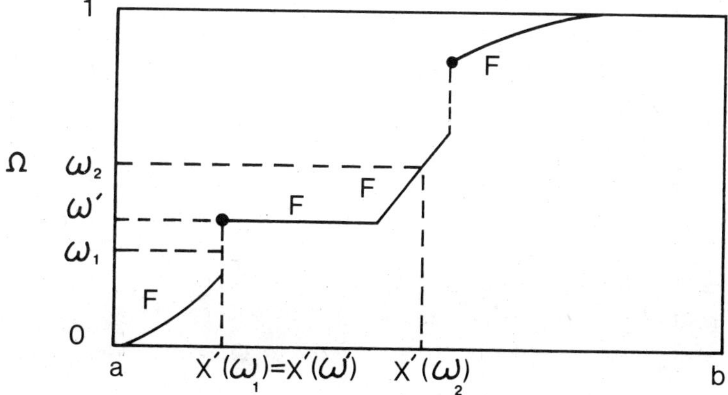

Figure 2-9. Construction of X' from F

I as the entire line Re with the understanding that random variables may be confined with probability one to finite intervals in Re. Given H on Re x Re, extended in the natural way if I in the preceding paragraph is not Re, the distribution function S of X + Z is

$$S(t) = P(X + Z \leq t) = \int_{\{(x,z):x+z\leq t\}} dH(x,z)$$

$$\text{for all } t \in \text{Re}. \qquad (2.60)$$

Depending on circumstances, S(t) may be written in more convenient ways. For example, if (X,Z) is concentrated with probability one on the finite set $\{(a_1,b_1),\ldots,(a_m,b_m)\}$ with $h(a_i,b_i) = P(X = a_i, Z = b_i)$ then

$$S(t) = \sum_{\{i:a_i+b_i\leq t\}} h(a_i,b_i).$$

In the continuous case, if H has a bivariate probability density function h on Re^2, then

$$S(t) = \int_{x=-\infty}^{\infty} \int_{z=-\infty}^{t-x} h(x,z)dz\ dx.$$

With G the distribution function for Y, $Y \overset{d}{=} X + Z$ simply means that $G(t) = S(t)$ for all real t. Suppose in fact that in the context of Theorem 2.5, there is a Z such that $Y \overset{d}{=} X + Z$ and $H(\infty,0) = 1$, so that $Z \leq 0$ with probability one. Then for every $u \in U_1$, $Eu(Y) = Eu(X + Z) < Eu(X)$, where the strict inequality follows from $H(\infty,0) = 1$ and the continuing presumption that $F \neq G$, and hence $F >_1 G$. Conversely, if $F >_1 G$, then with X' and Y' as guaranteed by Theorem 2.5, we can define $Z'(\omega) = Y'(\omega) - X'(\omega)$ so that $Z' \leq 0$ on Ω with $Z'(\omega) < 0$ for some $\omega \in \Omega$ and such that $Y' = X' + Z'$. It is then possible to define Z so that $Y \overset{d}{=} X + Z$ and $H(\infty,0) = 1$.

Somewhat more intricate results obtain for SSD. Theorem 2.6, stated below, is true also for unbounded random variables having finite means under presumption of the existence of Eu(X) and Eu(Y) for all $u \in U_2$ as shown by Strassen (1965). We shall confine our statement to bounded random variables and then briefly indicate how the theorem is proved.

THEOREM 2.6. *Let* X *and* Y *be random variables confined to finite intervals with probability one and with distribution functions* F *and* G *respectively. Then* $F >_2 G$ *if and only if there is a random variable* Z *(jointly distributed with* X *as explained earlier) such that* $Y \overset{d}{=} X + Z$ *and such that* $E[Z|X] \leq 0$ *with probability one. Furthermore, if* $E(X) = E(Y)$ *then the latter condition--that* $E[Z|X] \leq 0$ *with probability one--can be replaced by the condition that* $E[Z|X] = 0$ *with probability one.*

The statement that $E[Z|X] \leq 0$ with probability one means that the set of all X values for which $[Z|X] \leq 0$ includes a subset that has probability one under F.

Suppose $F \neq G$, $Y \overset{d}{=} X + Z$ and $E[Z|X] \leq 0$ with probability one. Then for all $u \in U_2$,

$$\begin{aligned} Eu(Y) &= Eu(X + Z) = EE[u(X + Z)|X] \\ &\leq Eu(X + E[Z|X]) \leq Eu(X), \end{aligned}$$

where the first inequality arises from Jensen's inequality (2.22), and the second inequality comes from the monotonicity of u and $E[Z|X] \leq 0$ with probability one. Therefore by the necessity proof of Theorem 2.2, $D^2(x) = G^2(x) - F^2(x)$ is nonnegative for all x. Since $G \neq F$, $D^2(x) > 0$ for some x and it then follows that $Eu(Y) < Eu(X)$ for all $u \in U_2$, or $F >_2 G$. The converse proof of Theorem 2.6--that $F >_2 G$ implies the existence of Z as stated--requires the existence or construction of a bivariate distribution function H(x,z), which possesses the requisite properties. A constructive proof for H can be patterned on the approach taken by Rothschild and Stiglitz (1970), proving the result first for finite discrete random variables and then using limiting procedures for the general case.

2.20 Stochastic Dominance for Multivariate Random Variables

This section provides a brief outline of stochastic dominance for multidimensional variables in Re^n for $n \geq 2$. Except for Theorem 2.11, proofs will be omitted. Unless noted otherwise, $I = [0,1]^n$ or $I = Re^n$, and in all cases I is a convex subset of Re^n that contains all possible outcomes. All utility functions are presumed to be measurable in the sense that $\{x \in I: u(x) \in J\}$ is a Borel subset of I for every real interval J.

Generalizing slightly from previous developments in this chapter, we shall let U_1 be the set of all nondecreasing u on I, so that $u \in U_1$ if and only if u is measurable and $u(x + h) \geq u(x)$ whenever $x = (x_1,\ldots,x_n)$ and $x + h = (x_1 + h_1,\ldots,x_n + h_n)$ are in I and $h_i \geq 0$ for $i = 1,\ldots,n$. With u concave whenever $u[\alpha x + (1 - \alpha)y] \geq \alpha u(x) + (1 - \alpha)u(y)$ for all $x,y \in I$ and all $\alpha \in [0,1]$, we let U_2 be the subset of functions in U_1 that are concave.

Working with nonstrict instead of strict stochastic dominance we shall define $\geq_1$ and $\geq_2$ by

$$F \geq_1 G \text{ if and only if } Eu(X) \geq Eu(Y) \text{ for all } u \in U_1,$$
$$F \geq_2 G \text{ if and only if } Eu(X) \geq Eu(Y) \text{ for all } u \in U_2, \tag{2.61}$$

whenever F and G are respectively multivariate distribution functions of n-vector random variables X and Y with $P(X \in I) = P(Y \in I) = 1$. These definitions presume that F and G are such that Eu(X) and Eu(Y) exist for all relevant u. Paradoxically, it appears easier to characterize $\geq_2$ than $\geq_1$ in the multivariate case. Lehmann (1955) seems to have given the most general results for $\geq_1$; he has proved theorems essentially similar to Theorems 2.7 and 2.8. In the first of these, $S \subseteq I$ is increasing if $x + h \in S$ whenever $x \in S$, $x + h \in I$ and $h_i \geq 0$ for $i = 1,\ldots,n$.

THEOREM 2.7. *F $\geq_1$ G if and only if $\int_S dF \geq \int_S dG$ for all increasing Borel subsets $S \subseteq I$.*

Since increasing subsets of I when n = 1 are simply upper intervals of I, Theorem 2.7 is similar in spirit to Theorem 2.1 although it is not very useful in the multivariate setting. But if the components of X and Y are independent--so that $F(x_1,\ldots,x_n) = F_1(x_1)\ldots F_n(x_n)$, for example--then more useful results apply.

THEOREM 2.8. *If the components of X and Y are independent and the marginal distributions of F (for X) and G (for Y) are respectively $F_1,\ldots,F_n$ and $G_1,\ldots,G_n$, then F $\geq_1$ G if and only if $F_i \geq_1 G_i$ for $i = 1,\ldots,n$.*

This shows that, under independence, the test for multivariate $\geq_1$ reduces to tests for univariate $\geq_1$ component by component.

Turning to the nonstrict second-degree stochastic dominance relation $\geq_2$, Strassen (1965) has proved the next two theorems, the first of which Sherman (1951) established earlier for discrete random variables.

THEOREM 2.9. *If I is a compact, convex subset of Re^n and F and G are respectively distribution functions for X and Y that assign probability one to I, then F $\geq_2$ G if and only if there exists a random vector Z such that $Y \overset{d}{=} X + Z$ and $E[Z|X] = (E[Z_1|X],\ldots,E[Z_n|X]) \leq (0,\ldots,0)$ with probability one.*

As explained in the previous section, the last part of the statement of this theorem says that a random vector Z has a joint distribution function H(x,z) with X whose marginal on X is F, such that $Y \overset{d}{=} X + Z$ and such that the set of all X values for which $E[Z|X] \leq (0,\ldots,0)$ includes a subset of I that has probability one under F. Theorem 2.9 with I an n-dimensional rectangular subset in Re^n also has been proved by Brumelle and Vickson (1975) using simpler and more accessible methods than Strassen's.

THEOREM 2.10. <u>If</u> $I = Re^n$, $n \geq 2$, <u>and if the mean vectors</u> μ_F <u>and</u> μ_G <u>are finite and equal</u>, <u>then</u> $E(u,F) \geq E(u,G)$ <u>for all measurable and concave</u> u (<u>whether nondecreasing or not</u>) <u>if and only if there is a random vector</u> Z <u>such that</u> $Y \overset{d}{=} X + Z$ and $E[Z|X] = (0,\ldots,0)$ <u>with probability one</u>.

The question of the validity of Theorem 2.9 for unbounded random variables with unequal means appears to be unresolved except for the univariate case in which $n = 1$.

Before stating our final multivariate theorem, which applies to SSD with independent components, we note an algorithm based on Theorem 2.9 that can be used to test for $F \geq_2 G$ when X and Y are discrete multivariate random variables concentrated on a finite number of points. For illustration, consider $n = 2$ with X and Y concentrated on the m-point set $\{a_1,\ldots,a_m\}$ with $a_i = (a_{i1}, a_{i2}) \in Re^2$ for each i. Let

$$f_i = P(X = a_i), \quad \sum_{i=1}^{m} f_i = 1;$$

$$g_i = P(Y = a_i), \quad \sum_{i=1}^{m} g_i = 1.$$

If $F \geq_2 G$, then there is a Z such that $Y \overset{d}{=} X + Z$ and $E[Z|X = a_i] \leq (0,0)$ for all i for which $f_i > 0$. (If $f_i = 0$ then $E[Z|X = a_i]$ is undefined.) Consequently, by setting

$$d_{ij} = P[Z = a_j - a_i | X = a_i] \quad \text{if } f_i > 0$$
$$d_{ij} = 0 \quad \text{if } f_i = 0,$$

$F \geq_2 G$ shows that

(a) $d_{ij} \geq 0$ for $i,j = 1,2,\ldots,m$;

(b) $\sum_{j=1}^{m} d_{ij} = 1$ for all i such that $f_i > 0$;

(c) $g_j = \sum_{i=1}^{m} f_i d_{ij}$ for $j = 1,\ldots,m$;

(d) $\sum_{j=1}^{m} d_{ij} a_{j1} \leq a_{i1}$ and $\sum_{i=1}^{m} d_{ij} a_{j2} \leq a_{i2}$ for all i having $f_i > 0$.

Properties (a) and (b) follow from probability axioms, (c) expresses $Y \overset{d}{=} X + Z$, and (d) represents $E[Z|X_i = a_i] \leq (0,0)$.

Conversely, if there exists an m-by-m matrix $[d_{ij}]$ that satisfies (a) through (d), then an application of Jensen's inequality (2.22) in nonstrict form shows that $F \geq_2 G$. Thus (a) through (d) expresses necessary and sufficient conditions for dominance. Application of standard feasibility tests of linear programming can determine whether there are d_{ij} that satisfy (a) through (d).

As with $\geq_1$, the test for $\geq_2$ simplifies greatly when the components of X and Y are independent. According to Bessler and Veinott (1966), Veinott proved a result analogous to Theorem 2.11 for convex rather than concave functions. Since Veinott's proof is unpublished, we will prove Theorem 2.11 by a simple application of Theorem 2.6.

THEOREM 2.11. If the mean vectors μ_F and μ_G are finite and the marginal distribution functions of X and Y are respectively $F_1,\ldots F_n$ and $G_1,\ldots,G_n$ with $F(x_1,\ldots,x_n) = F_1(x_1)\ldots F_n(x_n)$ and $G(x_1,\ldots,x_n) = G_1(x_1)\ldots G_n(x_n)$ for all $x \in Re^n$, then $F \geq_2 G$ if and only if $F_i \geq_2 G_i$ for $i = 1,\ldots,n$.

Proof: Suppose first that $F \geq_2 G$. Then if $u_i \in U_2$ (one-dimensional), $u(x_1,\ldots,x_n) = u_i(x_i)$ is in U_2 (n-dimensional) and consequently $Eu(X) \geq Eu(Y)$ yields $Eu_i(X_i) \geq Eu_i(Y_i)$, so that $F_i \geq_2 G_i$, regardless of whether the components of X and Y are independent. Conversely, suppose independence holds and $F_i \geq_2 G_i$ for all i. Then by the generalized version of Theorem 2.6, there exist $Z_1,\ldots,Z_n$ such that $Y_i \overset{d}{=} X_i + Z_i$ for all i, with $E[Z_i|X_i] \leq 0$ with probability one. Letting H_i be the bivariate distribution function of (X_i,Z_i), define

$$H(x,z) = H[(x_1,\ldots,x_n),(z_1,\ldots,z_n)] = H_1(x_1,z_1)\ldots H_n(x_n,z_n).$$

Since $F_i(x_i) = H_i(x_i,\infty)$, independence of the X_i implies that $F(x) = H(x,\infty)$. In addition, $G(x_1,\ldots,x_n) = G_1(x_1)\ldots G_n(x_n) = S_1(x_1)\ldots S_n(x_n)$, where S_i is the distribution function of $X_i + Z_i$ obtained from H_i in the manner described by Eq. (2.60). Since the (X_i,Z_i) are independent by the definition of H, $S_1(x_1)\ldots S_n(x_n)$ is the distribution function of $X + Z = (X_1 + Z_1,\ldots,X_n + Z_n)$, and therefore $Y \overset{d}{=} X + Z$. Finally, $E[Z_i|X] = E[Z_i|X_i] \leq 0$ with probability one for each i. It then follows from Jensen's inequality (2.22) in the nonstrict form that $E(u,F) \geq E(u,G)$ for all $u \in U_2$, so that $F \geq_2 G$.

2.21 Nondimensional Stochastic Dominance

Having considered univariate and multivariate stochastic dominance, the main part of this chapter concludes with nondimensional versions of stochastic dominance for probability distributions defined on a finite set C of consequences. In this development C replaces I, and the notion of an increasing utility function on I is replaced by a utility function that preserves the decision-maker's preference order on C. It is immaterial whether the consequences are single-attribute consequences or multiattribute consequences; but it is important that the probabilities assigned to the consequences in C sum to unity for each risky decision alternative.

To develop first-degree stochastic dominance in the C context we assume that the decision-maker can order the consequences in C according to increasing preference and that he is never indifferent between distinct consequences. (The latter assumption can be relaxed by working with ordered indifference classes in place of ordered consequences.) With $C = \{c_1, c_2, \ldots, c_{n+1}\}$, we use an obvious subscripting convention and write

$$c_1 <_p c_2 <_p \cdots <_p c_n <_p c_{n+1} \tag{2.62}$$

where $c_k <_p c_{k+1}$ means that consequence c_{k+1} is preferred to c_k. A utility function u on C is congruent with (2.62) if and only if

$$u(c_1) < u(c_2) < \ldots < u(c_{n+1}). \tag{2.63}$$

Now let f and g be probability mass functions on C that characterize two risky decision alternatives, with $f(c_k) \geq 0$ and $g(c_k) \geq 0$ for $k = 1,\ldots,n + 1$, $\Sigma f(c_k) = \Sigma g(c_k) = 1$, and $f \neq g$. Regardless of whether f and g have natural cumulative distribution functions, we shall use the preference order (2.62) to define preference-cumulative distribution functions:

$$\begin{aligned} F(c_k) &= f(c_1) + f(c_2) + \ldots + f(c_k), \\ G(c_k) &= g(c_1) + g(c_2) + \ldots + g(c_k) \end{aligned} \tag{2.64}$$

for $k = 1,\ldots,n + 1$, with $F(c_{n+1}) = G(c_{n+1}) = 1$. The difference in expected utility between the two risky prospects will then be

$$E(u,F) - E(u,G) = \sum_{k=1}^{n} [G(c_k) - F(c_k)][u(c_{k+1}) - u(c_k)], \tag{2.65}$$

which, like Eq. (2.50), follows from Abel's identity (2.49). Then it is easily seen from Eq. (2.65) that $E(u,F) > E(u,G)$ for all u that satisfy (2.63) if and only if $G(c_k) \geq F(c_k)$ for $k = 1,\ldots,n$. This result expresses a form of first-degree stochastic dominance that is similar to the result of Theorem 2.1.

Although it may not be immediately clear how we can define a form of second-degree stochastic dominance in the C context that will be related to Theorem 2.2, Fishburn (1964:205) has suggested a natural way of doing so. In particular, given (2.62) we shall work with a ranking of the differences $u(c_{k+1}) - u(c_k)$ of adjacent utilities from (2.63). Because there is no natural reason to have $u(c_2) - u(c_1) > u(c_3) - u(c_2) > \ldots > u(c_{n+1}) - u(c_n) > 0$--as would have been the case if the c_i were equally spaced points of the line for a risk-averse investor--the resultant ranking of adjacent utility differences could look, for example, like $u(c_4) - u(c_3) > u(c_2) - u(c_1) > u(c_5) - u(c_4) > \ldots$.

In line with our discussion of (2.23), the utility-difference comparisons are obtained by comparing simple 50-50 or even-chance gambles. For example, if the investor prefers a 50-50 gamble between c_2 and c_4 to a 50-50 gamble between c_1 and c_5, then his utility function must satisfy $\frac{1}{2} u(c_2) + \frac{1}{2} u(c_4) > \frac{1}{2} u(c_1) + \frac{1}{2} u(c_5)$, or $u(c_2) - u(c_1) > u(c_5) - u(c_4)$. If he is indifferent between c_7 with certainty and a 50-50 gamble between c_6 and c_8, then $u(c_7) = \frac{1}{2} u(c_6) + \frac{1}{2} u(c_8)$, or $u(c_7) - u(c_6) = u(c_8) - u(c_7)$.

Given (2.63) and comparisons between adjacent utility differences as described above, we shall write the resultant order of first differences as

$$u(c_{\sigma(1)+1}) - u(c_{\sigma(1)}) \geq u(c_{\sigma(2)+1}) - u(c_{\sigma(2)}) \geq \ldots \geq u(c_{\sigma(n)+1}) - u(c_{\sigma(n)}) > 0, \qquad (2.66)$$

where σ is a permutation on $\{1,\ldots,n\}$ and each $\geq$ might be either = or >. For example, if n = 3, if $[\sigma(1),\sigma(2),\sigma(3)] = (3,1,2)$, and if all inequalities in (2.66) are strict, then (2.66) is $u(c_4) - u(c_3) > u(c_2) - u(c_1) > u(c_3) - u(c_2) > 0$.

Given (2.63) and the preference-cumulative distribution functions F and G defined by Eqs. (2.64), we form cumulatives of these cumulatives according to the particular permutation σ that is used in (2.66). This step replaces the definitions of F^2 and G^2 from Eqs. (2.31). Thus we define

$$F_\sigma^2(c_{\sigma(k)}) = \sum_{j=1}^{k} F(c_{\sigma(j)}) \quad \text{for } k = 1,\ldots,n,$$

$$G_\sigma^2(c_{\sigma(k)}) = \sum_{j=1}^{k} G(c_{\sigma(j)}) \quad \text{for } k = 1,\ldots,n. \tag{2.67}$$

For example, if n = 3, $[f(c_1),f(c_2),f(c_3),f(c_4)] = (.3,.1,.4,.2)$ and $[\sigma(1),\sigma(2),\sigma(3)] = (3,1,2)$, then $[F(c_1),F(c_2),F(c_3),F(c_4)] = (.3,.4,.8,1.0)$ and

$$F_\sigma^2(c_{\sigma(1)}) = F(c_{\sigma(1)}) = F(c_3) = .8,$$

$$F_\sigma^2(c_{\sigma(2)}) = F(c_{\sigma(1)}) + F(c_{\sigma(2)}) = F(c_3)+ F(c_1) = 1.1,$$

$$F_\sigma^3(c_{\sigma(3)}) = F(c_{\sigma(1)}) + F(c_{\sigma(2)}) + F(c_{\sigma(3)}) = F(c_3) + F(c_1) + F(c_2) = 1.5.$$

Using Abel's identity (2.49) on Eq. (2.65) after Eq. (2.65) is rewritten as

$$E(u,F) - E(u,G) = \sum_{k=1}^{n} [G(c_{\sigma(k)}) - F(c_{\sigma(k)})][u(c_{\sigma(k)+1}) - u(c_{\sigma(k)})],$$

we obtain

$$E(u,F) - E(u,G) = \sum_{k=1}^{n-1} [G_\sigma^2(c_{\sigma(k)}) - F_\sigma^2(c_{\sigma(k)})][u(c_{\sigma(k)+1}) - u(c_{\sigma(k)}) - u(c_{\sigma(k+1)+1}) + u(c_{\sigma(k+1)})] + [G_\sigma^2(c_{\sigma(n)}) - F_\sigma^2(c_{\sigma(n)})][u(c_{\sigma(n)+1}) - u(c_{\sigma(n)})]. \tag{2.68}$$

Suppose all inequalities in (2.66) are strict. Then all u terms in brackets in (2.68) will be strictly positive. Consequently, E(u,F) > E(u,G) for all utility functions u on C that satisfy (2.66) with strict inequalities if and only if

$$G_\sigma^2(c_{\sigma(k)}) \geq F_\sigma^2(c_{\sigma(k)}) \quad \text{for } k = 1,\ldots,n. \tag{2.69}$$

If some of the inequalities in (2.66) are in fact equalities, then minor but obvious changes are required in the statement of this second-degree theorem.

A short example will illustrate the use of the second-degree stochastic dominance criterion given by (2.69). Following our earlier illustrations, suppose $C = \{c_1,c_2,c_3,c_4\}$ witn $n = 3$, $c_1 <_p c_2 <_p c_3 <_p c_4$ and $[\sigma(1),\sigma(2),\sigma(3)] = (3,1,2)$ with

$$u(c_4) - u(c_3) > u(c_2) - u(c_1) > u(c_3) - u(c_2) > 0. \tag{2.70}$$

Let two risky decisions have point probabilities on C as follows:

Preference Increases to the Right

	c_1	c_2	c_3	c_4
f	.3	.1	.4	.2
g	.2	.2	.5	.1

To check the first-degree situation, form the preference-cumulative distribution functions:

	c_1	c_2	c_3	c_4
F	.3	.4	.8	1.0
G	.2	.4	.9	1.0

Since $F(c_1) > G(c_1)$ and $F(c_3) < G(c_3)$, (2.63) allows no definite conclusion about the sign of $E(u,F) - E(u,G)$. Next, to check the second-degree situation against (2.69), rearrange the first three c_i according to σ and take "cumulatives" of F and G as indicated:

	c_3	c_1	c_2
F_{σ}^{2}	.8	1.1	1.5
G_{σ}^{2}	.9	1.1	1.5

Since (2.69) holds, the expected utility for F exceeds the expected utility for G for all utility functions u that satisfy (2.70).

Appendix 2A

In generalizing the SD theorems of Section 2.14, we shall treat classes of utility functions that are as general as possible, consistent with the basic ideas underlying the U_i classes of Section 2.9 through 2.11 and allow the interval I to be unbounded below. To cover cases such as $I = [0,1]$ or $[0,\infty)$, we shall speak for example of conditions on the interior I^0 of I even though $I^0 = I$ when $I = Re$.

Our utility function classes are:

$$\underset{\sim}{U}_1 = \{u:u \text{ is finite on } I^0 \text{ and nondecreasing on } I\}; \tag{2A.1}$$

$$\underset{\sim}{U}_2 = \{u:u \in \underset{\sim}{U}_1 \text{ and } u \text{ is concave on } I\}; \tag{2A.2}$$

and

$$\underset{\sim}{U}_3 = \{u:u \in \underset{\sim}{U}_2,\ u' \text{ is convex on } I \text{ and finite on } I^0\}. \tag{2A.3}$$

Note that all "strictness" has been dropped in defining the $\underset{\sim}{U}_i$, and boundedness is not assumed. Continuity of u is not assumed in the definition of $\underset{\sim}{U}_1$, but it follows automatically on I^0 from concavity for $\underset{\sim}{U}_2$ and $\underset{\sim}{U}_3$ on I. Also, $\underset{\sim}{U}_2$ and $\underset{\sim}{U}_3$ may be defined equivalently using simple gambles:

$$\underset{\sim}{U}_2 = \{u:u \in \underset{\sim}{U}_1,\ u(x) + u(x + 2\delta) - 2u(x + \delta) \leq 0 \text{ for } x \in I,\ \delta > 0,\ x + 2\delta \in I\}; \tag{2A.4}$$

$$\underset{\sim}{U}_3 = \{u: u \in \underset{\sim}{U}_2,\ u(x + 3\delta) + 3u(x + \delta) - u(x) - 3u(x + 2\delta) \geq 0 \text{ for } x \in I,\ \delta > 0,\ x + 3\delta \in I\}. \quad (2A.5)$$

The equivalence of (2A.2) and (2A.4) is shown by Hardy et al. (1967), while that of (2A.3) and (2A.5) is more difficult. An argument like that of Section 2.12 shows that (2A.3) implies (2A.5). To go the other way, we must show that (2A.5) forces u' to exist, and to be continuous and convex.

For $u \in \underset{\sim}{U}_3$ as given in (2A.5), concavity and monotonicity imply that there exists a nonnegative, nonincreasing Lebesgue integrable function m such that

$$\begin{aligned} u(x) &= u(0) + \int_0^x m(t)dt \quad \text{for } x \geq 0 \\ u(x) &= u(0) - \int_x^0 m(t)dt \quad \text{for } x < 0. \end{aligned} \quad (2A.6)$$

As in Section 2.12, the defining condition in (2A.5) can be written as

$$2\int_{x-\delta}^{x} m(t)dt \leq \int_{x-2\delta}^{x-\delta} m(t)dt + \int_{x}^{x+\delta} m(t)dt$$

$$\text{for } [x - 2\delta, x + \delta] \subset I. \quad (2A.7)$$

Define the left-hand and right-hand limit functions of m as follows: $m^{\pm}(t) = \lim_{h \downarrow 0} m(t \pm h)$, which exist for all $t \in I^0$. By monotonicity of m, we have $m^-(x) \geq m^+(x)$ for all $x \in I^0$. But (2A.7) gives $2m^-(x) \cdot \delta \leq 2\int_{x-\delta}^{x} m(t)dt \leq m^+(x - 2\delta) \cdot \delta + m^+(x) \cdot \delta$, or $2m^-(x) \leq m^+(x - 2\delta) + m^+(x)$. As $\delta \downarrow 0$, $m^+(x - 2\delta) \to m^-(x)$; hence $m^-(x) \leq m^+(x) \leq m^-(x)$ for all $x \in I^0$. Thus m is continuous, which implies that u is continuously differentiable on I^0, and that u' = m. [This result, called the fundamental theorem of integral calculus for Lebesgue integrals, is not completely trivial. A general proof is in Hewitt and Stromberg (1965).]

To show that u' is convex on I when $u \in \underset{\sim}{U}_3$ by (2A.5), we take any closed subinterval J in the interior of I and show that u' is convex on J. This will show that u' is convex on I^0, and we are permitted to extend this property to the end-points of I without affecting u. It may be true that $u' = \infty$ at the left-hand endpoint of I. Without loss in generality assume that $[0,1] \subseteq I^0$ and take J = [0,1]. Then for n sufficiently large, $[-1/n, 1 + (1/n)] \subseteq I^0$. Define

$$c_j = n[u\left(\frac{j}{n}\right) - u\left(\frac{j-1}{n}\right)], \quad j = 0,1,\ldots,n+1 \qquad (2A.8)$$

and note that

$$\int_{(j-1)/n}^{j/n} c_j \, dt = u(j/n) - u((j-1)/n)$$
$$= \int_{(j-1)/n}^{j/n} u'(t)dt, \quad j = 0,1,\ldots,n+1. \qquad (2A.9)$$

According to (2A.5)

$$c_j \geq 0, \qquad j = 0,1,\ldots,n+1;$$

$$c_j - c_{j+1} \geq 0, \qquad j = 0,1,\ldots,n;$$

and

$$c_j - c_{j+1} \geq c_{j+1} - c_{j+2}, \quad j = 0,1,\ldots,n-1. \qquad (2A.10)$$

It then follows from (2A.9), (2A.10) and u' nonincreasing and continuous that

$$c_j \geq u'(t) \geq c_{j+2}$$
$$\text{if } t \in [j/n,(j+1)/n], \quad j = 0,1,\ldots,n-1. \qquad (2A.11)$$

Let m_n be the piecewise linear function on J such that $m_n(j/n) = c_j$ for $j = 0,1,\ldots,n$, and m_n is linear on $[j/n,(j+1)/n]$ for $j = 0,1,\ldots,n-1$. See Figure 2A-1. The function m_n is convex, nonnegative, and nonincreasing on J. We now show that

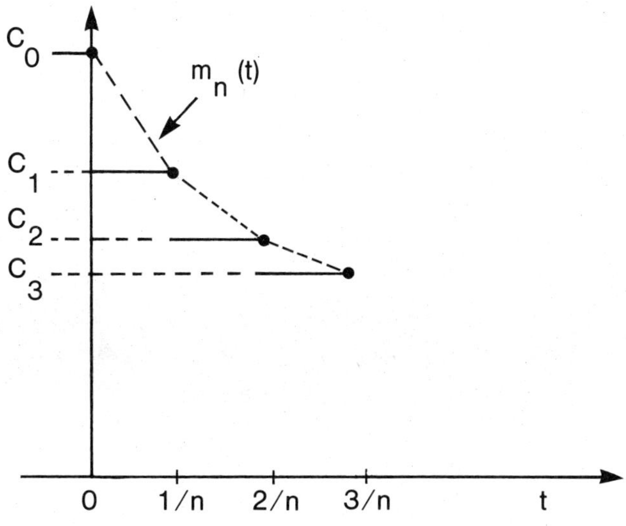

Figure 2A-1. Construction of $m_n(t)$

$$\lim_{n\to\infty} m_n = u'$$

uniformly on J, so u' is convex. For $j = 0,1,\ldots,n - 1$ and $t \in [j/n,(j + 1)/n]$, (2A.10) and (2A.11) imply

$$|u'(t) - m_n(t)| \le c_j - c_{j+2} = c_j - c_{j+1} + c_{j+1} - c_{j+2} \le 2(c_j - c_{j+1})$$

$$\le 2(c_0 - c_1) = 2\{n[u(0) - u(-\tfrac{1}{n})] - n[u(\tfrac{1}{n}) - u(0)]\}. \tag{2A.12}$$

As $n \to \infty$, the right-hand side of (2A.12) approaches $2[u'(0) - u'(0)] = 0$. Thus $m_n(t) \to u'(t)$ as $n \to \infty$, uniformly for $t \in J$.

Corresponding to the classes $\underset{\sim}{U}_i$ there are classes $\underset{\sim}{U}_i^s$ with "strictness" conditions restored:

$$\underset{\sim}{U}_1^s = \{u{:}u \text{ is strictly increasing on I and finite on } I^0\}; \tag{2A.13}$$

$$\underset{\sim}{U}_2^{\,s} = \{u : u \in \underset{\sim}{U}_1^{\,s} \text{ and } u \text{ is strictly concave on } I\}; \tag{2A.14}$$

and

$$\underset{\sim}{U}_3^{\,s} = \{u : u \in \underset{\sim}{U}_2^{\,s},\ u' \text{ is strictly convex on } I \text{ and finite on } I^0\}. \tag{2A.15}$$

In the SD theorems, $\underset{\sim}{U}_i$ and $\underset{\sim}{U}_i^{\,s}$ will be treated simultaneously.

Before going on to the SD theorems in Appendix 2B, we indicate our approach to their proofs. The basic idea is to approximate any u $\in \underset{\sim}{U}_i$ by a positive linear combination of simple elements in $\underset{\sim}{U}_i$. The simple elements are precisely those that produce the test quantities in the SD theorems. That is, if u is approximated as $u \simeq \Sigma_j c_j u_j$ with $c_j > 0$, then $E(u_j,F) \geq E(u_j,G)$ for all j implies $E(u,F) \geq E(u,G)$, by fairly straightforward limiting procedures. For example, every $u \in \underset{\sim}{U}_1$ can be approximated by a nondecreasing step function, and any such step function is a positive linear combination of step functions that are zero below some point x and unity above it. Similarly, every u $\in \underset{\sim}{U}_2$ can be approximated by a positive linear combination of ramp functions in $\underset{\sim}{U}_2$ of the form given in Eq. (2.42), and every $u \in \underset{\sim}{U}_3$ can be approximated by a positive linear combination of piecewise quadratic functions in $\underset{\sim}{U}_3$ of the form given in Eq. (2.44). In geometric terms, the sets $\underset{\sim}{U}_i$ are convex cones in the sense that $u_1, u_2 \in \underset{\sim}{U}_i$ and $c_1, c_2 \geq 0$ imply $c_1u_1 + c_2u_2 \in \underset{\sim}{U}_i$. The simple elements of $\underset{\sim}{U}_i$ correspond to points on the extreme rays of the cones $\underset{\sim}{U}_i$, and the SD tests are merely the dominance relations applied to these rays. There is, in this sense, an intimate connection between stochastic dominance and sum or integral representations of convex cones. This viewpoint clarifies why SD theory is poorly developed for the DARA utility functions and for multivariate distributions. For the class U_d of decreasing (or nonincreasing) absolute risk-averse utility functions, which is a convex cone, the extreme rays are not known explicitly. Indeed, there is a close connection between the class U_d and the class of log-convex or log-concave functions: for $u \in U_d$, log u' is concave. The appropriate integral representation theory for such cones appears to be undiscovered. In practical terms, we thus are forced to attack each problem of stochastic dominance over U_d separately. Similarly, in the multivariable case, the extremal elements of the convex cone of concave functions are not known in explicit terms.

Appendix 2B

As in Section 2.14, we define functions D^i related to F and G:

$$D^1(x) = G(x) - F(x);$$

$$D^2(x) = \int_{-\infty}^{x} G(y)dy - \int_{-\infty}^{x} F(y)dy;$$

$$D^3(x) = \int_{-\infty}^{x} \int_{-\infty}^{y} G(z)dz\,dy - \int_{-\infty}^{x} \int_{-\infty}^{y} F(z)dz\,dy.$$

We shall deal only with random variables having finite means μ_F and μ_G so that $D^2(x)$ is finite for all x. When random variables are unbounded below, it will be assumed that D^3 is defined, i.e., is not of the form $\infty - \infty$. A sufficient condition for this is that one or both of σ_F^2 and σ_G^2 is finite.

We now state the general SD theorems. For the strict inequalities pertaining to $\underset{\sim}{U}_i^s$ to be applicable when neither E(u,F) nor E(u,G) is finite, we make the convention that $\infty > \infty$, $\infty > -\infty$ and $-\infty > -\infty$. As before, we presume that $F \neq G$.

THEOREM 2B.1. <u>The following conditions are equivalent</u>:

(a) $D^1(x) \geq 0$ <u>for all</u> $x \in Re$;

(b) $E(u,F) \geq (>) E(u,G)$ <u>for all</u> $u \in \underset{\sim}{U}_1$ $(\underset{\sim}{U}_1^s)$ <u>for which</u> E(u,F) <u>and</u> E(u,G) <u>exist</u>.

THEOREM 2B.2. <u>The following conditions are equivalent</u>:

(a) $D^2(x) \geq 0$ <u>for all</u> $x \in Re$;

(b) $E(u,F) \geq (>) E(u,G)$ for all $u \in \underset{\sim}{U}_2(\underset{\sim}{U}_2^s)$ for which $E(u,F)$ and $E(u,G)$ exist.

THEOREM 2B.3. The following conditions are equivalent:

(a) $D^3(x) \geq 0$ for all $x \in Re$, and $\mu_F \geq \mu_G$;

(b) $E(u,F) \geq (>)$ for all $u \in \underset{\sim}{U}_3(\underset{\sim}{U}_3^s)$ for which $E(u,F)$ and $E(u,G)$ exist.

The necessity proofs have essentially been carried out in Section 2.15: $D^1(x) = E(f_x,F) - E(f_x,G)$, where

$$f_x(t) = \begin{cases} 0, & t < x \\ 1, & t \geq x; \end{cases} \tag{2B.1}$$

$D^2(x) = E(g_x,F) - E(g_x,G)$, where

$$g_x(t) = \begin{cases} t - x, & t \leq x \\ 0, & t > x; \end{cases} \tag{2B.2}$$

and $2D^3(s) = E(h_x,F) - E(h_x,G)$, where

$$h_x(t) = \begin{cases} -(t - x)^2, & t \leq x \\ 0, & t \geq x. \end{cases} \tag{2B.3}$$

For all $x \in I$, $f_x \in \underset{\sim}{U}_1$, $g_x \in \underset{\sim}{U}_2$, and $h_x \in \underset{\sim}{U}_3$. Although these functions are not in the $\underset{\sim}{U}_i^s$ classes, there are functions in the $\underset{\sim}{U}_i^s$ that are arbitrarily close to them; hence the conditions are necessary also for the case of "strict" SD.

Sufficiency of the conditions will be established now. Consider $\underset{\sim}{U}_1$ first. Given $u \in \underset{\sim}{U}_1$ for which $E(u,F)$ and $E(u,G)$ are defined, let u^+ and u^- denote the positive and negative parts of u:

$$u^+(x) = \max\{u(x),0\}, \quad u^-(x) = \min\{u(x),0\}.$$

Note that $u = u^+ + u^-$ and recall that $E(u,F)$ is <u>defined</u> as $E(u^+,F) + E(u^-,F)$ unless $E(u^+,F) = \infty$ and $E(u^-,F) = -\infty$, in which case $E(u,F)$ is undefined. Also note that if $E(u^+,F) = \infty$ and $E(u^-,G) = -\infty$, then $E(u,F) > E(u,G)$ is trivially true. Thus we assume henceforth that $E(u^-,G) > -\infty$. (The arguments for $E(u^+,F) < \infty$ are similar.) We treat u^+ and u^- separately, setting $u(0) = 0$ without loss of generality. First, define

$$u_n^+(x) = \begin{cases} u(i/2^n) & \text{if } x \in [i/2^n,(i+1)/2^n) \\ & \text{for } i = 0,1,\ldots,n2^n, \text{ and} \\ \\ u(n) & \text{if } x \geq n \\ 0 & \text{if } x < 0. \end{cases} \tag{2B.4}$$

Clearly, u_n^+ is a positive linear combination of functions of the form (2B.1). Thus $D^1 \geq 0$ implies $E(u_n^+,F) \geq E(u_n^+,G)$ for all n. Since $u_n^+ \uparrow u^+$ as $n \to \infty$, the monotone convergence theorem implies that

$$E(u^+,F) = \lim_n E(u_n^+,F) \geq \lim_n E(u_n^+,G) = E(u^+,G).$$

Next, define

$$u_n^-(x) = \begin{cases} u(i/2^n) & \text{if } x \in [(i-1)/2^n,i/2^n) \\ & i = -n2^n,\ldots,-1,0 \\ \\ u(-n) & \text{if } x \leq -n \\ 0 & \text{if } x \geq 0. \end{cases} \tag{2B.5}$$

Each u_n^- is a positive linear combination of step functions of the form $f - 1$, where f is of the form (2B.1). Thus $E(u_n^-,F) \geq E(u_n^-,G)$. Since $u_n^- \downarrow u^-$ and $E(u^-,G) > -\infty$, the dominated convergence theorem implies that

$$-\infty < E(u^-,G) = \lim_n E(u_n^-,G) \le \lim_n E(u_n^-,F) = E(u^-,F).$$

Since $u = u^+ + u^-$, we have $E(u,F) \ge E(u,G)$.

To show that $E(u,F) > E(u,G)$ for all $u \in \underset{\sim}{U}_1^s$ for which $E(u,F)$ and $E(u,G)$ are defined, let J be any closed interval in I for which $D^1(x) \ge \delta > 0$ for all $x \in J$. Take $J = [0,1]$ and $u(0) = 0$ without loss of generality and define

$$u_1(x) = \begin{cases} u(x), & x < 0 \\ 0, & x \in [0,1] \\ u(x) - u(1), & x > 1, \end{cases}$$

$$u_2(x) = \begin{cases} 0, & x < 0 \\ u(x), & x \in [0,1] \\ u(1), & x > 1. \end{cases} \tag{2B.6}$$

Then $u_1, u_2 \in \underset{\sim}{U}_1$ and $u = u_1 + u_2$. We now show that $E(u_2,F) > E(u_2,G)$.

Let $u_2^n(x)$ be defined as follows:

$$u_2^n(x) = \begin{cases} 0, & x < 1/n \\ u_2(j/n), & x \in [j/n,(j+1)/n), \quad j = 1,\dots,n-1 \\ u_2(1), & x > 1. \end{cases} \tag{2B.7}$$

Then $u_2^n \uparrow u_2$ as $n \to \infty$. Since

$$u_2^n(x) = \sum_{j=1}^{n} \left[u_2\left(\frac{j}{n}\right) - u_2\left(\frac{j-1}{n}\right)\right] f_{j/n}(x),$$

where f is as in (2B.1), we have

$$E(u_2^n,F) - E(u_2^n,G) = \sum_{j=1}^{n} \left[u_2\left(\frac{j}{n}\right) - u_2\left(\frac{j-1}{n}\right)\right]\left[G\left(\frac{j}{n}\right) - F\left(\frac{j}{n}\right)\right]$$

$$\ge \delta\left\{\sum_{j=1}^{n} \left[u_2\left(\frac{j}{n}\right) - u_2\left(\frac{j-1}{n}\right)\right]\right\} = \delta[u(1) - u(0)] > 0.$$

As $n \to \infty$ we get $E(u_2,F) - E(u_2,G) > 0$.

Next consider $\underset{\sim}{U}_2$. Assume without loss of generality that $u \in \underset{\sim}{U}_2$ has $u(0) = 0$ and that $E(u,F)$ and $E(u,G)$ are defined. By (2A.6), there exists a nonnegative, nonincreasing function m such that

$$u(x) = \int_0^x m(t)dt,$$

where $\int_0^x$ is interpreted as $-\int_x^0$ if $x < 0$. Let

$$m_n(t) = \begin{cases} m((i+1)/2^n) & \text{if } t \in (i/2^n, (i+1)/2^n], \\ & \text{for } i = -n2^n, \ldots, -1, 0, 1, \ldots, n2^n \\ m(-n) & \text{if } t \leq -n \\ 0 & \text{if } t > n. \end{cases} \tag{2B.8}$$

Then $m_n \uparrow m$ as $n \to \infty$. Each m_n is a positive linear combination of functions p_w of the form $p_w(t) = 1$ for $t \leq w$ and $p_w(t) = 0$ for $t > w$. Define $u_n(x) = \int_0^x m_n(t)dt$. Since m_n is a positive linear combination of p_w functions as just described, u_n is a positive linear combination of functions of the form $\int_0^x p_w(t)dt = g_w(x) + w$, where g_w is as in (2B.2). Note that $u_n^+(x) \uparrow \int_0^x m(t)dt = u^+(x)$ for $x \geq 0$.

Let v_n and v be:

$$v_n(x) = \begin{cases} m(0) \cdot x, & x \leq 0 \\ u_n^+(x), & x \geq 0, \end{cases}$$

$$v(x) = \begin{cases} m(0) \cdot x, & x \leq 0 \\ u^+(x), & x \geq 0. \end{cases} \tag{2B.9}$$

By the monotone convergence theorem, $E(v_n,F) \to E(v,F)$ and $E(v_n,G) \to E(v,G)$ as $n \to \infty$. If $D^2(x) \geq 0$ for all $x \in Re$ and $E(u^+,F) < \infty$ [arguments for $E(u^-,G) > -\infty$ are similar], then since $v_n \in \underset{\sim}{U}_2$ is a positive linear combination of functions of the form g in (2B.2), we obtain $E(v_n,G) \leq E(v_n,F)$ for all n. Thus $E(v,G) \leq E(v,F) \leq E(u^+,F) < \infty$.

Similarly, $u_n^-(x) \downarrow \int_0^x m(t)dt = u^-(x)$ for $x \leq 0$. The function $e_n(x) = u_n^-(x) - m(0)\, g_0(x)$ is a positive linear combination of functions of the form $g_w(x)$ + constant. Defining $e(x) = u^-(x) - m(0)g_0(x)$, we have $0 \geq e_n \downarrow e$. By the monotone convergence theorem, $E(e_n,G) \to E(e,G) \geq E(u^-,G)$, and $E(e_n,F) \to E(e,F) > E(e,G)$. Since $u(x) = e(x) + v(x)$, it follows that $E(u,F) \geq E(u,G)$ for every $u \in \underset{\sim}{U}_2$ for which $E(u,F)$ and $E(u,G)$ are defined.

To show that $D^2 \geq 0$ implies $E(u,F) > E(u,G)$ for $u \in \underset{\sim}{U}_2^s$ [given $F \neq G$ and the existence of $E(u,F)$ and $E(u,G)$], let $D^2(x) \geq \delta > 0$ for all $x \in [0,1]$ with no loss in generality. Given $u \in \underset{\sim}{U}_2^s$ with $u(x) = \int_0^x m(t)dt$, m is a positive, strictly decreasing function.

Let

$$m_1(t) = \begin{cases} m(t) + m(1) - m(0), & t \leq 0 \\ m(1) & t \in [0,1] \\ m(t) & t \geq 1, \end{cases}$$

$$m_2(t) = \begin{cases} m(0) - m(1), & t \leq 0 \\ m(t) - m(1), & t \in [0,1] \\ 0, & t \geq 1 \end{cases} \tag{2B.10}$$

and note that m_1, m_2 are nonnegative and nonincreasing, with $m = m_1 + m_2$. Thus $u_1(x) = \int_0^x m_1(t)dt$ and $u_2(x) = \int_0^x m_2(t)dt$ are in $\underset{\sim}{U}_2$. We shall show that $E(u_2,F) > E(u_2,G)$.

Let $m_2^n(t)$ be:

$$m_2^n(t) = \begin{cases} m_2(t), & t \leq 1/n \\ m_2(j/n), & t \in (j/n,(j+1)/n],\ j = 1,\ldots,n-1 \\ m_2(t) = 0, & t > 1. \end{cases} \tag{2B.11}$$

Then $m_2^n \downarrow m_2$ as $n \to \infty$, and $u_2^n(x) \equiv \int_0^x m_2^n(t)dt \downarrow u_2(x)$ as $n \to \infty$. Since

$$u_2^n(x) = \int_0^x \sum_{j=1}^n [m_2\left(\frac{j-1}{n}\right) - m_2\left(\frac{j}{n}\right)]p_{j/n}(t)dt$$

$$= \sum_{j=1}^{n} [m_2\left(\frac{j-1}{n}\right) - m_2\left(\frac{j}{n}\right)][g_{j/n}(x) + j/n],$$

we have

$$E(u_2^{\,n},F) - E(u_2^{\,n},G) = \sum_{j=1}^{n} \left[m_2\left(\frac{j-1}{n}\right) - m_2\left(\frac{j}{n}\right)\right] D^2(j/n)$$

$$\geq \delta \sum_{j=1}^{n} \left[m_2\left(\frac{j-1}{n}\right) - m_2\left(\frac{j}{n}\right)\right] = \delta[m(0) - m(1)] > 0,$$

for all n. As $n \to \infty$, we obtain $E(u_2,F) - E(u_2,G) > 0$.

Finally, consider $u \in \underset{\sim}{U}_3$, for which E(u,F) and E(u,G) exist, and without loss in generality let u(0) = 0. Then $u(x) = \int_0^x m(t)dt$, where m is a nonnegative, nonincreasing convex function. By arguments identical to those above, the function m can be approximated by a sequence m_n of nonnegative, nonincreasing functions, each of which is a positive linear combination of piecewise-linear convex ramp functions of the form $q_w(t) = \frac{1}{2}(w - t)$ for $t \leq w$, $q_w(t) = 0$ for $t \geq w$, with $m_n \downarrow m$ as $n \to \infty$. Since $\int_0^x q_w(t)dt = h_w(x) + w^2$, where h is as in (2B.3), we have: $\mu_F \geq \mu_G$ and $D^3 \geq 0$ imply that $E(u_n,F) > E(u_n,G)$ for all n, where $u_n(x) = \int_0^x m_n(t)dt$. Since $u_n \uparrow u$ on $(-\infty,0]$ and $u_n \downarrow u$ on $[0,\infty)$, the monotone and the dominated convergence theorems imply that $E(u,F) = \lim E(u_n,F) \geq \lim E(u_n,G) = E(u,G)$, if either $E(u^+,F) < \infty$ or $E(u^-,G) > -\infty$. We shall leave it to the reader to prove that $E(u,F) > E(u,G)$ if $u \in \underset{\sim}{U}_3^{\,s}$, using methods similar to those above.

Note on the Proofs. The point x = 0 that is singled out in the proofs has no significance other than its being an interior point of I. The same mode of proof can be used for $I = [0,\infty)$ or $I = [0,1]$. Note that boundedness of the u or finiteness of E(u,F) and E(u,G) is not assumed. The versions of the monotone and the dominated convergence theorems used are those of Loeve (1963:124-125). The proofs are adapted from Brumelle and Vickson (1975).

Introduction to Chapter 3
Portfolio Applications: Empirical Studies

In this chapter, R. Burr Porter reviews a number of empirical studies of portfolio selection and performance that have employed stochastic dominance methodology. As Porter has made a large contribution to this literature, he is in a unique position to survey it.

Many of these studies deal with comparisons of stochastic-dominance (SD) and mean-variance (EV) efficient sets. Porter begins with a discussion of the Porter, Wart, and Ferguson (1973) algorithms that allow the SD efficient set to be determined for large-scale empirical comparisons. Although these algorithms have not gone uncriticized (cf. Chapter 2, Section 2.16), they have been used effectively in a number of SD studies. Porter then discusses several studies that tested the discriminating power of SD, EV, and other criteria on samples of individual securities and industrial groupings. Following this, his review considers studies of mutual fund performance in which the discriminating power of the criteria among diversified portfolios and between portfolios and average market experience was investigated.

Porter considers methodology next. He reports the differences in results produced by altering the length of holding periods and by grouping data to estimate frequency distributions. The efficiency of diversification is also considered. He then introduces mean-semivariance as an operationally feasible compromise between the computational ease of EV and the theoretical superiority of SD (Richard C. Burgess expands this theme in Chapter 4). Next, the effects of nonstationarity and sample size are discussed. Finally, Porter considers the significance of the lack of an SD portfolio selection algorithm and presents some provisional suggestions.

3 Portfolio Applications: Empirical Studies

R. Burr Porter

A considerable volume of empirical work on SD efficiency has been generated. This chapter examines the majority of studies currently available and considers some methodological problems associated with SD empirical applications.

3.1 Introduction

A major feature of empirical work involving SD is the processing of substantial data. Many more observations are required to estimate a probability function than to estimate a mean and variance. One result of this feature has been the development by Porter, Wart, and Ferguson (1973) of several algorithms that allow efficient processing of data required for empirical tests involving large numbers of portfolios. This chapter first reviews the PWF algorithms.

Following the discussion of algorithms, the major empirical studies are examined. They fall logically into three categories: studies of individual securities, studies involving mutual funds, and studies involving other portfolios. In addition, the studies cover a variety of time periods with rates of return determined monthly, quarterly, semiannually, and annually. In most cases, aspects of SD efficient sets--size membership, etc.--are compared to the same aspects of EV efficient sets derived from the same sample.

The chapter concludes with the examination of two serious reservations that have been expressed about SD methodology. The first concerns the reliability of the sample probability functions upon which SD analysis is based. The second makes the point that EV methodology includes optimizing algorithms that build efficient portfolios while SD criteria are suitable only as screening devices for existing samples of portfolios.

3.2 Computer Algorithms for Empirical SD Tests

In empirical studies, a major problem with SD, as opposed to EV, tests of portfolio efficiency based on historical data is the need to generate and process significantly more data. First, more data points are needed to obtain a reliable estimate of the entire probability function than are needed to generate reasonable estimates of the mean and variance. Second, the application of the EV test to any two portfolios requires only two comparisons--E_1 vs. E_2 and V_1 vs. V_2--while the SD test may require a total number of comparisons equal to the sum of the number of sample observations on each of the portfolios. Finally, to conduct tests of SSD efficiency, all the calculations required for the FSD test must be made regardless of whether one is interested in FSD results. And for TSD experiments, all the calculations required for FSD and SSD tests are required.

As an example, consider a sample of 100 portfolios for each of which there are 50 monthly return observations. To determine either the EV or the SSD efficient set, each portfolio must be compared to every other portfolio, a total of 4950 pairwise comparisons. For the EV test, every pairwise comparison involves two parameters for a total of 9900 individual comparisons. For the SSD test, every pairwise comparison may involve 100 points (50 for each portfolio) for a total of 495,000 comparisons, or 50 times the EV requirement. Moreover, since the FSD numbers must be calculated before the SSD numbers can be determined, a total of 990,000 calculations (495,000 for each of FSD and SSD) may be required to generate SSD tests of efficiency as opposed to the 9900 for the EV test. As the number of portfolios or data points increases, the difference in required calculations becomes enormous.

Recognizing these problems, Porter, Wart, and Ferguson developed computer algorithms that employ several SD properties to make feasible SD tests of the efficiency of large numbers of portfolios.

The first step in processing the data for SD tests is the approximation of the true underlying distribution functions by finite (and therefore discrete) sets of sample observations. For this purpose, the three dominance criteria must be redefined in terms of these discrete observations. This result is obtained by first listing the sample observations in ascending order such that if x_i and x_j are the _i_th and _j_th observations, then $x_i \leq x_j$ if and only if $i < j$. Note that although it is possible for two or more observations to have the same numerical value, for consistency in labeling, each observation is considered to be distinct. If there are K distinct observations of return on a given portfolio, then each occurs with a relative sample frequency $f(x_i) = 1/K$. The corresponding distribution function $F_1(x_n)$ is generated directly by summing these sample frequencies for all x_i, $i \leq n$. Finally, in the comparison of two probability functions, f(x) and g(x), there are a total of N = 2K distinct observations. If the _i_th observation belongs to portfolio f, then $f(x_i) = 1/K$ and $g(x_i) = 0$; if it belongs to portfolio g, then $g(x_i) = 1/K$ and $f(x_i) = 0$.

With this framework the SD rules can be restated as follows:

FSD: The probability function f(x) is said to dominate the probability function g(x) by FSD if and only if $F_1(x_n) \leq G_1(x_n)$ for all $n \leq N$ with strict inequality for at least one $n \leq N$, where

$$F_1(x_n) = \sum_{i=1}^{n} f(x_i) \qquad n = 1,2,3,\ldots,N$$

and

$$G_1(x_n) = \sum_{i=1}^{n} g(x_i) \qquad n = 1,2,3,\ldots,N$$

SSD: The probability function f(x) is said to dominate the probability function g(x) by SSD if and only if $F_2(x_n) \leq G_2(x_n)$ for all $n \leq N$ with strict inequality for at least one $n \leq N$, where

$$F_2(x_n) = \sum_{i=2}^{n} F_1(x_{i-1})(x_i - x_{i-1}) \qquad n = 2,3,\ldots,N$$

and

$$F_2(x_1) = 0.$$

$G_2(x_n)$ is similarly defined.

TSD: The probability function f(x) is said to dominate the probability function g(x) by TSD if and only if $F_3(x_n) \leq G_3(x_n)$ for all $n \leq N$ with strict inequality for at least one $n \leq N$, and $F_2(x_N) \leq G_2(x_N)$, where

$$F_3(x_n) = 1/2 \sum_{i=2}^{n} [F_2(x_i) + F_2(x_{i-1})](x_i - x_{i-1})$$

$$n = 2,3,\ldots,N$$

and

$$F_3(x_1) = 0.$$

$G_3(x_n)$ is similarly defined.

By way of example, consider two portfolios f and g, for which the following observed rates of return obtain:

Portfolio	% Return
f	6, 2, 1.8, 7
g	6, 3, 1, 3

Using the notation given above, K = 4, N = 2(4) = 8, and the complete matrix of data required for the application of the three SD rules is presented in Table 3-1. The values $F_2(x_8)$ and $G_3(x_8)$ can be calculated as follows:

Table 3-1
Matrix of Values Required for SD Tests

Value of	Observation Number (n)							
	1	2	3	4	5	6	7	8
x_n	1.0	1.8	2.0	3.0	3.0	6.0	6.0	7.0
$f(x_n)$	0	1/4	1/4	0	0	1/4	0	1/4
$g(x_n)$	1/4	0	0	1/4	1/4	0	1/4	0
$F_1(x_n)$	0	0.25	0.50	0.50	0.50	0.75	0.75	1.00
$G_1(x_n)$	0.25	0.25	0.25	0.50	0.75	0.75	1.00	1.00
$F_2(x_n)$	0	0	0.05	0.55	0.55	2.05	2.05	2.80
$G_2(x_n)$	0	0.20	0.25	0.50	0.50	2.75	2.75	3.75
$F_3(x_n)$	0	0	0.005	0.305	0.305	4.205	4.205	6.630
$G_3(x_n)$	0	0.080	0.125	0.500	0.500	5.375	5.375	8.625

Source. Porter, Wart, and Ferguson (1973:75). Used with permission.

$$\begin{aligned} F_2(x_8) &= 0(1.8 - 1) + .25(2 - 1.8) + .5(3 - 2) + .5(3 - 3) \\ &\quad + .5(6 - 3) + .75(6 - 6) + .75(7 - 6) \\ &= 2.80 \\ G_3(x_8) &= .5[(.2 + 0)(1.8 - 1) + (.25 + .2)(2 - 1.8) \\ &\quad + (.5 + .25)(3 - 2) + (.5 + .5)(3 - 3) \\ &\quad + (2.75 + .5)(6 - 3) + (2.75 + 2.75)(6 - 6) \\ &\quad + (3.75 + 2.75)(7 - 6)] \\ &= 8.625 \end{aligned}$$

Inspection of Table 3-1 reveals that portfolio f dominates portfolio g by TSD but not by FSD or SSD.

To conduct SD tests on large numbers of portfolios, the actual procedures for applying the algorithms must be much more efficient than those just illustrated. Three tricks have the effect of increasing the algorithms' efficiencies. The first trick (see Figure 3-1) is based on listing the portfolios in descending order of expected values. Since Hadar and Russell (1969) have shown that for one portfolio to dominate another the expected return of the dominant portfolio must be at least as large as that of the dominated portfolio, we know that none of the portfolios in the sample can be dominated by any listed below them. For the case in which two or more have the same mean, the one with the smallest variance is listed first. Porter (1971) has shown that in such cases one portfolio can dominate another only if the former has a smaller variance than the latter. The algorithms take advantage of this information in the following manner:

1. Begin with the portfolio listed first, and refer to it as the base.

2. Select the next listed portfolio, and refer to it as the challenger.

3. If the smallest data point (rate of return) for the challenger is larger than the smallest data point for the base, conclude that the challenger cannot be dominated by the base portfolio.

4. Since the base portfolio cannot be dominated by the challenger, record the fact that neither portfolio dominates the other, and proceed to compare the base to the next challenger.

For each such case the SD result is determined without any calculations at all. Therefore the more often such cases occur in the sample, the faster the algorithms perform their duties.

The second trick relies on the fact that the SD relationships are transitive by eliminating from further consideration any portfolio that already has been dominated by a predetermined degree of dominance. For example, if portfolio 1 dominates portfolio 10 by FSD, then there is no reason to allow portfolio 10 to challenge portfolios 2 through 9 since it cannot dominate them and since it is not a member of any of the SD efficient sets. Moreover, portfolio 10 should not be allowed to serve as a base portfolio since it will not dominate any portfolio that is not also dominated by portfolio 1. As a result of this step, the actual number of portfolio comparisons might well be less than one-half the potential required number.

The effectiveness of this step is a function of the predetermined degree of SD by which a portfolio is allowed to be eliminated from further consideration. If only FSD-dominated portfolios are

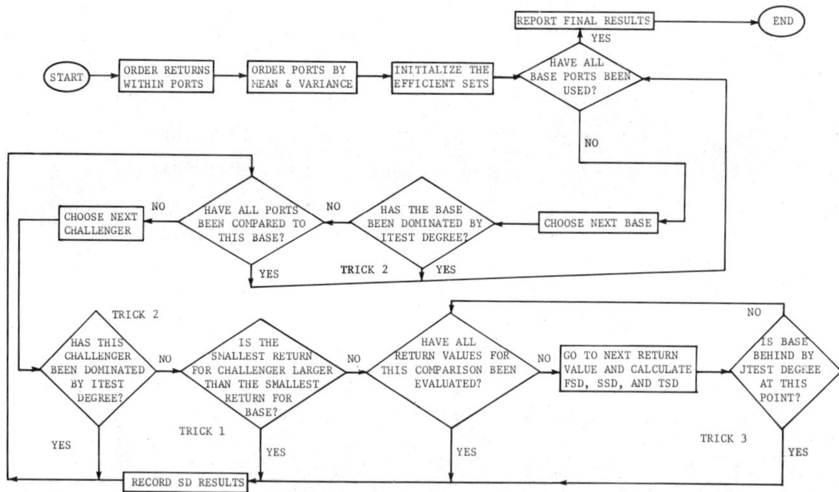

Figure 3-1. Flowchart [from Porter, Wart, and Ferguson (1973:78)]. Used with permission.

eliminated, one would expect to receive substantially less benefit than if SSD-dominated portfolios are eliminated. The choice of degree by which portfolios are dropped from further consideration is made when the decision-maker sets an input parameter of the program. The reason for leaving the user with the option of elimination by FSD, SSD, or TSD is that elimination by SSD renders the FSD results useless and elimination by TSD destroys both the FSD and the SSD results. That is, if portfolio B is dropped because it is SSD-dominated by portfolio A, it is possible that there exists a portfolio C that is

FSD-dominated only by B (A would dominate C by SSD but not necessarily by FSD). Since B would never be compared to C, C would be reported incorrectly as being a member of the FSD efficient set.

The third trick combines the facts (1) that the base portfolio must at least be even with the challenger at all points (i.e., all return values) if it is to dominate the challenger and (2) that if the base does not dominate the challenger by TSD, then it does not dominate the challenger by either FSD or SSD. With this understanding, the rule is added that if the base portfolio falls behind the challenger by TSD at any point, the comparison is terminated, the fact that neither dominates the other by any degree is recorded, and the program proceeds to the next challenger. If the base falls behind at the third data point, for example, FSD, SSD, and TSD values need not be calculated for the remaining, say, 97 points.

This trick also can be made more effective by stopping the comparison if the base portfolio falls behind at any point by SSD. Since any portfolio is more likely to fall behind by SSD than by TSD, the algorithm would stop sooner, more often. To use the SSD stopping rule instead of TSD, however, the user would have to be willing to forego the results of the TSD test.

The benefit of these algorithms is that they facilitate the SD analysis of relatively large numbers of portfolios, each having many data points with only a few seconds of computer time. In addition, they are flexible enough to allow the user to adjust the tests, output, and speed of operation to suit his circumstances. Versions of these algorithms were used in several of the studies examined below.

3.3 Empirical Studies

3.3.1 SD Studies of Individual Securities

Primarily as a means to illustrate the use of SD rules in testing the efficiency of individual securities, Porter and Carey (1974) randomly selected 16 common stocks from the Compustat Tapes (see Table 3-2). Monthly rates of return were calculated for the 54 periods from the last quarter of 1963 through the first quarter of 1968 and frequency

Table 3-2
Companies Included in the Study

Company No.	Company Name
1	Federal Paper Board
2	American Machine and Foundry
3	Smith Kline/French Laboratories
4	Rayonier, Inc.
5	American Tobacco
6	Crowell-Collier and Macmillan
7	American Seating Co.
8	Emerson Electric Co.
9	Riegel Textile Corp.
10	Cerro Co.
11	American Distilling Co.
12	American Investment Co.
13	Johnson and Johnson
14	United Aircraft Corp.
15	Dresser Industries, Inc.
16	Schering Corp.

Source: Porter and Carey (1974:18). Used with permission.

distributions were developed following a histogram method with 10 outcome intervals evenly spaced from -18 percent to 22 percent.

The results summarized in Table 3-3 indicate that with FSD only three securities--3, 5, and 7--were eliminated by any of the others. Thus the investor who started with 16 securities to compare would still have 13 from which to choose. FSD would not have helped him very much. Actually, this rather weak result should have been anticipated because FSD represents a fairly stringent test of superiority of one security or portfolio over another. With SSD all but 2 of the securities, 8 and 12, were eliminated, and 8 almost eliminated 12. By applying SSD, the investor would have reduced the size of the set of investment alternatives from 16 to 2. If the investor had been selecting individual securities, he could have been certain that 8 and 12 were the 2 best securities. Moreover, the cumulative probability functions for securities 8 and 12 (Figure 3-2) are such that many investors probably would agree that 8 is the single best security.

Table 3-3
Results of First- and Second-Degree Stochastic Dominance Tests

By First-Degree Stochastic Dominance

Company number		Company number
2	dominated	3
5	dominated	3
8	dominated	3, 5, 7

By Second-Degree Stochastic Dominance

Company number		Company number
2	dominated	3
4	dominated	10
5	dominated	1, 2, 3, 7
7	dominated	1
8	dominated	1, 2, 3, 4, 5, 6, 7, 9, 10, 11, 13, 14, 15, 16
9	dominated	10
11	dominated	3
12	dominated	3, 11
13	dominated	1, 10
14	dominated	10
15	dominated	6, 9, 10, 14
16	dominated	1, 4, 6, 9, 10, 13, 14, 15
1, 3, 6, 10	dominated	none

Source: Porter and Carey (1974:18). Used with permission.

By way of comparison, if the EV rule had been applied to those 16 securities solely as a screening device, all but 5, 8, and 12 would have been eliminated. Securities 8 and 12 are consistent with SSD; but it is noteworthy that although 5 is included in the EV efficient set, it is one of the few securities eliminated by FSD. It is clear from these results that the EV rule can make serious errors of choice as suggested by the theoretical analysis of EV and SD.

In another study of individual securities, Levy and Hanoch (1970) determined efficient sets by eight different criteria. Since several criteria were variations on the quadratic utility function, we consider here the results only for FSD, SSD, EV, and a three-moment rule. Using 138 securities traded on the Israeli market, quarterly

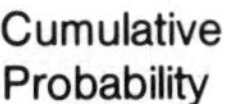

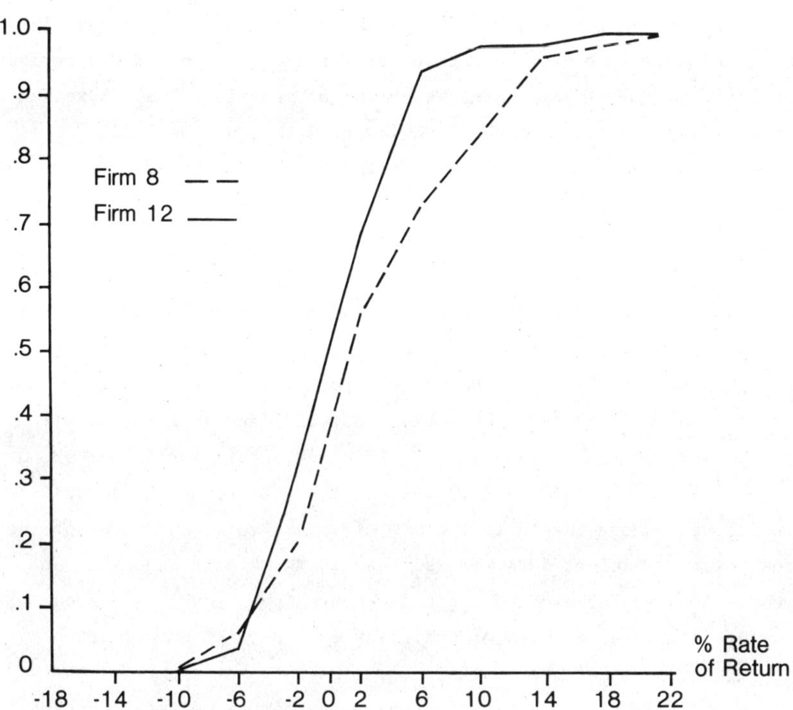

Figure 3-2. Cumulative Probability Function of Rate of Return for Firms 8 and 12 [from Porter and Carey (1974:19)]. Used with permission.

rates of return were computed for 1958-1968. Since few securities were available in 1958, the total period was divided into two subperiods, 1962-1968 and 1965-1968.

For the shorter periods, each distribution is estimated on the basis of fewer observations, but more distributions are available for comparisons. Table 3-4 summarizes the number of distributions and observations for each period. Table 3-5 compares results for FSD, SSD, EV, and the three-moment rule. As in the Porter and Carey study (1974) the FSD rule was not very effective for selection in the longer periods 1958-1968 and 1962-1968. When the number of securities was increased (and fewer observations were available for each), however, FSD eliminated more than half the securities.

The results with SSD were much better for the entire period: only 4 of 16 securities were efficient, while for the shortest period (1965-1968) only 7 of 138 securities were efficient.

The size of the efficient sets for the EV criterion were similar to those of sets based on SSD for the different periods, but the membership for any given period was not identical.

In 1965-1968, only 4 securities (out of 7 and 9, respectively) were the same in the SSD and the EV efficient sets. For 1958-1968, 3 out of 4 were identical. For 1962-1968, the 6 EV efficient securities were included among the 10 in the SSD efficient set. The sizes of the three-moment efficient sets were similar to those of EV and SSD, but no comparison was made of the actual memberships. Levy and Hanoch also noted that the members of efficient sets by a given criterion were quite dissimilar over different periods.

As part of a study of the potential gains from diversification on the London Stock Exchange, Sarnat (1972a) examined the SD relationships among 14 categories of investments listed on the exchange. The categories, their mean returns, and their standard deviations based on annual data covering the period 1963 to 1970 are shown in Table 3-6.

The conclusions of the main part of the study are that "intra-industry diversification captures most of the gain from diversification among domestic ordinary shares"; and "the potential gain is greatest when the English investor combines ordinary shares with fixed-interest securities (preferred shares) and/or with commodity shares."

Table 3-4
Number of Securities, Number of Observations on Each Security, and Period of Inquiry

Period[a]	No. of Securities Included	No. of Observations (Quarters) for Each Security
1958-1968	16	41
1962-1968	37	25
1965-1968	138	13

Source: Levy and Hanoch (1970:71). Used with permission.

[a]For 1968, only the first quarter is included.

Table 3-5
Number of Securities in the Efficient Set

Period		Total No. of Securities	Size of Efficient Sets			
			FSD	SSD	EV	Three-moment
1958-1968	41	16	15	4	4	5
1962-1968	25	37	32	10	6	11
1965-1968	13	138	66	7	9	11

Source: Levy and Hanoch (1970:71-74). Used with permission.

Having derived these results, Sarnat considered whether any individual investment categories would dominate others by FSD or SSD. When the FSD test was applied, only 6 of the original 14 categories survived. The survivors included consumer durables, chemicals, oils, shipping, rubber, and coppers. It is worth noting that none of the fixed-interest securities survived the FSD test. This means that at least one of the other categories had annual rates of return in excess of the return on fixed-interest securities in each of the years included in the study. Of course the significance of the results is limited by the extremely small size of the sample on which the distribution functions are based.

Table 3-6
Mean Rates of Return and Standard Deviations of Selected Security Groups, 1963-1970 (in percent)

	Mean Rate of Return[a]	Compounded Annual Average Rate of Return[b]	Standard Deviation
Ordinary shares			
1) Capital goods	9.3	7.7	20.3
2) Consumer durables	11.7	9.0	26.9
3) Consumer non-durables	9.8	8.4	19.4
4) Chemicals	11.8	9.6	24.1
5) Oil	20.9	16.2	40.0
6) Shipping	21.3	19.2	24.1
7) Finance	9.6	8.2	19.3
8) Rubber	21.2	20.5	14.5
9) Tea	14.6	12.4	24.4
10) Coppers	25.5	21.0	36.8
11) Tins	7.5	6.8	12.7
Fixed-interest securities			
12) Consols	0.1	0.1	3.1
13) 20-year Government bonds	1.3	1.2	3.4
14) Preferred shares	1.9	1.8	5.5

Source: Sarnat (1972:54). Used with permission. Calculated from data on security prices and yield; compiled by the *Financial Times*, The Institute of Actuaries and the Faculty of Actuaries in Edinburgh and published daily in the *Financial Times*.

[a]Arithmetic mean.

[b]Geometric mean.

When the SSD criterion was applied to the investment categories, only shipping, rubber, and copper shares survived. Thus the risk-averse investor making mutually exclusive choices among the 14 categories would limit his consideration to these 3. Again, however, the significance of the results must be evaluated in the light of the limited sample size.

Discussion. We have considered three different studies of the efficiency of individual securities from three different sources: the Compustat Tapes, the Israeli Stock Exchange, and the London Stock Exchange. Several results were common to each study. The FSD test of efficiency was of rather limited effectiveness in reducing the original sample, often eliminating almost no securities. The SSD test was much more effective than FSD, producing an efficient set 5 percent to 30 percent of the sample size. The EV efficient set was very similar to that of SSD in both size and membership, but there were some significant differences.

In considering these studies, one should remember their limitations. First, they are tests of individual securities rather than portfolios; second, the number of securities included in each study was relatively small; and finally, in the studies by Levy and Hanoch (1970) and by Sarnat (1972a), some of the probability functions are based on so few return observations that they are of questionable validity.

3.3.2 Stochastic Dominance and Mutual Fund Performance

A study by Joy and Porter (1974) presented the results of a stochastic dominance test of the performance of mutual funds relative to the market as measured by the Dow-Jones Industrial Average. In an earlier paper, using the reward-to-variability ratio as the performance criterion, Sharpe (1966) found that from 1954 to 1963 only 11 of 34 funds outperformed the Dow-Jones Industrial Average (DJIA) while 23 funds were outperformed by the DJIA. Annual performance was measured as return to stockholders: the sum of dividend payments, capital gains distributions, and changes in net asset value. This is a measure of _net_ performance, i.e., gross yield less management and administrative expenses. Sharpe pointed out that on a _gross_ performance basis--before deducting expenses--the funds performed, on average, as well as the DJIA. He concluded that the mutual funds were inferior investments during the period. Arditti (1971) theorized that since investors prefer positive skewness, assets with relatively low reward-to-variability ratios would not be inferior investments _if_ they also have relatively high third moments (high positive skewness) since positive skewness implies a greater probability of higher return. Empirically reexamining the Sharpe data with this additional test, Arditti found that average fund performance was _not_ inferior to DJIA performance since the skewness of the DJIA return distribution was significantly less than fund skewness.

The Joy and Porter study was based on the premise that a proper test of mutual fund performance relative to the market (DJIA) is a test employing stochastic dominance principles. Such a test necessitates a pairwise comparison between each fund and the DJIA. The first step of their analysis was to collect performance data for the 34 funds analyzed by both Sharpe and Arditti for the 10 year period 1954-1963. Price and dividend data were also collected for the DJIA over the same period.

The null hypothesis was: that there would be no difference between fund and market performance, against the alternate hypothesis: that the market would outperform the fund. For this study the null hypothesis was operationalized by hypothesizing that the number of funds that dominated the DJIA should equal the number of funds that were dominated by the DJIA. That is, of the total number of pairwise comparisons that exhibit dominance--either for or against the funds--half should show the DJIA dominating the fund and half should show the opposite result. This hypothesis, which utilizes the binomial distribution, was tested under all three stochastic dominance criteria using computer programs developed by Porter, Wart, and Ferguson. Results are presented in Table 3-7.

Under FSD, there were no funds that dominated the DJIA, nor were any dominated by the index. Under SSD, 6 funds were dominated by the DJIA, but no fund dominated the DJIA. Therefore 28 funds neither dominated the DJIA nor were dominated by it. Applying the binomial test, the probability that the observed event (the event being all 6 dominance pairs favoring the DJIA) could have occurred by chance is only 1.56 percent. This constitutes a rejection of the null hypothesis of no difference between fund and market performance for most significance levels. Similarly, under TSD, there were 9 instances in which funds were dominated by the DJIA, none in which the DJIA was dominated, and 25 instances of no dominance. The probability that the observed event (all 9 dominance pairs favoring the DJIA) could have occurred by

Table 3-7
Stochastic Dominance Results

Type of Dominance	Funds Dominating the DJIA	Funds Dominated by the DJIA
First-degree	None	None
Second-degree	None	1. Delaware Fund 2. Equity Fund 3. Financial Industrial Fund 4. Fundamental Investors 5. Incorporated Investors 6. Selected American Shares
Third-degree	None	1. Delaware Fund 2. Equity Fund 3. Financial Industrial Fund 4. Fundamental Investors 5. Incorporated Investors 6. Massachusetts Investors Trust[a] 7. National Securities-Income Series[a] 8. Selected American Shares 9. United Funds-Income Fund[a]

Source: Joy and Porter (1974:29). Used with permission.

[a] Funds dominated by DJIA under third-degree stochastic dominance that were not so dominated under second-degree stochastic dominance.

chance is only 0.2 percent. This, too, supports a rejection of the null hypothesis. Under both SSD and TSD, each incorporating conventional economic assumptions, the conclusion is that the funds were inferior investments.

Joy and Porter pointed out that the binomial test is deficient in that it ignores the "no dominance" cases. Nevertheless, the raw data speak for themselves, and they clearly indicate that the funds fail to outperform the market.

A second study, by Levy and Sarnat (1970), examined the size and composition of efficient sets of mutual funds generated by the FSD, SSD, and EV criteria. The empirical analysis was based on the open-end mutual funds appearing in the annual editions of Investment Companies, published by Arthur Wiesenberger and Company. Levy and Sarnat pointed out that mutual funds are a particularly appropriate subject since, for the purposes of such a test, an individual mutual fund provides an excellent analog for a particular portfolio of securities, the return on mutual fund shares is readily available, and the data are available for a relatively large group of funds over a 20-year period. Moreover, mutual funds constitute the investment medium through which a significant proportion of investors seek to diversify their holdings.

The sample of funds employed is summarized in Table 3-8. The distribution of returns was estimated for each mutual fund on the basis of its past performance during three periods: 1946-1967, 1956-1967, and 1958-1967. Within each period the sample population is exhaustive, and it includes all funds for which data were available over the entire period. Since the number of funds increased substantially from 1946 to 1967, the total period was divided into two shorter periods to increase the size of the test population from 58 for 1946-1967 to 149 for 1958-1967. Thus while for the shorter periods each distribution is estimated on the basis of fewer observations, more funds become available for comparison.

Table 3-9 presents the results of the application of the three efficiency criteria to the mutual fund returns for each period. The FSD criterion was not a very effective tool for selection in the longest period considered; only about 15 percent of the funds were eliminated by this criterion for 1946-1967. When the number of funds was increased and the number of data points decreased (i.e., in the shorter periods), however, FSD was more effective and 30 percent of the funds for 1956-1967 and 40 percent of the funds for 1958-1967, were eliminated.

When the assumption of risk aversion (i.e., the SSD criterion) was introduced, the number of funds remaining in the efficient set was greatly reduced in each period, with the proportionately greatest reduction again coming in the shortest period (1958-1967). For this period, SSD eliminated all but 18 of the funds, i.e., almost 90 percent

Table 3-8
Number of Mutual Funds Included in Samples, (by Time Periods)

	1958-1967	1956-1967	1946-1967
Growth funds	44	20	8
Diversified common stock funds	50	37	29
Balanced funds	26	22	16
Income funds	17	7	4
Specialized funds	12	1	1
Total	149	87	58

Source: Levy and Sarnat (1970:1156). Used with permission.

of the total population.

Although the use of EV reduced the size of the efficient subset in each period, these reductions were only slightly greater than the reductions achieved by SSD. In fact, in the period 1958-1967, the EV criterion resulted in a slightly larger subset (21) than that obtained by SSD (18).

The memberships of the corresponding EV and SSD efficient sets also were quite similar. For 1946-1967, 9 out of 12 funds were in both sets. For 1956-1967, 8 out of 14 were common to both sets. For 1958-1967, the result was only 11 of 21. One additional important result noted by Levy and Sarnat is that all efficient sets had an unusually high proportion of funds from the growth category.

A similar study by Sarnat (1972b) used four different criteria to determine the efficiency of mutual funds in two different time periods. The first three criteria were the familiar FSD, SSD, and EV. The fourth criterion consisted of a two stage application: first the EV rule was applied, then the FSD rule was applied to the EV test results. The two periods were 1946-1957 and 1958-1969, and the methodology for generating the return data and conducting the tests was similar to that employed in the Levy and Sarnat study (1970).

Table 3-10 sets out the size composition of the efficient sets using the four criteria, as well as the number of funds that were in

Table 3-9
Distribution of Mutual Funds Included in the Efficient Set (by Time Periods)

	Total Population		FSD		SSD		EV	
	Number of funds	%	Number of funds	%	Number of funds	%	Number of funds	%
				1958-1967				
Growth funds	44	30	40	45	14	77	10	47
Diversified common stock funds	50	34	26	29	2	11	2	10
Balanced funds	26	17	7	8	--	--	6	29
Income funds	17	11	10	11	1	6	3	14
Specialized funds	12	8	6	7	1	6	--	--
Total	149	100	89	100	18	100	21	100
				1956-1967				
Growth funds	20	23	17	27	7	44	7	50
Diversified common stock funds	37	43	26	42	3	19	--	--
Balanced funds	22	25	16	26	6	37	7	50
Income funds	7	8	2	3	--	--	--	--
Specialized funds	1	1	1	2	--	--	--	--
Total	87	100	62	100	16	100	14	100
				1946-1967				
Growth funds	8	14	8	16	4	24	3	25
Diversified common stock funds	29	50	26	52	6	35	4	33
Balanced funds	16	27	13	26	7	41	5	42
Income funds	4	7	2	4	--	--	--	--
Specialized funds	1	2	1	2	--	--	--	--
Total	58	100	50	100	17	100	12	100

Source: Levy and Sarnat (1970:1156). Used with permission.

the efficient sets of both periods for each criterion. The main results are similar to those just described. Of the 56 funds included in the study, over two-thirds were efficient by FSD. With SSD and EV, the efficient sets were closer to 20 percent of the original sample.

Table 3-10
Number of Mutual Funds Included in Efficient Sets
for Selected Efficiency Criteria in the Years 1946-1957 and 1958-1969

Efficiency Criterion	No. of Funds in Efficient Set 1946-57 (1)	1958-69 (2)	No. of Funds Included in Both Sets (3)
FSD	38	48	33
SSD	12	13	5
EV	9	9	2
EV/FSD	9	9	2

Source: Sarnat (1972:904). Used with permission.

No indication of the similarities of membership among efficient sets of different criteria was given. The two-stage rule proved to be fruitless since the application of FSD to the EV efficient set had no effect. Membership in efficient sets for the different periods was quite similar for FSD, but since the FSD set included most funds, the result could not have been otherwise. Relatively few funds were common to efficient sets of both periods with the other criteria. It is worth pointing out that SSD might have been more effective than FSD in the two-stage criterion.

Discussion. The efficiency tests of mutual funds considered here are of two different kinds. The Joy and Porter study (1974) examined the ability of mutual funds to outperform the DJIA and found them to be, at best, no better than the DJIA. The studies by Levy and Sarnat (1970) and by Sarnat (1972b) were comparisons of EV, SD, and other efficiency criteria employing mutual funds as a sample base for reasons given by Levy and Sarnat. Generally their results are similar to those found in tests of individual securities. FSD was less effective than EV and SSD. The EV and SSD efficient sets were quite similar in size but had some important differences. Sarnat also showed that neither the EV nor the SSD sets were very consistent over time in terms of set membership.

3.3.3 SD Test of Portfolio Efficiency

In an extensive test of portfolio efficiency, Porter (1973a) generated (by means of a stratified random sampling procedure) 893 different combinations of individual stocks from a sample composed of the 925 stocks from the CRISP Price Relative File with complete data for 1960-1965. The major aspects of SD and EV efficiency under investigation included the following:

1. the relative magnitudes of the SD and EV efficient sets;
2. the nature and extent of other differences in the respective efficient sets;
3. the relative effectiveness of FSD, SSD, and TSD in reducing the size of the efficient set;
4. the effect on the EV and SD efficient sets of switching from monthly data to quarterly, semiannual, and annual data;
5. the effect on the various SD efficient sets of using a frequency interval approach (as opposed to a point-by-point approach) to generate the necessary distribution functions.

Point-by-Point Approach. Monthly results showed that of the 893 portfolios examined, 67 were efficient by the EV rule, 216 by SSD, and 146 by TSD (see Table 3-11). The FSD efficient set was too large to be measured given available computer facilities. There were substantial differences in the sizes of the various efficient sets: the TSD set was approximately twice the size of the EV set, and the SSD set was approximately three times the size of the EV set. The EV rule clearly seemed to be the most powerful discriminator of the four rules. Only 7.5 percent of all portfolios were included in the EV efficient set.

Of more importance, however, is the evaluation of other differences in the efficient sets. Further examination showed that of the 67 EV efficient portfolios, 61 also were efficient by SSD. Thus the SSD set contained most (91 percent) of the EV set. Since this same 61 is only 28 percent of the total membership of the SSD efficient set, the major difference in EV and SSD efficiency revealed

Table 3-11
Size of the Efficient Set

	Efficiency Criteria					
Period	EV (%)[a]	SSD (%)	TSD (%)	FSD (%)	EV & SSD (%)	EV & TSD (%)
Monthly	67 (7.5)	216 (24.2)	146 (16.3)	NA (NA)	61 (6.8)	56 (6.3)
Quarterly	65 (7.3)	127 (14.2)	69 (7.7)	676 (75.7)	45 (5.0)	32 (3.6)
Semiannual	56 (6.3)	82 (9.2)	44 (4.9)	404 (45.2)	29 (3.2)	21 (2.4)
Annual	41 (4.6)	32 (3.6)	12 (1.3)	101 (11.3)	16 (1.8)	10 (1.1)

Source: Porter (1973a:593). Used with permission.

[a]Size of efficient set as a percent of the total number of portfolios examined.

by Table 3-11 is that the EV set excluded a number of portfolios that were included in the SSD efficient set. Similar conclusions also hold for the comparison of EV and TSD. The TSD efficient set included 56 (84 percent) of the 67 EV efficient portfolios but had many more portfolios that were EV inefficient.

With quarterly rates of return, the EV, SSD, and TSD efficient sets were more similar with regard to their respective sizes. The TSD set included 69 portfolios--almost exactly the same as the 65 portfolios in the EV set. The SSD set was about twice as large with 127 members. The EV set with quarterly data was almost as large as with monthly data, but the SSD and TSD sets were only 50 percent as large as with monthly data. Both the number and percent of portfolios common to both the EV and SSD (or EV and TSD) efficient sets were smaller than with monthly data. Only 45 of the 65 members of the EV set were included in the SSD set (32 of 65 for TSD). This result indicates that while the relative sizes of the different efficient sets were more similar, the differences in specific membership were more marked than those observed with monthly data. The virtual uselessness of the FSD rule was indicated by the fact that the FSD efficient set included 676 (or 75.7 percent) of 893 possible portfolios.

Results with semiannual data show that the TSD efficient set, with 44 portfolios, was smaller than either the EV set, with 56, or the SSD set, with 82. In addition, the conflicts were in some respects more severe. Only 21 of the 44 members of the TSD efficient set were included among the 56 members of the EV set. Twenty-nine portfolios were common to the SSD and EV efficient sets. The FSD efficient set included 404 portfolios, or 45 percent of the total number of portfolios in the study.

With annual data the changes noted in moving from monthly to quarterly and semiannual data were even more pronounced. Both the SSD and the TSD efficient sets were smaller--32 and 12 portfolios, respectively--than the EV set with 41 members. Exactly one-half the members of the SSD efficient set were included in the EV set. The TSD set was just over one-fourth the size of the EV set, and all but 2 of the TSD efficient portfolios were EV efficient. The FSD set included 101 portfolios, more than twice as many as the SSD set, and eight times as many as the TSD set.

Frequency Interval Approach. The efficient sets derived from frequency interval data differ significantly from those based on the point-by-point approach. For example, the SSD efficient set on a frequency interval basis included 85 portfolios with monthly data and 30 with quarterly data as opposed to 216 and 127 derived on the point-by-point approach. The TSD set had 61 monthly and 27 quarterly, as opposed to 146 and 69 before. The FSD efficient set, which was too large to be determined on a point-by-point basis, included only 208 portfolios for monthly data and 54 quarterly when the frequency interval approach was used.

In addition, the composition of the frequency-interval efficient sets was significantly different from that of the corresponding point-by-point efficient sets. For example, only 7 of the 30 members of the new SSD efficient set based on quarterly data were also in the point-by-point SSD set. Six of the 27 members of the new TSD set based on quarterly data were in the point-by-point TSD set. These differences appear to be more significant than the corresponding differences between EV and either SSD or TSD efficiency. While the new sets were not completely different, it is clear that the class interval efficient sets were not subsets of the point-by-point efficient sets.

EV/SD Graphical Analysis. A unique feature of Porter's study was the analysis of differences between EV and SD efficient sets in terms of their location on an EV graph. The intent was simply to provide a visual comparison of the various sets rather than to set up EV location as a standard of validity.

As an example we have included a graphical analysis of efficiency based on semiannual data and the point-by-point approach (Figure 3-3). Examination of the figure reveals several significant points. First, no SSD or TSD efficient portfolio lies far from the EV efficient frontier. That is, all portfolios that were efficient by any rule lie along a fairly tight band, one border of which is the familiar EV frontier. If all SSD efficient portfolios were also EV efficient, then no SSD efficient portfolio would lie off the frontier. In this case,

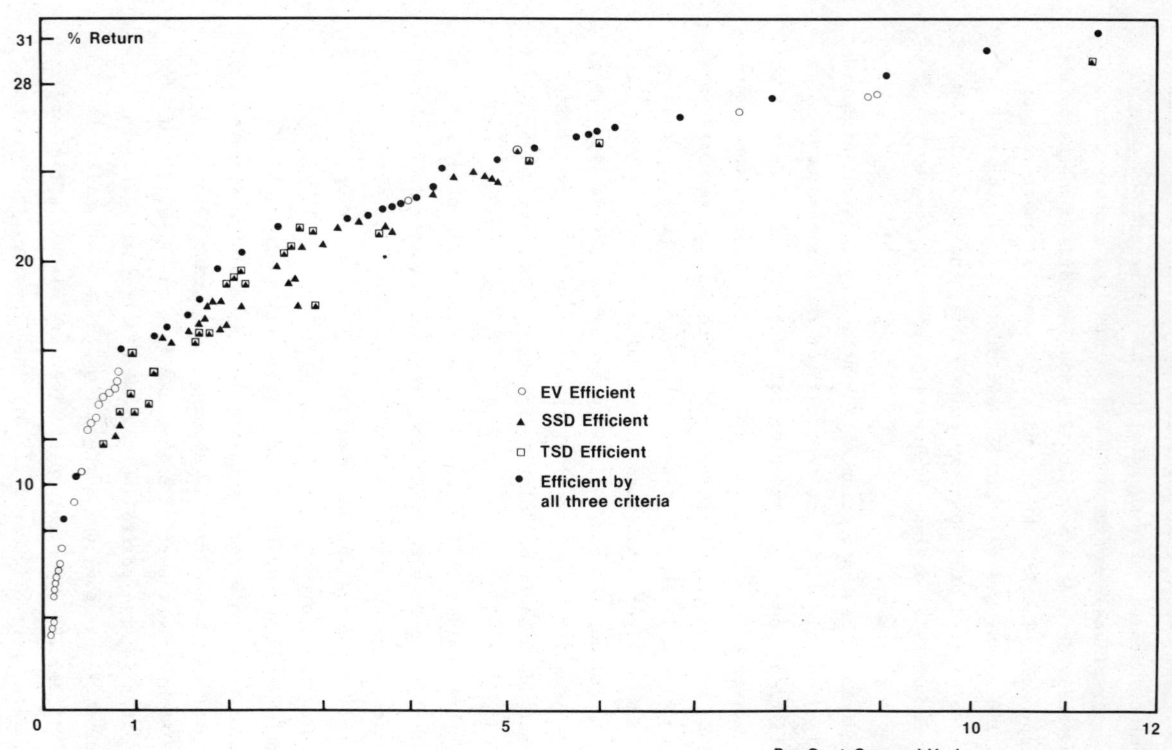

Figure 3-3. EV, SSD, and TSD Efficient Sets--Semiannual Rates of Return [from Porter (1973a:599)]. Used with permission.

some portfolios are clearly not on the frontier; on the other hand, no SSD efficient portfolio is very far from the EV frontier.

Another point is that the number of conflicts between EV and either SSD or TSD efficiency is a decreasing function of the magnitude of the mean. That is, the three sets are virtually identical in the upper range of mean and variance. Most of the SSD and TSD efficient portfolios that are EV inefficient occur in the middle range of mean and variance. Most of the portfolios that are EV but not SSD efficient occur in the lower range of mean and variance. In fact, 14 members of the EV efficient set have means (and variances) smaller than the smallest mean (and variance) found in the SSD efficient set. The significance of this result is that the more risk-averse an investor is, the more likely he is to choose incorrectly if he applies the mean-variance test to semiannual data because he will concentrate his search for EV efficient portfolios on the low-variance--and thus low-mean--portion of the EV frontier. This result is quite similar to Baumol's conclusion (1963) derived on the basis of his EL selection rule.

This study supports conclusions that follow from studies of individual securities and mutual funds. FSD is relatively ineffective. SSD is more useful and produces efficient sets that bear remarkable similarity to EV efficient sets in many cases. TSD efficient sets are similar to those of EV and SSD. On the other hand, the nature of the data--monthly, quarterly, etc. and point-by-point versus frequency interval--can have a substantial impact on the results of efficiency tests.

In a related study, Porter and Gaumnitz (1972) conducted several different tests of EV and SD efficiency. In part of their study, monthly data (i.e., monthly rates of return) from 140 stocks of the largest firms in Fortune's 500 as of December 31, 1964, for 1960-1963 were used to generate an EV efficient set of portfolios based on an index version of Markowitz's portfolio model. The output from this model gave at each specified value of expected return the corresponding portfolio with the smallest variance. The EV efficient set was generated under two different sets of restrictions: (1) where full investment was not required (cash holdings allowed); and (2) where full investment was required with a maximum of 5 percent invested in any one security (cash holdings not allowed). The 5-percent limitation was representative of the normal restriction placed on open-end investment companies and might be considered normal for many other institutional investors.

The means and standard deviations of the six EV efficient portfolios generated under the two sets of requirements are presented in Table 3-12. The returns are reported as total percent return for the holding period rather than as percent per month or per year. With one exception, portfolios with identical mean returns showed considerably smaller standard deviations when cash holdings were permitted.

The same data from which the means and variances were determined above were used to develop the necessary frequency distributions upon which the FSD, SSD, and TSD tests were applied. In developing these distributions, the computationally efficient procedure of classifying observed returns into frequency intervals of equal length was employed.

The results of the stochastic dominance evaluation of the EV efficient sets differ drastically depending on whether one is considering the full investment set or the set of portfolios that allow cash holdings. When cash holdings were permitted, the EV efficient set was identical with each of the three stochastic dominance efficient sets. The reason for this result was that the portfolios with higher expected returns and greater variability inevitably had at least one outcome smaller than the smallest return observed on any portfolio with a lower expected return. Consequently, no member of the EV efficient set was dominated by another when the stochastic dominance criteria were applied.

With full investment required, the results were significantly different (see Table 3-13). FSD eliminated portfolios B, C, and D, leaving only A, E, and F--the highest and two lowest return portfolios--in the efficient set. SSD and TSD eliminated portfolio E, leaving A and F to constitute the efficient set.

Another aspect of this study was an SD analysis of the efficiency of diversification. One of the important applications of EV analysis has been the test of the efficiency of diversification where efficiency has been measured in terms of the rate of decrease of the variance as

Table 3-12
Portfolio Selection Summary of Expected Returns and Standard Deviations, 1960-1963

	Portfolio					
	A	B	C	D	E	F
I. Full investment not required[a]						
Expected net return for 1960-63[b]	118.0	30.0	25.0	20.0	10.0	5.0
Standard deviation	42.0	9.0	7.5	6.0	2.9	1.5
Efficient portfolio held in cash[b]	0	63.6	67.5	73.4	85.6	93.0
II. Full investment required[a]						
Expected net return for 1960-63[b]	118.0	30.0	25.0	20.0	10.0	5.0
Standard deviation	42.0	11.6	10.4	9.4	7.4	6.4

Source: Porter and Gaumnitz (1972:440). Used with permission.

[a]Maximum of 5 percent in any security.

[b]Percent.

Table 3-13
Summary of Portfolio Dominance with Full Investment Required, 1960-1963

	Dominated Portfolios by:	
Dominating portfolios	First-degree dominance	Second- and Third-degree dominance
A	B,C,D	B,C,D,E
B	D	C,D
C	D	D
D	none	none
E	none	none
F	none	none

Source: Porter and Gaumnitz (1972:441). Used with permission.

the number of different securities in the portfolio is increased. The results--as reported by Evans and Archer (1968) and Lintner (1965), for instance--indicate that most of the gain from diversification is obtained with somewhere between 10 and 20 securities. Since increasing the number of securities in the portfolio generally lowers the expected return, an efficient portfolio should not have more than, say, 12 securities.

Since these tests do not explicitly measure the loss in expected return as variance is reduced, a stochastic dominance test of the efficiency of diversification seems to be more reasonable. To effect this test of efficiency of diversification through FSD and SSD rules, 7 sets of 20 portfolios each were selected at random from the same 925 stocks employed in Porter's study (1973a). The first set of 20 portfolios included only 1 stock each, the next set of 20 portfolios included 6 stocks each, then 11, 16, 21, 26, and finally 31 stocks in each portfolio for a total of 140 portfolios (20 in each group). Each portfolio in a given set was compared by FSD and SSD with each portfolio in every other set. Consequently, there were 400 possible comparisons at a given level. For example, in comparing 6-security portfolios with 11-security portfolios, the distribution of returns for each portfolio in the latter group was compared to the distribution of each of the portfolios in the former group and checked for stochastic dominance. This process was repeated for all portfolios and at all levels and involved a grand total of 8400 different comparisons. If most of the portfolios with a given number of securities dominated those with a smaller number of securities, presumably the additional naive diversification obtained with the larger number of securities was justified. On the other hand, if the opposite effect occurred, one might conclude that the practical limit of diversification had been reached.

The FSD results were too weak for meaningful analysis, in that few portfolios were dominated using the FSD criterion. The results of the SSD test are presented in Table 3-14. The first entry for paired values in the table indicates the number of times out of 400 total comparisons that the larger-numbered portfolio exhibited second-degree dominance over the smaller-numbered portfolio listed on the left. For

Table 3-14
Second-degree Dominance Comparisons of Random Portfolios with Varying Number of Securities

	Number of Securities							
	1	6	11	16	21	26	31	
Portfolio	A	B	C	D	E	F	G	Totals
A		144, 31	127, 26	150, 11	126, 23	135, 10	131, 13	813, 114
B			94, 107	127, 56	102, 97	119, 58	110, 76	552, 394
C				166, 50	127, 111	157, 43	143, 64	593, 268
D					71, 167	103, 94	78, 147	252, 408
E						160, 69	129, 99	289, 168
F							73, 126	73, 126

Source: Porter and Gaumnitz (1972:444). Used with permission.

instance, B portfolios (6 securities each) exhibited second-degree dominance over A portfolios (1 security each) on 144 occasions, while the opposite result occurred only 31 times. (The remaining portfolio comparisons out of 400 failed to exhibit second-degree dominance).

Looking at the totals column of Table 3-14, one can see that most portfolios composed of 6 securities or more generally exhibited second-degree dominance over 1 security portfolio; that is, on 813 occasions larger-numbered portfolios dominated 1-stock portfolios and in only 114 cases did the reverse occur. The results of higher-level portfolios were ambiguous. The first reversal of second-degree dominance in total (last column, Table 3-14) occurred where portfolios composed of 16 securities dominated portfolios composed of more securities. That is, portfolios with 16 securities had 408 instances of second-degree dominance over larger-numbered portfolios, compared with only 252 occasions where the opposite result obtained. On the other hand, portfolios composed of 21 securities were generally dominated by larger-numbered portfolios (289 versus 168). From these results it is difficult to conclude precisely what is the optimum number of securities in a naively diversified portfolio. Nevertheless, the overall performance of the 16-stock portfolios tends to reinforce the feeling that relatively few securities give ample diversification in common stocks.

In a third study, Porter (1974a) employed the same basic data he used in an earlier study (1973a) to conduct empirical tests of EV, SD, and ES_h efficiency. (Here ES_h denotes "mean-semivariance" where semivariance is measured about position h on the return scale--for a formal definition of semivariance, see Section 4.2). In each of 893 randomly generated portfolios, 72 monthly rates of return were used in calculating the means, variances, semivariances, and distributions required for the different tests. ES_h efficient sets were derived with three different values for h: 0, .1, and E.

The results shown in Table 3-15 were basically consistent with what theoretical analysis suggests. The $ES_{0.0}$ set contained 50 members, all of which were included in the SSD set. The $ES_{0.1}$ set contained 49 members, all of which were included in the SSD set and 43 of which also were in the $ES_{0.0}$ set. In comparison, the EV

Table 3-15
Size of the Efficient Set and Members Common to Both Sets

Type of data	SSD	EV	ES_E	$ES_{0.0}$	$ES_{0.1}$
			Efficiency Criteria		
Monthly	216	69	70	50	49
Quarterly	127	65	62	33	33

Type of data	$ES_{0.0}$ & $ES_{0.1}$	SSD & EV	SSD & ES_E	SSD & $ES_{0.0}$	SSD & $ES_{0.1}$
			Efficiency Criteria		
Monthly	43	61	70	50	49
Quarterly	26	45	55	33	33

Source: Porter (1974a:203). Used with permission.

efficient set included 69 members, 8 of which were excluded by the SSD rule. The one surprise is that all 70 members of the ES_E set also were members of the SSD set. Theoretical analysis had suggested that discrepancies might exist between ES_E and SSD efficient sets, but they failed to materialize in this sample. In addition, the ES_E set included most members of the $ES_{0.0}$ and $ES_{0.1}$ sets.

As a further check on the consistency of the different efficiency criteria, the monthly observations for each of the 893 portfolios were converted to quarterly rates of return, and the efficiency tests were repeated. These results, also shown in Table 3-15, are quite similar to the results using monthly data. The major differences are that all the efficient sets were smaller than before and the ES_E set contained 7 members (out of a total of 62) that were not efficient by the SSD rule. With quarterly data, therefore, some difference between ES_E and SSD efficiency was found, but this discrepancy still was not so significant as that between EV and SSD in which 20 out of 65 EV efficient portfolios were dominated by the SSD rule.

3.3.4 Commentary

The main results of the empirical studies of efficiency among individual securities, mutual funds, and other portfolios tend to support several important conclusions:

1. The FSD criterion is relatively ineffective in reducing an original sample to a manageable efficient set; apparently it is rather difficult for one security or portfolio to dominate another by FSD.

2. The EV, SSD, TSD, and ES_h criteria are quite effective in reducing the sample to a manageable efficient set, and the sets actually chosen by each rule often have much in common in terms of both size and membership.

3. While the different criteria do give similar results, there are important cases in which the EV set includes members that are eliminated by one of the SD rules.

4. All the efficiency criteria (with the possible exception of FSD) are highly sensitive to the type of data from which security and portfolio return distributions are generated. Both size and membership in the efficient set according to any of the rules differ substantially as quarterly or annual data are substituted for monthly data covering the same time period, for example. Grouping individual return observations into frequency intervals similarly influences the outcome of the study. Different periods yield different results. One especially interesting result is that the size of the efficient set by any criterion is an increasing function of the number of data points used to estimate the probability functions.

Given these results as well as related questions about the appropriate methodology for efficiency studies, several papers have attempted to raise and/or answer procedural points relevant to the proper testing for efficiency. The next section of this chapter examines several of these questions.

3.4 Methodological Problems Associated With EV and SD Tests

Two questions about test methodology that have been raised are especially important. One concerns the reliability of the data on which the tests are based, and the other concerns the manner in which the different rules are applied to determine efficiency. The point of both questions is that while the theoretical advantages of SD over EV are clear, the EV model has substantial technical advantages whenever the rules are applied to determine efficiency among securities and portfolios.

3.4.1 Data Reliability

Critics of SD methodology have questioned the reliability of data used in SD studies. They argue that estimation of a probability function requires substantially more data than the estimation of a mean and variance for a given desired level of accuracy and, since more data may mean more time periods, any nonstationarity in the underlying distributions is more damaging to SD tests than to EV tests. As an example, Frankfurter and Phillips (1975) argue that without stationarity, use of historical data can produce misleading results with both EV and SD approaches but, while minor departures from stationarity would have a slight effect on EV tests, they would be devastating for SD tests.

Objections to this argument can be made on two grounds. In the first place, it qualifies as a conjecture. It remains necessary to demonstrate empirically that SD tests are in fact less reliable than EV tests. In the second place, historical data are merely proxies for expectational data. To the extent possible, actual decisions should be based on the decision-maker's assessment of probability functions of return over the holding period in question. In that case nonstationarity may be irrelevant. Since empirical studies continue to rely upon historical data, however, it would seem appropriate to test the adequacy of historical data.

Several of the studies already discussed contain evidence on the effect of data on efficiency decisions. Sarnat (1972b), for example, divided his mutual fund sample into two subperiods (1946-1957 and 1958-1969), found the efficient set for each period, and recorded for each efficiency criterion the number of funds common to the efficient sets in both periods. The results were better for SSD than for EV. The EV set had 9 funds in each period, but only 2 (slightly over 20 percent) were in both sets. With SSD, the efficient set included 12 funds in the first period and 13 in the second period. Nine funds (approximately 40 percent) were in both sets. While these results are interesting, their implications are not clear because no information was given on the nature of the intertemporal changes in the underlying distributions. Since all the data are from unknown population distributions, no definite conclusions can be drawn.

Several of the studies contain evidence that the sizes of efficient sets for all criteria are an increasing function of the number of data points in the sample. Porter (1973a), for example, broke one common time period into monthly data, then quarterly data, then semiannual and annual data. As the data changed, the number of points decreased sharply--from 72 monthly observations to 5 annual observations. In every case the size of the efficient set decreased significantly as the number of data points decreased. The size of the EV set, however, changed less than that of any SD set: from 67 to 41 for EV and from 216 to 32 for SSD. As a further test of the tendency of SSD and TSD sets to increase rapidly in size as the number of data points increases, Porter performed SSD and TSD tests on the first 6 months of the monthly data, then the first 12 months, then 18, 24, 30, and 36 months. The results (see Table 3-16) support the suggestion that the size of the efficient set is an increasing function of the number of data points.

These results suggest more questions than they answer concerning correct procedures in performing EV and SD tests of portfolio efficiency. Since the size of the efficient set is affected so much by the type of data used, which data and which criteria are most appropriate? The obvious need is for a more direct attack on this problem. Two summary comments on data might be useful, however.

First, if the underlying process that generates the rates of return is stable over time, then the more data points one incorporates the more accurately one approximates the true probability function and the more valid are the results. Alternatively, if the underlying process is not stable over time, one should use only the most recent data. Both the focus on recent data and the need for enough points to develop a reliable probability function argue for the use of monthly

Table 3-16
Size of Efficient Sets as a Function of the Number of Data Points

Criterion	Number of Monthly Data Points					
	6	12	18	24	30	36
SSD	10	24	52	54	120	188
TSD	8	21	38	36	45	86

Source: Porter (1973a:603). Used with permission.

data. On the other hand, one might argue that all historical data are irrelevant, and thus the discussion of which type of past data to use is pointless. Only data concerning future expectations should be used. While these results may be interesting, they do not deal directly with the problem of determining the reliability of the data on which efficiency tests have been and are being based. Direct studies of this question would be quite valuable.

3.4.2 Appropriateness of Application

The second question concerning SD tests makes the point that SD criteria are appropriate only for "screening" an existing set of securities or portfolios. In particular, there exists nothing in the SD methodology that permits one to build or search systematically for efficient portfolios. On the other hand, as indicated by Frankfurter and Phillips (1975), one virtue of EV methodology is that it is based on an optimization algorithm that guarantees that from a given set of individual securities the best combinations--in the EV sense--will be found. With SD, one is never sure that one is looking at the best combinations that could have been found.

Two points are noteworthy in light of this criticism of SD. It is necessary first to acknowledge that prior empirical studies of SD versus EV clearly do not answer the question of which approach is superior. Their major direct result is simply to demonstrate the kinds of quantitative and qualitative differences that can occur when SD and

EV criteria are used to <u>screen</u> given samples of portfolios and securities. Presumably there exist circumstances under which such knowledge would be of benefit. Second, it is essential to conduct direct tests of the significance of the portfolio-building algorithms and to seek methods of adding such algorithms to SD methodology.

To gain perspective on the problem resulting from the lack of an SD optimization algorithm, Porter and Bey (1974) used several different procedures to select a number of portfolios from a basic population of 100 securities randomly chosen from the Chicago Price Relative Tapes. They used monthly returns for the period 1965-1967 (i.e., 36 observations) to generate the input data for the EV and SSD models.

An ideal test of the value of an optimization algorithm would require that one develop such an algorithm and then observe its performance on a security base. Since no one has yet made significant progress in this direction, Porter and Bey resorted to several imperfect but nevertheless revealing procedures. The first step was to generate randomly a number of different sets of portfolios containing different numbers of securities. For this test, they selected portfolios with 2, 5, 10, 20, and 30 securities, assuming equal investment in each security. For each size class, 10 portfolios were selected, then 25, then 50, and then 100. In addition, they selected 300 portfolios of size 2 and 10. The purpose was to observe the kinds of changes in the SSD efficient set that would result as the number and size of the portfolios varied. Markowitz (1959), for example, suggested that with a basic population of 100 securities, a randomly generated sample of size 200 should provide a reasonable approximation to the true efficient set.

Porter and Bey's second step was to employ the EV rule to find the actual EV efficient frontier. For this step they used the Sharpe index model to find corner portfolios, and they choose combinations of adjacent corner portfolios to fill large gaps in the frontier. Since the EV rule has an optimization algorithm and the SSD rule does not, a comparison of the results of these first two steps should provide a clue to the significance of the lack of the algorithm. In pursuit of this comparison, the SSD efficient sets from each of the randomly selected groups were plotted on an EV graph for comparison with the EV frontier. Porter and Gaumnitz (1972) and Porter (1973a) have shown that when the EV and SSD rules are employed strictly as screening devices on randomly generated portfolios, the EV and SSD efficient sets are remarkably similar (in spite of some significant differences). If in Porter and Bey's test procedure a substantial gap were to exist between the EV and SSD efficient sets, then the absence of an optimization algorithm for SSD would seem important. A further test was provided by mixing the EV and SSD efficient portfolios and running SSD tests on this set. If many of the EVs dominated SSDs by the SSD rule, the importance of the algorithm would be more obvious.

The third step of Porter and Bey's test procedure was to examine the original 100 securities to see if there appeared to be any logical procedures for selecting portfolios that might perform better than portfolios selected on a purely random basis.

The results of the tests center around three figures. Figure 3-4 indicates the EV location of the SSD efficient two-stock portfolios and the EV corner portfolios. The number of SSD efficient two-stock portfolios depended on the number that were randomly generated. These numbers are summarized as follows:

Number Generated	Number Efficient	Graph Symbol
10	3	□
25	5	Δ
50	14	*
100	20	•
300	22	0

Several conclusions seem reasonable. First, there appears to be a significant gap (a visual space) between the SSD portfolios and the EV frontier. Second, the gap is greater for the SSD portfolios from the 10 and 25 randomly selected groups than for the groups of 50, 100, and 300 portfolios. Third, while the efficient members from the 300 randomly chosen portfolios provide the best results, the gap remains significant. It is considerably larger than the gaps reported by Porter and Gaumnitz (1972) and by Porter (1973a). On the basis of this information one tends to conclude that the lack of the algorithm

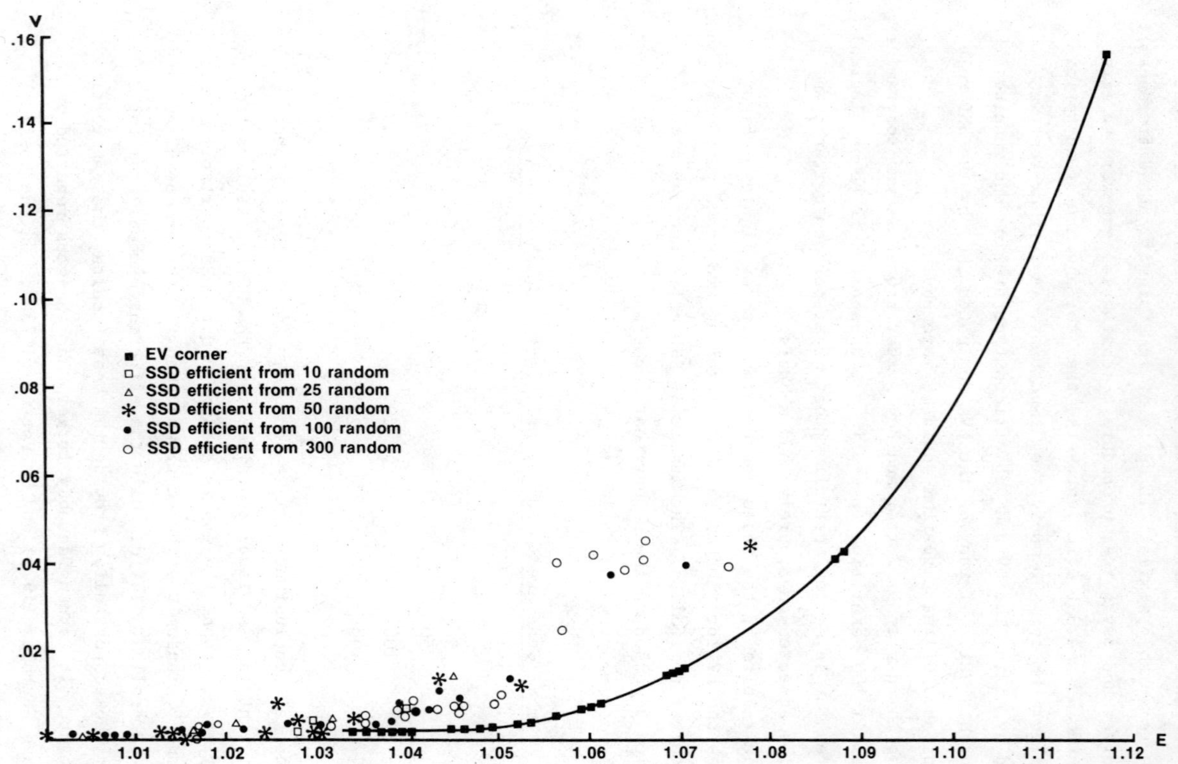

Figure 3-4. Comparison of Efficient Random Portfolios with EV Corner Portfolios [from Porter and Bey (1974:1483)]. Used with permission.

may have very serious consequences.

Only the results for the two-security portfolios are presented in Figure 3-4. The reason for omitting the results obtained with portfolios of larger size is that they were basically the same as those for two-stock portfolios except in the high-return area. No randomly chosen portfolios with more than two securities fell in the high-return, high-variance area. The larger portfolios naturally tended to converge toward the minimum variance range, but they did not have variances smaller than some of the two-security portfolios. Overall, the procedure of selecting a large number of portfolios with a few securities seemed to work best. Increasing the number of securities in the portfolio did not improve the results.

When the EV corner portfolios were added to the randomly chosen two-stock portfolios, the preliminary conclusions received substantial support. Of the 64 SSD efficient two-security portfolios, only 13 survived the SSD test when mixed with the EV efficient portfolios. In other words, approximately 80 percent of the portfolios that had been declared to be efficient by the SSD rule were found to be inefficient when tested against the EV portfolios. An error of this magnitude is clearly intolerable, and it is an error that results from the lack of an algorithm for building efficient combinations.

The value of the EV search algorithm was supported by the fact that not one of the EV efficient portfolios failed the SSD test. The result stands in contrast to Porter and Gaumnitz's result (1972) in which both the EV rules and SSD rules were used as screening devices on a set of randomly chosen portfolios. There some portfolios that were EV efficient were not SSD efficient.

The results to this point represent a serious indictment against the operational capability of the SSD rule for portfolio selection. Given the conceptual superiority of the SSD rule as compared with the EV rule, however, a search for a better selection procedure for the SSD method would seem to be justified. As a first step in this direction, the 100 randomly selected individual securities were plotted on the EV graph (Figure 3-5). An examination of this graph reveals three main points. First, most securities are clustered in a relatively small portion of the total space. Since most securities

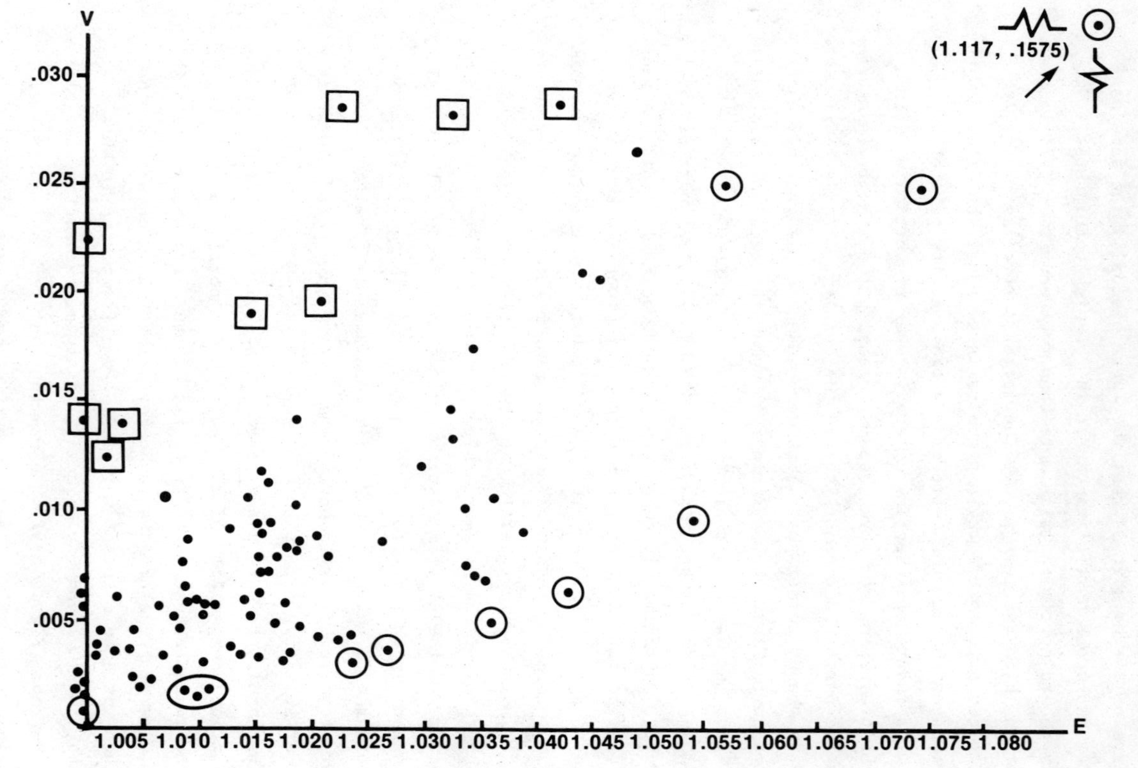

Figure 3-5. EV Location of 100 Randomly Selected Securities [from Porter and Bey (1974:1484)]. Used with permission.

are positively correlated, the potential benefit from mixing these clustered securities is relatively small. Given that most of the securities fell in this group, the majority of the randomly selected portfolios were likely to be inefficient.

The second observation is that some securities had such large variances and small expected values that they were relatively unlikely to be part of an efficient portfolio (see the boxed points on the graph). It seems rather pointless to include them in portfolios. Finally, several securities had combinations of expected return and variance, which suggested that they might contribute much toward a portfolio's efficiency. These securities are enclosed by circles on the graph. One security in particular had such a high expected value that it should be forced to appear in many of the test portfolios.

As a result of the graphical analysis, Porter and Bey selected a new set of 207 portfolios composed of weighted combinations of the securities circled on the graph. These securities were combined in pairs with the weights varying from 10 percent to 90 percent by units of 10. That is, 10 percent of one security was combined with 90 percent of another, then 20 percent with 80 percent etc. These newly selected portfolios were combined with the 51 EV efficient portfolios and the 13 randomly selected portfolios that survived the SSD test when combined with the EV portfolios. The SSD test was then applied to this new sample of 271 portfolios.

The results of this test, presented in Figure 3-6, were encouraging. Of the 207 weighted combinations, 67 survived the SSD test. Moreover, these 67 were very close (graphically) to the EV efficient frontier. The gap that was observed earlier no longer existed. Finally, more than half of the 13 randomly chosen portfolios that had survived to this point were eliminated by the newly selected portfolios. An interesting result is that the new portfolios did not eliminate any of the EV efficient portfolios. Since there existed the potential for some EV efficient portfolios to be inefficient by the SSD rule, it was expected that the relatively simple selection procedure would produce at least one such occurrence.

In summary, it appears that a relatively simple selection procedure can make a dramatic improvement in the results of the SSD

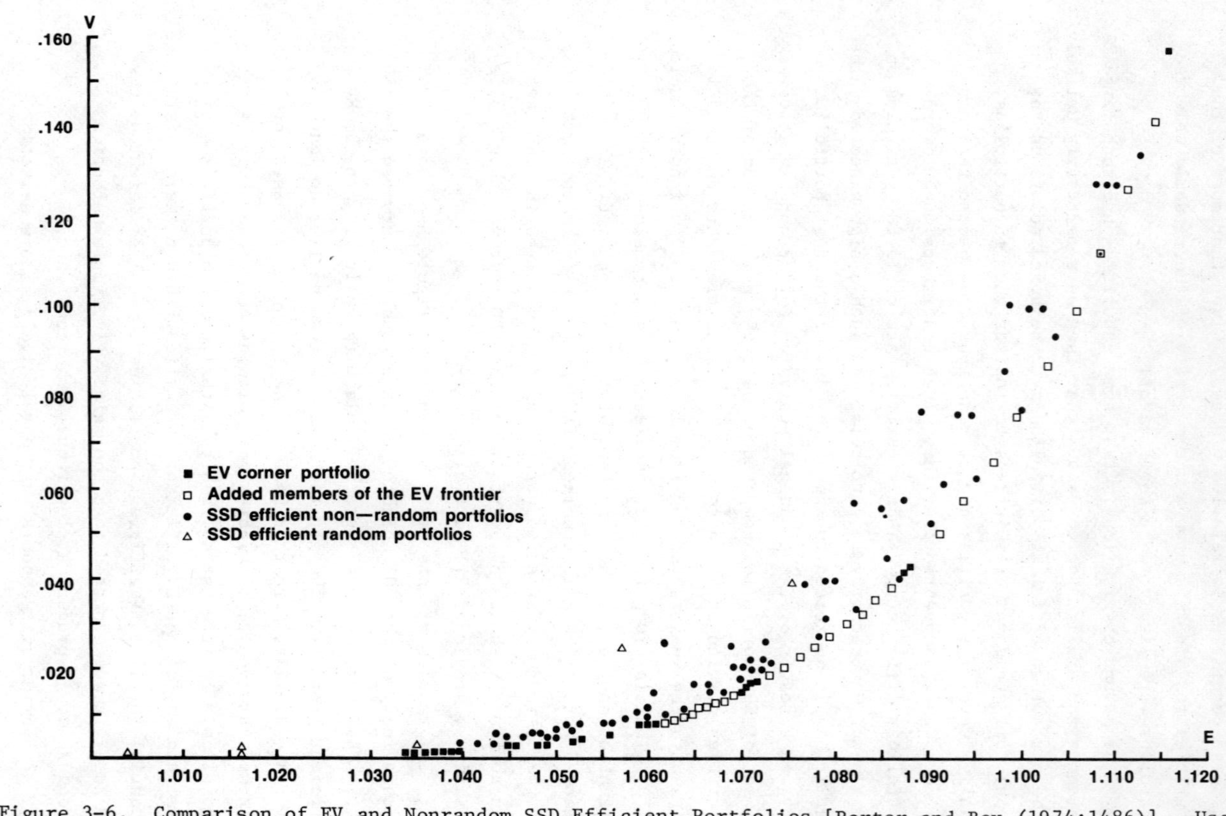

Figure 3-6. Comparison of EV and Nonrandom SSD Efficient Portfolios [Porter and Bey (1974:1486)]. Used with permission.

approach to portfolio selection even in the absence of an optimization algorithm. Further gains might be made by recombining portfolios into portfolios of portfolios, by generating larger numbers of deliberately mixed securities, by making partial use of a sample of correlation or regression coefficients to determine which securities to mix, or by some other means. Given the attractive theoretical properties of the SSD rule and the results presented here, further investigation in this direction seems warranted.

Introduction to Chapter 4
Portfolio Applications: Comparison of Selection Models

Richard C. Burgess presents some original results of the application of the mean-semivariance (ES_h) model in this chapter. These results are especially significant in view of the facts that (1) Porter has shown that the ES_h efficient set is a proper subset of the second-degree stochastic dominance (SSD) efficient set and (2) ES_h portfolio selection algorithms exist whereas an SSD selection algorithm does not. Thus at least in the near term, ES_h may be an operational approach to the implementation of SSD.

After a discussion of the appropriate ES_h objective function, Burgess reports the results of his EV and ES_h simulation studies. The relative superiority of the latter is found to depend significantly on the asymmetry of the return data. As discussed in Chapter 3, Arditti (1971) found positive skewness in mutual fund return data; work by Miller and Scholes (1972) also attests to the presence of skewness in return data. If such findings are correct, they amplify the importance of Burgess's revealing investigation.

4 Portfolio Applications: Comparison of Selection Models

Richard C. Burgess

4.1 Introduction

The first application of quadratic programming to the problem of asset selection under conditions of risk was introduced by H. M. Markowitz (1952). He later expanded his concepts into a book published in 1959. The following assumption was made in these two early works:

> For any given expected portfolio return, the portfolio with the smallest variance is preferred to all others; and for any given portfolio variance, the portfolio with the maximum expected return is preferred to all others.

The above mean-variance criterion is essential for the application of the quadratic programming model to the problem of efficient asset selection. Extensions of the mean-variance criterion have been the basis of a large body of theoretical work.

In addition to variance, Markowitz suggested five other alternative measures of risk: (1) the expected value of loss; (2) the probability of loss; (3) the expected absolute deviation; (4) the maximum expected loss; and (5) the semivariance.

Until recently these alternative measures of risk have been largely ignored. The computational ease of the quadratic programming model has made the assumption of the mean-variance criterion very desirable.

Empirical investigations of executive utility functions by Mao (1970a) and Swalm (1966) suggest that the concept of risk is better described by semivariance than variance. The notion that variance is not a valid quantitative risk surrogate is not a unique insight; it has long been discussed and was summarized by Lorie (1966:108):

> I might say in passing, without intending special application to Sharpe's article that further work needs to be done on the measurement of risk. All of the methods with which I am familiar seem conceptually deficient since they are based on variation from year to year in the price of a security or in the value of a portfolio. It is not variation per se which constitutes risk; it is the decline in price or value. I believe that we will ultimately find an objective measure of sensitivity to decline which avoids the inherent absurdity of calling a stock risky because in the past it has gone up much faster than the market in some years and only as fast in others, whereas we call a security which never varies in price not risky at all.

The exploration of semivariance as an alternative measure of risk has been ignored for two reasons: (1) because of the unexplored difficulties associated with the semivariance based objective function, and (2) because it was thought that the alternative measure would yield the "same" results as variance if empirical distributions were normal. Two works addressed themselves to the computation of the efficient boundary in the mean-semivariance portfolio selection model. Ilano (1969) and Hogan and Warren (1972) demonstrated that the mean-semivariance-based allocation model retains sufficient tractability to permit construction of efficient mean-semivariance combinations of assets. (I will review these works in detail later in this section.)

The use of semivariance can be defended intuitively and mean-semivariance efficient portfolios can be computed, but neither fact implies an overwhelming need for the use of semivariance as a risk surrogate. The main motivation for the use of the mean-semivariance-based allocation model derives from the result developed by Porter (1974a), who demonstrated that with the exception of identical means and semivariances, the efficient set of portfolios based on the mean-semivariance model (calculated about a fixed point) is a subset of the SSD efficient set.

For the practical application of the stochastic dominance approach to decision-making under conditions of risk, Porter's result combined with that of Hogan and Warren (1972) are essential. There does not and may never exist an algorithm for developing weighted combinations of risky assets that are efficient by any of the stochastic dominance rules. Therefore without the above results, the conceptually superior SSD rule cannot be implemented practically. With them, the computation of a subset of the SSD efficient set becomes possible.

4.2 The Semivariance Objective Function

The semivariance of a portfolio return about a fixed target T may be defined as

$$S_T(X) = E\{[\min(0, RX' - T)]^2\}$$

Here ' denotes vector transposition; X represents a vector of n possible investment amounts, $X = (x_1, x_2, \ldots, x_n)$; and R is a vector of random rates of return, $R = (r_1, r_2, \ldots, r_n)$, so the inner product RX' is the return on portfolio X. An efficient portfolio is a vector X that achieves a specified expected return and minimizes the semivariance of the portfolio $S_T(X)$ over all possible values of X. As in the mean-variance model (EV), the mean-semivariance (ES) model restricts each x_i to be greater than or equal to zero and

$$\sum_{i=1}^{n} x_i = 1.$$

Hogan and Warren (1972) analyzed the above semivariance objective function in detail and showed it to be convex and continuously differentiable if $E(RR') < \infty$. Their computational procedure was based on a discrete case where R takes on a finite number of values R^k, k = 1,2,...,K each with probability p_k, and was formulated as follows:

$$\text{Minimize} \qquad S_T(X) = \sum_{k=1}^{K} p_k \left[\min\left(0, \sum_{j=1}^{n} r_j^k x_j - T\right)\right]^2$$

$$\text{subject to} \qquad E(RX') = E = \sum_{k=1}^{K} p_k \sum_{j=1}^{n} r_j^k x_j$$

and $$\sum_{j=1}^{n} x_j = 1$$

The above formulation of the ES model corresponds in form to the EV model. Since the objective function is a convex differentiable function of the investment alternatives, a number of algorithm routines for numerical studies are available. Hogan and Warren developed a FORTRAN computer code based on the Frank-Wolfe (1956) algorithm, which they have made available to the public upon request.

The ES-based model requires the joint probability distribution of the rates of return for all assets under consideration as inputs for the development of an ES efficient frontier. It does not have the advantage of the EV model of using index-based inputs (Sharpe 1963), although preliminary work has been done on an equilibrium capital market model based on semivariance (Hogan and Warren 1974). The necessary estimates of the rates of return must then come from historical observations of these rates. Even with this possible limitation, semivariance appears to be theoretically and intuitively superior to variance as a surrogate for risk.

4.3 A Simulation Study of EV-Based and ES-Based Allocation Models

The purpose of this study was to test the EV and ES allocation models first when the distributions of returns are normal and then under varying degrees of asymmetry of the distributions of returns of the individual assets. This empirical testing would determine the relationship between the EV and ES allocation models and how this relationship is influenced by controlled departures from normality. Clearly if returns were highly skewed, one would not accept the EV-based allocation model. The fundamental empirical question is, how highly must they be skewed before ES proves to be a superior allocation model? This degree of skewness may then be compared to that observed for common stocks.

A simulation approach was chosen to analyze the EV and ES relationship. The simulation approach has two distinct advantages over an approach based on historical data. First and primarily, simulation permits the degree of asymmetry to be manipulated as an independent variable. If the relationship between the EV and ES allocation models is a function of the degree of asymmetry of the distributions of returns, then the relationship between EV and ES allocation models and the degree of asymmetry may be determined. Second, simulation permits stationary data to be generated. Each set of period-by-period returns will be generated to follow specified means and variances. Estimates of the specifications may be made from "historical" patterns of returns for a predefined period. Simulation is the ideal vehicle to determine the exact effects of semivariance as a measure of risk versus variance under various degrees of asymmetry (skewness).

Actual data were used to determine realistic expected returns and variance-covariance values. These values were used to generate the period-by-period returns used in the analysis. The generated data set is composed of period-by-period returns for a given number of assets. These returns follow the mean variance-covariance specification and all have the same approximate degree of asymmetry (skewness).

The foregoing approach adds realism to the generated results. If statistically independent sets of variables had been used with specific means, the portfolios formulated would have had unrealistic characteristics.

Using actual data to formulate the expected returns and variance-covariance matrix generated realistic data, even though the observations generated were statistically independent over time. The data generation problem therefore was to specify expected returns and a variance-covariance matrix of returns and to generate period-by-period returns that conform to this specification but have varying degrees of skewness.

4.4 The Generation Technique

Let Σ be the specified variance-covariance matrix and μ the vector of specified expected returns. To generate normally distributed period-by-period returns we start with a p-component column vector Z of random normal deviates where p equals the number of assets. Here $Z \sim N(0,I)$, i.e., independent normal deviates that have a mean of zero and a standard deviation of one. I is a pth order identity matrix. All the random deviates were drawn from a random number generator and standardized to have a mean of zero and a standard deviation of one.

Σ was factored into $\Sigma = A'A$ where A' is a lower triangular matrix. [The subroutine utilized for the factorization was DMFSD using Cholfsky's square-root method. The subroutine was taken from the System/360 Scientific Subroutine Package (360-CM-03X), Version 111 (1968).] The following rescaling procedure was then used (Rao 1965: 521):

$$R = \mu + A'Z,$$

where R is a column vector of p observations (p assets). The random normal deviates initially had a mean of zero and a standard deviation of one, but the rescaling process adjusts the size of the deviates so that they follow the desired mean and variance-covariance specifications, that is:

$$R \sim N(\mu,\Sigma) \quad \text{where } \Sigma = A'A$$

Repeat the above process of generating vectors R until the desired number of period-by-period returns is generated.

The generation of period-by-period returns that are significantly skewed involves several difficulties, but the same principles are applied: start with a set of skewed standardized random deviates and perform the same rescaling procedure so the desired means and variance-covariance relationships are obtained. Specifically, an array of chi-square random deviates was developed by summing n squared random normal deviates where n is the degrees of freedom of the chi-square distribution. These values were then standardized to have a mean of zero and standard deviation of one.

The vector Z is now a vector of nonnormal independent standardized random deviates. The alteration of the skewness of the random deviate in turn alters the skewness of the rescaled values that represent period-by-period returns.

The selection of the form of the distribution of random deviates is particularly important. It is desirable to have a distribution for which one can easily adjust the skewness.

The chi-square distribution's skewness is a function of its degrees of freedom n; it is easily adjusted to achieve different degrees of skewness. More specifically:

$$E[\chi^2_n] = n$$

$$Var[\chi^2_n] = 2n$$

$$Skewness[\chi^2_n] = \sqrt{8/n} = b_1$$

The measure of skewness used was the standardized skewness b_1 defined in the next section.

4.5 Results of the Generation Procedure

For the specification of a realistic vector of means μ and a realistic variance-covariance matrix Σ, a random selection of 25 stocks from the New York Stock Exchange was drawn. Monthly observations were taken for prices and dividends for the period 6/24/63 through 7/24/67. Returns for each stock were calculated as follows:

$$r_t = \frac{(P_{t+1} - P_t) + D_t}{P_t}$$

where P_t and D_t represent prices and dividends in period t, respectively, and r_t represents the one period rate of return for the common stock in period t.

The mean and variance of these rates of return are shown in Table 4-1. The jth central moment of the distribution of rates of return is defined as follows (Pearson and Hartley 1954:61):

$$m_j = \sum_{t=1}^{T} \frac{(r_t - \bar{r})^j}{T} \quad (j \geq 2),$$

Table 4-1
Monthly Return Characteristics of 25 Randomly Selected Stocks from 6/24/63 Through 7/24/67

Stock	Mean	Variance (m_2)	Standardized Skewness[a] (b_1)
1	-1.4139	222.864	1.1921
2	0.6770	39.323	0.7441
3	1.6866	65.308	0.8808
4	-0.4916	36.892	0.2502
5	1.8336	38.243	-0.3233
6	0.4264	100.644	2.1933
7	1.1194	27.766	-0.2387
8	3.4240	161.384	-0.5449
9	-1.0653	27.569	0.1592
10	0.3807	31.733	0.9052
11	0.8052	37.254	0.4407
12	4.1671	84.086	0.8032
13	3.4256	260.654	1.5524
14	1.9075	54.754	0.7872
15	2.5929	88.536	0.6209
16	3.1812	88.509	0.3638
17	3.3522	90.851	0.6043
18	0.1524	15.300	0.3615
19	1.2266	10.325	0.1515
20	1.3812	67.271	-0.0610
21	1.4832	41.459	0.2442
22	0.4086	25.920	0.5172
23	2.9445	49.645	-0.2194
24	3.5407	84.129	-0.5634
25	1.0567	115.156	0.8506

Note: Average skewness = $\overline{b_1}$ = 0.4753.

[a]For the 50 monthly observations taken, a standardized skewness statistic, $|b_1| \geq 0.533$, is significant at the .05 level (Pearson and Hartley, 1954:183).

where $\bar{r}$ is the arithmetic mean of the T observations.

The standardized skewness or the first moment ratio b_1 is shown in Table 4-1 and is defined by

$$b_1 = \frac{m_3}{m_2^{3/2}} .$$

The matrix of correlation coefficients of these actual rates of return is shown in Table 4-2. This is the variance-covariance matrix Σ that is used in the data-generation technique.

The highest degree of skewness, b_1, that was used with the generation technique was .9066. This is an average of all b_1 for the 25 assets with chi-square variates with two degrees of freedom. The average degree of skewness for the actual data was .4753, which corresponds to an average degree of skewness of .4863 for data generated with chi-square variates with nine degrees of freedom.

For the analysis of the EV and ES allocation models, three sets of 25 returns, 100 periods in length, were generated. These sets of returns corresponded to variates with normal distributions and scaled chi-square distributions with nine and two degrees of freedom. (Since scaled χ_n^2 approaches normality as n approaches infinity, the normal distribution may be viewed as a scaled chi-square with n = ∞.) The average degree of skewness in the observed returns was approximated, and an average level of skewness approximately twice that observed was generated. Summary statistics for the three sets of 100 returns generated for each of the 25 stocks are shown in Tables 4-3 through 4-8.

Several interesting observations can be made based on these tables. First, even though the chi-square variates used in the generation technique have the same degree of skewness, i.e., $b_1 = \sqrt{8/n}$ where n equals the degrees of freedom (d.f.), the resulting variables generated have different degrees of skewness. This peculiarity of the generation technique could not be eliminated. Considering Table 4-1, however, different degrees of skewness do exist in reality and with the type of range that was generated by the technique. Consequently, the realism desired for the generation process has been maintained. Second, an examination of the correlation matrices indicates that not only do the specified means and variances closely match those generated, but the correlation elements follow the desired pattern rather well.

Table 4-2
Actual Correlation Matrix of 25 Monthly Stock Returns, 6/24/63 Through 7/24/67

	1	2	3	4	5	6	7	8	9	10	11	12	13	14	15	16	17	18	19	20	21	22	23	24	25
1.	1.0																								
2.	.16	1.0																							
3.	-.05	.17	1.0																						
4.	.16	.06	.13	1.0																					
5.	.16	.21	.28	.23	1.0																				
6.	.53	.16	.27	-.06	.14	1.0																			
7.	.05	.24	.31	.28	.10	.38	1.0																		
8.	.37	.06	.30	.40	.51	.37	.20	1.0																	
9.	.30	.36	.13	.15	.48	.28	.44	.27	1.0																
10.	.43	.09	.29	.17	.43	.49	.21	.41	.23	1.0															
11.	.05	.20	.32	.35	.05	.04	.34	.34	.23	.10	1.0														
12.	.26	.12	.19	.07	.03	.24	.05	.12	.13	.16	.21	1.0													
13.	.18	.31	.03	-.23	.11	.10	-.03	.04	.05	.05	.05	.31	1.0												
14.	.19	.22	.24	-.04	.38	.30	.12	.10	.25	.24	-.04	.41	.32	1.0											
15.	.23	.16	.22	.13	.36	.46	.28	.27	.32	.39	.12	.15	.09	.25	1.0										
16.	.07	.13	.19	-.04	.39	.32	-.03	.41	.07	.24	.13	.30	.29	.24	.23	1.0									
17.	.18	.49	.28	.11	.21	.31	.31	.15	.34	.38	.35	.42	.28	.31	.33	.30	1.0								
18.	.30	.10	.15	-.03	.32	.40	.32	.31	.17	.50	.07	.06	-.02	.19	.43	.01	.17	1.0							
19.	.09	.06	.24	.24	.30	.03	.20	.30	.09	.24	.40	.12	.27	.18	.18	.33	.22	.15	1.0						
20.	.33	.12	.27	.28	.21	.21	.31	.32	.30	.25	.39	.61	.14	.16	.23	.07	.33	.12	.09	1.0					
21.	.25	.48	.16	.29	.32	.22	.25	.49	.42	.21	.30	.12	.18	.07	.19	.16	.37	.32	.36	.10	1.0				
22.	.02	.03	.08	.39	.17	.01	.39	.15	.32	.19	.16	.05	-.17	.14	.08	-.01	.03	.13	.37	.02	.14	1.0			
23.	.28	.21	.35	.16	.32	.31	.24	.20	.30	.49	.13	.24	.29	.37	.27	.31	.59	.23	.17	.27	.32	.12	1.0		
24.	.18	.11	.33	.06	.50	.18	.13	.39	.19	.28	.24	.39	.30	.32	.33	.54	.32	.22	.21	.45	.20	.04	.52	1.0	
25.	.30	.13	.40	.12	.40	.52	.44	.38	.27	.52	.21	.34	.24	.23	.38	.42	.37	.38	.33	.37	.29	.22	.43	.46	1.0

Table 4-3
Summary Data: Generated Returns for 25 Assets for 100 Periods--Normal

Assets	Specified Mean	Actual Mean	Specified Variance	Actual Variance	Standardized Skewness: b_1[a]
1	-1.4140	-1.4140	222.86	222.86	-0.1266
2	0.6770	0.6770	39.32	39.78	-0.2266
3	1.6866	1.6866	65.31	65.34	0.0522
4	-0.4916	-0.4916	36.89	35.94	0.1296
5	1.8336	1.8336	38.24	39.93	-0.5009
6	0.4264	0.4263	100.64	95.64	0.0902
7	1.1194	1.1194	27.77	32.19	-0.0181
8	3.4239	3.4239	161.38	144.27	-0.2399
9	-1.0653	-1.0653	27.56	34.05	-0.0899
10	0.3807	0.3807	31.77	30.47	-0.0216
11	0.8052	0.8052	37.25	39.62	-0.0367
12	4.1671	4.1670	84.09	81.70	0.0558
13	3.4256	3.4255	260.65	252.11	0.0973
14	1.9075	1.9075	54.75	47.37	-0.0486
15	2.5929	2.5929	88.53	85.35	0.0276
16	3.1812	3.1812	88.51	92.91	-0.2951
17	3.3522	3.3522	90.85	103.78	0.0461
18	0.1524	0.1524	15.30	16.50	0.0312
19	1.2266	1.2266	10.33	12.89	-0.2097
20	1.3813	1.3812	67.27	74.83	0.1719
21	1.4832	1.4832	41.46	46.69	0.0122
22	0.4086	0.4086	25.92	28.08	-0.1224
23	2.9445	2.9445	49.64	54.64	-0.0352
24	3.5408	3.5407	84.13	94.77	-0.1310
25	1.0567	1.0567	115.16	114.71	-0.1374

Note: Average skewness = $\overline{b_1}$ = -0.0610

[a] For the 100 returns generated, a standardized skewness statistic, $|b_1| \geq 0.389$, is significant at the .05 level [Pearson and Hartley (1954:183)].

Table 4-4
Correlation Matrix for Generated Returns--Normal

	1	2	3	4	5	6	7	8	9	10	11	12	13	14	15	16	17	18	19	20	21	22	23	24	25
1.	1.0																								
2.	.20	1.0																							
3.	.03	.20	1.0																						
4.	.04	.01	.21	1.0																					
5.	.29	.26	.28	.23	1.0																				
6.	.57	.23	.24	-.02	.14	1.0																			
7.	.05	.35	.34	.40	.14	.38	1.0																		
8.	.35	.09	.39	.42	.46	.32	.30	1.0																	
9.	.37	.55	.12	.13	.50	.32	.48	.19	1.0																
10.	.36	.26	.36	.22	.55	.37	.16	.48	.19	1.0															
11.	-.01	.22	.44	.35	.09	.02	.37	.41	.17	.21	1.0														
12.	.23	.22	.23	.07	.06	.15	.18	.23	.21	.16	.34	1.0													
13.	.18	.23	-.03	-.31	.13	.04	-.04	.14	.03	.13	.15	.21	1.0												
14.	.18	.27	.15	-.06	.25	.31	.17	.08	.24	.19	-.02	.45	.22	1.0											
15.	.27	.14	.20	.12	.31	.47	.20	.19	.31	.35	.08	.15	.10	.36	1.0										
16.	.19	.16	.07	.04	.46	.26	.01	.38	.15	.35	.19	.42	.33	.25	.24	1.0									
17.	.26	.63	.26	.08	.34	.36	.30	.17	.45	.47	.31	.44	.23	.40	.32	.38	1.0								
18.	.26	.28	.30	.07	.23	.46	.41	.35	.09	.54	.20	.15	.05	.25	.49	.09	.35	1.0							
19.	.09	.18	.35	.34	.36	.04	.34	.44	.12	.39	.61	.22	.30	.16	.03	.29	.29	.26	1.0						
20.	.34	.23	.44	.21	.35	.22	.40	.42	.37	.28	.39	.61	.12	.15	.16	.20	.32	.22	.23	1.0					
21.	.16	.54	.25	.30	.27	.23	.44	.47	.51	.27	.48	.98	.15	.03	.17	.12	.43	.31	.47	.13	1.0				
22.	.13	.18	.06	.37	.15	.02	.51	.23	.26	.17	.16	.15	.15	.26	.01	.08	.20	.24	.42	.04	.30	1.0			
23.	.30	.32	.27	.06	.37	.39	.23	.14	.36	.47	.12	.27	.32	.33	.40	.40	.67	.32	.12	.31	.29	.04	1.0		
24.	.19	.01	.31	.01	.43	.11	.13	.34	.13	.25	.37	.43	.30	.21	.29	.56	.28	.19	.22	.52	.06	.05	.51	1.0	
25.	.24	.14	.43	.21	.55	.38	.48	.48	.34	.56	.27	.26	.20	.15	.29	.43	.34	.31	.39	.47	.33	.22	.43	.49	1.0

Table 4-5
Summary Data: Generated Returns for 25 Assets for 100 Periods--Chi-Square = 9 d.f.

Assets	Specified Mean	Actual Mean	Specified Variance	Actual Variance	Standardized Skewness: b_1[a]
1	-1.4140	-1.4140	222.86	222.86	0.6815
2	0.6770	0.6770	39.32	40.12	0.1494
3	1.6866	1.6866	65.31	63.99	0.4113
4	-0.4916	-0.4916	36.89	36.94	0.9638
5	1.8336	1.8336	38.24	40.15	1.0482
6	0.4264	0.4264	100.64	93.47	0.5367
7	1.1194	1.1194	27.77	25.69	0.4501
8	3.4240	3.4239	161.38	165.94	0.4557
9	-1.0653	-1.0653	27.57	23.76	0.6260
10	0.3807	0.3807	31.77	36.02	0.4773
11	0.8052	0.8052	37.25	28.44	0.3745
12	4.1671	4.1669	84.09	83.96	1.1211
13	3.4256	3.4256	260.65	288.84	0.5547
14	1.9076	1.9075	54.75	45.36	0.3038
15	2.5929	2.5928	88.54	77.46	0.5904
16	3.1812	3.1812	88.51	81.01	0.0863
17	3.3522	3.3522	90.85	72.39	0.2854
18	0.1525	0.1524	15.30	14.20	0.2486
19	1.2266	1.2266	10.32	11.44	0.2743
20	1.3812	1.3812	67.27	67.63	0.4049
21	1.4832	1.4832	41.46	40.89	0.7089
22	0.4086	0.4086	25.92	24.10	0.4707
23	2.9445	2.9445	49.64	41.94	0.4572
24	3.5407	3.5407	84.13	83.40	-0.0804
25	1.0567	1.0567	115.16	121.58	0.5608

Note: Average skewness = $\overline{b}_1$ = 0.4863

[a]For the 100 returns generated, a standardized skewness statistic, $|b_1| \geq 0.389$, is significant at the .05 level [Pearson and Hartley (1954:183)].

Table 4-6
Correlation Matrix for Generated Returns--Chi-Square = 9 d.f.

	1	2	3	4	5	6	7	8	9	10	11	12	13	14	15	16	17	18	19	20	21	22	23	24	25
1.	1.0																								
2.	.22	1.0																							
3.	-.12	.08	1.0																						
4.	.23	.07	.03	1.0																					
5.	.19	.22	.30	.26	1.0																				
6.	.52	.08	.16	-.07	.06	1.0																			
7.	.04	.06	.20	.16	-.07	.42	1.0																		
8.	.49	.19	.23	.45	.47	.38	.12	1.0																	
9.	.25	.26	.02	.07	.42	.21	.33	.14	1.0																
10.	.42	.05	.23	.35	.50	.40	.31	.44	.13	1.0															
11.	-.03	.09	.16	.20	.12	-.10	.20	.30	.17	.12	1.0														
12.	.34	.14	.00	.04	.00	.14	-.01	.21	.13	.01	.30	1.0													
13.	.22	.27	-.12	-.27	.06	.07	-.09	.16	.05	-.02	.26	.43	1.0												
14.	.11	.20	.22	.04	.43	.10	.02	.10	.21	.16	.12	.27	.25	1.0											
15.	.24	.06	.11	.13	.25	.33	.31	.08	.35	.44	.07	.12	-.01	.24	1.0										
16.	.26	.05	.10	.18	.44	.30	-.02	.44	.10	.36	.20	.36	.33	.14	.07	1.0									
17.	.23	.35	.20	.15	.26	.20	.17	.25	.19	.42	.26	.35	.33	.20	.31	.40	1.0								
18.	.37	.08	.10	.06	.40	.38	.28	.32	.20	.60	-.06	.01	-.09	.18	.42	.15	.20	1.0							
19.	.06	-.13	.10	.17	.32	-.09	.02	.37	-.12	.33	.45	.20	.30	.22	.16	.43	.24	.21	1.0						
20.	.38	.21	.12	.21	.20	.10	.19	.29	.32	.22	.38	.64	.20	.04	.19	.18	.36	.06	.07	1.0					
21.	.31	.40	-.01	.24	.25	.24	.09	.58	.24	.14	.20	.18	.24	.08	.03	.19	.26	.28	.35	.07	1.0				
22.	-.06	-.11	.14	.46	.12	-.10	.28	.16	.25	.28	.26	.03	-.22	.11	.20	.07	.03	.09	.33	.09	-.02	1.0			
23.	.33	.07	.19	.33	.33	.18	.15	.25	.19	.52	.12	.15	.21	.16	.22	.42	.58	.31	.23	.26	.20	.15	1.0		
24.	.30	.08	.27	.03	.40	.05	-.02	.27	.17	.25	.38	.45	.38	.25	.22	.50	.38	.10	.28	.57	.03	.08	.51	1.0	
25.	.35	.01	.38	.05	.24	.59	.50	.37	.18	.55	.11	.27	.20	.00	.36	.39	.31	.38	.16	.35	.13	.11	.33	.33	1.0

Table 4-7
Summary Data: Generated Returns for 25 Assets for 100 Periods--Chi-Square = 2 d.f.

Asset	Specified Mean	Actual Mean	Specified Variance	Actual Variance	Standardized Skewness: b_1[a]
1	-1.4140	-1.4140	222.86	222.86	2.1059
2	0.6770	0.6770	39.32	40.14	1.7147
3	1.6866	1.6866	65.31	63.65	1.3261
4	-0.4916	-0.4916	36.89	36.32	1.0008
5	1.8336	1.8336	38.24	36.60	0.9418
6	0.4264	0.4264	100.64	104.84	1.5191
7	1.1194	1.1194	27.76	28.83	1.2306
8	3.4239	3.4239	161.38	177.21	1.3301
9	-1.0653	-1.0653	27.57	25.27	0.3756
10	0.3807	0.3807	31.77	31.93	0.7374
11	0.8052	0.8052	37.25	38.19	0.6943
12	4.1671	4.1670	84.09	73.65	1.2024
13	3.4256	3.4256	260.65	287.40	0.9219
14	1.9075	1.9075	54.75	47.96	0.7548
15	2.5929	2.5929	88.54	87.46	0.7388
16	3.1812	3.1812	88.51	97.82	0.4616
17	3.3522	3.3522	90.85	85.94	0.4289
18	0.1525	0.1525	15.29	17.65	0.9667
19	1.2266	1.2266	10.32	11.73	1.8635
20	1.3812	1.3812	67.27	63.75	0.1849
21	1.4832	1.4832	41.46	46.91	0.6766
22	0.4086	0.4086	25.92	25.87	0.5961
23	2.9445	2.9445	49.64	43.66	0.7098
24	3.5407	3.5407	84.13	105.85	0.4288
25	1.0567	1.0567	115.16	77.76	-0.2464

Note: Average skewness = $\overline{b}_1$ = 0.9066

[a]For the 100 returns generated, a standardized skewness statistic, $|b_1| \geq 0.389$, is significant at the .05 level [Pearson and Hartley (1954:183)].

Table 4-8
Correlation Matrix for Generated Returns--Chi-Square = 2 d.f.

	1	2	3	4	5	6	7	8	9	10	11	12	13	14	15	16	17	18	19	20	21	22	23	24	25
1.	1.0																								
2.	.23	1.0																							
3.	-.24	.02	1.0																						
4.	.03	.05	.19	1.0																					
5.	.08	.27	.20	.18	1.0																				
6.	.59	.26	.11	-.08	.10	1.0																			
7.	.09	.28	.25	.41	.08	.34	1.0																		
8.	.35	.07	.15	.41	.53	.38	.13	1.0																	
9.	.27	.35	-.01	.24	.41	.21	.47	.19	1.0																
10.	.39	.13	.27	.07	.30	.56	.18	.42	.04	1.0															
11.	-.11	.04	.32	.52	.06	-.05	.37	.28	.18	.11	1.0														
12.	.24	.02	.13	.08	.31	.24	.12	.28	.23	.24	.14	1.0													
13.	.35	.35	-.09	-.21	.22	.15	-.13	.04	.03	.01	-.04	.32	1.0												
14.	.14	.16	.17	.08	.39	.17	.16	.16	.18	.06	-.04	.51	.31	1.0											
15.	.16	.15	.19	.13	.40	.41	.30	.28	.15	.49	.10	.08	.02	.06	1.0										
16.	.13	.14	.12	-.04	.43	.34	-.10	.53	.01	.36	.14	.35	.29	.10	.13	1.0									
17.	.06	.52	.20	.05	.20	.32	.37	.01	.39	.33	.26	.29	.12	.11	.25	.25	1.0								
18.	.41	.09	-.02	-.10	.29	.57	.28	.33	.13	.56	-.04	.18	.05	.17	.57	.08	.20	1.0							
19.	.08	.13	.19	.27	.24	-.05	.14	.21	-.02	.29	.45	.15	.34	.14	.16	.32	.18	.12	1.0						
20.	.16	.07	.31	.25	.38	.16	.36	.34	.28	.18	.32	.61	.14	.31	.27	.13	.21	.09	.06	1.0					
21.	.34	.46	-.04	.31	.34	.23	.21	.50	.40	.26	.34	.12	.23	.01	.14	.25	.34	.31	.47	-.01	1.0				
22.	.05	.04	.01	.52	.14	-.09	.36	.17	.24	.20	.27	.07	-.08	.16	.15	-.01	-.02	.11	.45	.04	.19	1.0			
23.	.32	.17	.29	.06	.17	.32	.20	.06	.28	.34	.16	.24	.20	.17	.10	.25	.55	.23	.19	.23	.27	.10	1.0		
24.	.15	.98	.26	.01	.63	.15	.08	.43	.15	.22	.21	.51	.34	.39	.34	.54	.19	.26	.26	.59	.16	.06	.41	1.0	
25.	.33	.07	.33	.17	.33	.47	.38	.37	.22	.52	.21	.36	.22	.03	.41	.33	.23	.36	.34	.31	.26	.20	.30	.31	1.0

In this section the data generation technique was presented along with the source of the specified means and specified variance-covariance matrix. Results of the data generation procedure were presented for two different degrees of skewness and normally distributed returns. It was demonstrated that the technique did indeed produce generated returns that compare favorably to the initial mean and variance-covariance specifications. We now have three sets of period-by-period returns for 25 assets with which to test the EV and ES allocation models.

4.6 Performance of the EV-Based and ES-Based Allocation Models

As outlined previously, it is desired to compare the mean-variance (EV) and the mean-semivariance (ES) allocation models. More specifically, does the application of the ES model to the portfolio choice decision yield results that differ significantly from the results that would be obtained using the EV analysis? It is the purpose of this section to examine the similarities and differences in the performance results in EV and ES efficient portfolios.

The evaluation of results is based on the three data sets generated with the technique described in the previous section. The data sets are identical from an EV viewpoint but contain different underlying degrees of skewness. EV and ES portfolios can be compared first when these returns are normal, and then when they are skewed at two different degrees. The skewed data sets will be identified by their degrees of freedom, i.e., skew 2 and skew 9 will be data sets based on chi-square distributions with two and nine degrees of freedom, respectively.

Thirty-six of the 100 time periods were used to estimate the distribution of returns for each asset. Since the initial mean and variance-covariance specification was based on monthly data, this time period represents three years. The required number of observations of historical rates of return to accurately estimate the efficiency frontier has not been studied extensively. Burgess and Johnson (1976), however, through simulation studies, have indicated that a minimum of 30 observations of monthly rates of return are required to yield efficient ex post portfolio performance.

The object of this study is to investigate the ex post portfolio performance of each model. These data were developed using the following procedure: The generated returns for periods 1-36 were used to estimate the vector of means and variance-covariance matrix for the 25 assets. These were used as inputs into the quadratic programming model, first with a variance objective function and then a semivariance objective function. The weights developed were applied to the actual individual asset returns in the 37th period to calculate the ex post portfolio return. The entire procedure was advanced one period and repeated, i.e., periods 2-37 for estimation and period 38 for evaluation, and so on.

The quadratic solution technique utilized in this project was Wolfe's modified simplex algorithm (1959). This is a similar solution technique to that made available by Hogan and Warren (1972).

The quadratic programming algorithm requires a requested return constraint. The levels of requested return chosen for this project were 2.0, 3.0, and 4.0. These levels of return may appear to be high for monthly data but are necessary to prevent being to the left of the minimum variance point in a particular period.

In total, 40 periods were evaluated for each of the three data sets. Of the total of 120 evaluations, only one failed to result in a feasible solution for a requested return of 4.0. An infeasible solution is one where no combination of individual assets can satisfy the requested return. Consequently, given the two tradeoffs of being to the left of the minimum variance (semivariance) point on one hand, and beyond a feasible solution on the other, the requested returns of 2.0, 3.0, and 4.0 appeared to be quite reasonable and thus were adopted.

4.7 The Allocation Results

Tables 4-9, 4-10, and 4-11 summarize the results of the ex post portfolio returns for 40 periods using the three data sets. In total, 10 different portfolios were developed for each of the 40 periods. The first 3 represent the conventional mean-variance allocations with the three different levels of requested return. The second 3 represent

Table 4-9
Summary Data: Ex Post Portfolio Returns, Normal Data Set

	Model	Ex Post Mean	Ex Post Variance	Geometric Mean	Standardized Skewness: b_1[a]	Average Portfolio Size
1	EV RR = 2.0	0.9971	13.1208	0.9336	-0.0120	8.225
2	EV RR = 3.0	1.1876	19.1867	1.0958	0.3373	7.625
3	EV RR = 4.0	1.5413	31.3793	1.3919	0.3316	6.325
4	ES @ $\overline{X}$ RR = 2.0	0.9716	13.2592	0.9075	0.0210	5.675
5	ES @ $\overline{X}$ RR = 3.0	0.9924	18.7710	0.9021	0.2113	5.325
6	ES @ $\overline{X}$ RR = 4.0	1.2418	29.4848	1.1008	0.2794	4.400
7	ES @ RR RR = 2.0	0.9581	13.8886	0.8909	-0.0030	5.450
8	ES @ RR RR = 3.0	1.0486	19.6831	0.9540	0.2159	5.525
9	ES @ RR RR = 4.0	1.2087	29.0442	1.0699	0.3092	4.650
10	Equal allocation 1/N	1.0289	18.7158	0.9385	0.0944	25

[a] For the 40 portfolio returns, a standardized skewness statistic, $|b_1| \geq 0.587$, is significant at the .05 level [Pearson and Hartley (1954:183)].

semivariance allocations with semivariance calculated about the mean. The third 3 also represent semivariance allocations, but they are calculated about a fixed point, specifically, the requested portfolio returns. The last portfolio is a naive portfolio involving an equal allocation to all 25 stocks. This numbering system will be maintained

Table 4-10
Summary Data: Ex Post Portfolio Returns, Skew 9 Data Set

	Model	Ex Post Mean	Ex Post Variance	Geometric Mean	Standardized Skewness: b_1[a]	Average Portfolio Size
1	EV RR = 2.0	2.3791	7.5506	2.3433	0.2644	8.875
2	EV RR = 3.0	3.1322	11.9125	3.0763	0.3157	8.050
3	EV RR = 4.0	3.4843	19.3466	3.3930	-0.0252	6.550
4	ES @ $\overline{X}$ RR = 2.0	2.4802	10.2758	2.4321	0.7493[a]	5.950
5	ES @ $\overline{X}$ RR = 3.0	3.2512	13.4637	3.1884	0.5184	4.725
6	ES @ $\overline{X}$ RR = 4.0	3.3974	22.9448	3.2903	0.3677	4.050
7	ES @ RR RR = 2.0	2.4735	9.9853	2.4267	0.7583[a]	6.125
8	ES @ RR RR = 3.0	3.1786	13.2598	3.1166	0.5022	5.400
9	ES @ RR RR = 4.0	3.4696	22.5717	3.3641	0.3062	4.600
10	Equal allocation 1/N	2.1290	15.2634	2.0563	0.0878	25

[a]For the 40 portfolio returns, a standardized skewness statistic, $|b_1| \geq 0.587$, is significant at the .05 level [Pearson and Hartley (1954:183)].

throughout the balance of the report.

The summary tables contain many anticipated results. Evans and Archer (1968) demonstrated that naive diversification reduced risk ex post, and Markowitz (1959) and later Francis and Archer (1971) developed the relationships of efficient diversification through the

Table 4-11
Summary Data: Ex Post Portfolio Returns, Skew 2 Data Set

	Model	Ex Post Mean	Ex Post Variance	Geometric Mean	Standardized Skewness: b_1[a]	Average Portfolio Size
1	EV RR = 2.0	1.9907	14.4316	1.9227	0.6303[a]	8.975
2	EV RR = 3.0	2.4828	23.7045	2.3729	0.9143[b]	8.000
3	EV RR = 4.0	2.3697	21.8967	2.2668	0.5066	6.050
4	ES @ $\overline{X}$ RR = 2.0	1.9861	12.3504	1.9277	0.5515	5.475
5	ES @ $\overline{X}$ RR = 3.0	2.6009	21.9839	2.5015	1.7697[b]	4.687
6	ES @ $\overline{X}$ RR = 4.0	2.4509	18.2072	2.3657	0.6317[a]	3.775
7	ES @ RR RR = 2.0	2.0971	11.5748	2.0423	0.4174	5.675
8	ES @ RR RR = 3.0	2.6931	21.9718	2.5935	1.6912[b]	5.425
9	ES @ RR RR = 4.0	2.4935	19.0986	2.4040	0.5782	4.125
10	Equal allocation 1/N	1.7811	18.9664	1.6904	0.1205	25

[a]For the 40 portfolio returns, a standardized skewness statistic, $|b_1| \geq 0.587$, is significant at the .05 level.

[b]For the 40 portfolio returns, a standardized skewness statistic, $|b_1| \geq 0.869$, is significant at the .01 level [Pearson and Hartley (1954:183)].

application of the quadratic programming algorithm. However, most of the previous work was ex ante, i.e., it was not based on portfolio performance results in subsequent periods. Tables 4-9, 4-10, and 4-11 show how the efficient allocation models actually perform in subsequent periods. There is a positive relationship between risk and return, and as we have higher requested returns, we do indeed realize higher returns in subsequent periods that are associated with higher variances. These statements are true for all the allocation models except for equal allocation, which does not have a requested return.

At this point it appears that the two allocation models using the quadratic programming algorithm behave as one would expect. Initially, it appears that EV and ES allocation have much in common. Even though semivariance is a partial dispersion measure, it still behaves similarly to its full variance counterpart.

The geometric mean return is shown on the tables to demonstrate that diversification of any kind will increase a portfolio's geometric mean rate of return over time (Francis and Archer 1971). The geometric mean rate of return increases as the variance of the period-by-period rates of return increases. The geometric mean rate of return is thus a composite measure that reflects a portfolio's arithmetic mean and variance.

The skewness data demonstrate that when period-by-period returns of individual assets are asymmetric, the portfolio period-by-period return distributions may be asymmetric. This effect is not pronounced until we move to the skew 2 data set (Table 4-11), which represents a degree of skewness twice that of the actual conditions observed in the market.

The tables indicate that there may be one systematic difference between the EV and ES portfolios, i.e., the portfolio size. This relationship was examined, and it was found that approximately the same assets were in each corresponding portfolio (based on corresponding requested returns), but the ES-based portfolios did not contain the assets in the EV portfolios that carried low weights. This resulted in slightly smaller portfolio sizes for the ES models.

The three generated sets of 100 returns for the 25 assets have the same mean and variance-covariance specification. Each data set of 100 returns for the 25 assets was generated independently of the other, with only the specification being common across data sets. Due to sampling error, the 40 periods of returns for the 25 assets used for ex post evaluation will not be the same across data sets. Comparisons of the ex post portfolio performance results must be restricted to within each data set and not across data sets.

4.8 Comparisons of the Allocation Models

Comparisons of the individual allocation models, particularly those with corresponding levels of requested return, were conducted using the techniques of regression and analysis of variance. The results of each approach will be discussed individually.

The regression analysis used the EV model as the independent variable and the corresponding ES model as the dependent variable. The results of the regression analysis are shown in Tables 4-12, 4-13, and 4-14.

The constant terms were insignificant for all three data sets; however, they become larger as the skewness increases. On the basis of the observed data, one cannot reject the hypothesis that the intercept term is equal to zero. The portfolio implication is that when the EV model has a return of zero, the corresponding ES model also has a return of zero.

The value of B_1 measures the average proportion that the ex post return in the ES allocation model is of the ex post return of the corresponding EV allocation model. For the portfolios based on the normal and skew 9 data sets, this proportion is approximately one. None of the B_1 coefficient was found to be significantly different from one. For the portfolios based on the skew 2 data set (the highest degree of skewness), all the estimated regression coefficients (Table 4-14) are significantly less than one at the .05 level. A unit change of return in the corresponding EV model produces less on average than a unit change of return in the ES model.

The interpretation of the tables presented thus far indicates that the corresponding EV and ES portfolios are highly related, particularly under the normal and moderately skewed (skew 9) data sets. They are highly correlated and have the same approximate magnitude of returns. Only when the returns are highly skewed are differences observed in the corresponding allocation models.

Table 4-12
Summary of Regression Results: Semivariance Model as a Function of its Full Variance Counterpart, Normal Data Set

Dependent Variable	Independent Variable	Constant Term: B_0 (t-ratio)[a]	Slope: B_1 (t-ratio)[b]	R-Square
4 ES @ $\overline{X}$ RR = 2.0	1 EV RR = 2.0	0.0093 (0.0547)	0.9651 (0.7645)	0.9218
5 ES @ $\overline{X}$ RR = 3.0	2 EV RR = 3.0	-0.1402 (0.7346)	0.9537 (1.0883)	0.9297
6 ES @ $\overline{X}$ RR = 4.0	3 EV RR = 4.0	-0.1987 (0.8299)	0.9346 (1.5676)	0.9297
7 ES @ RR RR = 2.0	1 EV RR = 2.0	-0.0171 (0.0887)	0.9780 (0.4240)	0.9037
8 ES @ RR RR = 3.0	2 EV RR = 3.0	-0.1055 (0.5083)	0.9718 (0.6086)	0.9206
9 ES @ RR RR = 4.0	3 EV RR = 4.0	-0.2155 (0.8638)	0.9240 (1.7483)	0.9225

[a]The t-ratio shown is for hypothesis test of significant difference from zero.

[b]The t-ratio shown is for hypothesis test of significant difference from one.

Critical values: t @ .05 level = 2.02, t @ .01 level = 2.70.

The regression portion of the analysis was limited to a consideration of the relationships between the EV and ES allocation models. The next portion of this section will test more precisely for differences that may exist between the allocation models. The statistical technique used was a single-factor analysis of variance design with repeated measures. The selection of the repeated measures design was based on the violation of the independence assumption commonly made in

Table 4-13
Summary of Regression Results: Semivariance Model as a Function of its Full Variance Counterpart, Skew 9 Data Set

Dependent Variable	Independent Variable	Constant Term: B_0 (t-ratio)[a]	Slope: B_1 (t-ratio)[b]	R-Square
4 ES @ $\overline{X}$ RR = 2.0	1 EV RR = 2.0	0.0097 (0.0312)	1.0384 (0.4453)	0.7924
5 ES @ $\overline{X}$ RR = 3.0	2 EV RR = 3.0	0.3209 (0.8464)	0.9355 (0.7872)	0.7744
6 ES @ $\overline{X}$ RR = 4.0	3 EV RR = 4.0	-0.1239 (0.3380)	1.0106 (0.1611)	0.8612
7 ES @ RR RR = 2.0	1 EV RR = 2.0	0.0013 (0.0045)	1.0391 (0.4897)	0.8165
8 ES @ RR RR = 3.0	2 EV RR = 3.0	0.2286 (0.6402)	0.9418 (0.7515)	0.7969
9 ES @ RR RR = 4.0	3 EV RR = 4.0	-0.0195 (0.0534)	1.0014 (0.0829)	0.8595

[a]The t-ratio shown is for hypothesis test of significant difference from zero.

[b]The t-ratio shown is for hypothesis test of significant difference from one.

Critical values: t @ .05 level = 2.02, t @ .01 level = 2.70.

an analysis of variance. Specifically, the returns from the allocation models were correlated within each period.

The repeated measures analysis of variance was performed on the ex post portfolio returns of each of the 10 allocation models. The computational procedures used are those suggested by Winer (1971). The results of this analysis indicate that the observed F ratios of 0.62 and 0.78 for the normal and skew 2 (highest degree of skewness)

Table 4-14
Summary of Regression Results: Semivariance Model as a Function of its Full Variance Counterpart, Skew 2 Data Set

	Dependent Variable	Independent Variable	Constant Term: B_0 (t-ratio)[a]	Slope: B_1 (t-ratio)[b]	R-Square
4	ES @ $\overline{X}$ RR = 2.0	1 EV RR = 2.0	0.3957 (1.2315)	0.7989 (2.6578)	0.7454
5	ES @ $\overline{X}$ RR = 3.0	2 EV RR = 3.0	0.5153 (1.2468)	0.8400 (2.0945)	0.7609
6	ES @ $\overline{X}$ RR = 4.0	3 EV RR = 4.0	0.5012 (1.5133)	0.8228 (2.7790)	0.8141
7	ES @ RR RR = 2.0	1 EV RR = 2.0	0.5116 (1.8136)	0.7965 (3.0641)	0.7909
8	ES @ RR RR = 3.0	2 EV RR = 3.0	0.5876 (1.4688)	0.8480 (2.0554)	0.7759
9	ES @ RR RR = 4.0	3 EV RR = 4.0	0.5144 (1.4608)	0.8315 (2.4310)	0.7996

[a]The t-ratio shown is for hypothesis test of significant difference from zero.

[b]The t-ratio shown is for hypothesis test of significant difference from one.

Critical values: t @ .05 level = 2.02, t @ .01 level = 2.70.

data sets do not exceed the critical value for the .05-level test. Therefore, for these two data sets the hypotheses that the performance results of the 10 allocation models are the same cannot be rejected.

The observed F ratio for the skew 9 data set, 3.62, does exceed the critical value for the .05-level test of 1.88. Since it does exceed the critical value for the .05-level test, the hypothesis that the effects of the 10 allocation models are all equal is rejected. To determine the exact location of the differences, a more systematic probing procedure was used.

A convenient test procedure for this systematic probing is the Newman-Keuls test (Winer 1971:191). The method uses the studentized range statistic for simultaneous tests on a set of means obtained in the analysis of variance. The Newman-Keuls test was conducted on the allocation means for the skew 9 data set. The results of this test are summarized as follows:

```
10   1   7   4   2   8   5   6   9   3
___________________________
     _____________________________________
```

The numbers shown correspond to the allocation model numbering system used throughout the chapter and are ranked in order of means, lowest to highest. The results are presented in the above ranked manner because the test procedure focuses on a series of ranges rather than a collection of differences between means. The schematic representation of the results is interpreted in the following manner: Allocation models underlined by a common line do not differ from each other; allocation models not underlined by a common line do differ. Thus allocation model 10, the equal allocation model, is significantly different from the EV allocation and the two ES allocation models with all three having requested returns of 4.0. For this data set, high levels of requested return yield significantly different results from equal allocation at the .05-level test.

The comparisons between the EV and the two ES models showed no evidence to reject the null hypothesis. The analysis of variance results support the conclusions of the regression analysis. The EV and the two ES allocation models perform in approximately the same manner.

4.9 Efficiency Analysis

Stochastic dominance (SD) and mean-variance (EV) efficiency analysis were conducted on the ex post portfolio returns. One could justify the use of an EV efficiency criterion by reviewing Tables 4-9 through 4-11 and noting that the portfolio returns developed on the skew 9 data set have two departures from normality using a .05-level test, and those based on the skew 2 data set have four departures from normality using a .05-level test. Therefore the moment-free criterion of SD should yield approximately the same results as the EV criterion for the portfolio returns based on the normal data set, and differences may be observed as we experience departures from symmetry of portfolio returns. Clearly, the SD analysis will yield the superior results when departures from normality are observed. As a method for evaluating operational allocation models, it does not depend on the shape of the distribution of portfolio returns. Using both analyses, however, permits the determination of the level of skewness that yields different rankings by the two efficiency criteria.

The EV results were obtained by (1) ranking the portfolio performance results in order of ascending means and (2) at any given level of ex post mean, checking if there is a portfolio with a higher mean and a lower variance. If this condition occurs, the second portfolio dominates the first. The SD tests were conducted using an efficient algorithm developed by Porter, Wart, and Ferguson (1971). The program DOMIN2 was adapted to analyze the portfolio returns developed by the allocation process, and all three levels of SD were evaluated.

The results of the SD tests and a summary of the EV efficiency results are shown in Table 4-15. As other studies have shown, the first-degree stochastic dominance (FSD) criterion assumes such a general specification of an investor's utility function (a positive first derivative) that as a decision criterion it is relatively ineffective (Porter and Gaumnitz 1970).

The general pattern of differences between the EV- and ES-based portfolios was what one would expect given the relationship between semivariance calculated about a fixed point and SSD demonstrated by Porter (1974a). The ES efficient portfolios with the semivariance calculated about the requested portfolio return, a fixed target, were SSD efficient across all three data sets. Even considering the sampling problems inherent in this empirical study, the ES-based portfolios calculated about a fixed point performed well according to the SSD rule.

Summary of Mean-Variance and Stochastic Dominance Efficiency Results, All Data Sets

Model		Results from Normal Data				Results from Skew 9 Data				Results from Skew 2 Data			
		EV	FSD	SSD	TSD	EV	FSD	SSD	TSD	EV	FSD	SSD	TSD
1	EV RR = 2.0	*	*	*	*	*	*	*	5,8	7	*	*	*
2	EV RR = 3.0	*	*	*	*	*	*	*	*	5,9	*	8	5,8,9
3	EV RR = 4.0	*	*	*	*	*	*	*	*	6,9	*	5,6,8,9	5,6,8,9
4	ES @ $\overline{X}$ RR = 2.0	1	*	*	*	*	*	*	5	7	*	7	7
5	ES @ $\overline{X}$ RR = 3.0	1,10	*	1,2	1,2	*	*	*	*	8	*	*	8
6	ES @ $\overline{X}$ RR = 4.0	*	*	*	3	3,9	*	*	*	*	*	8	5,8
7	ES @ RR RR = 2.0	1,4	*	*	1,4	*	*	*	*	*	*	*	*
8	ES @ RR RR = 3.0	2	*	*	2	*	*	*	*	*	*	*	*
9	ES @ RR RR = 4.0	*	*	*	*	3	*	*	*	*	*	*	5,8
10	Equal allocation 1/N	*	*	2	2	1,2,4,5,7,8	*	1,2,4,5,7,8	All	1,4,6,7	*	All	All

Note: *Indicates an efficient portfolio allocation model. Numbers indicate the portfolios that dominate the inefficient portfolio allocation models.

The ES-based portfolios calculated about the mean--portfolios 4, 5 and 6--were not SSD-efficient across the data sets; no consistent performance pattern was present for these portfolios. They were not uniformly efficient by the EV or any of the SD rules, although the criterion did result in portfolios that were dominated by relatively fewer portfolios than the EV-based allocation model.

The EV-based allocation model also performed as one would expect. It resulted in efficient portfolios for the normal data set, whose portfolio returns were also normal, and inefficient portfolios, even by the EV rule, when the portfolio returns became more skewed. It is interesting to note that the portfolios that dominate the EV-based portfolios resulted from the ES-based allocation models and that the converse is not true. None of the ES-based portfolios was dominated by EV-based portfolios when the individual assets were skewed.

4.10 Summary and Conclusions

Portfolios were formulated and evaluated in subsequent periods. The analysis of the ex post portfolio returns indicated that the EV and ES allocation models performed much in the same manner. There was a positive relationship between risk and return. As higher returns were requested, higher returns were realized in subsequent periods and these were associated with higher variances.

The statistical analysis of the ex post portfolio returns indicated that the returns from the EV and ES allocation models were not significantly different at the predefined confidence level. The returns of the ES-based portfolios were regressed on those of the EV-based portfolios that had the same corresponding requested return. For the portfolios based on individual returns that are skewed twice that observed in the returns of common stocks, the skew 2 data set, significant differences were found. The slope terms were found to be significantly less than one. A unit change in return in the corresponding EV model produced less than a unit change in the ES model, i.e., the ES model exhibited less variance.

The efficiency analysis conducted on the ex post portfolio returns demonstrated the primary advantage of the ES-based allocation model calculated about a fixed point. As the skewness of the individual assets was increased, the portfolio returns based on these assets exhibited increasing levels of skewness. As the skewness of the data sets increased the relative efficiency of the ES, fixed-point, model increased by all efficiency rules. In all cases the ES, fixed-point model resulted in SSD efficient portfolio returns. The skewness of the individual assets was twice that realized on the actual distributions of common stock returns to dramatize the differences. However, the ES, fixed-point model can be consistently depended on to result in SSD efficient returns while the EV and ES, mean models cannot.

Scaled chi-square distributions were used to introduce the third moment into the generated returns while holding the mean and variance-covariance specifications constant. As the skewness of the individual assets was increased, the skewness of the ex post portfolio returns increased. Given that other parameters were held constant, as demonstrated by the comparison section, investors would prefer portfolio returns skewed to the right, thus providing downside protection and potential for upside gain.

Generally, the EV and SSD rules will result in similar relationships for common stocks, but the EV rule may not be generalized to other types of assets as may the SSD rule. The ES, fixed-point model is theoretically superior because it may be generalized to assets with nonnormal returns, while this may lead to inefficient results with the EV or the ES, mean models.

Introduction to Chapter 5
Portfolio Applications: Computational Aspects

The two previous chapters are concerned with empirical applications of stochastic dominance methodology to security and portfolio data. In this chapter W. T. Ziemba considers computational aspects of optimal portfolio construction. In his very thorough treatment of the subject, he considers two modes of attack on the portfolio problem. In brief:

1. With assumed explicit knowledge of the investor's utility function, find by direct computation (using a suitable algorithm) the portfolio mix that maximizes expected utility.

2. With knowledge only that the investor's utility function belongs to a certain class (e.g., the class of increasing, concave functions), find the SD efficient set of portfolio mixes for that class. Then, with assumed explicit knowledge of the investor's utility function, find the optimum portfolio mix in the SD efficient set.

In Section 5.1, Ziemba considers the first approach. He provides an extensive discussion of the mathematical algorithms available for solving the portfolio problem by direct assault on the expected utility expression. In Section 5.2, he considers the second approach with its two stages. Here he limits his attention to the case where return distributions correspond to symmetric stable Paretian random variables (including, of course, normal variates), and the investor is permitted to invest in a risk-free asset. In this case mean-dispersion analysis is optimal in the SD sense.

5 Portfolio Applications: Computational Aspects

W. T. Ziemba

5.1 Expected Utility Portfolio Selection Problems

5.1.1 Introduction

A number of authors (see Chapter 1 for more detail and specific references) have presented sets of "reasonable" behavioral assumptions that imply that a decision-maker faced with the choice among risky investments behaves as if he maximized the expectation of a continuous utility function u. The function u, commonly called a von Neumann-Morgernstern cardinal utility function, is unique up to a positive linear transformation, so that $v(\cdot) = au(\cdot) + b$ for any $a > 0$ and b produces the same ordering as u. Suppose that the investor's initial wealth is B dollars, and that for each dollar invested in asset i he receives the random return ξ_i dollars at the end of the investment period. If x_i represents the number of dollars invested in asset i, the return from all n investments is

$$\sum_{i=1}^{n} \xi_i x_i .$$

The investor's problem then is to choose optimal allocation $\{x_i\}$ to

---

In this chapter I have made extensive use of the results in Ziemba (1972, 1974a). This research was partially supported by the National Research Council of Canada. I would like to thank M. J. Brennan, E. U. Choo, C. C. Huang, S. J. Press, and G. A. Whitmore for helpful comments on an earlier version of this chapter; I assume responsibility for any errors that may appear here, however.

$$\text{maximize} \quad E_{\xi_1,\ldots,\xi_n} u\left\{\sum_{i=1}^{n} \xi_i x_i\right\},$$

$$\text{subject to} \quad \sum_{i=1}^{n} x_i = B,$$

$$x_i \geq 0, \; i = 1,\ldots,n, \tag{5.1}$$

where E denotes mathematical expectation.

If the investment choices must satisfy certain size-purchase constraints related to the minimum and maximum investment in particular assets, then one has the additional constraints that $\alpha_i \leq x_i \leq \beta_i$. If the investor wishes to include the possibility of short sales, in which he sells x_i dollars ($x_i < 0$) of investment i and must buy (repay) at ξ_i, then $\alpha_i < 0$. Borrowing margin funds yB at cost c(yB) is also accommodated in the problem[1]

$$\text{maximize} \quad E_{\xi_1,\ldots,\xi_n} u\left\{\sum_{i=1}^{n} \xi_i x_i - c(yB)\right\},$$

$$\text{subject to} \quad \sum_{i=1}^{n} x_i = B(1 + y),$$

$$\alpha_i \leq x_i \leq \beta_i, \quad i = 1,\ldots,n,$$

$$0 \leq y \leq \delta \,. \tag{5.2}$$

The investor's problem can be further complicated by supposing that he wants to guard against ruination and hence he would like

$$P_r\left\{\sum_{i=1}^{n} \xi_i x_i \geq 0\right\}$$

to be at least ϕ, where ϕ is a number strictly below but close to 1. Suppose that $\xi \equiv (\xi_1,\ldots,\xi_n)'$ has a multivariate normal distribution with mean vector $\bar{\xi}$ and variance-covariance matrix Σ. Let F be the cumulative distribution of a normally distributed random variable with zero mean and unit variance, i.e.,

$$F(z) = \int_{-\infty}^{z} \frac{1}{\sqrt{2\pi}} \exp\{-t^2/2\}dt,$$

and D_ϕ is the ϕ-fractile of F, thus $F(D_\phi) = \phi$. Let $x \equiv (x_1,\ldots,x_n)'$. It is well known in the chance-constrained programming literature [see e.g., Wagner (1969)] that $P_r\{\xi'x \geq 0\} \geq \phi$ if and only if $h(x) \equiv \bar{\xi}'x - D_\phi(x'\not{\Sigma}x)^{\frac{1}{2}} \geq 0$. The function h is concave if $\phi \geq .5$. (Similar expressions may be developed if ξ has a multivariate stable distribution; see Section 5.2.2.) Under this specification the problem is to solve (5.2) with the additional nonlinear restriction that $\bar{\xi}'x - c(yB) - D_\phi(x'\not{\Sigma}x)^{\frac{1}{2}} \geq 0$. This yields the problem

$$\text{maximize} \quad E_\xi u\{\xi'x - c(yB)\},$$

$$\text{subject to} \quad \sum_{i=1}^{n} x_i = B(1 + y),$$

$$\alpha_i \leq x_i \leq \beta_i, \quad i = 1,\ldots,n,$$

$$0 \leq y \leq \delta,$$

and

$$\bar{\xi}'x - c(yB) - D_\phi(x'\not{\Sigma}x)^{\frac{1}{2}} \geq 0. \qquad (5.3)$$

Since u is a utility function over wealth, it is monotone nondecreasing. If the investor is risk-averse, then u is concave. Problem (5.3) will then be a concave program,[2] i.e., the maximization of a concave function over a convex set as long as $c(\cdot)$ is convex (the marginal cost of margin funds is nondecreasing).

It will be convenient to consider problems (5.1)-(5.3) and other related problems to be special cases of the portfolio problem

$$\text{maximize} \quad E_{\xi}u(\xi'x),$$

$$\text{subject to} \quad e'x = 1,$$

$$x \in D, \tag{5.4}$$

where $e \equiv (1,\ldots,1)'$, D is a closed convex subset of Euclidean n-space, and the returns ξ_i have been rescaled so that the investor's initial wealth may be taken as 1. That is, the x_i represent the proportion of total wealth invested in asset i. Let $K \equiv \{x | e'x = 1, x \in D\}$.

For problem (5.4) let $U_1, U_2, \ldots, U_S$ represent sets of admissible utility function classes from which the investor might choose a particular utility function u.

We shall discuss two approaches to the solution of (5.4):

1. With knowledge of u, find an x* that solves (5.4);
2. With only knowledge that $u \in U_s$, find that subset X_s of K that contains all the points that are optimal for some $u \in U_s$; then with knowledge of u find an x* that maximizes the expectation of u over all $x \in X_s$.

Problem (2) has two stages: first find the efficient set via stochastic dominance constructs, then find an optimal point in this set. Clearly this procedure has its primary advantage, from a computational point of view, when the set X_s has a very simple structure. A detailed discussion of this approach is given in Section 5.2.

5.1.2 Finiteness of Expected Utility

We now turn our attention to the solution of problems having the form of (5.4) when u is assumed to be known. To begin, we develop some of the mathematical properties of the objective function $Z(x) \equiv E_{\xi}u(\xi'x)$.

We develop conditions on u (assumed only to be monotone nondecreasing) and P(w), the distribution of wealth w, such that expected utility is finite. The simplest case is when u is bounded.

THEOREM 5.1. *If u is bounded between* $-\infty < \alpha$ *and* $\beta < \infty$, *then expected utility is finite.*

Proof: Since
$$\beta \geq u(w) \geq \alpha,$$
$$\beta \geq E(u,P) \geq \alpha.$$

Another simple case is when P has either a finitely distributed discrete distribution or a bounded distribution.

THEOREM 5.2. *Suppose* u *is finite for finite wealth. If the investor's wealth has either:*

(a) *the finite discrete distribution* $P_r\{w = w_j\} = P_j > 0$, $j = 1,\ldots,J$ *where each* $|w_j| < \infty$ *and* $\Sigma_{j=1}^{J} P_j = 1$; *or*

(b) *the bounded distribution* $P_r\{-\infty < a \leq w \leq b < \infty\} = 1$, *then expected utility is finite.*

Proof: (a) Let

$$\gamma \equiv \min_{j=1,\ldots,J} w_j$$

and

$$\delta \equiv \max_{j=1,\ldots,J} w_j.$$

Then

$$-\infty < \gamma \leq E(u,P) = \sum_{j=1}^{J} P_j u(w_j) \leq \delta < \infty.$$

(b) Since u is nondecreasing,

$$u(a) \leq u(w) \leq u(b).$$

Hence $-\infty < u(a) \leq E(u,P) \leq u(b) < \infty$.

When u is unbounded and P(w) ranges over the entire real line, it is quite possible that expected utility is infinite. Suppose, for example, that $u(w) = w^3$ and that w has the uniform distribution P(w) $= 1/(b - a)$ on the interval [a,b], then by Theorem 5.2 E(u,P) is bounded and equals $(b^4 - a^4)/4(b - a)$. If the uniform distribution is over the entire real line $(-\infty,\infty)$, however, then

$$E(u,P) = \lim_{\substack{b\to\infty \\ a\to-\infty}} \frac{b^4 - a^4}{4(b - a)} = \infty$$

As a further example suppose, u(w) is $e^{w^3/2}$ and that P(w) is the standard normal distribution

$$\frac{1}{\sqrt{2\pi}} \int_{-\infty}^{w} e^{-w^2/2}\, dw \ .$$

Then

$$E(u,P) = \frac{1}{\sqrt{2\pi}} \int_{-\infty}^{\infty} e^{(w^3-w^2)/2}\, dw = \infty.$$

It is customary to assume that the investor displays aversion to risk and hence to assume that u is concave. Under a concavity assumption, values of u(w) do not become too great for large positive w because u can always be supported from above by a linear function. For large negative values of w, however, u(w) can be an arbitrarily large negative number. Hence one would suspect that expected utility would be finite for concave functions if wealth was bounded from below and the expected utility of a linear utility function was finite, that is, the mean is finite.[3]

THEOREM 5.3. *Suppose an investor's wealth is defined on the interval* $[A,\infty)$, *where* $A > -\infty$, *with the distribution function* P(w) *possessing a finite mean* $\bar{w}$. *Assume in addition that the investor's utility function over wealth* u(w) *is nondecreasing and concave and that utility is finite at* A *and at some* $w_0 \in (A,\infty)$. *Then expected utility is finite.*

Proof: Since u is concave, it is continuous on (A,∞); hence utility is finite for any finite w. Let $\ell(w)$ denote a line that supports u at an arbitrary point $\hat{w} \in (A,\infty)$. The slope of ℓ is any $s(\hat{w}) \in [u'_L(\hat{w}), u'_R(\hat{w})]$, where $u'_L(\hat{w})$ and $u'_R(\hat{w})$ denote the left- and right-hand derivatives of u at $\hat{w}$ [which exist because u is continuous and concave (Rockafellar 1970:218)]. Since $\ell(\hat{w}) = u(\hat{w})$, it follows that $\ell(w) = sw + u(\hat{w}) - s\hat{w}$. Since $u(w) \leq \ell(w)$ for all w, it follows that $E(u,P) \leq E(\ell,P) = s\bar{w} + u(\hat{w}) - s\hat{w} < \infty$. Hence expected utility is bounded from above.

If $u(A) \geq 0$ then $E(u,P) \geq 0$. Suppose $u(A) = \beta < 0$. Let $v(w) \equiv u(w) + \beta$. Then $E(v,P) \geq 0$, which implies that $E(u,P) \geq \beta > -\infty$. Hence expected utility is bounded from below.

Theorem 5.3 is quite powerful in establishing the boundedness of expected utility. For example, it immediately indicates that expected utility is finite when wealth is lognormal or a nonnegative sum of lognormal variates for essentially all interesting concave utility functions. However, there still are many instances not covered by Theorem 5.3, nor by Theorems 5.1 and 5.2. For example, if w has the Cauchy distribution

$$p(w) = \frac{k}{\pi[k^2 + (w - \mu)^2]}, \quad 0 < k, \; -\infty < \mu < \infty,$$

then expected utility is infinite for any strictly concave u. We shall return to the study of the boundedness of expected utility for normal and stable distributions in Section 5.2.2.

5.1.3 General Algorithmic Solution Methods

We now take up the discussion of the development of methods to solve (5.4) when u is known. For a given u, problem (5.4) is a nonlinear program with a stochastic objective function, and there are at least five solution approaches that one may utilize. (For some u more than one of these approaches may be utilized, but there are u for which none of these approaches may be utilized.) First, one may utilize certain properties of u, the feasible region K, and $P(\xi)$, the distribution function of ξ, to determine the optimal x_i^* directly. Second, one may use certain properties of u and $P(\xi)$ to reduce the problem to a deterministic program whose solution may be sought via a nonlinear programming algorithm. Third, one may integrate $u(\xi'x)$ with respect to ξ to obtain an explicit deterministic program in x--say, Z(x)--whose solution may be sought via a nonlinear programming algorithm. Fourth, one may approximate either u or $P(\xi)$ to reduce the problem to one of the above cases. Lastly, one may modify a nonlinear programming algorithm to solve the problem without explicitly calculating Z(x). A summary of some of the available possibilities for each of these five solution approaches appears in Table 5-1.

We now describe how one can modify standard nonlinear programming algorithms to solve problems having the form of (5.4), and develop the details for one such algorithm. Rewrite problem (5.4) in the more compact form

$$\begin{aligned} &\text{maximize} && Z(x) \equiv E_{\xi} u(\xi'x) \\ &\text{subject to} && g_j(x) \geq 0,\ j = 1,\ldots,m, \end{aligned} \qquad (5.5)$$

where $x \in R^n$, ξ is a random n-vector defined on the probability space (Ξ, F, P) that is distributed independently of x, $u, g_1, \ldots, g_m$ and Z are real valued scalar functions, and $K \equiv \{x | g_1(x) \geqq 0, \ldots, g_m(x) \geqq 0\}$ is the feasible region.

Feasible direction algorithms [see, e.g., Zoutendijk (1960) and 1970) and Zangwill (1969) for details] proceed via the following procedure:

0. Initialization. Find an $x^1 \in K$. Set $k = 1$.
1. Find an n-dimensional direction vector d^k that is:

   (a) feasible. $\exists \lambda^0 > 0$: $\forall\ 0 \leqq \lambda \leqq \lambda^0, (x^k + \lambda d^k) \in K$; and

   (b) usable.[4] $\nabla Z(x^k)'d^k > 0$.
2. Find a step length λ^k:

   $Z(x^k + \lambda^k d^k) = \max_{\lambda \geqq 0} \{Z(x^k + \lambda d^k) | (x^k + \lambda d^k) \in K\}$.

Table 5-1
Some Expected Utility Solution Possibilities

Utility function u(w)		Random vectors	Deterministic equivalent Z(x)
1. Strictly concave Twice continuously differentiable	 $u'(w) > 0$ $u''(w) < 0$	Symmetric, $P(\xi_1,\ldots,\xi_n)$ is symmetric in $\xi_1,\ldots,\xi_n$; $\bar{\xi}_1 < \infty$, $\sigma_{ij} < \infty$; or P is identical, independent $P(\xi) = P_1(\xi_1)P_1(\xi_2)\ldots P_1(\xi_n)$; $\lvert\xi_1\rvert < \infty$, $\lvert\sigma_{11}\rvert < \infty$.	
The optimal solution in this case is $x_i^* = \frac{1}{n}$, $i = 1,\ldots,n$. Samuelson (1967a) proves these results. He also provides sufficient conditions for x_i^* to be > 0, in particular for independent investments with $\bar{\xi}_1 = \ldots = \bar{\xi}_n$, $x_i^* > 0$, $i = 1,\ldots,n$. Hicks (1962) shows that for u quadratic and independent investments, x_i^* is proportional to $(\bar{\xi}_i - \xi_0)/\sigma_i^2$, where investment "0" is nonrandom. Hadar and Russell (1971,1974a) prove these results and others via stochastic dominance constructs. See Chapter 7 for additional results.			
2. Exponential	$u(w) = 1 - e^{-aw}$ $a > 0$	Joint normal, $\lvert\xi_i\rvert < \infty$, $\lvert\sigma_{ij}\rvert < \infty$	$\left(\sum_{i=1}^{n} \xi_i x_i - \frac{a}{2} \sum_{i=1}^{n} \sum_{j=1}^{n} x_i x_j \sigma_{ij}\right)$ $\equiv \bar{\xi}x - \frac{a}{2} x'\Sigma x$
u is concave in w and hence in x, i.e., this investor is a risk-averter and Z is concave and continuously differentiable and hence is easy to maximize on K. Freund (1956) presented this model. Press (1972a) presents a similar result when ξ has a multivariate stable distribution.			

Table 5-1 Continued

Model	Utility function	Distribution	Deterministic equivalent
3. General		Discrete, $\Pr(\xi = \xi^{\ell}) = P_{\ell} > 0$, $\sum_{\ell=1}^{L} P_{\ell} = 1, \quad L < \infty$	$\sum_{\ell=1}^{L} P_{\ell} u\left[\sum_{i=1}^{n} \xi_i^{\ell} x_i\right] \equiv \phi(x)$

ϕ will have the useful properties of continuity, continuous first and second differentiability, non-negativity, concavity, and strict concavity if u has these respective properties. For L large (the usual case), the computations are severe as the objective has a large number of terms. For convenient u, some form of decomposition type algorithm may be computationally attractive. El-Agizy (1967), Dantzig and Madansky (1961), Pye (1967), and other authors have discussed this model using the discrete assumption.

Model	Utility function	Distribution	Deterministic equivalent
4a. Polynomial	$u(w) = \gamma_0 + \gamma_1 w + \gamma_2 w^2 + \ldots + \gamma_K w^K$	General, first K moments finite	$\sum_{k=1}^{K} \sum_{j=1}^{k} \alpha_{jk} x_1^{\gamma_{jk}^1} \ldots x_n^{\gamma_{jk}^n}$ α's and γ's constant
4b. Quadratic	$u(w) = \gamma_0 + \gamma_1 w + \gamma_2 w^2$	General, first two moments finite	$\gamma_1 \bar{\xi}' x + \gamma_2 x' Z_0 x$ Z_0 is the matrix of second moments about the origin

Richter (1959) first presented this model, which shows that for u a polynomial of degree K only the first K moments count. The converse--namely, that if only the first K moments count then u is a polynomial of degree K--is not true; see Chipman (1973:168). The expressions for Z are derived in Ziemba (1970). Borch (1968) has noted that u polynomial is not a feasible choice for an expected utility maximizer who is risk-averse since polynomial functions have convex and concave portions. Friedman and Savage (1948) have used such a utility function to explain gambling and insurance purchases by an investor.

Table 5-1 Continued

5. Separable asymmetric polynomial	$u(w) = \sum_{i=1}^{n} u_i(w_i)$ $u_i(w_i) = \begin{cases} \alpha_{0i} + \alpha_{1i}w_i + \dots + \alpha_{Ki}w_i^K & \text{if } w_i \geqq 0 \\ \beta_{0i} + \beta_{1i}w_i + \dots + \beta_{Ki}w_i^K & \text{if } w_i < 0 \end{cases}$	General, first K moments finite	$Z(x) = \sum_{i=1}^{m} Z_i(x_i)$ $Z_i(x_i) \equiv \sum_{k=0}^{K} \gamma_{ki}x_i^k$ γ_{ki} constant

When u is separable, only the marginal distributions of the ξ_i enter the calculation of Z(x). Such a function allows for a kink at the origin, which may be of interest when the ξ_i have negative occurrences or when investments are sold short. The mathematics carries through for any finite number of break points. See Ziemba (1970) for details.

6a. Separable; approximated by polynomial		General	Analogous to 4a
6b. General		General; approximated by discrete distribution	Analogous to 3

If u is separable (and continuous) it can be approximated to any degree of accuracy by a polynomial (Stone 1948). Any probability distribution can be approximated to any degree of accuracy by a discrete distribution (Feller 1962,1966).

Table 5-1 Continued

7a. Concave, continuously differentiable	
7b. Concave and continuous	General
7c. Continuous	

Under 7a and mild regularity assumptions, Z is concave and continuously differentiable; see Theorem 5.4. An assumption that one can numerically evaluate $\nabla Z(x) = E_{\xi}u'(\xi'x)$ for all $x \in K$ provides the basis for modification of feasible direction algorithms. See the discussion in Section 5.1.3. Under 7b, Z is concave and an assumption that one can evaluate Z(x) for all $x \in K$ provides the basis for modification of certain nonlinear programming algorithms that do not utilize gradients. The use of the Generalized Programming algorithm for such a purpose is illustrated in Section 5.1.4. Under 7c and mild regularity assumptions, Z is continuous and certain penalty function and methods-of-centers algorithms can be modified as in 7a and 7b and will find the x_i^* if they exist and a number of certain subproblems may be solved; see Ziemba (1972).

Set $x^{k+1} = x^k + \lambda^k d^k$.

3. Terminate if the stopping criteria is satisfied. Otherwise go to (1) with $k = k + 1$.

It is clear then that such algorithms may be used to solve problems having the form of (5.5) as long as Z and ∇Z can be _evaluated_ at any feasible point.

The initialization step may proceed, e.g., by a repeated application of a standard algorithm (Fiacco and McCormick 1968) or by a Simplex Phase 1 procedure (if the g_j are linear). Feasible direction vectors d^k have the property that they do not point out of K, i.e., $\nabla g_j(x^k)'d^k \geqq \varepsilon$ $(\varepsilon > 0)$ for constraints that are active at x^k, i.e., $g_j(x^k) = 0$. The direction-finding subproblem can take a number of forms such as a simplex pivot (in the convex simplex method), or a linear or quadratic program (in various first- and second-order gradient methods, respectively). These calculations may require that Z, ∇Z, and the Hessian matrix $\nabla\nabla Z$ be evaluated at x^k. The step-length calculation, of which that suggested in (2) is one of several possibilities, usually proceeds via a search procedure or an explicit calculation.

Topkis and Veinott (1967, Theorem 2) and Zangwill (1969:281) have proved general convergence theorems for feasible direction methods. Under appropriate assumptions, convergence is guaranteed to a stationary point that will be an optimal point if u is concave and the g_j are concave or quasi-concave.[5] The essential conditions these authors utilize in their convergence proofs that are relevant here is that Z must be continuously differentiable. A set of sufficient conditions implying that ∇Z is continuous and can be easily calculated is contained in Theorem 5.4.

THEOREM 5.4. _Suppose that_ u _is continuously differentiable on_ R _and_

$$|u(\xi'x)| \le d_0(\xi), \quad \left|\frac{\partial u(\xi'x)}{\partial x_i}\right| \le d_i(\xi)$$

for every $\xi \in \Xi$, $x \in K$ _where the_ d_i, $i = 0,\ldots,n$ _are integrable (i.e.,_ have finite integrals) over Ξ. Then Z is continuously differentiable on K and

$$\frac{\partial Z}{\partial x_i} = E_\xi\left[\frac{\partial u(\xi'x)}{\partial x_i}\right], \qquad i = 1,\ldots,n.$$

Proof: See Fleming (1964:199).

The theorem indicates that Z is continuously differentiable (as long as mild regularity assumptions are satisfied) whenever u is continuously differentiable and that the partial derivatives may be calculated by reversing the order of expectation and differentiation.[6] It may be noted that at boundary points of K, $\partial Z/\partial x_i$ is taken to be the one-sided partial derivative.

A number of algorithms such as various penalty function methods, some cutting plane algorithms, and various methods of centers do not utilize direction vectors and converge to an optimal point even if Z (and the g_j) are not continuously differentiable--concavity is required only for the cutting plane methods.[7] These algorithms proceed by solving a sequence of problems that approximate either K or Z.

The convergence proofs given in Zangwill (1969) assume in particular that Z and the g_i are continuous (and that K satisfies certain regularity assumptions). The following theorem presents sufficient conditions for Z to be continuous on K:

THEOREM 5.5. Suppose that u is continuous on R and $|u(\xi'x)| \leq d_0(\xi)$, for every $\xi \in \Xi$, $x \in K$, where d_0 is integrable over Ξ. Then Z is continuous on K.

Proof: See Fleming (1964:198).

5.1.4 Application of the Generalized Programming Algorithm to the Portfolio Selection Problem

In portfolio selection problems, although the optimization problem is to choose n investment allocations, the utility function depends on only the single random variable, wealth. It is clear that in the use of first- and second-order methods, one will need to evaluate multivariate integrals (if the ξ_j do not have discrete distributions). If one considers methods that utilize only function evaluations, however, only univariate integrations are required. One such method that appears to be particularly well suited for such problems is the Dantzig-Wolfe generalized programming algorithm (Dantzig 1963). Let us consider the portfolio problem

$$v_0 = \text{maximum } Z(x) \equiv E_\xi u(\xi'x),$$

$$\text{subject to} \quad Ax \leq b, \; x \geq 0, \tag{5.6}$$

where u is a concave utility function over wealth, $\xi'x$; x is an n x 1 decision vector; A is an m x n matrix of constants; and b is a m x 1 vector of constants. Assume that Z(x) is finite for finite x, that (5.6) has an optimal solution, and that at each iteration the linear program (5.8) (see below) has at least one nondegenerate basic feasible solution.

THEOREM 5.6. (a) *Z is concave in x if u is concave in R*; (b) *Z is strictly concave in x if u is strictly concave in R, and $\xi'x^1 = \xi'x^2$ for all $\xi \in \Xi$ implies*[8] $x^1 = x^2$.

Proof: By the concavity of u,

$$u\{\xi'[\lambda x^1 + (1 - \lambda)x^2]\} \geq \lambda u(\xi'x^1) + (1 - \lambda)u(\xi'x^2)$$

for $0 \leq \lambda \leq 1$, fixed ξ and all $x^1, x^2 \in K$. Taking the expectation of both sides of this inequality gives

$$Z\{\lambda x^1 + (1 - \lambda)x^2\} \geq Z(x^1) + (1 - \lambda)Z(x^2);$$

hence Z is concave. The same argument applies for strict concavity with $x^1 \neq x^2$ and strict inequalities replacing inequalities, under the assumptions.

Thus under reasonable assumptions, Z is continuous and hence (5.6) has a maximum if $\{x|Z(x) \geq \alpha\}$ is nonempty and bounded for all scalers α (Zoutendijk 1960). Since Z is concave, local maxima to (5.6) will be global maxima and the Kuhn-Tucker saddle-point conditions are necessary and sufficient for a global maxima. The maximizing point will be unique in the strict concavity case.

It is our purpose to solve (5.6) without explicitly calculating Z(x) when Z is concave and continuous (but not necessarily continuously differentiable) and Z(x) can be numerically evaluated for any feasible x. The generalized programming algorithm utilizes the simplex method to solve a sequence of linear programs. At each step the linear program adds an additional column that is chosen from a convex set. The determination of this column involves an unconstrained maximization and the discussion here utilizes the cyclic coordinate ascent method [see, e.g., Zangwill (1969] for this purpose.[9]

A generalized linear program that is equivalent to (5.6) is

$$\begin{aligned} &\text{maximize} && \theta\lambda, \\ &\text{subject to} && Ax \leq b,\ x \geq 0, \\ &&& \lambda = 1, \end{aligned} \tag{5.7}$$

where the column

$$\begin{bmatrix} \theta \\ \\ x \end{bmatrix}$$

is to be chosen from the convex set

$$T \equiv \{(\theta, x)|Z(x) \geq \theta\}.$$

Let $(\theta^1, x^1), \ldots, (\theta^L, x^L)$ be L points in T. Then in the Lth iteration one solves the linear program

$$\begin{aligned} \text{maximize} \quad & W = \theta^1\lambda^1 + \ldots + \theta^L\lambda^L , \\ \text{subject to} \quad & A(\lambda^1 x^1 + \ldots + \lambda^L x^L) \leq b \quad : \alpha^L, \\ & \lambda^1 + \ldots + \lambda^L = 1 \quad : \beta^L, \\ & \lambda^1 \geq 0, \ldots, \lambda^L \geq 0. \end{aligned} \tag{5.8}$$

For any value of x^ℓ, $\ell = 1,\ldots,L$, $Z(x^\ell)$ is the largest value θ^ℓ can take in the set T, and it is clear that θ^ℓ does achieve this value.

Let (α^L,β^L) be an optimal dual solution to (5.8) having solution value W^L. By duality

$$W^L = b'\alpha^L + \beta^L.$$

To test for the optimality of the solution $(x^*)^L = \lambda^1 x^1 + \ldots + \lambda^L x^L$, one solves the subproblem

$$\begin{aligned} \text{maximize} \quad & \theta - \alpha^L Ax - \beta^L, \\ \text{subject to} \quad & (\theta,x) \in T \end{aligned} \tag{5.9}$$

Since β^L is a constant and since θ can achieve its largest value $Z(x)$, (5.9) is equivalent to

$$S^L = \text{maximize } S(x) = Z(x) - \alpha^L Ax. \tag{5.10}$$

If $S^L \leqq \beta^L$, then $(x^*)^L$ is optimal. Otherwise any x^{L+1}, such that $S(x^{L+1}) > \beta^L$ with corresponding $\theta^{L+1} = Z(x^{L+1})$ represents a column to be entered into the master program (5.8) for iteration L + 1.

The calculation of an x^{L+1} may proceed via the cyclic coordinate ascent method as follows: Let e_i, $i = 1,\ldots,n$ be unit n-vectors having all coordinates zero except the ith coordinate, which is unity. Given a point x^1, set $x^{10} = x^1$. Determine x^{11} by maximizing $S(x)$ in the positive and negative direction e_2 from x^{11}. Continuing in this manner, after determining x^{12}, determine x^{21}, etc.

The x^{ij} may be determined via a one-dimension Golden Sections search (Zangwill 1969). Under the assumption, it can be shown (Dantzig 1963) that the method converges to an optimal solution to

(5.6) and that at each iteration the following bounds obtain

$$W^L \leq Z[(x^*)^L] \leq v_0 \leq S^L + W^L - \beta^L. \qquad (5.11)$$

Hence one may stop at an ε-optimal solution when $S^L - \beta^L \leqq \varepsilon$.

A flowchart of the procedure appears in Figure 5-1. A similar procedure may be developed for cases in which the constraints are nonlinear (Dantzig 1963).

The use of generalized programming or any other algorithm for the solution of the expected utility portfolio selection problem involves the numerical evaluation of univariate or multivariate integrals (unless the random variables have discrete distributions). The development of approximation schemes for evaluating such integrals as those encountered in the problems considered here is a standard problem in numerical analysis. A number of these methods are presented in Davis and Rabinowitz (1967). The multivariate calculations are usually difficult and computationally time-consuming if one demands high accuracy. The level of difficulty rises much more than linearly with the number of dimensions. Univariate calculations are relatively easy; numerous computer codes exist that will perform univariate numerical integrations quickly with high accuracy. Given the distribution function of the ξ_i, $P(\xi_1,\ldots,\xi_n)$ and a given vector x, one may generate the distribution function of W--say, $G(W|x)$--and the numerical evaluations may utilize G. In general G will not have a simple parametric form unless P is multivariate normal or stable. These later cases are discussed in Section 5.2.

5.1.5 Existence of Optimal Portfolio Policies

Leland (1972) and Bertsekas (1974) have studied the problem of the existence of optimal portfolio policies. In this section we briefly present some of their results that pertain to problems discussed in this chapter. Leland shows that several standard assumptions on the random returns and the utility function are sufficient to guarantee existence of an optimal policy. His conditions are easily checked on any given problem. Bertsekas presents necessary and sufficient

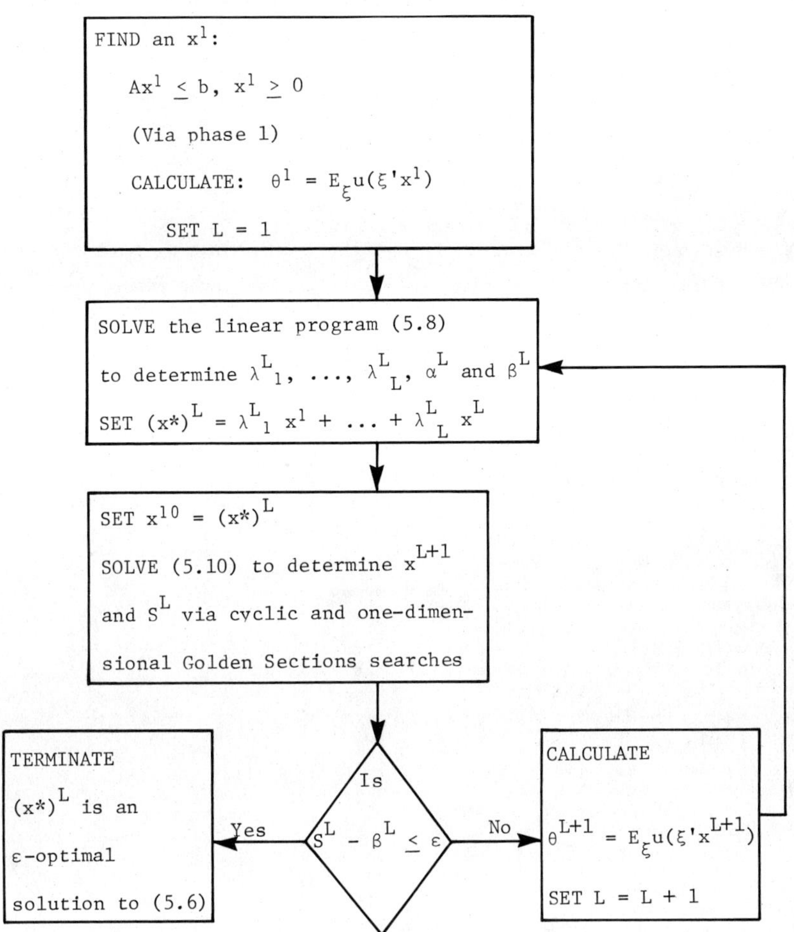

Figure 5-1. Generalized Programming Algorithm Flowchart

conditions that are developed using constructs from the theory of convex analysis (Rockafellar 1970). His conditions have a natural economic interpretation; however, they are generally more difficult to check.

Suppose the problem is

$$\begin{aligned} &\text{maximize} && Z(x) \equiv E_{\xi} u(\xi' x) \\ &\text{subject to} && x \in K \equiv \{x \mid g_j(x) \geq 0,\ j = 1,\ldots,m\}, \end{aligned} \tag{5.5}$$

where u is the investor's utility function over wealth w, there are n risky assets having random returns $\xi_1,\ldots,\xi_n$, the investment in asset i is x_i, i = 1,...,n and the g_j represent constraints on the choice of the x_i. Consider the following assumptions:

A1. K is a closed convex set that contains the origin;

A2. There exists a finite H such that there is no $x^k \in K$ that has the property that $\xi' x^k \geq 0$ except on a set of probability measure zero and

$$\left\{ \sum_{i=1}^{n} (x_i^k)^2 \right\}^{\frac{1}{2}} \geq H;$$

A3. u is strictly increasing and strictly concave;

A4a. Each investment i has a finite mean, i.e.,

$$|\bar{\xi}_i| < \infty \quad \text{and} \quad \lim_{w \to \infty} u'(w) = 0;$$

and

A4b. u(w) is bounded from above.

THEOREM 5.7. <u>If problem (5.5) satisfies assumptions A1-A3 and either A4a or A4b, then an optimal solution</u> x^* <u>exists</u>.

<u>Proof</u>: See Leland (1972).

Remarks:

1. Assumption A2 is equivalent to Hakansson's (1970) no-easy-money assumption and states that no arbitrarily large investment position exists that offers a nonnegative return with probability 1.

2. The theorem indicates that if the means of the random returns are finite, then existence is guaranteed (given A1-A3) if limiting marginal utility is 0, such as when $u(w) = \log w$. Alternatively, if u is bounded above, then existence is guaranteed even if the mean returns are infinite. Hence existence is guaranteed when u is negative-exponential and w has a log stable distribution.

3. If u is not concave, then even if u is bounded an optimal portfolio may fail to exist; for example, an investor with zero initial wealth and the utility function $u(w) = w/(w + 1)$ for $w \geq 0$ and $-w/(w + 1)$ if $w < 0$ will want to partake in an arbitrarily large amount of a gamble to receive \$1 with probability 3/4, lose \$1 with probability 1/4. If K is bounded, then obviously by Weierstrass's Theorem x^* will exist as long as Z is continuous.

4. Leland's theorem indicates that an optimal portfolio may exist even if $Z(x)$ is unbounded from below for all $x \neq 0$. For example, $x = 0$ is an optimal portfolio when the returns have Cauchy distributions and u is linear.

   Bertsekas uses different assumptions than Leland does, but they are neither weaker nor stronger. In particular, he assumes that:

   B1. K is a nonempty closed convex set;

   B2. u is monotone nondecreasing and concave; and

   B3. For every $x \in R^n$ the expected return and expected utility are finite, i.e., $E|\bar{\xi}'x| < \infty$ and $E|u(\xi'x)| < \infty$.

The analysis utilizes the notion of a direction of recession of a convex set, that is, a direction along which the set is unbounded. Formally, a vector $d \neq 0$ is a direction of recession of a closed convex set $K \subset R^n$ if $x^0 + \lambda d \in K$ for some (and hence for every) x^0 and all $\lambda \geq 0$. For the concave function Z, the vector $c \neq 0$ is a direction of recession of Z if $Z(x^0 + \lambda c)$ is a monotonically nondecreasing function of λ for some (and hence for every) $x^0 \in R^n$. Let

$$s^+ \equiv \lim_{w\to\infty} \frac{du(w)}{dw}$$

and

$$s^- \equiv \lim_{w\to-\infty} \frac{du(w)}{dw}$$

be the asymptotic slopes of u, where $0 \leq s^+ \leq s^- \leq \infty$. Define $s^* \equiv s^-/s^+$, using the conventions $s^* = \infty$ if $s^- = \infty$ or $s^- > 0$ and $s^+ = 0$, and $s^* = 0$ if $s^- = s^+ = 0$. The scalar s^* may be interpreted as a measure of risk aversion associated with the utility function u because s^* is related to the Arrow-Pratt risk-aversion index via

$$\ell n s^* = \lim_{a\to\infty} \int_{-a}^{a} \left[\frac{-u''(w)}{u'(w)}\right] dw.$$

It may be noted that s^* is invariant to positive linear transformations of u.

For $d \in R^n$, $d \neq 0$ let

$$p(d) \equiv \frac{E\{\xi'd \mid \xi'd > 0\}P_r\{\xi'd > 0\}}{E\{-\xi'd \mid \xi'd < 0\}P_r\{\xi'd < 0\}},$$

using the convention $p(d) = \infty$ if $P_r\{\xi'd < 0\} = 0$.

The ratio p(d) may be interpreted as a measure of expected profitability of holding assets in fixed ratios specified by the direction d. Let $p^* = \{\max p(d) \mid d$ is a direction of recession of K$\}$.

THEOREM 5.8. (a) Problem (5.5) has a nonempty and compact solution set if and only if the convex set K and the concave function Z have no common direction of recession.

(b) A vector $d \neq 0$ such that $Z(x^0 + \lambda d)$ is a direction of recession of Z if and only if $p(d) \geq s^*$.

(c) Problem (5.5) has a nonempty and compact solution set, and hence an optimal policy x^*, if and only if $p^* < s^*$.

(d) Suppose in B3 it is not assumed that the expected return is finite, but only that expected utility is finite. Then optimal policy x^* exists if $s^+ = 0$, $s^- > 0$, and $P_r(\xi'd < 0) > 0$ for all directions of recession d of K.

Proof: (a) See Rockafellar (1970:Theorems 27.1, 27.3); (b)-(d) see Bertsekas (1974).

Remarks:

1. The main result (c) provides a test for the existence of x^* and states that an optimal policy exists whenever there is no direction in which the expected profitability p(d) is exceeded by the measure s^* of the investor's risk aversion.

2. Under assumptions B1-B3, (c) implies Leland's theorem 5.7, which is the case when $s^+ = 0$, and $P_r\{\xi'd < 0\} > 0$ for all directions of recession d of K.

3. Existence is guaranteed if $s^- = \infty$ and $P_r\{\xi'd < 0\} > 0$ for all directions of recession d of K. Such a result is useful if u is logarithmic.

4. When $p^* = s^*$, problem (5.5) either has no feasible solution or there is a nonempty but unbounded solution set.

5. The calculation of s^* is extremely simple, but the calculation of p^* is more complicated, because in general the ratio p(d) must be computed for many d.

5.2 The Two-Stage Approach: Mean-Dispersion Analysis Is Optimal

5.2.1 Introduction

In this section we shall discuss the so-called two-stage approach to portfolio selection in the case when the returns have normal or symmetric stable distributions and the investor is permitted to invest in a risk-free asset. Let $\hat{x} \equiv (x_1,\ldots,x_n)'$ denote the vector of portfolio allocations made for the n risky assets and let x_0 be the allocation made to the safe asset. The vector of risky asset returns is $\hat{\xi} \equiv (\xi_1,\ldots,\xi_n)'$ and the safe asset has the fixed return $\bar{\xi}_0$. For notational convenience let $x' \equiv (x_0,\hat{x}')$ and $\xi' \equiv (\bar{\xi}_0,\hat{\xi}')$. We suppose that there are no constraints on x_0, save the budget constraint. The constraints on $\hat{x}$ are assumed to be described by the homogeneous inequalities,[10] $g_j(\hat{x}) \geq 0$, $j = 1,\ldots,m$, as well as the budget constraint. The investor's problem is

$$\begin{array}{ll} \text{maximize} & E_\xi u(\xi' x), \\ \text{subject to} & x_0 + e'\hat{x} = 1,\ g_j(\hat{x}) \geq 0,\ j = 1,\ldots,m, \end{array} \tag{5.12}$$

where u, the investor's utility function is assumed to be monotone nondecreasing, and concave, and $e \equiv (1,\ldots,1)'$. The two-stage procedure operates as follows: (1) with knowledge only that u is concave and nondecreasing, find the subset X of the feasible region that contains all the points that are optimal for some u in this class; (2) with a specific u in this class, find an x* that solves (5.12). The two-stage procedure was suggested by Lintner (1965). Ziemba et al. (1974) showed how to perform the second stage calculations.

The results may be summarized as follows: The normal distribution has an important place in the theory of portfolio selection because the Markowitz (1959) mean-variance theory is then consistent with expected utility maximization. In this case it is known that an optimal solution to problems having the form of (5.12) must lie on a mean-standard deviation efficient surface.

Stable distributions have increasing interest for the empirical explanation of asset price changes and other economic phenomena. An important reason for this is that all limiting sums (that exist) of independent identically distributed random variables are stable. If the variance exists, they are normally distributed. Thus it is reasonable to suspect that empirical variables that are sums of random variables conform to stable laws. Such an observation has led to a substantial body of literature concerned with the estimation of the distributions of stock price changes [see Fama (1965a, 1970a) for a survey of this work] and other economic variables [see, e.g., Mandelbrot (1963a,b)] utilizing stable distributions. Much of this literature focuses on the fact that the empirical distributions have more "outliers" and hence "fatter" tails than one would expect to be generated by a normal distribution. This leads to the conclusion that variance does not exist and that a normal distribution will not adequately fit the data.[11]

Utilizing the fact that linear combinations of symmetric stable distributions (having the same characteristic exponent, see Section 5.2.2) have symmetric univariate stable distributions, it follows that a mean-dispersion (μ - d) analysis is consistent with expected utility maximization as long as the mean exists. The calculation of the μ - d curve is generally quite difficult because one must solve a parametric concave program. When a risk-free asset exists, however, the efficient surface is a ray in (μ - d) space and a generalization of Tobin's (1958) separation theorem obtains. One may then calculate the optimal proportions of the risky assets by solving a fractional program. The character of the fractional program depends, of course, on the assumptions made about the joint distribution of the stable random variables. In fairly general circumstances, however, the fractional program has a pseudo-concave objective function and hence may be solved via a standard nonlinear programming algorithm. Typically the optimal solution is unique. The fractional program has an objective that is homogeneous of degree zero, and hence the budget constraint may be deleted from the calculation of the optimal proportions of the risky assets. The proportions found are then scaled to sum to one to form the optimal proportions. In the normal distribution case the fractional program is equivalent to a simple quadratic program (if the g_j are linear).

In the second stage one introduces the investor's utility function and an optimal ratio between a stable composite asset and the risk-free asset must be chosen. The composite asset is a sum of the risky stable assets where the weights are determined from the solution of the fractional program in stage one. The problem to solve is a stochastic program having a single random variable and a single decision variable. Such problems are generally easy to solve if the density of the random variable is known as it is in the normal distribution case. One simply combines a univariate numerical integration scheme with a procedure designed to search an interval such as the Golden Sections or Bisecting search procedures. Some numerical calculations using this procedure appear in Ziemba et al. (1974).

For certain utility functions--such as the quadratic, cubic, and exponential--an explicit deterministic equivalent exists whose solution may be easily found by differentiation. The situation with the stable composite asset is more complicated because its density is known only in a few special cases. However, Fama and Roll (1968) using series approximations due to Bergstrom, have tabulated, at discrete points, the density and cumulative distributions of a standardized symmetric stable distribution. These tables may be used to obtain a good non-linear programming approximation to the stochastic program. The solution of the nonlinear program generally provides a good approximation to the optimal solution of the stochastic program and hence of the portfolio problem. Some numerical calculations appear in Section 5.2.4.

5.2.2 Elementary Properties of Normal and Stable Distributions[12]

Let $\xi \equiv (\xi_1,\ldots,\xi_n)'$ be random variables having a joint cumulative distribution function $P(\xi_1,\ldots,\xi_n)$ and density $p(\xi_1,\ldots,\xi_n)$. If ξ has a joint normal distribution then

$$p(\xi) = \frac{1}{(2\pi)^{n/2}|\Sigma|^{\frac{1}{2}}}\exp\{-\tfrac{1}{2}(\xi - \bar{\xi})'\Sigma^{-1}(\xi - \bar{\xi})\} ,$$

where $\bar{\xi}$ denotes the mean vector and Σ denotes the n x n variance-covariance matrix having typical element $\sigma_{ij} = E(\xi_i - \bar{\xi}_i)'(\xi_j - \bar{\xi}_j)$. The notation $N(\bar{\xi},\Sigma)$ refers to a set of joint normally distributed random variables having mean vector $\bar{\xi}$ and variance-covariance matrix Σ. The assumption that individual assets have normal distributions is tantamount to assuming that these assets are composed of the summation of many independent effects. Mathematically, if $y_1,y_2,\ldots$ is a sequence of independent identically distributed random variables with mean μ and variance σ^2 and

$$\bar{y}_m = \sum_{k=1}^{m} \frac{y_k}{m} ,$$

then the limiting distribution of $\sqrt{m}(\overline{y}_m - \mu)$ as $m \to \infty$ is $N(0,\sigma^2)$, as long as the sequence converges and has finite variance. The expression

$$\mu + \sqrt{m}(\overline{y}_m - \mu) \to N(\mu,\sigma^2) \quad \text{as } m \to \infty.$$

The result in the multivariate case may be stated as follows: if $y_1, y_2, \ldots$ is a sequence of independent identically distributed vectors with mean vector μ and variance-covariance matrix Σ and

$$\overline{y}_m = \sum_{k=1}^{m} \frac{y_k}{m},$$

then the limiting distribution of $\mu + \sqrt{m}(\overline{y}_m - \mu) \to N(\mu,\Sigma)$, as long as the sequence converges and the components of Σ are finite. Other weaker central limit theorems are of course available; see, e.g., Feller (1962, 1966). In each case one is concerned with the summation of many independent or weakly correlated random variables.

An important property of normal distributions of particular relevance for the portfolio selection problem is that normal distributions are closed on addition. Hence the linear sum

$$w \equiv \sum_{i=1}^{n} \xi_i x_i \equiv \xi' x \sim N(\overline{\xi}' x, x' \Sigma x)$$

has a univariate normal distribution having mean $\overline{\xi}'x$ and variance $x'\Sigma x$.

Since $x'\Sigma x \geq 0$ because it is a variance, the matrix Σ is positive semidefinite. Throughout this chapter we shall assume that Σ is in fact positive definite so that $x'\Sigma x > 0$ for all $x \neq 0$, for otherwise one or more of the assets are merely linear combinations of the other assets. It is often useful to utilize the standardized normal variate

$$z \equiv \frac{w - \overline{\xi}' x}{(x' \Sigma x)^{\frac{1}{2}}} \sim N(0,1).$$

It will be necessary to assume that expected utility is finite. For an unbounded u, Theorems 5.1-5.3 are not general enough to cover this case. The difficulty is that u(w) can be too small (approaching $-\infty$) for very small values of w(approaching $-\infty$). Chipman (1973) has shown that a sufficient condition for expected utility to be finite is that there exist positive constants A and B such that

$$|u(w)| \leq Ae^{Bw^2}$$

and the convergence applies whenever $x'\Sigma x < 1/\sqrt{2B}$. Since u is concave, it is continuous on R; the condition may be generalized to read that

$$\lim_{w \to -\infty} \frac{|u(w)|}{Ae^{Bw^2}} = L$$

for some $0 \leq L < \infty$.

If u is continuously differentiable, then Chipman's condition is also sufficient to guarantee the existence of continuous partial derivatives of $Z(x) \equiv E_\xi u(\xi'x)$. One may differentiate under the integral sign to calculate the partial derivatives via

$$\partial Z(x)/\partial x_i = E_\xi\left[\frac{du(\xi'x)}{dw}\ \xi_i\right].$$

Many common utility functions satisfy Chipman's condition. In cases when u(w) is undefined for $w \leq 0$, however, it is necessary to append a concave segment to u in the range $(-\infty, w_0]$ for some $w_0 > 0$. In the logarithmic case, using a linear segment one obtains

$$u(w) = \begin{cases} \log w & \text{if } w \geq w_0 \\ \frac{w}{w_0} + \log(w_0) - 1 & \text{if } w \leq w_0. \end{cases}$$

Many assets have empirical distributions in which the probability of either a very small or a very large change is much greater than could be explained using a normality assumption. One explanation, which retains the closed-on addition property, is to assume that the assets have stable Paretian distributions. Stable distributions are generalizations of the normal distribution to the case where the variance is not finite. They may be supposed to be of practical relevance where asset prices are assumed to be composed of many independent effects. If ξ is a stable variate, then its distribution function $P(\xi)$ has parameters $\bar{\xi}$, S, β, and α, written $P(\bar{\xi},S,\beta,\alpha)$. Mathematically P is stable if and only if for all $a_1 > 0$, $a_2 > 0$, and b_1, b_2 there exists an $a > 0$ and b such that

$$P\left(\frac{\xi - b}{a}\right) = P\left(\frac{\xi - b_1}{a_1}\right) * P\left(\frac{\xi - b_2}{a_2}\right),$$

where * denotes the convolution operation. Thus stable variates are precisely those distributions that are closed upon addition of independent identically distributed random variables. Indeed one has the following central limit theorem result: Suppose $y_1, y_2, \ldots$ is a sequence of independent identically distributed random variables with mean μ, characteristic exponent $\alpha > 1$, skewness parameter β and dispersion S. Let

$$\bar{y}_m = \sum_{k=1}^{m} \frac{y_k}{m} .$$

Then the limiting distribution of

$$m^{1-(1/\alpha)}(\bar{y}_m - \mu)$$

as $m \to \infty$ is $P(0,S,\beta,\alpha)$, as long as the sequence converges. The expression

$$\mu + m^{1-(1/\alpha)}(\bar{y}_m - \mu) \to P(\mu,S,\beta,\alpha) \quad \text{as } m \to \infty.$$

[See Gnedenko and Kolmogorov (1954) for more detail and a discussion of multivariate stable central limit theorems.]

If the variance is finite, then it necessarily follows that $\alpha = 2$, $\beta = 0$, $S = \frac{1}{2}\sigma^2$, and $P(\mu,S,0,2) = N(\mu,\sigma^2)$.

Stable variates are unimodal and absolutely continuous, and they have continuous densities p. The density is, unfortunately, known in only the cases when α, the characteristic exponent, is $\frac{1}{2}$ (the arc sine), 1 (the Cauchy) and 2 (the normal). Absolute moments or order less than α exist, where $0 \leq \alpha \leq 2$. Variances fail to exist if $\alpha < 2$. The parameter $-1 \leq \beta \leq 1$ is related to the skewness of the distribution. When $\beta > 0$ (< 0), the distribution is skewed to the right (left). We shall assume that P is symmetric, hence $\beta = 0$. The parameter $\bar{\xi}$ is called the central tendency and is the mean if $\alpha > 1$. We shall assume that $1 < \alpha \leq 2$. The parameter $S \geq 0$ refers to the dispersion of the distribution. When P is normal (i.e., $\alpha = 2$, $\beta = 0$) S is half the variance. In general, $S^{1/\alpha}$ is approximately equal to the semi-interquartile range. We shall assume that $S > 0$; hence the stable variate is nontrivial. The expression $S^{1/\alpha}$ is called the α-dispersion and is proportional to the mean absolute deviation $E|\xi - \bar{\xi}|$. The α-dispersion plays the same role in a stable variate that the standard deviation plays in a normal distribution. If $\xi \sim P(\bar{\xi},S,0,\alpha)$, then $(\xi - \bar{\xi})/S^{1/\alpha}$ has the standardized distribution $P(0,1,0,\alpha)$.

Since p is known in closed form in only very special cases, one most conveniently studies the stable family using the characteristic function

$$\psi_\xi(t) \equiv \int_{-\infty}^{\infty} e^{it\xi}\, p(\xi)d\xi$$

where $i = \sqrt{-1}$. The log of the characteristic function of a symmetric stable variate $P(\bar{\xi},S,0,\alpha)$ is

$$\ln \psi_\xi(t) = i\bar{\xi}t - S|t|^\alpha .$$

A portfolio

$$\sum_{i=1}^{n} \xi_i x_i$$

of independent stable variates $P(\bar{\xi}_i, S_i, 0, \alpha)$ having the same characteristic exponent may be easily shown (by multiplying the individual characteristic functions) to have the stable distribution

$$P\left(\sum_{i=1}^{n} \bar{\xi}_i x_i, \quad \sum_{i=1}^{n} S_i |x_i|^{\alpha}, \ 0, \ \alpha\right).$$

A set of random variables $\xi \equiv (\xi_1, \ldots, \xi_n)'$ is said to be multivariate stable if every linear combination of ξ is univariate stable. The characteristic function of ξ is

$$\psi_{\xi}(t) \equiv Ee^{it'\xi} = \int_{-\infty}^{\infty} \cdots \int_{-\infty}^{\infty} e^{it'\xi} \, p(\xi) d\xi_1, \ldots, d\xi_n ,$$

where p is the density of ξ. If $p(\xi)$ is symmetric, then the log characteristic function [see Ferguson (1955)] is

$$\ln \psi_{\xi}(t) = i \, \delta(t) - \gamma(t) ,$$

where the dispersion measure $\gamma(\lambda t_1, \ldots, \lambda t_n) = |\lambda|^{\alpha} \gamma(t_1, \ldots, t_n)$, is positively homogeneous of degree α, $\gamma > 0$ and the central tendency measure δ is homogeneous. The characteristic exponent α is assumed to satisfy $1 < \alpha \leq 2$. With specific choices of δ and γ, one may generate many classes of (symmetric) multivariate stable laws. We shall mention those classes of multivariate stable variates due to Press and Samuelson.

Press (1972b,c) has developed a statistical theory along with associated estimation procedures for particularly convenient choices of δ and γ. Let $\bar{\xi}' \equiv (\bar{\xi}_1, \ldots, \bar{\xi}_n)$ be the mean of ξ, which will exist if $\alpha > 1$. Press sets

$$\delta(t) = \bar{\xi}'t$$

and

$$\gamma(t) = \tfrac{1}{2} \sum_{j=1}^{m} (t'\Omega_j t)^{\alpha/2}$$

where $n \geqq m \geqq 1$ and each Ω_j is a positive semidefinite matrix of order $n \times n$. The log characteristic function is then

$$\ln \psi_\xi(t) = i\bar{\xi}'t - \tfrac{1}{2} \sum_{j=1}^{m} (t'\Omega_j t)^{\alpha/2} \ .$$

The m indicates the number of independent partitions of the random variables $(\xi_1, \ldots, \xi_n)$. Hence if $m = 1$, all the random variables are dependent (as long as Ω_1 is positive definite). Then if $\alpha = 2$ (the case of normal distributions) one obtains

$$\gamma(t) = \tfrac{1}{2} t'\Omega_1 t \ ,$$

which is precisely half the variance of the linear sum $t'\xi$. If $m = n$, the random variables are independent. In this case with $\alpha = 2$, one may interpret $\gamma(t)$ as half the variance by setting the jjth coefficient of Ω_j equal to $\omega_j > 0$ (and all other coefficients equal to zero). Then

$$\gamma(t) = \tfrac{1}{2} \sum_{j=1}^{m} (t'\Omega_j t) = \tfrac{1}{2} \sum_{j=1}^{n} \omega_j t_j^2 \ .$$

If $x \equiv (x_1, \ldots, x_n)'$, then the linear form $\xi'x$ has the symmetric univariate stable distribution

$$P(\bar{\xi}'x, \tfrac{1}{2} \sum_{j=1}^{m} (x'\Omega_j x)^{\alpha/2}, 0, \alpha) \ .$$

The standardized variate

$$z \equiv \frac{\xi'x - \bar{\xi}'x}{\left[\tfrac{1}{2} \sum_{j=1}^{m} (x'\Omega_j x)^{\alpha/2}\right]^{1/\alpha}} \sim P(0, 1, 0, \alpha) \ .$$

Samuelson (1967b) has developed an additional class of multivariate stable variates. Suppose each

$$\xi_i = \sum_{j=1}^{k} b_{ij} y_j$$

where each y_j has the independent stable distribution $P(\bar{y}_j, S_j, 0, \alpha)$ and the b_{ij} are known constants. Then the portfolio

$$\sum_{i=1}^{n} \xi_i x_i$$

has the univariate stable distribution

$$P(\sum_{i=1}^{n} \bar{\xi}_i x_i, \sum_{j=1}^{k} | \sum_{i=1}^{n} b_{ij} x_i|^{\alpha} S_j, 0, \alpha) .$$

Finally we assume that expected utility is finite. For the univariate stable variate $w \sim P(\bar{w}, S, 0, \alpha)$ with $0 \leq S < \infty$, $|\bar{w}| < \infty$ and $1 < \alpha \leq 2$, $|E\ u(w)| < \infty$ if $|u(w)| \leq L_1 |w|^{\gamma_1}$ for some $\gamma_1 < \alpha$ and $0 \leq L_1 < \infty$. Thus the expected utility integral is convergent if the utility function is never steeper than a polynomial of order $< \alpha$. As in the normal distribution case, the hypothesis may be generalized to read that

$$\lim_{w \to -\infty} \frac{|u(w)|}{|w|^{\gamma}} = v_1$$

for some $0 \leq v_1 < \infty$ and $\gamma < \alpha$. If u is continuously differentiable, then the following assumptions are sufficient for the existence of continuous partial derivatives of $Z(x)$:

$$|u'(w)| \leq L_2 |w|^{\gamma_2}$$

for some $\gamma_2 < \alpha - 1$ and some $0 \leq L_2 < \infty$; or more generally,

$$\lim_{w \to -\infty} \frac{|u'(w)|}{|w|^{\gamma_2}} = v_2$$

for some $\gamma_2 < \alpha - 1$ and some $0 \leq v_2 < \infty$. If $w = \xi'x$, then

$$\frac{\partial Z}{\partial x_i} = E_\xi \left[\frac{du(\xi'x)}{dw} \xi_i \right] .$$

See Ziemba (1974a) for proofs. Most common utility functions either do not satisfy the convergence conditions [e.g., $-e^{-w}$, $w - \beta w^2 (\beta > 0)$] or are undefined for $w \leq 0$ [e.g., log w, $w^\alpha (0 < \alpha < 1)$]. Hence one must append concave sections to these utility functions from below and/or above. In the exponential case, using a linear segment one obtains

$$u(w) = \begin{cases} -e^{-w} & \text{if } w \geq w_0 \\ -(1 + w_0)e^{-w_0} + (e^{-w_0})w & \text{if } w \leq w_0 \end{cases} \quad \text{where } 0 > w_0 > -\infty .$$

5.2.3 Separation, Efficiency, and Properties of the First- and Second-Stage Problems

The problem is

$$\begin{aligned} &\text{maximize} && E_\xi u(\xi'x), \\ &\text{subject to} && x_0 + e'\hat{x} = 1,\ g_j(\hat{x}) \geq 0,\ j = 1,\ldots,m, \end{aligned} \tag{5.12}$$

where u is a monotone nondecreasing concave function, the g_j are homogeneous concave functions that contain the constraints $\hat{x} \geq 0$, $e \equiv (1,\ldots,1)'$, x_0 is the investment allocation in the safe asset at return $\bar{\xi}_0$, and $\hat{x}$ is the n-vector of investment allocations in the risky assets returning $\hat{\xi}$, and $x' \equiv (x_0, \hat{x}')$ and $\xi' \equiv (\bar{\xi}_0, \hat{\xi}')$. Assume that $\hat{\xi}$ has either the joint normal distribution $N(\hat{\bar{\xi}}, \Sigma)$ or a symmetric jointly dependent stable distribution with mean $\hat{\bar{\xi}}$, characteristic exponent $\alpha (1 < \alpha \leq 2)$ and dispersion

$$\gamma(t) = \tfrac{1}{2} \sum_{j=1}^{m} (t'\Omega_j t)^{\alpha/2} .$$

The following stochastic dominance result indicates that it is sufficient to limit consideration to only those feasible points that lie on a mean-standard deviation (normal case) or a mean-α-dispersion (stable case) efficient surface.

THEOREM 5.9. *Suppose* $E(x) \sim P(\mu_1,S_1,0,\alpha)$ *and* $H(y) \sim P(\mu_2,S_2,0,\alpha)$ *are distinct stable (or in the case* $\alpha = 2$, *normal) distributions, where* $|\mu_i| < \infty$, $0 < S_i < \infty$, $1 < \alpha \leq 2$, $\mu_1 \geq \mu_2$, *and* $E(z) > H(z)$ *for some* z. *Then* $Eu(w)dE(w) \geq Eu(w)dH(w)$ *for all convergent*[13] *concave nondecreasing* u *if and only if* $S_1^{1/\alpha} \leq S_2^{1/\alpha}$.

Proof: Sufficiency: (a) Suppose $\mu_1 = \mu_2 = 0$. Let $k = S_2^{1/\alpha}/S_1^{1/\alpha} \geq 1$. Then

$$\begin{aligned} &Eu(w)dH(w) - Eu(w)dE(w) \\ &= \int_{-\infty}^{\infty} [u(kw) - u(w)]dE(w) \quad \text{(by symmetry)} \\ &= \int_0^{\infty} \underbrace{\{[u(kw) - u(w)] - [u(-w) - u(-kw)]\}}_{\leq\, 0 \text{ (by concavity)}} dE(w) \leq 0. \end{aligned}$$

(b) Suppose $\mu_1 \geq \mu_2$. Let $\tilde{E}$ and $\tilde{H}$ be the cumulative distributions for x and y, respectively, when their means are translated to zero. Let $\varepsilon \equiv \mu_1 - \mu_2 \geq 0$. Then

$$\begin{aligned} \int u(w)dH(w) &= \int u(w + \mu_2)d\tilde{H}(w) \leq \int u(w + \mu_2)d\tilde{E}(w) \\ &\leq \int u(w + \mu_2 + \varepsilon)d\tilde{E}(w) = \int u(w)dE(w) \end{aligned}$$

where the first inequality follows from (a).

Necessity: For any $\mu_1 \geq \mu_2$ having $S_1 > S_2$ and a given α, a concave nondecreasing u can be found such that $Eu(w)dE(w) < Eu(w)dH(w)$, since E and H cross only once, see Theorem 3 in Hanoch and Levy (1969).

Theorem 5.9 provides validity for a mean-dispersion approach to the expected utility portfolio selection problem (5.12). Proofs of this result in the normal distribution case appear in Hanoch and Levy (1969), Hillier (1969), and elsewhere. The (sufficiency) proof is a slight generalization of that given by Hillier to apply for stable distributions as well. The result indicates that mean-variance or mean-dispersion analysis is optimal whenever the returns have a two-parameter distribution where the two parameters are independent functions of mean and dispersion (or variance). Hence uniform or even chance two-point distributions over wealth are allowed. However, for wealth defined as $w = \Sigma\xi_i x_i$ for general x_i, the normal or stable assumption is a strict requirement for the validity of the mean-standard deviation (mean-variance) or mean-α-dispersion approach.[14] Hence investments with higher means and smaller variances are not generally preferable for all risk-averse investors unless the returns are normal. Also, investments having a higher mean and a higher dispersion may be preferable for all risk-averse investors if $P(\xi)$ is non-stable. See Hanoch and Levy (1969) for counterexamples.

We shall assume that the measure of α-dispersion, $f(\hat{x}) = [\gamma(\hat{x})]^{1/\alpha}$, is positive, positively homogeneous [i.e., $f(\lambda\hat{x}) = \lambda f(\hat{x})$ for $\lambda > 0$] and convex. Some facts concerning the convexity of f for specific P are given in Theorem 5.10:

THEOREM 5.10. (a) _Suppose_ $P(\hat{\xi}) \sim N(\bar{\xi},\not{\Sigma})$, _where_ $\not{\Sigma}$ _is positive definite. Then_

$$f(\hat{x}) = \frac{1}{\sqrt{2}}(\hat{x}'\not{\Sigma}\hat{x})^{\frac{1}{2}}$$

is strictly convex on the feasible set $F \equiv \{\hat{x} | e'x = 1 - x_0, g_j(\hat{x}) \geq 0, j = 1,\ldots,m\}$, _for_ $-\infty < x_0 \leq 1$.

(b) _Suppose the_ ξ_i _have mutually independent stable distributions_ $P(\xi_i) = P(\bar{\xi}_i, S_i, 0, \alpha)$, $S_i > 0$, _then_

$$f(\hat{x}) = \left\{ \sum_{i=1}^{n} \bar{\xi}_i x_i^{\alpha} \right\}^{1/\alpha}$$

is strictly convex on F.

(c) *Suppose the* ξ_i *have a "totally dependent" stable distribution with* m = 1 *and* Ω_1 *positive definite, then*

$$f(\hat{x}) = \left(\frac{1}{2}\right)^{1/\alpha} (\hat{x}'\Omega_1\hat{x})^{1/2}$$

is strictly convex on F.

(d) *Suppose the* ξ_i *have a partially "dependent" stable distribution, with* n > m > 1 *and each* n x n *matrix* Ω_j *is positive semidefinite and some* Ω_j *is positive definite, then*

$$f(\hat{x}) = \left\{ \tfrac{1}{2} \sum_{j=1}^{m} (\hat{x}'\Omega_j\hat{x})^{\alpha/2} \right\}^{1/\alpha}$$

is convex on F.

(e) *Suppose the* ξ_i *belong to Samuelson's class of stable distributions where each* S_j > 0. *Then*

$$f(\hat{x}) = \left\{ \sum_{j=1}^{k} \left| \sum_{i=1}^{n} a_{ij}x_i \right|^{\alpha} S_j^{\alpha} \right\}^{1/\alpha}$$

is convex on F.

Proof: See Ziemba (1974a).

The efficient surface may be obtained by solving

$$\phi(\beta) \equiv \text{maximize} \quad \bar{\xi}'x,$$
$$\text{subject to} \quad x_0 + e'\hat{x} = 1,$$
$$g_j(\hat{x}) \geq 0, \ j = 1,\ldots,m,$$
$$f(\hat{x}) \leq \beta, \tag{5.13}$$

for all $\beta > 0$. If $x_0 = 0$, the optimal objective value, say, $\phi_0(\beta)$, is a concave function of β (see Figure 5-2). For general x_0, $\phi(\beta)$ consists of all points on the ray L that evolves from the point (mean $= \bar{\xi}_0$, α-dispersion = 0) and supports the function $\phi_0(\beta)$ at the point M having mean $= \bar{\xi}_c$ and α-dispersion $= S_c^{1/\alpha}$. Since both $\bar{\hat{\xi}}'\hat{x}$ and $f(\hat{x})$ are positively homogeneous, points on L are linear combinations of $x_0 = 1$ (total investment in the safe asset assuming $\hat{x} \geq 0$) and the point M. Since L is a ray, it is clear that the optimal ratios of the risky assets, namely,

$$x_i^* \Big/ \sum_{j=1}^{n} x_j^*, \quad i \neq 0$$

are independent of u. Hence all investors having concave, nondecreasing utility functions will invest their wealth in a combination of the risky composite asset, i.e., mutual fund M and the safe asset i = 0. This is Tobin's (1958) famous separation theorem[15] that was initially proved for the normal distribution case. Breen (1968) and Stone (1970) have presented separation theorems in which it is shown that separation crucially depends on the homogeneity of f. Our statement and proof is motivated by Bradley (n.d.) who has shown that the result still obtains when homogeneous g_j type constraints are included in the formulation.

THEOREM 5.11. Let the efficiency problem be given by (5.13), where it is assumed that the g_j are homogeneous concave functions and contain the constraints $\hat{x} \geq 0$, f is positive, convex, and positively homogeneous, $\beta > 0$, and also that u is nondecreasing and concave and (5.12) has an optimal solution x^*.

Then the relative proportions invested in the risky assets

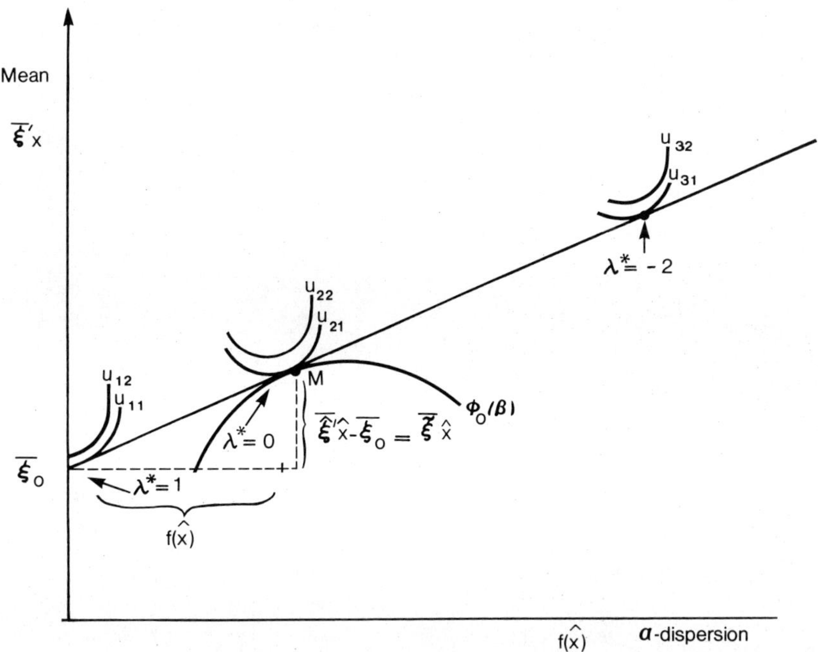

Figure 5-2. Geometry of the Generalized Tobin Separation Theorem

$$x_i^* \Big/ \sum_{j=1}^{n} x_j^*, \quad i \neq 0$$

are independent of u.

Proof: Suppose $x_0^* \neq 0$. Since x* solves (5.12), it must solve (5.13) for some β. Hence it must satisfy the Kuhn-Tucker conditions for (5.13) (which are necessary[16] and sufficient under the assumptions):

(a) $$f(\hat{x}) \leq \beta, \; g_j(\hat{x}) \geq 0,$$

$$j = 1,\ldots,m, \quad x_0 + e'\hat{x} = 1,$$

(b) (i)
$$\bar{\xi}_i - \lambda \frac{\partial f(\hat{x})}{\partial x_i} - \mu + \sum_{j=1}^{m} \alpha_j \frac{\partial g_j(\hat{x})}{\partial x_i} = 0,$$

$$i = 1,\ldots,n,$$

(ii)
$$\bar{\xi}_0 - \mu = 0,$$

and

(c)
$$\lambda \geq 0,\ \alpha_j \geq 0, \quad j = 1,\ldots,m.$$

It will suffice to show that for all $\sigma > 0$ there exists a $\gamma \neq 0$ such that $x^{**} \equiv (\gamma x_0^*, \sigma x_1^*,\ldots,\sigma x_n^*)$ also solves the Kuhn-Tucker conditions for all $\beta^{**} \geqq \beta\sigma$. Conditions (a) are satisifed because

$$f(\hat{x}^*) \leq \beta \Rightarrow f(\sigma\hat{x}^*) = \sigma f(\hat{x}^*) \leq \sigma\beta$$

$$g_j(\hat{x}^*) \geq 0 \Rightarrow g_j(\sigma\hat{x}^*) = \sigma g_j(\hat{x}^*) \geq 0,$$

$$x_0^* + e'\hat{x}^* = 1 \Rightarrow \gamma x_0^* + \sigma e'\hat{x}^* = 1$$

for

$$\gamma \equiv \frac{1 - \sigma e'\hat{x}^*}{x_0^*} \neq 0.$$

Now $\partial f/\partial x_i$ and $\partial g_j/\partial x_i$ are homogeneous of degree zero; hence

$$\bar{\xi}_i - \lambda\frac{\partial f(\hat{x}^*)}{\partial x_i} - \mu + \sum_{j=1}^{m} \alpha_j\frac{\partial g_j(\hat{x}^*)}{\partial x_i} = 0$$

if and only if

$$\bar{\xi}_i - \lambda\frac{\partial f(\sigma\hat{x}^*)}{\partial x_i} - \mu + \sum_{j=1}^{m} \alpha_j\frac{\partial g_j(\sigma\hat{x}^*)}{\partial x_i} = 0 \quad .$$

Suppose $x_0{}^* = 0$, then $\hat{x}^*$ corresponds to a portfolio associated with the point M having mean $\bar{\xi}_c$ and α-dispersion $S_c{}^{1/\alpha}$, which is independent of u even if M is not unique.

One may find the slope of L and the point M by solving

$$\text{maximize} \qquad g(\hat{x}) \equiv \frac{\bar{\xi}'\hat{x} - \bar{\xi}_0}{f(\hat{x})}$$

$$\text{subject to} \qquad e'\hat{x} = 1,$$

$$g_j(\hat{x}) \geq 0, \quad j = 1,\ldots,m. \tag{5.14}$$

By letting $\bar{\tilde{\xi}}_i = \bar{\xi}_i - \bar{\xi}_0$, $i = 1,\ldots,n$, (5.14) becomes

$$\text{maximize} \qquad g(\hat{x}) = \frac{\bar{\tilde{\xi}}'\hat{x}}{f(\hat{x})}$$

$$\text{subject to} \qquad e'\hat{x} = 1,$$

$$g_j(\hat{x}) \geq 0, \quad j = 1,\ldots,m. \tag{5.15}$$

We shall assume that $\bar{\tilde{\xi}}'\hat{x} > 0$ for all "interesting" feasible $\hat{x}$. Since the $\bar{\tilde{\xi}}$ are the risk premiums, and $\hat{x} \geq 0$, this assumption is extremely mild because an optimal solution to (5.12) is $\hat{x}^* = 0$, $x_0{}^* = 1$ if $\bar{\tilde{\xi}}'\hat{x} \leq 0$ for all feasible $\hat{x}$. See Merton (1972) for some discussion related to this assumption in a different context. Conditions will now be presented that guarantee that (5.15) has a unique solution.

A differentiable function $r(y) : Y \to R$ is said to be strictly pseudo-concave (spc) on Y a subset of R^n if for all y, $\bar{y} \in Y$, $y \neq \bar{y}$ we have that

$$(y - \bar{y})' \nabla r(\bar{y}) \leq 0 \Rightarrow r(y) < r(\bar{y}),$$

where $\nabla r(y)$ denotes the gradient operation $(\partial r/\partial y_1,\ldots,\partial r/\partial y_n)'$. Geometrically, functions are spc if they strictly decrease in all directions that have downward or horizontal pointing derivatives. Univariate and bivariate normal distributions are spc. The main facts relating problem (5.15) and the spc of g are contained in Theorem 5.12.

THEOREM 5.12. (a) Suppose $Y \subset R^n$ is a convex set, $q(y) : Y \to R$ is a positive differentiable concave function, $r(y) : Y \to R$ is a positive differentiable strictly convex function. Then $\ell(y) \equiv q(y)/r(y) : Y \to R$ is spc.

(b) Suppose $\ell(y) : Y \to R$ is spc on the convex set Y. Then ℓ either has a unique maximum on Y or no maximum exists.

(c) Suppose $\bar{\bar{\xi}}'\hat{x} > 0$ and f is strictly convex. Then g is spc on $\{\hat{x} | e'\hat{x} = 1, g_j(\hat{x}) \geq 0, j = 1,\ldots,m\}$ and g has a unique[17] maximum $\hat{x}^*$ on this set.

Proof: (a) Since $\ell = q/r$, $\nabla\ell = (r\,\nabla q - q\,\nabla r)/r^2$. Let $\bar{y} \in Y$, then

$$\nabla\ell(\bar{y})'(y - \bar{y}) = \left\{\frac{r(\bar{y})\ \nabla q(\bar{y}) - q(\bar{y})\ \nabla r(\bar{y})}{[r(\bar{y})]^2}\right\}'(y - \bar{y})$$

$$\leq 0 \quad \text{for all } y \in Y,\ y \neq \bar{y},$$

$$\Rightarrow \left\{r(\bar{y})\ \nabla q(\bar{y}) - q(\bar{y})\ \nabla r(\bar{y})\right\}'(y - \bar{y})$$

$$\leq 0 \quad \text{since } r(\bar{y}) \neq 0,$$

$$\Rightarrow r(\bar{y})\left[q(y) - q(\bar{y})\right] - \left[q(\bar{y})\ \nabla r(\bar{y})\right]'(y - \bar{y})$$

$$\leq 0 \quad \text{since q is concave and } r(\bar{y}) > 0,$$

$$\Rightarrow r(\bar{y})\left[q(y) - q(\bar{y})\right] + q(\bar{y})\left[r(\bar{y}) - r(y)\right]$$

$$< 0 \quad \text{since r is strictly convex and } q(\bar{y}) > 0,$$

$$\Rightarrow r(\bar{y})\ q(y) - q(\bar{y})\ r(y) < 0\ ,$$

which implies that

$$\ell(y) - \ell(\bar{y}) < 0$$

since $r(y) > 0$ and $r(\bar{y}) > 0$.

(b) We utilize the following:

LEMMA. <u>Suppose</u> $\ell(y) : R^n \to R$ <u>is differentiable at</u> y <u>and there is a direction</u> d <u>such that</u> $\nabla\ell(y)'d > 0$. <u>Then</u> a $\sigma > 0$ <u>exists such that for all</u> $\tau \in (0,\sigma]$ $\ell(y + \tau d) > \ell(y)$.

<u>Proof</u>: See Zangwill (1969).

<u>Case 1</u>: There exists a $y \in Y$ such that $\nabla\ell(y) = 0$. Then since ℓ is spc, i.e., $\nabla\ell(y)'(\bar{y} - y) \leq 0 \Rightarrow \ell(\bar{y}) < \ell(y)$ for all $\bar{y} \in Y$, y is the unique maximizer.

<u>Case 2</u>: There does not exist a $y \in Y$ such that $\nabla\ell(y) = 0$. Suppose y maximizes ℓ over Y. Then for all $\bar{y} \neq y$, $\nabla\ell(y)'(\bar{y} - y) \leq 0 \Rightarrow \ell(\bar{y}) < \ell(y)$ and y is clearly the unique maxima unless there exists $\bar{y} \in Y$ such that $\nabla\ell(y)'(\bar{y} - y) > 0$. But by the lemma that would imply that there exists a $\tau > 0$ such that $\ell[y + \tau(\bar{y} - y)] > \ell(y)$, which contradicts the assumed optimality of y. Note that the point $[y + \tau(\bar{y} - y) = [\tau\bar{y} + (1 - \tau)y] \in Y$, for $\tau \leq 1$, by the convexity of Y.

<u>Proof (cont.)</u>: (c) Now $g(\hat{x}) = \bar{\tilde{\xi}}'\hat{x}/f(\hat{x})$ is spc by (a). Since g is a continuous function on a compact set, it has a maximum $\hat{x}^*$, which by (b) is unique.

It is important to note that $g(\hat{x})$ is positively homogeneous of degree zero, i.e., $g(\hat{x}) = g(\lambda\hat{x})$ for all $\lambda > 0$, hence one may delete the constraints $e'\hat{x} = 1$ from (5.15) and solve the simpler problem

$$\begin{array}{ll} \text{maximize} & g(\hat{x}) = \bar{\xi}'\hat{x}/f(\hat{x}) \\ \text{subject to} & g_j(\hat{x}) \geq 0,\ j = 1,\ldots,m, \end{array} \tag{5.16}$$

and then rescale the optimal solution to (5.16)--say, $\hat{x}^0$--so that its components sum to 1 and $x_i^* = x_i^0/e'\hat{x}^0$. The problem (5.16) simplifies further for specific g_j and f. For example, if only the constraints $\hat{x} \geq 0$ are present and ξ has a joint normal distribution, then $f(\hat{x}) = (1/\sqrt{2})(\hat{x}'\not{Z}\hat{x})^{\frac{1}{2}}$. The Kuhn-Tucker conditions of (5.16) (which are necessary and sufficient) indicate after some substitutions that an equivalent problem is the quadratic program

$$\begin{array}{ll} \text{maximize} & \bar{\xi}'\hat{x} - \tfrac{1}{2}\hat{x}'\not{Z}\hat{x} \\ \text{subject to} & \hat{x} \geq 0. \end{array} \tag{5.17}$$

See Ziemba et al. (1974) for details and other special cases when the returns have a joint normal distribution.

Bradley and Frey (1974) have studied the solution and equivalence properties of fractional programming problems involving homogeneous functions. Their general results indicate that (5.16) is equivalent (has the same set of optimal solutions) to the convex program

$$\begin{array}{ll} \text{minimize} & f(\hat{x}), \\ \text{subject to} & g_j(\hat{x}) \geq 0,\ j = 1,\ldots,m,\ \bar{\xi}'\hat{x} = 1. \end{array} \tag{5.18}$$

Problem (5.18) is generally easier to solve than (5.16). When ξ is joint normal and only $\hat{x} \geq 0$ constraints are present, (5.18) yields

$$\begin{array}{ll} \text{minimize} & \hat{x}'\not{Z}\hat{x}, \\ \text{subject to} & \hat{x} \geq 0,\ \bar{\xi}'\hat{x} = 1, \end{array} \tag{5.19}$$

a problem equivalent to (5.17).

Suppose the first-stage problem (5.15) has been solved to obtain $\hat{x}^*$. The second-stage problem is then to determine the optimal ratios of risky to nonrisky assets. The risky composite asset is

$$R \equiv \hat{\xi}'\hat{x}^* \sim P(\overline{\xi}_c, S_c, 0, \alpha),$$

where

$$\overline{\xi}_c \equiv \overline{\hat{\xi}}'\hat{x}^* \quad \text{and} \quad S_c^{1/\alpha} \equiv f(\hat{x}^*).$$

The best combination of R and the risk-free asset may be found by solving (see Figure 5-2)[18]

$$\begin{aligned} &\text{maximize} \quad \phi(\lambda) \equiv E_R u[\lambda\overline{\xi}_0 + (1-\lambda)R] \\ &\text{subject to} \quad -\infty < \lambda \leq 1 \end{aligned} \tag{5.20}$$

Problem (5.20) is a stochastic program with one random variable (R) and one decision variable (λ). Since u is concave in w, it follows that ϕ is concave in λ (see note 2). Under the assumptions described in Section 5.2.2, $\phi(\lambda)$ and $d\phi(\lambda)/d\lambda$ are bounded. Now

$$\phi(\lambda) = \int_{-\infty}^{\infty} u[\lambda\overline{\xi}_0 + (1-\lambda)\{\overline{\hat{\xi}}'\hat{x}^* + f(\hat{x}^*)z\}]p(z)dz \tag{5.21}$$

where the standardized stable or normal variate is

$$z \equiv \frac{R - \overline{\hat{\xi}}'\hat{x}^*}{f(\hat{x}^*)} \sim P(0,1,0,\alpha) \ .$$

The continuous derivative of ϕ (assuming u is continuously differentiable) is

$$\frac{d\phi(\lambda)}{d\lambda} = \int_{-\infty}^{\infty} \left\{\overline{\xi}_0 - \overline{\hat{\xi}}'\hat{x}^* - f(\hat{x}^*)z\right\} \frac{du[\lambda\overline{\xi}_0 + (1-\lambda)\{\overline{\hat{\xi}}'\hat{x}^* + f(\hat{x}^*)z\}]}{dw} p(z)dz. \tag{5.22}$$

Problems having the form of (5.20) are generally easy to solve by combining a univariate numerical integration scheme with a search procedure that uses function or derivative evaluations. See Ziemba et al. (1974) for some specific calculations and a comparison of different utility functions in the normal distribution case. For the stable case f(z) is not known in closed form unless $\alpha = 2$ or 1. However, one may obtain a good approximation to (5.21) and/or (5.22) using the tables compiled by Fama and Roll (1968) based on series expansions of p(z) due to Bergstrom (1952). The tables consider $\alpha = 1.0, 1.1, \ldots, 2.0$ and $R = \pm 0, .05, \ldots, 1.0, 1.1, \ldots, 2.0, 2.2, \ldots, 4.0, 4.4, \ldots, 6, 7, 8, 10, 15$, and 20 (a grid of 50 points). One then has the approximation to (5.21):

$$\phi(\lambda) \cong \sum_{j=1}^{100} P_j u[\lambda\bar{\xi}_0 + (1 - \lambda)\{\bar{\hat{\xi}}'\hat{x}^* + f(\hat{x}^*)z_j\}] \tag{5.23}$$

where

$$P_j = P_r[z = z_j] > 0 \quad \text{and} \quad \sum_{j=1}^{100} P_j = 1 \, .$$

One may similarly approximate (5.22). The solution to the approximate versions of (5.21)--say, λ^a--may proceed via any known univariate search method such as the golden sections or bisecting search techniques; see Zangwill (1969). The approximate optimal portfolio is then

$$x_0^a = \lambda^a \quad \text{and} \quad x_i^a = (1 - \lambda^a)\hat{x}_i^*, \; i = 1, \ldots, n.$$

5.2.4 Example: Independent Stable Distribution Case

In this section we illustrate the use of the results in Section 5.2.3 for the determination of optimal portfolios consisting of 25 independent stable assets and one safe asset.[19] We utilized 500 monthly observations from the CRSP tape (Center for Research in Security Prices, University of Chicago) during the period January 1926-September 1967 for each security. The estimates of the $\bar{\xi}_i$, S_i, and α_i were made using the techniques described in Fama and Roll (1971). The theory in

Section 5.2.3 is valid only if all α_i are equal. Nearly all the estimates obtained had little variation around their mean of $\hat{\alpha} = 1.5162$. Hence it was assumed that this value of α prevailed for all the stable assets. The risk-free asset return was taken to be $\bar{\xi}_0 = 1.004$ corresponding to a 5-percent interest rate. The various stable assets and their means, dispersions, and optimal proportions are listed in Table 5-2. The composite asset $R \sim P[\bar{\xi}_c, S_c, 0, \alpha] = P[1.0100, 0.002254, 0, 1.5162]$.

Unfortunately λ^* tended toward large negative values because our choice of $\bar{\xi}_0 = 1.004$ was too low in comparison with $\bar{\xi}_c = 1.010$, given that the α-dispersion was only 0.002254. For example, when $u(w) = -e^{-aw}$, λ^* ranged between -20.00 and -17.11 when a ranged between 0.25 and 4; see Table 5-3. Hence to obtain more realistic values of λ^*, we parameterized[20] $\bar{\xi}_0$. The results for $\bar{\xi}_0$ ranging from 1.0040 to 1.01010 for $u(w) = -e^{-aw}$ when $\underline{a}$ ranged between 0.25 and 4 appear in Table 5-3. Similar calculations[21] for

$$u(w) = \begin{cases} w^{\beta} & \text{if } w \geq w_0 \\ (1-\beta)w_0^{\beta} + (\beta w_0^{\beta-1})w & \text{if } w < w_0 \end{cases}$$

when $w_0 = \frac{1}{2}$, β ranged from 0.1 to 0.9, and $\bar{\xi}_0$ ranged from 1.0089 to 1.01010 appear in Table 5-4. The results suggest that for fixed $\underline{a}$ or β, λ^* is an increasing function of $\bar{\xi}_0$ and that $\lambda^* \to 1$ as $\bar{\xi}_0 \to 1.01$ (actually because of the approximations involved, λ^* did not generally reach 1 until $\bar{\xi}_0$ had slightly surpassed 1.01). For fixed $\bar{\xi}_0$, λ^* is an increasing function of $\underline{a}$ and a decreasing function of β, hence the investor is more risk-averse with increasing $\underline{a}$ and decreasing β.[22]

5.2.5 Dropping the Risk-Free Asset Assumption

The case when the risk-free asset is not available is more complicated because one is not able to decompose the problem using the separation theorem. The optimal solution must still be mean-α-dispersion efficient, but it is simplest not to compute the function $\phi_0(\beta)$ but rather

Table 5-2
Description of the Stable Assets

Name of Asset	$\bar{\xi}_i$	$\tilde{\bar{\xi}}_i \equiv \bar{\xi}_i - \bar{\xi}_0$
ACF Industries	1.0089	0.0049
AJ Industries	0.9960	negative
ABEX Corporation	1.0074	0.0034
Allegheny Power System	1.0075	0.0035
Allis-Chalmers Mfg.	1.0060	0.0020
Barber Oil	1.0050	0.0010
Bayuk Cigar Inc.	1.0050	0.0010
Beech-Nut Life Savers	1.0083	0.0043
Bethlehem Steel Corp.	1.0099	0.0059
Burroughs Corp.	1.0117	0.0077
CF & I Steel Corp.	1.0010	negative
CIT Financial Corp.	1.0107	0.0067
Calumet & Hecla, Inc.	1.0050	0.0010
Canadian Pacific Ry.	1.0030	negative
J.I. Case Co.	1.0050	0.0010
Freeport Sulphur Co.	1.0132	0.0092
Gen. Dynamics Corp.	1.0080	0.0040
Gen. Electric Co.	1.0109	0.0069
Gen. Motors	1.0130	0.0090
Gen. Refractories	1.0070	0.0030
Gen. Signal Corp.	1.0098	0.0058
Helme Products	1.0060	0.0020
Homestake Mining Co.	1.0079	0.0039
Howmet Corp.	1.0099	0.0059
Inland Steel Co.	1.0113	0.0073

Note: (1) The optimal solution to the fractional program

$$\text{maximize} \quad \tilde{\bar{\xi}}'\hat{x} / \sum_{i=1}^{25} S_i x_i^{\alpha},$$

$$\text{subject to} \quad e'\hat{x} = 1, \ \hat{x} \geq 0$$

was found to be 0.3374 using the computer code Complex (Computer Centre, University of British Columbia). This calculation took less than one second of CPU time on the university's IBM 360-168 computer. (2) Three of the assets had $\tilde{\bar{\xi}}_i$ negative. These and four other assets had zero optimal proportions.

Table 5-2 Continued

s_i	$(\bar{\xi}_i - \xi_0)/s_i^{0.6595}$	x_i^*
0.01447	0.08005	0.08600
0.01352	negative	0
0.01079	0.06740	0.02878
0.02717	0.03774	0.00829
0.009324	0.04366	0.02506
0.01704	0.01467	0
0.009513	0.02154	0.03764
0.004499	0.15180	0.08695
0.001154	0.11189	0.07569
0.01108	0.15000	0.04365
0.0240	negative	0
0.01194	0.12425	0.04904
0.01075	0.01989	0
0.01699	negative	0
0.01698	0.01470	0
0.009024	0.20520	0.09496
0.02572	0.04472	0.01038
0.005649	0.20960	0.08536
0.008486	0.20910	0.10054
0.01626	0.04538	0
0.01276	0.10294	0.01692
0.004467	0.07093	0.01967
0.005483	0.12083	0.07237
0.01205	0.10875	0.05972
0.00631	0.20615	0.09898

to solve the expected utility problem directly by combining a numerical integration (or other numerical approximation) scheme with a nonlinear programming algorithm. This results in a problem having n decision variables and one random variable that is generally more difficult to solve than problem (5.12). Let the problem be

$$\begin{aligned} &\text{maximize} \quad E_{\xi}u(\xi'x), \\ &\text{subject to} \quad e'x = 1, \ g_j(x) \geq 0, \ j = 1,\ldots,m, \end{aligned} \tag{5.23}$$

where u is monotone nondecreasing and concave, $x = (x_1,\ldots,x_n)'$, $\xi \equiv (\xi_1,\ldots,\xi_n)'$, $e \equiv (1,\ldots,1)'$, and each g_j is concave. Suppose ξ has a symmetric stable or normal distribution P with characteristic exponent $\alpha \in (1,2]$ having the log characteristic function

Table 5-3
Optimal Values of λ When $u(w) = -e^{-aw}$

$\bar{\xi}_0$	a = 0.25	0.5	0.75	1.00	1.50	2.00	3.00	4.00
1.0040	-20.00	-20.00	-20.00	-20.00	-19.998	-19.998	-19.994	-17.11
1.0050	-20.00	-20.00	-20.00	-20.00	-19.997	-19.997	-19.994	-15.50
1.0060	-20.00	-20.00	-20.00	-20.00	-19.998	-19.998	-18.92	-13.9
1.0070	-20.00	-20.00	-20.00	-20.00	-19.997	-19.989	-16.03	-11.70
1.0089	-19.996	-19.98	-19.99	-19.97	-15.75	-11.34	- 7.124	- 5.110
1.0095	-19.998	-19.98	-14.57	-10.68	- 6.930	- 5.162	- 2.951	- 1.998
1.0098	-18.641	- 8.867	- 5.156	- 3.711	- 2.372	- 1.243	- 0.605	- 0.2267
1.0099	- 9.387	- 3.772	- 2.825	- 1.491	- 0.581	- 0.295	0.185	0.2604
1.00995	- 3.991	- 1.260	- 0.508	- 0.4706	0.0882	- 0.1928	0.5881	0.5414
1.00996	- 2.809	- 1.276	- 0.2419	0.1574	0.2624	0.5274	0.6917	0.7743
1.00997	- 1.9204	- 0.615	0.0484	0.3039	0.5616	0.7422	0.7802	0.7826
1.00998	- 0.8106	- 1.857	0.3294	0.4346	0.679	0.8242	0.8598	0.8701
1.00999	0.50167	0.2622	0.2604	0.7709	0.8501	0.7157	0.9201	0.9581
1.01000	0.54148	0.8090	0.9479	0.7157	0.9679	0.8804	0.9799	0.9779
1.01005	0.9362	0.9917	0.9824	0.9800	0.9763	0.9740	0.9877	0.9886
1.01010	0.9362	0.9935	0.9871	0.9859	0.9853	0.8854	0.9739	0.9739

Note: (1) u(w) is strictly increasing and strictly concave on R. (2) The calculation of λ^* utilized the Golden Section search method on the interval [-20,1] and took less than one second of CPU time on the University of British Columbia's IBM 360-168 computer for each value of $\bar{\xi}_0$ and a.

Table 5-4

Optimal Values of λ When $u(w) = \begin{cases} w^{\beta} & \text{if } w \geq \frac{1}{2} \\ (1 - \beta) \frac{1}{2}^{\beta} + \beta \frac{1}{2}^{\beta-1} w & \text{if } w < \frac{1}{2} \end{cases}$

$\overline{\xi}_0$	β = 0.1	0.2	0.3	0.4	0.5	0.6	0.7	0.8	0.9
1.0089	-17.64	-18.43	-19.59	-19.99	-20.00	-19.99	-20.00	-19.99	-20.00
1.0095	-11.25	-12.42	-13.59	-14.84	-17.02	-18.93	-20.00	-20.00	-20.00
1.0098	- 5.170	- 5.893	- 6.319	- 7.773	- 8.485	-10.81	-13.419	-18.09	-19.998
1.0099	- 2.825	- 2.372	- 4.004	- 7.072	- 3.705	- 5.893	- 7.320	-11.98	-17.36
1.00995	- 2.103	- 2.103	- 1.371	- 2.103	- 4.004	- 2.825	- 4.004	- 5.893	-11.98
1.00996	- 0.9238	- 0.9238	- 0.9238	- 2.103	- 2.103	- 1.650	- 2.825	- 5.171	- 8.938
1.00997	- 0.9238	- 0.1928	- 0.9238	- 0.9238	- 0.923	- 1.372	- 4.004	- 4.004	- 8.952
1.00998	- 0.1928	- 0.1928	0.2605	- 0.1928	- 0.923	- 0.9238	- 1.371	- 2.103	- 4.439
1.00999	- 0.1928	0.2605	0.2605	0.2604	- 0.1928	- 0.1928	0.8822	- 0.9234	- 2.103
1.0100	0.2605	0.2605	0.5414	0.7157	0.5414	0.2605	0.3415	0.5414	0.2605
1.01005	0.5415	0.7157	0.8907	0.7157	0.8237	0.9322	0.9740	0.9322	0.9580
1.01010	0.8907	0.8237	0.9740	0.9322	0.9739	0.9322	0.9840	0.9580	0.9580

$$\ell n\ \psi_\xi(t) = i\bar{\xi}t - \gamma(t),$$

where $\gamma(t)$ is positive, convex, and positively homogeneous of degree α. For any feasible x^k, $\xi' x^k$ has the univariate symmetric stable distribution $P[\bar{\xi}' x^k, \gamma(x^k), 0, \alpha]$. Hence one may evaluate

$$Z(x^k) = \int_{-\infty}^{\infty} u(\xi' x^k) dP(\xi' x^k) \tag{5.24}$$

by either a numerical integration scheme (normal case) or using a modification of the Fama-Roll tables. It may be noted that using standardized normal or stable variates is not particularly useful because

$$Z(x) = \int_{-\infty}^{\infty} u[\bar{\xi}' x + \{\gamma(x)\}^{1/\alpha} z] p(z) dz, \tag{5.25}$$

where $z \sim P(0,1,0,\alpha)$ is not generally a concave function of x. Also it seems preferable to apply algorithms directly to (5.24) and not its partials because they involve the bivariate distributions of ξ_i and $\xi' x^k$. The algorithm described in Section 5.1.4 would be particularly appropriate because $\xi' x$ has a univariate stable (or normal) distribution.

5.2.6 Separation Theorems in the Absence of a Risk-Free Asset

In this section we present two mutual fund separation theorems due to Merton (1972) and to Hart and Jaffee (1974). They obtain when rather special assumptions concerning the asset allocation constraints are invoked. Let the problem be

$$\begin{aligned} &\text{maximize} && E_\xi u(\xi' x), \\ &\text{subject to} && e' x = 1 , \end{aligned} \tag{5.26}$$

where u is monotone nondecreasing and concave, $x \equiv (x_1, \ldots, x_n)'$, $\xi \equiv (\xi_1, \ldots, \xi_n)' \sim N(\bar{\xi}, \Sigma)$, where Σ is positive definite and $e \equiv (1, \ldots, 1)'$. By Theorem 5.9 an optimal solution to (5.26) must be mean-variance efficient and thus lie on the efficient surface

$$f(\alpha) \equiv \text{minimize} \quad x'\Sigma x,$$
$$\text{subject to} \quad \bar{\xi}'x = \alpha,\ e'x = 1\ . \tag{5.27}$$

THEOREM 5.13.[23] (a) $f(\alpha) = b_1 + b_2\alpha + b_3\alpha^2$ and the unique optimal solution to (5.27) is $x^* = a_1 + a_2\alpha$, where

$$a_1 \equiv \frac{\Sigma^{-1}(d\bar{\xi} - ec)}{c(adc - b)}, \qquad a_2 \equiv \frac{\Sigma^{-1}(ac^2e - b\bar{\xi})}{c(adc - b)},$$

$$b_1 \equiv a_1'\Sigma a_1, \quad b_2 \equiv 2a_1'a_2, \quad b_3 \equiv a_2'a_2\ ,$$

$$a \equiv e'\Sigma^{-1}\bar{\xi},\ b \equiv e'\Sigma^{-1}e,$$

$$c \equiv \bar{\xi}'\Sigma^{-1}\bar{\xi}, \quad \text{and} \quad d \equiv \bar{\xi}'\Sigma^{-1}e.$$

(b) Let

$$A \equiv \sum_{i=1}^{n} a_{1i}\xi_i$$

and

$$B \equiv \sum_{i=1}^{n} (a_{1i} + a_{2i})\xi_i$$

be two mutual funds. For any utility function u an optimal solution to (5.26) can be found by choosing between A and B.

Proof: (a) These relations are easily established by eliminating the multipliers from the Kuhn-Tucker conditions of (5.27).
(b) Since $x^*(\alpha)$ is linear, any two $x^*(\alpha_1)$, $x^*(\alpha_2)$ will serve as mutual funds. The choice $\alpha_1 = 0$, $\alpha_2 = 1$ gives A and B.

The result (b) means that the investor can optimally choose among $\xi_1,\ldots,\xi_n$ by optimally choosing among A and B. Now $A \sim N(a_1'\bar{\xi}, a_1'\Sigma a_1)$ and B is $N[(a_1 + a_2)'\bar{\xi}, (a_1 + a_2)'\Sigma(a_1 + a_2)]$, hence the problem is to find a λ^* that solves

$$\begin{array}{ll} \text{maximize} & E_{AB}\, u(\lambda_1 A + \lambda_2 B), \\ \text{subject to} & (e'a_1)\lambda_1 + e'(a_1 + a_2)\lambda_2 = 1, \end{array}$$

which, assuming $e'a_1 \neq 0$, is equivalent to the unconstrained maximization problem

$$\text{maximize } E_{A,B}\, u\left[\left\{B - \frac{e'(a_1 + a_2)}{e'a_1} A\right\}\lambda_2 + \frac{A}{e'a_1}\right], \qquad (5.28)$$

a considerably simpler problem than (5.26).

The second separation theorem is due to Hart and Jaffee (1974). It arises in a portfolio problem involving financial intermediaries. It is assumed that there are n assets $x_i \geq 0$ and m liabilities $x_i \leq 0$ that are held in such quantities that the fixed component of the intermediaries' net worth is zero. The budget constraint is then

$$\sum_{i=1}^{n} x_i + \sum_{j=n+1}^{n+m} x_j = 0 .$$

It is assumed that there are reserve requirements for the liabilities, say, ρ_i per unit of liability, $0 \leq \rho_i \leq 1$, so that

$$x_1 \geq - \sum_{j=n+1}^{n+m} \rho_j x_j .$$

Let the ending value of one dollar of security i purchased or sold at the beginning of the period be ξ_i, where $\xi \equiv (\xi_1, \ldots, \xi_{n+m})' \sim N(\bar{\xi}, \Sigma)$. The portfolio problem is then

$$\text{maximize} \quad E_{\xi} u(\xi' x),$$

$$\text{subject to} \quad \sum_{i=1}^{n} x_i + \sum_{j=n+1}^{n+m} x_j = 0,$$

$$x_1 + \sum_{j=n+1}^{n+m} \rho_j x_j \geq 0,$$

$$x_i \geq 0, \qquad i = 1,\ldots,n,$$

$$x_j \leq 0, \qquad j = n+1,\ldots,n+m. \tag{5.29}$$

The separation theorem may be proved using the following parametric nonlinear programming result due to Huang, Wehrung and Ziemba (1976):

THEOREM 5.14. *Consider the random nonlinear program*

$$\phi(\xi) \equiv \{\min_x f(x) \mid Ax = b\xi,\ g_j(x) \geq 0,\ j = 1,\ldots,J\}, \tag{1}$$

where $x \in E^n$, A *is an* $m \times n$ *fixed matrix*, b *is an* $m \times 1$ *fixed vector*, f *and* g_j *are real valued functions, and the random variable* ξ *is distributed independently of the choice of* x *and defined on the probability space* $(\Xi, \mathcal{F}, F)$. *Assume that*

(a) ξ *is nonnegative, i.e.,* $\Pr\{\xi \geq 0\} = 1$, *and has finite moments of order* $n \geq 1$;

(b) *there exists* $\xi^0 > 0$, $\xi^0 \in \Xi$ *such that there exists an optimal solution* x^0 *to (1) when* $\xi = \xi^0$;

(c) f *is homogeneous of degree* $k_0 > 0$ *and each* g_j *is homogeneous of degree* k_j; *and*

(d) $\phi(0) = 0$.

Then an optimal solution to (1)--namely, $x(\xi)$*--exists for all* $\xi \in \Xi$; *moreover,*

$$x(\xi) = \frac{\xi}{\xi^0} x^0.$$

Proof: By assumption, x^0 is an optimal solution to (1) when $\xi = \xi^0$. Hence $\phi(\xi^0) = f(x^0) = \{\min f(x) | Ax = b\xi^0, g_j(x) \geq 0\}$. For general $\xi > 0$, problem (1) is $\phi(\xi) = \{\min f(x) | Ax = b\xi, g_j(x) \geq 0\}$. Let $\delta \equiv \xi/\xi^0$ and $x \equiv \delta y$, then

$$\begin{aligned}\phi(\xi) &= \{\min f(\delta y) | A\,\delta y = \delta b\xi^0,\ g_j(\delta y) \geqq 0\} \\ &= \{\min \delta^{k_0} f(y) | Ay = b\xi^0,\ \delta^{k_j} g_j(y) \geqq 0\} \\ &= \delta^{k_0}\{\min f(y) | Ay = b\xi^0,\ g_j(y) \geqq 0\} \\ &= \delta^{k_0} f(x^0) = (\xi/\xi^0)^{k_0}\ \phi(\xi^0) = f[(\xi/\xi^0)(x^0)].\end{aligned}$$

Thus $x(\xi) = (\xi/\xi^0)(x^0)$ solves (1) if $\xi > 0$. By assumption (d), it follows that $x = 0$ is optimal when $\xi = 0$.

Remarks:

1. Theorem 5.14 may be proved using the Kuhn-Tucker conditions with the additional hypotheses that f is differentiable and pseudo-convex and the g_j are differentiable and quasi-concave and $k_j > 1$ for $j = 1,\ldots,J$. In this version it is not necessary to assume that f is homogeneous; only its gradient must be homogeneous. Since homogeneous functions of degree $r > 1$ have partial derivatives that are homogeneous of degree $r - 1$ but not conversely, such a result is useful in problems such as $f(x) = \log a'x$ where the gradient but not the function is homogeneous.

2. Since an optimal solution exists for all $\xi \in \Xi$, the random variable $\phi(\xi) = f[x(\xi)]$ is well defined. Moments of order n/k_0 will exist because $f[x(\xi)] = f(x^0)(\xi/\xi^0)^{k_0}$. If f is convex (strictly convex) and the g_j are concave, then ϕ is a continuous, convex (strictly convex) function of ξ.

3. The nonpositive case may be handled by changing the signs of the components of b.

By Theorem 5.9 an optimal solution to (5.29) must lie on the mean-variance efficient surface

$$\begin{aligned}
\text{minimize} \quad & x'\mathcal{V}x, \\
\text{subject to} \quad & \bar{\xi}'x = \alpha \\
& \sum_{i=1}^{n} x_i + \sum_{j=n+1}^{n+m} x_j = 0, \\
& x_1 + \sum_{j=n+1}^{n+m} \rho_j x_j \geqq 0, \\
& x_i \geq 0, \qquad i = 1,\ldots,n, \\
& x_j \leq 0, \qquad j = n+1,\ldots,n+m. \qquad (5.30)
\end{aligned}$$

THEOREM 5.15. _A portfolio allocation_ x _is efficient if and only if_ $x = \lambda x^*$, _for some_ $\lambda \geq 0$ _and a mutual fund portfolio_ x^*.

Proof: Problem (5.30) satisfies the requirements of Theorem 5.14; thus

$$x(\alpha) = \frac{\alpha}{\alpha_0} x(\alpha_0).$$

The result then follows by defining $x^* \equiv x(\alpha_0)$ and $\lambda \equiv \alpha/\alpha_0$.

The theorem[24] indicates that each efficient point is yielded by expansion or contraction of a single efficient portfolio. Hence the optimal decision is to determine how much of this mutual fund to hold.

The mutual fund x^* may be found by solving

$$g \equiv \text{maximize} \quad \frac{\bar{\xi}'x}{(x'\mathcal{V}x)^{\frac{1}{2}}},$$

$$\text{subject to} \quad y \geq 0,\ v \leq 0,\ x_1 \geq -\rho'v,\ e'x = 0, \qquad (5.31)$$

where $y \equiv (x_1,\ldots,x_n)'$, $v = (x_{n+1},\ldots,x_{n+m})'$, $x' = (y',v')$, $\rho \equiv (\rho_{n+1},\ldots,\rho_{n+m})'$, and $e \equiv (1,\ldots,1)'$. Using the results in Bradley and Frey (1974) [see (5.18)], it follows that (5.31) is equivalent to

$$\begin{aligned}&\text{minimize} && x'\Sigma x,\\ &\text{subject to} && (1,0,\ldots,0,\rho)'x \geq 0,\ \bar{\xi}'x = 1,\\ &&& y \geq 0,\ v \leq 0,\ e'x = 0.\end{aligned} \tag{5.32}$$

Assuming that (5.32) has a unique[25] optimal solution x^*, the mutual fund is $B \equiv \xi'x^* \sim N(\bar{\xi}'x^*, x^{*\prime}\Sigma x^*)$. The problem[26] is then to choose λ to

$$\begin{aligned}&\text{maximize} && E_B\, u(\lambda B),\\ &\text{subject to} && \lambda \geq 0.\end{aligned} \tag{5.33}$$

Notes

1. In practice one usually has the further complication that the investor must put up ψ dollars security for each dollar in i sold short and x_i is received at the end, not the beginning, of the investment period. For convenience we assume that there are sufficient funds invested to provide the necessary security for short sales and hence (5.2) need not be altered. If such funds are not available, one may accommodate this short-sale regulation by letting $x_i = x_i^+ + x_i^-$, where $x_i^+ \geq 0$ and $x_i^- \leq 0$ represent investment and short selling in investment i, respectively. The essential changes in the formulation are that the budget constraint becomes

$$\sum_{i=1}^{n} \{x_i^+ - (1 + \psi)x_i^-\} \leq B(1 + y),$$

and the objective's argument becomes

$$\left[\sum_{i=1}^{n} \{\xi_i x_i^+ - (2 + \psi - \xi_i)x_i^- - c(yB)\}\right].$$

2. To prove this it is necessary to use the following well known properties of concave functions, see Mangasarian (1970). If $f(x)$ is a concave function defined on Euclidean n-space (R^n), then the

set $\{x|f(x) \geq \alpha\}$ is convex for all scalars α; the intersection of several convex sets is convex; if u is a concave nondecreasing function of the concave function $w(x)$, then $s(x) \equiv u[w(x)]$ is concave in x; and if $f(x,\xi)$ is concave in x for all fixed ξ then $\int f(x,\xi)dF(\xi)$ is concave in x.

3. Theorem 5.3 is a slight generalization of a result due to Arrow (1974). Arrow proved the result for nonnegative wealth ($A = 0$) using a somewhat different argument.

4. The gradient of Z, namely

$$\left(\frac{\partial Z}{\partial x_1},\ldots,\frac{\partial Z}{\partial x_n}\right)'$$

is denoted by ∇Z.

5. A function $f(x)$ defined on R^n is quasiconcave if and only if the set $\{x|f(x) \geq \alpha\}$ is convex for all $\alpha \varepsilon R$. All concave functions are quasi-concave but not conversely (for example x^3 for $x \varepsilon R$ is quasi-concave but not concave).

6. For absolutely continuous ξ, the continuous differentiability assumption can, with appropriate regularity assumptions, be replaced by a concavity assumption; see Ziemba (1974b).

7. The generalized programming algorithm considered in Section 5.1.4 is dual to a cutting plane algorithm.

8. This uniqueness property is satisfied by most distributions. In the joint normal distribution case it is required that the variance-covariance matrix be nonsingular.

9. In practice one would normally combine the cyclic coordinate ascent method with other methods such as that of conjugate directions or Stewart's modification of Davidson's method to improve the rate of convergence. See Fletcher (1969) and Zangwill (1969) for more discussion.

10. A function $h(\hat{x})$ defined on R^n is said to be homogeneous (of degree one) whenever $\lambda h(\hat{x}) = h(\lambda\hat{x})$ for any scalar λ. Hence constraints of the form $\hat{x} \geq 0$, $\bar{\xi}'\hat{x} - D_\phi(\hat{x}'\Sigma\hat{x})^{\frac{1}{2}} \geq 0$ are homogeneous, but $\beta \geq \hat{x} \geq \alpha$ is not homogeneous. As Bradley (n.d.) points out, any constraints that are homogeneous of degree k can be reduced to equivalent constraints that are homogeneous of degree one. For example suppose ℓ is

homogeneous of degree r then $[\ell(\hat{x})]^{1/r}$ is homogeneous of degree one and $\{\hat{x}|\ell(\hat{x}) \geq 0\} = \{\hat{x}|[\ell(\hat{x})]^{1/r} \geq 0\}$ since $(\cdot)^{1/r}$ is a monotone non-decreasing function.

11. See Blattberg and Gonedes (1974), Mandelbrot and Taylor (1967), Praetz (1972) and Press (1967, 1968, 1970) for discussions of some alternative distributions that may be used to fit this type of data. These distributions are not closed on addition.

12. In this section we make use of results pertaining to stable distributions found in Feller (1962, 1966), Ferguson (1955), Gnedenko and Kolmogorov (1954) and P. Levy (1954). The reader may also wish to consult Fama and Roll (1968, 1971) and Press (1972b,c) for discussions of estimation techniques for univariate and multivariate symmetric stable distributions. Press (forthcoming) has given a recent survey of the properties and recent results concerning stable distributions.

13. As Tesfatsion (1974) has pointed out in connection with the Hanoch-Levy article (1969) it is sufficient to assume that

$$\int_{-\infty}^{\infty} u(w)dH(w) - \int_{-\infty}^{\infty} u(w)dE(w)$$

is well defined,

$$\int_{-\infty}^{0} u(w)dH(w) > -\infty$$

and

$$\int_{-\infty}^{0} u(w)dE(w) > -\infty .$$

14. There are some exceptions to this, such as when the means must be equal [see Hadar and Russell (1971)], and when wealth has a lognormal distribution [see Levy (1973a), etc.]. In the lognormal case the mean-variance efficient set is sufficient for dominance but not necessary--it will contain all possible optimal portfolios. However, these results deal with assumptions on wealth that are not directly transferable to the ξ_i.

15. Cass and Stiglitz (1970), Hakansson (1969), Pye (1967), Vickson (1975b), and others have discussed a different type of

separation in which the optimal asset proportions are independent of initial wealth. These theorems hold for specific u rather than specific P, and are of interest in a variety of situations, but they are not of much computational value in this context.

16. Note that the homogeneity of f and the g_j guarantee satisfaction of Slater's constraint qualification.

17. If f is merely convex rather than strictly convex, then the maximizing point $\hat{x}^*$ can be shown to exist but it may fail to be unique. In that instance g is pseudo-concave, i.e., $(y - \bar{y})\,\nabla g(\bar{y})' \leq 0$ implies $g(y) \leq g(\bar{y})$ for all y, $\bar{y} \in Y$, and the Kuhn-Tucker conditions are necessary and sufficient. See Mangasarian (1970).

18. Note that λ values strictly between 0 and 1 correspond to purchase of both the risky composite and safe assets, while λ values that are negative correspond to borrowing at the risk-free rate for investment in the risky asset; when $\lambda = -2$, twice the investor's initial wealth is borrowed and this plus his initial wealth is invested in R.

19. These results were obtained in collaboration with C. E. Sarndal and J. N. Y. Yu.

20. To cut down the volume of computations we assumed that R $\sim P[1.0100, 0.002254, 0, \alpha]$ was independent of $\bar{\xi}_0$. Although not precisely true, there is reason to believe that this assumption is a reasonable approximation.

21. Since $u(w) = w^\beta$ is undefined for $w < 0$, this function appends a linear segment tangent to w^β at w_0 to provide values of u(w) for negative w. The resulting utility function is strictly increasing and concave on R.

22. These conclusions are consistent with those found by Ziemba et al. (1974) utilizing normal data using these utility functions.

23. This mutual fund result may be attributed to Merton (1972). Independently Ziemba derived this result for a problem in Ziemba and Vickson (1975) based on a suggestion by M. J. Brennan.

24. A rather devious alternative proof of Theorem 5.15 may be gleaned by noting that the separation Theorem 5.11 is valid if $\bar{\xi}_0 = 0$, in which case (5.30) will then satisfy the assumptions of Theorem 5.11.

25. An optimal solution to (5.32) will exist if Σ is positive definite and there exists a point having mean $g\sigma$ and standard deviation σ that is strictly preferred by the point (mean = 0, standard deviation = 0), where g is the slope of the mean-standard deviation frontier (5.31). See Hart and Jaffee (1974).

26. Theorem 5.7 may be used to provide conditions that will guarantee that (5.33) has an optimal solution λ^*. When $u(w) = w - \alpha w^2$, $\alpha > 0$, $\lambda^* = \overline{B}/(2\beta\overline{B^2})$, where $\overline{B}$ and $\overline{B^2}$ are the first two moments of B. When $u(w) = -e^{-aw}$, $a > 0$, $\lambda^* = \overline{B}/(a \text{ Var } B)$. However, λ^* does not exist if u is linear.

Introduction to Chapter 6
Applications to Financial Management and Capital Markets

Although many of the early finance applications of stochastic dominance (SD) concepts focused on securities and security portfolios, SD applications to financial management problems and capital market issues have been growing in number and importance. The three sections of this chapter concern applications of stochastic dominance to: (1) capital budgeting, (2) selecting optimal asset and liability structures for a commercial bank, and (3) testing the efficiency of capital markets.

In Section 6.1, Roger P. Bey and R. Burr Porter employ a "states of nature" device [see Stapleton (1971) for a similar approach in the EV framework] to derive data inputs for the capital budgeting decision. They then evaluate these data, for 10 hypothetical projects, by a number of choice criteria in various "decision environments." The resulting SSD efficient set differs sufficiently from the efficient sets of other criteria to imply a significant value of the former to firms employing portfolio approaches to capital budgeting (which would include firms following managerial or behavioral goal structures in imperfect capital markets and all firms in inefficient capital markets). Their study also shows that the mean-semivariance (ES_h) criterion provides an efficient set that is most like the SSD one. Thus in capital asset selection, as in security portfolio selection, the ES_h criterion provides an operational alternative where the SSD criterion cannot be implemented effectively.

In Section 6.2, Porter briefly discusses an application of SD to bank balance-sheet management. This section makes it clear that the area of financial intermediation provides a fertile field for applications of SD methodology.

In the last section, M. C. Findlay reviews recent empirical and theoretical studies that draw on SD concepts for an investigation of capital market efficiency. The studies considered include several reviewed (from a different perspective) by Porter in Chapter 3 and others concerned with the efficiency of several international stock markets and the reinsurance market. Findlay puts forward the appealing idea that the several degrees of stochastic dominance may provide an objective gauge by which a given market's prevailing level of efficiency can be assessed.

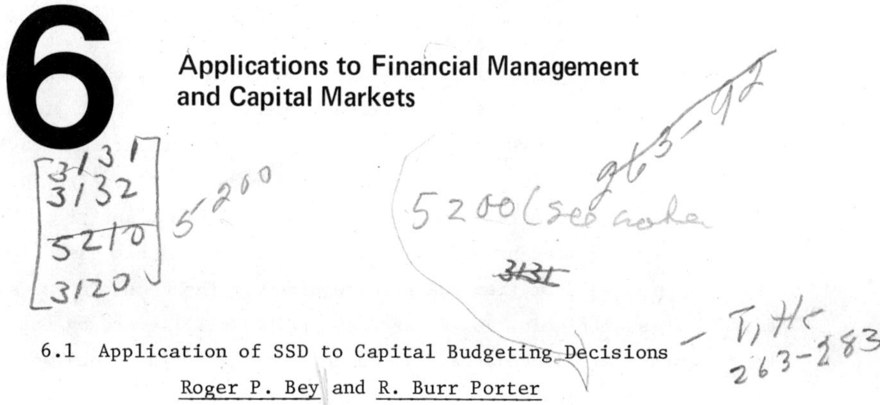

6 Applications to Financial Management and Capital Markets

6.1 Application of SSD to Capital Budgeting Decisions

Roger P. Bey and R. Burr Porter

The capital budgeting problem can be viewed as a portfolio problem that differs from the security portfolio problem in two major respects: firms normally will be considering relatively few large capital budgeting projects compared to the universe of individual securities that might be evaluated, and capital budgeting projects normally are not divisible and therefore must be accepted wholly or rejected. These two differences combine to limit the number of different possible combinations of projects to be considered in capital budgeting so that the absence of a stochastic dominance optimization algorithm becomes less important [see also Porter and Bey (1974)]. As a result, the capital budgeting problem represents an almost ideal forum for a test of SD efficiency criteria versus competing criteria for making decisions under risk.

A 1974 study by Bey and Porter examined two major points: (1) the feasibility of different schemes for estimating and processing the data required by the various portfolio models for capital budgeting and (2) the performance of several competing models in a variety of "decision environments" involving simulated data. The models included in the test are SSD, mean-semivariance (ES_h), chance-constrained programming (CCP), two different mean-variance models (EV-I and EV-II), and net present value (NPV). These two points are discussed in the next two sections.

6.1.1 Data Estimation and Processing Procedures

With the simplest version of NPV the decision-maker needs only the expected cash flows associated with each project and the "cost of capital." (These numbers are familiar to financial decision-makers.) If the decision-maker is to apply a portfolio model to the selection of capital budgeting projects, he must have some feasible means of estimating the required probability functions of annual net cash flow (NCF) and deriving from them the data required by the model to be used. The problem is difficult, but it is made particularly severe by the need to specify either covariances, joint probability functions, or other aspects of the statistical interrelationships among project returns. Moreover, the estimation process must be repeated for each future time period within the planning horizon. The problem is most severe with SD because the accurate determination of the true SD-efficient set requires that the decision-maker have the joint probability function for every possible combination of projects. Yet the difficulty is not insignificant for other portfolio models. We consider three methods for solving the data problem.

Direct Specification of Conditional Probabilities. The direct specification of conditional probability functions is one means of capturing the statistical interrelationships among random variables. The key to this approach to the capital budget problem is the specification of probability functions for new projects in terms of possible outcomes for the firm if no new projects are accepted. The steps in this procedure can be outlined as follows:

1. Estimate a discrete or histogram type of probability function of NCF for the firm for each time period within the planning horizon assuming that no new projects are accepted. Either assume independence over time or employ a Markov process to incorporate intertemporal dependencies.

2. Consider the first project and the first time period. For each possible NCF from Step 1, assign a conditional probability function of NCF for the project. In the simplest case, only the expected value of the probability function of return on the project is affected by the outcome for the firm. Even this case,

however, incorporates a broad range of positive and negative correlation. Further complexity can be added by allowing the degree of skewness (or some other characteristic) to depend on the outcome of the firm. That is, if NCF for the firm is better than expected, then greater NCF for the project is either more likely or less likely than if NCF for the firm is lower.

3. Repeat Step 2 for each time period. Following this procedure, the firm can allow for a variety of patterns of changes in the moments of the probability function over time.

4. Repeat Steps 2 and 3 for each project under consideration.

5. Apply Monte Carlo simulation to the data resulting from the above steps to estimate the joint probability function of return for each possible combination of projects.

The procedure has the advantage of considerable flexibility. The only limitations on the number and type of individual and conditional probability functions that the decision-maker includes are based on his personal ability, his time, and his computer facilities. Nevertheless, the approach becomes more difficult to handle as the number of projects, states, and time periods increases. The next approach helps alleviate this problem.

Direct Assignment of NCF to "States-of-the Economy." To simplify the procedures for capturing the statistical interrelationships among project cash flows, the second approach argues that the main influence on the result of most investments is the state of the economy. During recessions most projects will suffer but some may improve. When the total economy is experiencing rapid growth, most projects will be doing quite well, but some may not. If the general level of economic activity is the primary influence on the cash flows of projects, then an efficient manner for estimating outcomes in a way that incorporates statistical interrelationships among individual projects is to assign for each possible state of the economy in each relevant time period the outcome for the firm and for each project.

The steps in this approach are summarized as follows:

1. Select a measure of the state, choose the number of states to consider, and assign a probability of occurrence for each state

and each time period.

2. For each project and time period, estimate the NCF that will result from each particular state.

3. Determine the joint probability functions of NCF for combinations of projects, and evaluate according to the selected rule.

Consider an example based on three periods, three states, a firm, and two projects. The state probabilities and NCF values are given in Table 6-1. State 1 represents a low level of economic activity, state 2 an average level, and state 3 a high level. The NCF for the firm and for the projects are positively correlated with the level of economic activity, but the degree of correlation varies among projects and over time. Excluding the possibility that the firm might scrap its current activities, it must consider four alternatives: no change, add project 1, add project 2, add both projects.

The bottom of Table 6-1 lists the joint probability functions of NCF that result if both projects are added. The next step would depend on the decision rule to be applied. For SD, the period NCFs would be converted to probability functions of either NPV, net terminal value (NTV), or rate of return (ROR). How this step is completed depends on the decision-maker's assumption regarding the intertemporal relationships among the probability functions assigned to the economic states. The simplest case results from the assumption that the probability function assigned to any one period is independent of the probability function for any other period.

Formula Projection of NCF on Economic States. The third method is referred to as the formula approach to the assignment of NCF to a state-of-the-economy framework. The major difference between this method and the direct assignment of NCF to "states-of-the economy" is that it employs specified types of probability functions, a formula for determining variances, and simulation to assign cash flows to economic states. The required steps for one version of this approach can be summarized as follows:

1. Select a measure of the state of the world, choose a reasonable

Table 6-1
State-of-the-World Analysis of a Firm and Two Projects

	States	Periods		
		T_1	T_2	T_3
	S_1	.25	.10	.20
Probabilities	S_2	.50	.50	.60
	S_3	.25	.40	.20
	S_1	80	70	50
Firm NCF	S_2	100	100	100
	S_3	120	130	150
	S_1	0	5	10
Project 1 NCF	S_2	20	25	20
	S_3	25	30	30
	S_1	40	20	0
Project 2 NCF	S_2	50	60	30
	S_3	60	65	40
	S_1	120	95	60
The firm plus both projects	S_2	170	185	150
	S_3	205	225	220

number of states, and assign a probability of occurrence to each state in each time period. Either assume independence over time or employ a Markov process to incorporate intertemporal dependencies.

2. Assign to the firm and to each project under consideration a standard probability function such as uniform, exponential, normal, etc. Allow the parameters of the probability function to vary over time according to a formula that produces desired changes in mean, variance, skewness, and other moments.

3. Employ simulation to provide a sample frequency distribution for each project and time period that satisfies the parameters of the

assumed probability function.

4. For each project and time period, use the state probabilities to assign sample observations from Step 3 to states, and let the mean of the observations for each state represent the cash flow of that state. For example, if 200 observations are simulated for a project that has its lowest NCF in state 1 and the probability of state 1 is .10, then the lowest 20 observations are assigned to state 1 and their mean value becomes the cash flow for that project if state 1 occurs. Allow for the possibility that net cash flows from some projects may be negatively correlated with the level of economic activity. The result is a probability function over state net cash flows that closely approximates the assumed probability function.

5. Since state occurrences completely determine the NCF for each project, joint probability functions for combinations of projects can be determined directly from the results of Step 4. Evaluate these functions according to the chosen rule.

Since NCFs are assigned by selecting standard probability functions and allowing their parameters to vary over time according to a predetermined formula, this procedure requires less effort for a decision-maker than the first two procedures. For the same reason, however, it has limited flexibility and may be less realistic than direct specification of probabilities. The choice among methods depends on the decision-maker's needs, abilities, and resources. The next section examines a study in which the formula projection method was employed.

6.1.2 A Test of Several Portfolio Models Based on Hypothetical Data

In an effort to determine both the relative performance of different capital budgeting criteria--using the SSD efficient set of project combinations as a standard of comparison--and the feasibility of the formula projection of NCF distributions on an economic state framework, Bey and Porter (1974) conducted a test employing hypothetical data for a firm and 10 projects under a variety of "decision environments."

The capital budgeting models included in the study were a net present value model (NPV), a modification of the mean-variance model as adapted to capital budgeting by Weingartner (1966) (EV-I), Porter's (1973b) extension of the Lintner (1965) single-period mean-variance capital budgeting model to the multiperiod case (EV-II), a semivariance model (ES_h), and a chance-constrained model (CCP). An SSD model was used as a standard of comparison.

Data. The data required for capital budgeting portfolio models are the probability distribution of NPVs, NTVs, or RORs for each project and the joint probability distribution of NPVs for each combination of projects. Ideally, these estimates should be based on actual proposed investments of corporations. The nature of the analysis of this study, however, required that one set of proposed projects be evaluated over a wide variety of decision environments--a condition that could not be met with a corporation's actual investment data. Given the lack of real data and the need to examine the performance of the models under a variety of conditions regarding shape of probability functions and intercorrelation of project returns, we chose the logical alternative, a simulated environment in which the important parameters generating returns could be varied at will.

The development of the necessary data involved three steps: (1) establishment of an expected value and variance of NCF for each project in each year; (2) selection of the basic shape or type of probability function of NCF and determination of the correlation among returns of different projects; (3) simulation of joint probability functions of NPV for all possible combinations of projects. These steps were accomplished as follows:

1. Establishment of the mean and variance of NCF. The annual mean NCFs (see Table 6-2) are the annual cash flows from 10 of 30 projects employed in Weingartner's study (1963:180). We chose our 10 projects to emphasize a variety of starting and terminating dates, cash flows that were well mixed with both positive and negative values, and a wide range of cash flow amounts. All 26 periods of Weingartner's data base were utilized. In addition, we included an existing asset base to simulate the condition of an existing firm evaluating future investment projects. The expected NCFs for the firm and the projects are given in Table 6-2.

The standard deviation of the cash flows for each project i in period t is projected by the formula:

Table 6-2
Project Expected Cash Flows

	Project Number										
Years	1[a]	2	3	4	5	6	7	8	9	10	11
1	200	-100	-100	-200			- 50	-75			
2	210	20	15	25		-100	-100	-75		-200	
3	212	20	15	25		18	-175	-40		60	
4	215	20	15	25		17	50	40		40	
5	220	19	15	25		15	55	40		30	
6	215	19	15	25		12	60	40		15	
7	210	18	13	25		8	65	35		-25	
8	205	16	13	25		-10	60	35		-25	
9	200	14	13	25	-60	18	50	30		50	
10	195	11	13	25	-30	17	40	25	-40	40	
11	190	6	13	25	-10	15	30	15	15	30	-70
12	190	- 8	11	25	45	12	20	5	13	20	15
13	185		11	25	-34	8	10		9	10	13
14	185		11	25	25	- 10	- 25		7		11
15	180		11	25	16	18	50		5		10
16	180		11	25	12	17	41		2		9
17	175		9	25	8	15	35				7
18	175		9	25	-20	12	25				6
19	170		9	25	21	8	15				4
20	170		9	25	16		5				3
21	170		9	25	12						2
22	165			25	9						
23	165			25	7						
24	160			25	5						
25	160			25	3						
26	150			25							

[a]Project number 1 refers to the existing firm or the existing asset base.

$$\sigma(CF_{it}) = (X_i)(\overline{CF}_{it}) \exp[(TG_i)t],$$

where X_i reflects the degree of uncertainty associated with different types of projects, $(\overline{CF}_{it})$ is the expected cash flow, and TG_i is an annual growth factor representing the usual situation in which risk increases over time. The range of TG_i is from 0.04 to 0.08. It is assumed that X_i is constant over all time periods for a given project, but X_i ranges from 0.15 to 0.45 among projects. Low values of X_i may indicate projects closely related to the firm's current activities in which the firm is expected to be able to anticipate future cash flows with a relatively high degree of accuracy. On the other hand, high values of X_i may indicate cases in which the concept of the project is entirely new so that the firm lacks the expertise to estimate accurately either the costs or the revenues associated with the project.

2. Selection of shapes of probability functions and correlations among returns of different projects. A number of sets of data were required to enable us to evaluate the capital budgeting models over a variety of conditions. Each data set consists of a probability distribution for each project in each period, and each is considered to be a decision environment. That is, we have 20 different sets of assumptions regarding probability functions of project NCFs; each set of assumptions is referred to as a "decision environment." The 20 decision environments fall logically into the following five groups:

a. Each cash flow distribution (CF_{it}) for project i in period t is normally distributed. This situation is decision environment 1. No correlations among returns of different projects are negative.

b. Each CF_{it} is generated by an underlying distribution that is not normal. The general shape of CF_{it} is the same for all projects and is constant over time. Five sets of data were generated under these conditions. These are distributions that are highly skewed to the right (decision environment 2A), slightly skewed to the right (2B), highly skewed to the left (2C), slightly skewed to the left (2D), and uniform (2E). No correlations are negative.

c. The shape of CF_{it} varied among projects. Project 1 may have had a normal distribution; project 2, a distribution skewed to the right; and project 3, a uniform distribution. The distribution shape for each project is assumed to remain constant over time.

The four variations tested are denoted decision environments 3A, 3B, 3C, and 3D. No correlations are negative.

d. The distributions of CF_{it} varied among projects and over time. Project 1 may initially have a normal distribution and end up with a highly skewed distribution. Project 2 may have begun with a uniform distribution and terminated with a normal distribution. Four variations of these, decision environments 4A, 4B, 4C, and 4D, were tested. No correlations are negative.

e. The CF_{it} distribution shapes varied among projects and over time as with 4A through 4D. In addition, returns on some projects are negatively correlated with returns on other projects.

We used each portfolio model to select efficient combinations of the projects under each of the decision environments.

3. Simulation of joint probability functions of NPV for combinations of projects. Probability functions of NCF must be simulated for the firm as well as for the 10 projects; then probability functions of NPV must be simulated for all possible combinations of the firm and the projects. If, for convenience, we label the firm "Project 1" and the projects being evaluated as 2 through 11, we then have 11 projects in total and therefore 1024 possible combinations. Thus we have to generate 11 probability functions of NCF for each time period and for each of the 20 decision environments. Then we have to generate 1024 joint probability functions of NPV for each of the 20 decision environments.

A key element in the derivation of joint distributions for this investigation was the economic state framework. It was important because it provided a feasible mechanism for capturing the varying degrees of correlation among projects. That is, by assessing the probability functions of NCF on individual projects over a common set of economic states, we can determine easily the extent to which high returns on one project are associated with high returns on another project.

The steps required to simulate the probability functions were accomplished as follows:

a. Establish 10 economic states and assign a probability of occurrence to each state and each time period. Let state 1 represent the lowest level of economic activity while state 10 represents the highest level of economic activity.

b. For each project, time period, and decision environment (i.e., mean, variance, skewness, and type of probability function) employ simulation to determine the cash flow associated with each economic state. For example, if 200 observations are generated from the probability function of NCF for a given project and situation and the probability associated with state 1 is .05, then the smallest 10 observations (from the 200) are assigned to state 1. The same procedure is followed for states 2 through 10. Since a single number is desired for each state, the arithmetic mean of the numbers in each state is determined.

c. For decision environments involving some projects with negatively correlated returns, assign low simulated returns to high level economic states and vice versa.

d. Once the probability functions for individual project NCF have been imposed on the economic state framework under a given decision environment, use simulation to generate state sequences over time and the probability of occurrence of each sequence. Since the NCFs are functions of the state sequences, it is a relatively simple matter to determine the joint probability function of NPV for any combination of individual projects.

Results. The results of this study are reported primarily in terms of the consistency between the efficient sets selected by the decision models tested and the SSD efficient set. Since the results of the decision models are highly dependent on whether the projects' cash flows are positively or negatively correlated, the results are examined first in terms of the 16 decision environments that had all project cash flows positively correlated. A discussion of the results when some projects had negatively correlated cash flows follows.

Positively correlated cash flows. Since the SSD model was used as a standard of comparison, by definition it correctly classified all combinations. The SSD model selected relatively consistent efficient sets over the range of decision environments with the number of combinations varying between 27 and 34 (see Table 6-3), with one exception where it yielded 21 combinations. The exception occurred in decision environment 2A, which consisted of projects with highly positively skewed cash flow distributions. Examination of the major classes of decision environments revealed that the size of the SSD efficient set

Table 6-3
Number of Combinations Accepted by Decision Environment and Capital Budgeting Procedure

	Capital Budgeting Procedure						
					Chance-constrained[a]		
Decision Environment	SSD	EV-I	EV-II	ES_h[b]	h_1	h_2	h_3
1	32	10	8	15	10	13	14
2A	21	10	8	13	8	12	13
2B	28	10	8	16	9	11	13
2C	30	10	8	17	13	12	10
2D	31	10	8	16	8	13	13
2E	34	10	8	14	10	12	14
3A	32	10	8	16	10	14	15
3B	34	10	8	19	9	10	12
3C	27	10	8	16	10	12	13
3D	29	10	8	16	9	10	13
3E	29	10	8	16	9	12	13
3F	29	10	8	16	8	10	13
4A	34	10	8	18	9	13	13
4B	34	10	8	12	9	11	12
4C	28	10	8	19	9	10	11
4D	29	10	8	16	11	12	13
5A	4	7	6	1	5	5	3
5B	8	7	6	1	5	3	4
5C	6	7	6	1	4	4	5
5D	9	7	6	1	4	4	4

[a] The critical values--h_1, h_2, and h_3--equal the expected net present value of combination 1 minus 1σ, 2σ, and 3σ of the net present value of combination 1, respectively.

[b] The critical value h equals the expected net present value of combination 1.

varied as much within a decision class as among decision classes.

The SSD efficient set contained more combinations than the efficient set associated with any other model studied. The number of combinations in each of the efficient sets is as follows: SSD--21 to 34 combinations; ES_h--12 to 19 combinations, CCP--10 to 14 combinations; EV-I--10 combinations; EV-II--8 combinations; and NPV--1 combination. The larger SSD-efficient set apparently results from the less restrictive utility assumptions associated with the SSD model. The family of utility functions for this model includes all increasing concave functions and hence all degrees of risk-averse behavior. As additional restrictions are imposed on the utility functions, the resulting decision rule becomes more effective in ordering alternatives and the efficient set becomes smaller (Hadar and Russell 1969). The additional utility assumptions also mean that the criteria are appropriate for a smaller class of investors, or for a more restricted class of options. Levy and Sarnat (1972: Chapter 9) reach similar conclusions.

A total of 46 combinations were selected from a possible 1024 combinations by at least one capital budgeting method in at least one decision environment. The SSD model selected 44 of the 46 combinations at least once. Fourteen of the 46 combinations were always selected by the SSD model, while 12 other combinations were chosen at least 75 percent of the time. The 2 combinations never selected by SSD were the combinations with the lowest means and variances of any of the combinations chosen. None of the decision rules selected all 46 combinations.

Each of the models being examined was ranked on the basis of the extent to which its efficient set of project combinations agreed with the efficient set chosen by SSD model. The performance rankings were established in each of two ways. First, rankings were determined by counting the number of combinations included in the model's efficient set but not included by SSD plus the number excluded by the model but included by SSD. The total derived is referred to as the number of combinations "misclassified." Table 6-4 reports the rank of the models based on the number of combinations misclassified.

Table 6-4
Ranking of Capital Budgeting Procedures
Based on the Number of Combinations
Misclassified by Decision Environment

Decision Environment	EV-I	EV-II	ES_h [b]	Chance-constrained [a] h_1	h_2	h_3
1	5	6	1	4	3	2
2A	4	6	1	2	2	5
2B	5	6	1	4	3	2
2C	5	6	1	2	3	4
2D	4	6	1	4	2	2
2E	5	6	1	4	3	2
3A	5	6	1	2	2	3
3B	5	6	1	4	3	2
3C	5	6	1	3	3	2
3D	5	6	1	4	3	2
3E	4	6	1	5	3	2
3F	4	6	1	4	3	2
4A	5	6	1	3	2	3
4B	3	6	1	2	5	3
4C	5	6	1	4	3	2
4D	5	6	1	4	3	2
5A	4	3	4	1	1	4
5B	3	2	3	1	3	6
5C	4	2	4	2	6	1
5D	2	1	6	3	3	3

[a] The critical values--h_1, h_2, and h_3--equal the expected net present value of combination 1 minus 1σ, 2σ, and 3σ of the net present value of combination 1, respectively.

[b] Critical value h equals the expected net present value of combination 1.

Following this procedure, the semivariance model clearly outperformed all the others. In fact, it misclassified fewer combinations than any other model in each of the 16 decision environments with no negative correlations. The superior performance of the ES_h model is based partly on the fact that its efficient set was a proper subset of the SSD-efficient set in every case. That is, although the ES_h selected a smaller efficient set than did the SSD model, every combination in the ES_h efficient set was included in the corresponding SSD set. These results are consistent with Porter's (1974a) theoretical and empirical findings.

The next best performance was accomplished by the three different chance-constrained models. Although there was some variation of ranking within the chance-constrained models, all three of them misclassified more combinations than did the ES_h model but fewer than any of the other models. Only in 3 out of 16 decision environments did any chance chance-constrained model perform worse than a model ranked below it.

Both the mean-variance models fell below the semivariance and chance-constrained models with EV-I outperforming EV-II. In fact, EV-I was superior to EV-II in every decision environment and was superior to 1 chance-constrained model in 3 out of the 16 decision environments. It is interesting to notice that since the project means and variances were not affected by changes in the decision environments, the efficient sets chosen by the EV models did not vary as the decision environment changed. Thus the EV-I model selected the same 10 combinations in each decision environment. EV-II selected 8 of the same 10 in each decision environment. Therefore the EV-II efficient set was a proper subset of the EV-I-efficient set in every case. Seven of the 10 selected by EV-I and 5 of the 8 selected by EV-II were included in the SSD efficient set in every decision environment. In general, the EV efficient combinations not included in the SSD efficient set were those with the smallest mean and variance [see Porter (1973a) and Porter and Gaumnitz (1972) on this point].

Since the NPV model selects an efficient set consisting of the same single combination of projects--namely, all those with NPV greater than or equal to zero--and since this choice is unaffected by changes in the decision environment, a direct comparison of the NPV model with the others seems questionable. For this reason the NPV model is not ranked in Table 6-4. However, the fact that the combination selected by the NPV model appears in the SSD efficient set in only 7 out of 20 decision environments (including negative correlations) suggests that the performance of the NPV model was quite poor. It means, for example, that a risk-averse investor would have made a clearly incorrect choice with the NPV model in at least 13 out of 20 cases. The NPV model's performance seems even more suspect when it is revealed that the combination it selected was not selected by any of the other models (except SSD) in any decision environment at all.

The second method of ranking the performance of different models was to count only the number of combinations included in the efficient set of the model being tested but not included in the SSD efficient set. This criterion is referred to as "falsely included" and is reported in Table 6-5. On this basis the overall rankings were the same except that the two EV models had identical ranks in all decision environments. Since the ES_h model chose proper subsets of the SSD efficient sets, it falsely included no combinations. The performance of the chance-constrained models fell in between that of the ES_h model and that of the two EV models.

Negatively correlated cash flows. The introduction of some projects with negative correlated cash flows--numbers 2,3,6,7, and 11--had considerable impact on the SSD efficient sets selected. The size of the SSD efficient sets was reduced to between four and nine combinations. A reduction in the size of the SSD efficient set was expected since the mean of the combinations remained unchanged, while some of the combination variances decreased substantially. The reduction in the variance while the mean remained constant resulted in combinations with negatively correlated projects dominating combinations with all positively correlated projects and a smaller SSD efficient set. A similar reduction occurred in the size of the efficient sets for the other models. See Table 6-3 for details.

Eighteen combinations were selected by at least one of the decision rules when some of the projects had negatively correlated

Table 6-5
Ranking of Capital Budgeting Procedures
Based on Combinations Falsely Included by Capital Budgeting Procedure

	Capital Budgeting Procedure					
				Chance-constrained[a]		
Decision Environment	EV-I	EV-II	ES_h[b]	h_1	h_2	h_3
1	5	5	1	2	2	2
2A	3	3	1	2	1	6
2B	5	5	1	2	2	2
2C	5	5	1	2	2	2
2D	5	5	1	2	2	2
2E	5	5	1	2	2	2
3A	3	3	1	2	5	6
3B	5	5	1	2	2	2
3C	3	3	1	2	3	3
3D	5	5	1	1	1	1
3E	2	2	1	2	2	2
3F	5	5	1	2	2	2
4A	3	3	1	2	3	6
4B	3	3	1	2	5	5
4C	5	5	1	2	2	2
4D	2	2	1	2	2	2
5A	6	5	1	2	2	2
5B	6	4	1	2	2	4
5C	6	4	1	2	4	2
5D	6	2	1	2	2	2

[a]The critical values--h_1, h_2, and h_3--equal the expected net present value of combination 1 minus 1σ, 2σ, and 3σ of the net present value of combination 1, respectively.

[b]The critical value h equals the expected net present value of combination 1.

NPVs. The SSD model selected 14 of the 18 combinations. The 4 combinations not selected by SSD were selected by only the EV-I and EV-II models. The mean and variance of each of these 4 combinations were less than the smallest mean and variance of all combinations contained in the SSD efficient set. This result agrees with Porter (1973a) and Porter and Gaumnitz (1972), who found that SSD tended to eliminate low mean-variance portfolios that were included in the efficient set of a mean-variance decision rule.

The performance ranking of the models was changed considerably (see Tables 6-4 and 6-5) by the introduction of negatively correlated projects. Likewise, the models were more sensitive to changes in the characteristics of the models and the ranks of models showed more variability than when no projects were correlated negatively. Based on the number of combinations falsely included (Table 6-5), the rankings were the same as for decision environments with no negatively correlated projects; namely, ES_h, chance constrained, EV-I, EV-II (in decreasing order)--except that EV-I outperformed EV-II rather than tying it. When the ranking is based on total number of combinations misclassified (Table 6-4), however, no clear ranking of models emerges. In each decision environment a different model was ranked best, and in each decision environment a different model was ranked worst. With cases involving some negatively correlated project returns, then, no clear conclusion follows.

Other interesting findings. In addition to the performance rankings reported above, we observed a number of other interesting results concerning the impact of shifts in the decision environment and the consistency of efficient set membership among models. With the ES_h model, for example, 22 different combinations were selected over the 16 decision environments with nonnegative correlations, but 10 of the 22 were included in each environment. These same 10 were always in the SSD efficient set, and 7, 6, and 5 of them were always included by EV-I, the chance-constrained models, and EV-II, respectively.

The ES_h model was especially sensitive to skewness. When the set of possible combinations contained some NPV distributions that were negatively skewed and others that were positively skewed, the

ES_h efficient set selected only combinations with positive skewness. If all NPV distributions were positively skewed, the ES_h model tended to select the combinations with the higher degree of skewness. On the other hand, if all NPV distributions were negatively skewed, the ES_h model tended to choose those combinations with the least amount of negative skewness.

Although the CCP model was tested for three critical values, the discussion of the results of the CCP model considers only the h_2 critical value, i.e., the expected net present value of the existing firm minus 2σ of the net present value of the existing firm. The results of the CCP model for the three critical values were not identical, but were similar, and the h_2 critical value results are representative.

The size of the CCP efficient set ranged from 10 to 14 combinations, which was larger than the efficient set of the EV-II model, greater than or equal to the size of the EV-I efficient set, and always smaller than the efficient sets associated with the ES_h and SSD models. A total of 24 different combinations were selected by the CCP model. Only 7 of the 24 combinations were selected in all 16 decision environments. Six of the 7 combinations that were always in the CCP efficient set were also always in the SSD efficient set.

6.1.3 Summary and Conclusions

Positively Correlated NPVs. An important finding of this study was that for the three capital budgeting models that used a measure of risk other than the variance of returns, the composition of the efficient sets varied as the decision environments were altered. On the other hand, each EV-I and EV-II model selected an identical efficient set in all 16 decision environments with positively correlated cash flows. These models were insensitive to changes in the characteristics of project cash flow distributions.

Another significant result of this study is that the rankings of the models show ES_h to be superior to the rest. The ES_h model not only misclassified fewer combinations than any other model, but also included only combinations that were contained in the SSD efficient set. Since the ES_h efficient set is a subset of the SSD efficient set, a decision-maker who utilizes the ES_h model to determine an efficient set and then selects a combination from the ES_h efficient set is assured of choosing an SSD efficient combination--a choice that is consistent with risk aversion. None of the other capital budgeting models tested can give this assurance. The performance ranking of other models is as follows: CCP, EV-I, EV-II.

All models reduced the potential number of combinations (1024) to a manageable number, with EV-II having the smallest efficient set (other than that of the NPV model) of 8 combinations only. EV-I had 10, CCP had roughly 8 to 15, ES_h had roughly 12 to 19, and SSD had 21 to 34. A ranking according to smallest number of combinations included would be the reverse of the ranking based on performance.

Negatively Correlated NPVs. The interrelationships of the project returns were important in selecting the efficient set. If all project NPVs were positively correlated (as they were for the foregoing conclusions), each capital budgeting model selected one relatively consistent set of combinations for all decision environments. The introduction of some projects with negatively correlated cash flows resulted in an almost entirely different efficient set of combinations for each capital budgeting model. Very few combinations were common to the efficient sets generated when all project cash flows were positively correlated or when some project cash flows were positively correlated and others were negatively correlated. The number of combinations included was substantially smaller when negative correlations were admitted. The ranks of the capital budgeting models based either on the number of combinations misclassified or on the number of combinations falsely included in an efficient set varied considerably as the decision environment changed. No longer was it possible to give a definite superiority ranking to the capital budgeting models.

Data Processing Methodology. While no attempt was made to evaluate the cost of implementing the various models studied, several observations can be drawn from the methodology used in this study, which involved simulating cash flows and assigning them to economic states. The NPV model required the simplest input data--the expected cash flow of each project for each period and a risk-adjusted discount rate. Unfortunately, however, the NPV model gave the poorest results. The SSD, ES_h, CCP, EV-I, and EV-II models all require the same basic input information: estimates of the mean, variance, basic type of distribution (e.g., normal, uniform, gamma), and the amount of skewness of the cash flow distributions for each project in each period. A risk-free discount rate must be determined also. Each of the models, with the possible exception of NPV, requires a computer algorithm for solution. As long as complete enumeration is a feasible solution technique, the algorithms are neither complex nor difficult. Although SSD was used as a standard of comparison, it is no more difficult to operationalize than the other capital budgeting models tested. From an operational standpoint, there is no reason why it could not be used for capital budgeting purposes.

6.2 Application of SD to Bank Balance-Sheet Management

R. Burr Porter

The problem of bank balance sheet management is basically the problem of selecting a combination of assets, liabilities, and capital that maximizes some objective function while at the same time satisfying some constraint on the amount of risk to which the bank is exposed. The problem is made interesting by the facts that future outcomes of the bank's activities are subject to random fluctuations (risk) and the most profitable assets tend to be those with the greatest degree of risk. The problem is made difficult by the complexity required to provide a reasonably accurate statement of the relationships that account for the balance sheet changes from one observation point to the next. For example, in a standard portfolio problem, one invests specific amounts of money in each of a number of assets, waits some period of time, and observes the results. This problem is relatively easy to model. With the bank problem, however, one cannot even be certain at the beginning of the period how much ultimately will be invested in various loan categories during the period or how much cash will be available for investment. Loan demands and deposit balances are major random variables in the problem.

To clarify the bank's decision process, we assume that the bank has defined a basic time period of length such that changes in policies regarding balance sheet structure are not made during the period. That is, the only changes in balance sheet values that occur within the period either result from random fluctuations or deliberate changes that are specifically required to meet the constraints of the problem once the random fluctuations have occurred.

Each basic decision time period can be thought of as being divided into subperiods or "stages" as follows:

1. At the beginning of period t a decision model is employed to select the optimal set of beginning balances for the various balance sheet items, subject to the relevant constraints. Transactions are conducted to adjust balances of investments, assets and liabilities, certificates of deposit, and capital to the chosen amounts. The chosen balances of cash, loans, and deposits are somewhat fictitious in the sense that they are the expected values of random variables. They would be the actual balances only if expected values were realized exactly and immediately. In fact, changes in these balances occur throughout the period, and the actual results frequently deviate from the expected results. All qualified loan applications will be granted, and the actual volume of such applications--as well as the actual repayment of prior loans--is a random variable. In addition, the returns on all loans and investments are random variables. The values chosen by the decision model are defined to be the values at observation point 1, or the first-stage decisions.

2. Once the first-stage decisions have been made and a portion of period t elapsed, actual outcomes for the random variables are observed to determine if any of the constraints is violated. If violations are discovered, changes are made in the nonrandom variables to bring the bank into compliance with its constraints. The resulting random and nonrandom balances are referred to as the values at observation point 2. The changes in nonrandom balances are referred to as the second-stage decisions.

3. Following observation point 2, additional random fluctuations occur, period t concludes, and final results for balance sheet balances are observed. These balances are the values at observation point 3. Next, the decision model is applied again, and period "t + 1" has begun.

6.2.1 Models Proposed in Other Studies

A number of studies have shown that several stochastic programming models can be employed to solve this problem. Before discussing SD, we shall summarize the main approaches that have been employed and point out their deficiencies.

The Cohen and Hammer linear programming model (1966) maximizes either terminal value of equity, present value of net income during the horizon period, or the sum of these two amounts under the assumption that rates of return are known. Risk is brought into the analysis in the form of constraints or limits on the combinations of investments available to the bank. These constraints are designed to guarantee that the bank will be able to meet its loan demand and cash outflow from deposit withdrawals. They are based on the Federal Reserve Board liquidity/capital adequacy requirements as well as individual bank policy considerations. They require, for example, that the ratio of total capital to total assets increase as the asset structure becomes less liquid. In addition, the model includes market constraints such as the maximum demand for each class of loan.

Although this approach represents a rather limited and somewhat conservative view of risk, it remains an important analytical contribution to bank asset management. It is computationally feasible and, being tied to Federal Reserve guidelines, it has a degree of familiarity to bank managers. In addition, it is amenable to the use of sensitivity analysis for determining the effects of incorrect assessments of future returns on investments, loan demands, etc.

The two-stage programming model (Booth 1972; Crane 1971), frequently called "programming with recourse," begins where the linear programming models end and adds two new elements of risk. First is the substitution in the objective function of expected values of returns on assets for the assumed known values. This change has the advantage of admitting explicitly that investment outcomes cannot be known for certain. The second and more important addition is a focus on risk in terms of the expected cost of violating one or more of the liquidity/capital adequacy constraints. To accomplish this extension, the decision process is viewed as occurring in two steps (or stages).

First a set of investments is chosen. A period of time elapses, and the results of the investments are recorded. In addition, changes in the bank's liability structure are noted. If any of these results leaves the bank in the position of violating one or more of the accepted constraints, the bank must adjust its balance sheet accordingly and incur the costs associated with the adjustments. The unique feature of this approach is that the expected cost of the adjustments is included in the objective function that the bank maximizes in order to select its portfolio of assets at the beginning of the first stage.

This approach has the advantage of adding an appealing degree of flexibility and realism to the basic linear programming model. It significantly broadens the bank's view of uncertainty while retaining computational feasibility by restricting consideration to discrete probability functions. It is limited, however, in the number of variables and time periods that it can consider, and it requires a considerable degree of independence among the random variables. In addition, it still limits its measurement of risk to expected values of the random variables.

<u>The chance-constrained models</u> represent a significant departure from the traditional Federal Reserve view of risk. A model proposed by Charnes and Littlechild (1968), for example, maximizes return on investment subject to a limit on the probability that the bank will be unable to meet its loan demand. This probability limit is referred to as a "chance constraint." The liquidity/capital adequacy constraints are omitted. Risk is defined as the chance that otherwise acceptable loans will have to be refused because of inadequate reserves. The probability that this situation will occur depends on the set of assets chosen by the bank, so the bank controls risk by excluding any set of assets that results in a probability of loan refusal greater than the agreed-upon probability.

A more recent model by Fried (1970) broadens the chance constraint to include the probability that the total value of liquid assets will fall below some predetermined amount. This approach allows for uncertainty in the prices of liquid assets, volume of deposits, and demand for loans. In addition, expected returns are substituted for assumed known returns in the objective function. Computational efficiency is maintained by requiring that the random variables be normally distributed. Statistical interrelationships among variables is admitted through the inclusion of covariance terms.

This approach shares with the two-stage method the focus on risk in terms of constraint violations. It differs in the choice of constraints and particularly in ignoring the explicit measure of the cost of constraint violation. Finally, it requires normally distributed random variables.

6.2.2 SD Model

Stochastic dominance criteria overcome the risk-modeling deficiencies of the stochastic-programming approaches. It seems important, therefore, to conduct empirical tests of the SD model. The SD model focuses on the cumulative probability function of net return to the bank where the return function incorporates all possible inflows and outflows including costs associated with any intraperiod adjustments required to satisfy regulatory demands or, in fact, to avoid bankruptcy. Thus SD criteria avoid the narrow and unrealistic view of risk as the probability of not satisfying a constraint.

Since SD criteria do not contain procedures for generating efficient balance sheet combinations, Porter (1974b) has suggested that SD criteria be applied in either or both of two ways: (1) using a stochastic-programming model with varying risk-aversion coefficients to generate efficient sets of balance sheet structures and then applying SD criteria to screen the members of these sets; and (2) using experience and judgment to establish a large but finite number of feasible structures that can be screened by SD. The second suggestion might incorporate a controlled random-sampling procedure such as that used by Porter (1973a).

As an example of how this approach can be followed and of how serious the errors resulting from other decision rules can be, Porter applied FSD, SSD, and TSD to the joint distributions of four prespecified combinations of consumer and commercial loans. The results, shown in Figure 6-1, indicate that mixtures 1 and 2 (M1 and M2) are dominated by FSD, SSD, and TSD, while neither M3 nor M4 is dominated

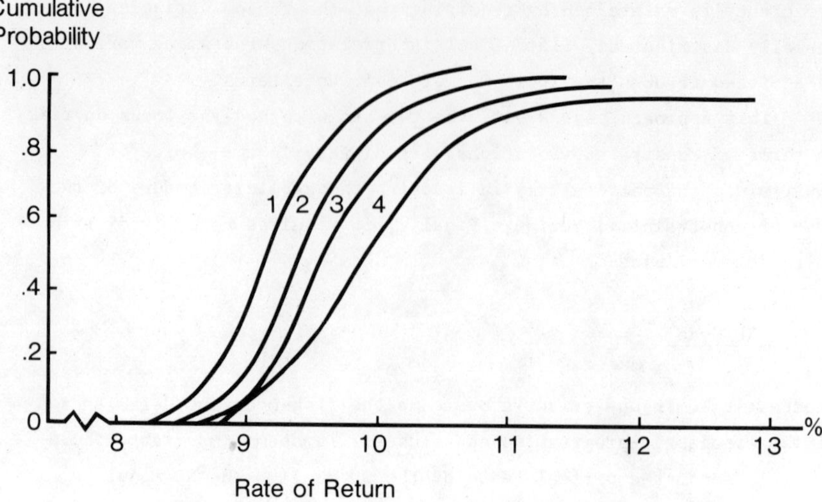

Figure 6-1. Simulated Distribution Functions of Return on Bank Assets

by any SD rule. Therefore the bank's manager must examine both M3 and M4 directly and make a choice. We would expect most observers to choose M4, since its distribution function lies to the right of M3's except for an almost unnoticeable part at the lower end of the range. Yet it is possible that a risk-constraint model would arbitrarily select M3 and M4. SD avoids this problem by presenting distribution functions for both M3 and M4 for the decision-maker to choose between.

6.3 Stochastic Dominance and Capital Market Efficiency

M. C. Findlay

Numerous theoretical and empirical studies of capital market efficiency have appeared in the last decade [cf. Fama (1970a) and Jensen (1972b)]. Most of these have been based on the EV market model of Markowitz, Sharpe, et al., although a few have also used the more elegant Arrow-Debreu state preference theory. Stochastic dominance has been employed in this context only recently and mostly as a tool for inefficiency proofs. This section will review some of these studies and propose a few conjectures for further research.

Sarnat (1974) computed the rates of return on seven U.S. investment media (U.S. government and corporate bonds and industrial, railroads, public utility, New York City bank, and property and liability insurance company common shares) for the period 1946-1969. He then investigated the strategies of investing solely in one medium and found that industrial shares eliminated both groups of bonds as well as railroad shares by FSD and further eliminated NYC bank shares by SSD. He also discovered that over the relevant range of pure interest rates, the EV efficient set consisted of various proportions of the three media (i.e., industrial, utility, and property and liability shares) that were, individually, members of the SSD set. From the analysis, Sarnat concluded (p. 1252) that "the findings suggest that some imperfections in the capital market have persisted over a significantly long period of time."

The Joy and Porter (1974) study, already described in Chapter 3, might also be viewed in this regard. Various studies of mutual fund performance, which find that the funds do not outperform the market, have been employed by some writers to advance the strong form of the efficient capital market hypothesis (EMH). This hypothesis posits that all private as well as public information is impounded in share price, and mutual funds are treated as sophisticated possessors of private information in these discussions. The latter assertion is subjected to considerable doubt by Joy and Porter's findings that the performance of the overall market dominates the performance of the funds at the .0156 significance level for SSD and .002 for TSD. It would thus appear that strong-form EMH advocates, if they wish to avoid charges of erecting a straw man, must find a more convincing class of sophisticated investors upon which to test their null hypothesis.

In regard to non-U.S. markets, results of tests on the Israeli and London exchanges have been reported already in Chapter 3. In addition, Findlay and Danan (1975) conducted an SD efficiency test on the Toronto Stock Exchange (TSE). In the latter study, stocks were ranked by their return variances over a 36-month period, divided into three risk groups, formed into 153 portfolios of 15 stocks each (50 random portfolios plus 1 portfolio with the stocks having the lowest beta coefficients in each risk group) and tracked over the succeeding 12-month period. This process was repeated annually over a decade and a comparison was made between the low beta strategy and random investment in each of the three total risk classes. In the two lower risk groups, the former strategy exhibited SSD over the latter and only a single outlier (which could be attributed to sampling error) prevented this conclusion from holding for the high-risk group as well. See Figure 6-2 for the monthly return cumulative distribution functions. Hence at least in terms of the EV return-generating market model, the TSE was not even weakly efficient over this period (1959-1971).

As we move from stock and bond markets to the broader concept of markets for contingent claims, a paper by Lippman (1972) becomes relevant. Lippman investigated the three types of reinsurance generally available (i.e., excess of loss, pro rata quota share, and sliding quota share) by holding constant the expected value of the ceder's liability. He then proved that excess of loss reinsurance exhibited SSD over the other two with regard to the ceder. Although as an empirical matter this was also the most prevalent form of reinsurance, the other two do continue to exist. Hence one can contend that an inefficiency persists in the reinsurance market.

Finally, the following conjecture can be advanced. Much is written about the relative efficiency of various markets and of markets becoming increasingly efficient without any empirical standards for such statements. It would appear that SD might provide at least an ordinal scale for this analysis. A market in which "representative" portfolios (i.e., the portfolios of significant market participants) could be shown to be FSD-inferior to other available portfolios would hardly seem a market at all. If this condition held for SSD, at least strong inefficiency claims could be made. Furthermore, at least for the purpose of demonstrating inefficiency vis-a-vis the EV return-generating market model, large random portfolios would seem to provide adequate proxies of "representative" portfolios. The jury is not in on TSD and DARA-SD, but there is some intuitive appeal in classifying a market's efficiency in terms of the level of SD required to reduce

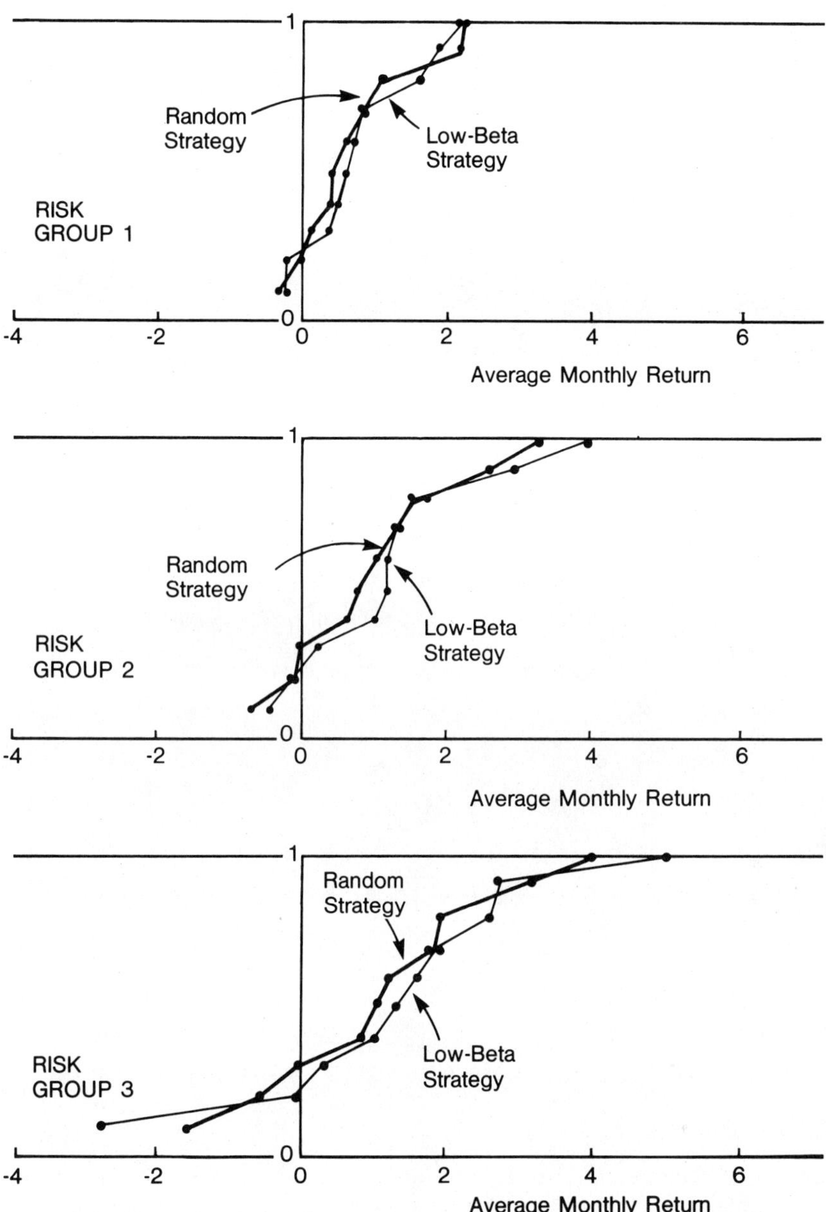

Figure 6-2. A Comparison of Random and Low-Beta Portfolios for Three Risk Groups Comprised of Stocks from the Toronto Stock Exchange.

the size of the efficient set "significantly" (the last an interesting empirical question also).

Introduction to Chapter 7
Applications in Economic Theory and Analysis

Stochastic dominance methodology can contribute to our understanding of various economic phenomena. This has been shown already by the important role that it plays in understanding and solving the portfolio selection problem. The discussion of applications in earlier chapters, however, has been concerned mainly with empirical results or computational characteristics. In this chapter SD methodology is used to investigate selected theoretical issues in economic analysis.

In Section 7.1. Josef Hadar and William R. Russell use stochastic dominance principles to study changes in economic behavior that are induced by changes in the uncertainty of the economic environment. For instance, in one application they consider, a firm is uncertain about the market price it will receive for its product. They derive conditions under which the firm will increase its production level with an upward (FSD or SSD) shift in the distribution of the market price.

In Section 7.2, they concern themselves with conditions under which diversification of an investment fund among several uncertain prospects is an economically optimal strategy. They present a number of theorems that relate the nature of the joint probability distribution of the prospects to the type of diversification that is optimal. These theorems draw heavily on SD theory.

7 Applications in Economic Theory and Analysis

Josef Hadar and *William R. Russell*

7.1 Comparative Statics of Uncertainty

Analysis of behavior under uncertainty is concerned, among other things, with the following two types of questions: (1) How does behavior under uncertainty differ from behavior in which the decision-maker has full information? and (2) How does a decision-maker under uncertainty change his behavior with changes in the nature of uncertainty? In cases in which uncertainty is expressed in terms of probability distributions, changes in uncertainty usually take the form of shifts in the probability distribution. It is the second problem with which we are concerned in this section. In the framework to be analyzed here, the decision-maker is assumed to maximize the expected value of an objective function that depends on a random variable and a decision variable. The central problem is to determine the direction of change in the optimal value of the decision variable following a shift in the distribution function of the random variable.

In most of the existing analyses of this type of problem, the shifts that are assumed to take place in the probability distributions are of a rather special class. In general, the approach has been to transform the random variable into a new one, and thereby to parameterize the distribution function. The most commonly used shifts are of two types. [For applications of the various shifts see Arrow (1971), Batra and Ullah (1974), and Sandmo (1971).]

1. Horizontal shifts in the distribution: If the original random variable is X, a new random variable Y is defined as $Y = X + k$, $k > 0$. Then the distribution function of Y differs from X by a horizontal displacement of length k. Thus if F(x) is the distribution

function of X, and G(x) is the distribution of Y, then $G(x) = F(x - k)$. Since $x - k < x$ for all finite x, it follows that $G(x) \leq F(x)$ for all x; in other words, distribution G dominates F in the sense of FSD. (See the definitions of FSD and SSD in Section 2.14.) Consequently, the above horizontal shifts are special cases of general FSD shifts.

2. Stretching the distribution: Stretching results when the random variable Y is defined as $Y = X + k\,(X - x_0)$, $k > 0$, and where x_0 is some fixed number. Here we have

$$G(x) = F\left(\frac{x + kx_0}{1 + k}\right) .$$

To analyze the effects of stretching, it may be helpful to consider two special cases.

Case (a): $0 \leq x,\ x_0 \leq 0$
In this case

$$G(x) = F\left(\frac{x + kx_0}{1 + k}\right) \leq F(x) ,$$

so that G dominates F in the sense of FSD.

Case (b): $E(X) \leq x_0$
To derive the implications of this case, we write X as a function of Y; that is,

$$X = A + BY,$$

where

$$A = \frac{kx_0}{1 + k}$$

and

$$B = \frac{1}{1 + k} .$$

Since $A \geq (1 - B)E(X)$, the relationship between X and Y satisfies Theorem 4 in Hadar and Russell (1971), according to which F dominates G in the sense of SSD. (Strictly speaking, the above-cited theorem assumes that X is non-negative. However, in part ii of that theorem the non-negativity assumption is not needed.)

We thus see that horizontal shifts and certain types of stretching of the distribution are special cases of stochastic dominance shifts; however, some types of stretching need not create stochastic dominance between the two distributions.

Shifts in distributions that create stochastic dominance but are otherwise arbitrary are more general than the cases considered above. Essentially, they admit a greater variety of patterns in which the probability mass may be redistributed as the distribution is shifted. In the present analysis we consider two general types of shifts in the distribution: FSD and SSD shifts. For convenience, the shifts will be made in a direction such that the shifted distribution is "better" than the original distribution; that is, the shifted distribution dominates the original distribution in the sense of either FSD or SSD, as the case may be.

7.1.1 A General Model

The decision-maker's objective function is denoted by $\phi(v,x)$, where v is the decision variable and x is the random variable. The function ϕ is assumed to be thrice continuously differentiable. Furthermore, it is assumed to be strictly concave in v (for every x), and strictly monotonic in x (for every v). The range of x is some interval [a,b]. The distribution function of the random variable is denoted by F(x,p), where p is a shift parameter. It will also be assumed that E(X) is finite for all p.

The decision-maker maximizes the expected value of $\phi(v,x)$, which is, of course, a function of v and p. We write this function as

$$E[\phi(v,x)] = \Phi(v,p). \tag{7.1}$$

We assume that for every p, the function Φ possesses an interior maximum at which the second derivative with respect to v does not vanish. Formally, we assume that for every p there exists v* such that

$$\Phi_v(v^*,p) = 0, \tag{7.2}$$

$$\Phi_{vv}(v^*,p) < 0. \tag{7.3}$$

Since the strict concavity of ϕ with respect to v implies strict concavity of Φ with respect to v, the optimal value v* is a single-valued function of p, which we write as

$$v^* = \theta(p). \tag{7.4}$$

Now if the distribution function of the random variable shifts as a result of a shift in the parameter p, in general, the decision-maker will respond by adjusting the optimal value of his decision variable. The nature of this response is given by the function θ defined in Eq. (7.4). Of course, since the model is specified only by general functions, one can deduce only general properties of the function θ, such as its slope. It is the purpose of the following analysis to determine the sign of θ'. This is an example of what in economic theory is known as "comparative static analysis." We shall investigate the sign of θ' for an FSD shift and an SSD shift in the distribution function of X.

7.1.2 FSD Shifts in the Distribution Function

If the shifted distribution function is to dominate the original distribution in the sense of FSD, the distribution function must be pulled downward at least at one point in its domain. Therefore we shall associate a small increase in the shift parameter p with a downward shift in the distribution function F, at least at some point. Formally we assume

$$F_p(x,p) \leq 0 \quad \text{for all p and x}, \tag{7.5}$$

the strict inequality holding for some x in the interior of [a,b]. To obtain an expression for θ', we differentiate Eq. (7.2) with respect to p, using Eq. (7.4). After rearranging terms, we get

$$\theta' = -\frac{\Phi_{vp}}{D}, \tag{7.6}$$

where $D = \Phi_{vv}[\theta(p),p] < 0$. Now if the left-hand side of Eq. (7.1) is written explicitly in terms of the distribution function and the equation is differentiated partially, first with respect to v and then with respect to p, Eq. (7.6) can be written as

$$\theta' = \frac{1}{D} \int_a^b \phi_{vx} F_p(x,p)dx. \tag{7.7}$$

It can be seen, in view of the assumptions in (7.3) and (7.5), that if ϕ_{vx} is of only one sign in its domain, then we have

$$\text{sgn } \theta' = \text{sgn } \phi_{vx}. \tag{7.8}$$

7.1.3 SSD Shifts in the Distribution Function

As in the case of an FSD shift, we shall again shift the distribution in such a way that the shifted distribution dominates the original one in the sense of SSD. Since the SSD condition is defined in terms of the integral of the distribution function, the latter integral must be made to shift downward as a result of a small increase in the shift parameter. We define

$$H(x,p) = \int_a^x F(t,p)dt, \tag{7.9}$$

and hence assume

$$H_p(x,p) \le 0, \quad \text{for all p and x,} \tag{7.10}$$

the inequality holding strictly for some x in the interior of [a,b].

To obtain an expression for θ', we integrate the integral appearing in Eq. (7.7), using integration by parts. This yields

$$\theta' = \frac{1}{D}\left[\phi_{vx}(v,b)\int_a^b F_p(t,p)dt - \int_a^b \phi_{vxx}(v,x)\int_a^x F_p(t,p)dt\, dx\right]. \tag{7.11}$$

We may note here that for any random variable with finite mean whose distribution function is given by F(x,p), the following holds:

$$E(X) = -\int_{-\infty}^{0} F(x,p)dx + \int_0^\infty [1 - F(x,p)]\, dx = \eta(p). \tag{7.12}$$

Upon differentiating the above equation we get

$$\eta' = -\int_{-\infty}^{\infty} F_p(x,p)\, dx = -\int_a^b F_p(x,p)\, dx. \tag{7.13}$$

Also, differentiating Eq. (7.9) yields

$$H_p(x,p) = \int_a^x F_p(t,p)dt. \tag{7.14}$$

Substituting in Eq. (7.11) from Eqs. (7.13) and (7.14), we have

$$\theta' = -\frac{1}{D}\left[\phi_{vx}(v,b)\eta' + \int_a^b \phi_{vxx}(v,x)H_p(x,p)dx\right]. \tag{7.15}$$

In the investigation of the sign of θ' as given by Eq. (7.15), two cases need to be considered: SSD shifts in which E(X) remains unchanged--so-called mean-preserving shifts, and shifts in which the mean increases. [SSD shifts with constant mean have been considered by Rothschild and Stiglitz (1971).] We again consider only those situations in which each of the functions ϕ_{vx} and ϕ_{vxx} is of only one sign in its domain since otherwise the results are indeterminate. For a mean-preserving shift ($\eta' = 0$) we get, in view of Eqs. (7.10) and (7.15),

$$\operatorname{sgn} \theta' = \operatorname{sgn}(-\phi_{vxx}). \tag{7.16}$$

For a mean-increasing shift we have

$$\operatorname{sgn} \theta' = \operatorname{sgn} \phi_{vx} \quad \text{if the product } \phi_{vx}\phi_{vxx} \text{ is nonpositive.} \tag{7.17}$$

If $\phi_{vx}\phi_{vxx} > 0$, the sign of θ' is indeterminate.

7.1.4 The Role of the Measure of Risk Aversion

As has been shown above, the results that we are concerned with in this analysis directly depend on the signs of the functions ϕ_{vx} and ϕ_{vxx}. These signs in turn are related to the properties of a generalized measure of risk aversion that will be introduced now. For this purpose we think of the decision-maker as maximizing the expected value of a utility function u(y), where y is a random variable. The latter is assumed to depend on the decision variable v and the random variable x through a relationship such as $y = f(v,x)$. The utility function is assumed to be strictly increasing and strictly concave in y; that is, $u' > 0$, and $u'' < 0$ for all y. The function f is assumed to be thrice differentiable, but the other properties of f may vary from one problem to another. In general, the function f will be monotonic in x.

We define the following measure of risk aversion:

$$R(x,v) = \frac{-f_v f_x u''[f(v,x)]}{u'[f(v,x)]}. \tag{7.18}$$

While a justification for this measure will not be given here, it can be seen immediately that for the two special cases $f_v f_x = 1$ and $f_v f_x = f(v,x)$, the measure R reduces to the Arrow-Pratt measures of absolute and relative risk aversion, respectively [see Arrow (1971) and Pratt (1964)]. The relationship between the general objective function ϕ and the utility function u is given by

$$\phi(v,x) = u[f(v,x)]. \tag{7.19}$$

Partial differentiation of the above gives

$$\phi_{vx} = f_{vx}u' + f_v f_x u'' = (f_{vx} - R)u', \tag{7.20}$$

where the second equation follows from (7.18). Differentiating once again with respect to x yields

$$\phi_{vxx} = f_x(f_{vx} - R)u'' + (f_{vxx} - R_x)u'. \tag{7.21}$$

In view of (7.20), we can restate the comparative static result for an FSD shift given in (7.8) as follows:

$$\operatorname{sgn} \theta' = \operatorname{sgn}(f_{vx} - R). \tag{7.22}$$

7.1.5 Some Economic Examples

In this section we investigate the effects of FSD and SSD shifts in the context of several simple economic decision models. Since all these problems are well known and have been analyzed extensively in the literature, we shall be quite brief in the description of these decision problems. The main purpose here is to illustrate the applicability of general FSD and SSD shifts in comparative static analysis.

A Portfolio Problem. One of the simplest portfolio problems is that of the optimal division of a fixed fund between a sure prospect and an uncertain prospect. The problem is formulated by means of the following notation:

m = size of fund (initial wealth),
v = amount to be invested in the uncertain prospect,
r = yield on the sure prospect,
z = yield on the uncertain prospect,
y = terminal wealth at the end of period.

Terminal wealth is defined as $y = (m - v)r + vz$, which can also be written as $y = mr + vx$, where $x = z - r$ is a random variable. The investor is assumed to maximize the expected utility of terminal wealth; that is, he maximizes $E[u(mr + vx)]$ with respect to the decision variable v. To guarantee an interior solution, i.e., $0 < v^* < m$, we assume $E(x) > 0$.

In this problem we have $f(v,x) = mr + vx$, and hence the following: $f_v = x$, $f_x = v$, $f_{vx} = 1$, and $f_{vxx} = 0$. Therefore the risk aversion measure takes the form $R = -xvu''/u$. [In this problem the function R is the same as what Menezes and Hanson (1970) have called "partial relative risk aversion function" and Zeckhauser and Keeler (1970) have called "size-of-risk aversion function."] Thus for this particular problem, Eq. (7.22) can be stated as

$$\operatorname{sgn} \theta' = \operatorname{sgn} (1 - R) \tag{7.23}$$

This leads to the following proposition:

PROPOSITION 7.1. _If_ $R < 1$ _for all_ v _and_ x, _then an FSD shift in the distribution of the return on the uncertain prospect induces the investor to invest more in the uncertain prospect_.

The assumption $R < 1$ places certain restrictions on the utility function u. For example, if the range of the random variable y is unbounded from above, and the utility function is defined on the entire range of the random variable, then, given the properties of $f(v,x)$ in the present problem, it can be shown that $u[f(v,x)] \to \infty$ as $y \to \infty$. In words, the utility function cannot be bounded from above if the range of the random variable is unbounded from above. [The upper unboundedness of the utility function need not jeopardize the existence of expected utility as has been shown by Ryan (1974) and Arrow (1974).]

To determine the effect of an SSD shift, we apply Eqs. (7.16) and (7.17), which requires us to establish the signs of the functions ϕ_{vx} and ϕ_{vxx}. Turning to Eqs. (7.20) and (7.21) and using the properties of the function f stated above, we find the following: $\phi_{vx} = (1 - R)u'$ and $\phi_{vxx} = v(1 - R)u'' - R_x u'$. This leads to the following results:

PROPOSITION 7.2. _If_ $R < 1$ _and_ $R_x > 0$ _for all_ v _and_ x, _then an SSD shift in the distribution of the return on the uncertain prospect induces the investor to invest more in the uncertain prospect_.

In this problem, it is reasonable to assume that $m > 0$ and $r \geq 1$. Therefore terminal wealth y is bounded away from zero, i.e., $y \geq mr > 0$. Consequently, two classes of utility functions satisfying Propositions 7.1 and 7.2 are $u = \alpha + \beta \ln y$ and $u = \alpha + \beta y^{\gamma}$, $\beta > 0$, $0 < \gamma < 1$.

Model of a Competitive Firm. In simple models of the firm, uncertainty may arise with respect to several aspects of the firm's operations. Two examples are a random element in the production process, and uncertainty with respect to the market price of the firm's product. The latter type of uncertainty may occur if the firm operates in a competitive market (i.e., the firm is a price-taker) and also is faced with a relatively long lag in production. In that case the firm must choose its level of production without having perfect knowledge of the price that will prevail in the market when the product is put on sale.

It is the case of price uncertainty that we shall consider here. In this model the firm is assumed to choose its level of output (its decision variable) so as to maximize expected utility of profit for the relevant planning period, given that the product price is a random variable. We use the following notation:

v = level of output,
$c(v)$ = total variable cost function,
c_0 = fixed cost,
x = market price,
y = profit for the period.

Profit is defined by $y = vx - c(v) - c_0$, so that the firm maximizes $E\{u[vx - c(v) - c_0]\}$ with respect to v. We shall assume that the average variable cost function $c(v)/v$ has a minimum for some non-negative level of output, and we shall denote this minimum by c_m. To ensure that the optimal value of v (assuming it exists) is strictly positive, we assume $E(X) > c_m$. Furthermore, in this problem $f(v,x) = vx - c(v) - c_0$, $f_v = x - c'(v)$, $f_x = v$, $f_{vx} = 1$, and $f_{vxx} = 0$, so that the risk aversion function is

$$R = \frac{-v(x - c')u''}{u'} .$$

Since the functions f_{vx} and f_{vxx} are the same as in the portfolio problem presented above, we can state results similar to those in Propositions 7.1 and 7.2, namely:

PROPOSITION 7.3. *If $R < 1$ for all v and x, then an FSD shift in the distribution of the market price causes the firm to increase its level of production.*

PROPOSITION 7.4. *If $R < 1$ and $R_x > 0$ for all v and x, then an SSD shift in the distribution of the market price causes the firm to increase its level of production.*

It is reasonable to assume that given the firm's plant, the amount of output that can be produced in a typical period is bounded from above, say, by v_0. Consequently, the profit y in a typical period is bounded from below by $-c(v_0) - c_0$, given the usual assumption that the cost function c is monotonically increasing, and assuming that the market price is bounded from below by zero. Propositions 7.3 and 7.4 therefore will be satisfied for utility functions of the form $u = \alpha + \beta \ln(k + y)$ and $u = \alpha + \beta(k + y)^\gamma$, where $\beta > 0$, $0 < \gamma < 1$, and $k > c(v_0) + c_0$.

In the remaining examples it will be assumed that the utility function depends on two arguments: a decision variable and a random variable. More specifically, the utility function is of the general form $u(v,y)$, where $y = f(v,x)$. As usual, the utility function is monotonically increasing in each argument, that is, $u_i > 0$, $i = 1,2$. The assumption of risk aversion is reflected in the restriction $u_{22} < 0$. Since the second argument of the utility function is the random variable, the risk-aversion function for this class of utility functions is defined as

$$R = \frac{-f_v f_x u_{22}}{u_2} \ . \tag{7.24}$$

We now set $\phi(v,x) = u[v,f(v,x)]$, and differentiate this equation with respect to v. Thus

$$\phi_v = u_1 + u_2 f_v \ . \tag{7.25}$$

Differentiating the above with respect to x yields

$$\phi_{vx} = u_{12} f_x + u_{22} f_x f_v + u_2 f_{vx} \ . \tag{7.26}$$

By substituting R, as defined in Eq. (7.24), into Eq. (7.26), it can be rewritten as

$$\phi_{vx} = f_x u_{21} + (f_{vx} - R) u_2 \ . \tag{7.27}$$

Differentiating once more with respect to x, we get

$$\phi_{vxx} = f_{xx} u_{21} + f_x^2 u_{212} + f_x (f_{vx} - R) u_{22} + (f_{vxx} - R_x) u_2 . \tag{7.28}$$

Because of the interrelationship between the two arguments of the utility function, the problem is quite a bit more complex than the one-dimensional case. Since the functions ϕ_{vx} and ϕ_{vxx} have several more terms than in the one-dimensional case, it is more difficult to determine their signs. So far, no theoretical justification is available for hypothesizing particular signs for such cross-partial derivatives as u_{12} and u_{122}. [For a discussion on this point see, for example, Sandmo (1969).] In each of the examples presented below we assume a sign pattern that yields intuitively reasonable conclusions.

Intertemporal Consumption with Uncertain Income. In this problem a consumer is assumed to plan for a horizon of two periods. In the first period he receives an income that he can allocate for consumption and/or saving in that period. He can also borrow in the first period in order to consume more than his income in that period. Borrowing and lending can be done at the same rate of interest and the rate is known with certainty. In the second period he receives an income the amount of which is unknown when the consumption plan for the entire horizon is decided. If the consumer borrows in the first period, the accruing debt must be paid out of the second-period income; otherwise, the income in the second period is used exclusively for consumption in that period. In other words, it is assumed that at the end of the second period the consumer's net worth should be zero. In this setting, utility is a random variable because consumption in the second period is random.

The following variables appear in the model:

v = consumption (in dollars) in the first period,
m = income in the first period,
t = rate of interest,
x = income in the second period,
y = consumption in the second period.

The consumer's asset position at the end of the first period is $(m - v)z$, where $z = 1 + t$, so the amount that he can consume in the second period is given by $y = x + (m - v)z$. His decision problem can be stated as maximizing $E\{u[v,x + (m - v)z]\}$ with respect to v. Since $f(v,x) = x + (m - v)z$, we get $f_v = -z$, $f_x = 1$, $f_{vx} = f_{xx} = f_{vxx} = 0$, and $R = zu_{22}/u_2 < 0$. In view of (7.27) and (7.28), we can state:

PROPOSITION 7.5. *If $u_{21} \geq 0$, then an FSD shift in the distribution of second-period income will cause the consumer to increase his*

<u>consumption in the first period (and hence decrease his saving)</u>.

Unlike the preceding propositions on FSD shifts, the above proposition imposes no restrictions on the risk-aversion measure. For an SSD shift we use, in addition to the above, Eqs. (7.28) and (7.17), and we state:

PROPOSITION 7.6. <u>If</u> $u_{212} \leq 0$, <u>and</u> $R_x > 0$, <u>then an SSD shift in the distribution of second-period income causes the consumer to increase his consumption in the first period (and hence to decrease his saving)</u>.

<u>Intertemporal Consumption with an Uncertain Return</u>. This problem is similar to the preceding one in that the consumer has a two-period utility function in which the second-period consumption is a random variable. In this problem, however, the incomes in both periods are known with certainty. The consumer may save a part of his income in the first period and invest it for one period, the return on the investment being a random variable. Consumption in the second period is again constrained so as to leave the consumer with a zero asset position at the end of the horizon. The notation for this model is as follows:

v = consumption in the first period,
m_i = income in period i, i = 1,2,
x = return on investment,
y = consumption in the second period.

According to the above specifications, the consumer's asset position at the end of the first period is $(m_1 - v)x$, so that consumption in the second period is given by $y = m_2 + (m_1 - v)x$. The consumer chooses v so as to maximize $E\{u[v, m_2 + (m_1 - v)x]\}$. We also have $f(v,x) = m_2 + (m_1 - v)x$ and hence $f_v = -x$, $f_x = m_1 - v$, $f_{vx} = -1$, and $f_{xx} = f_{vxx} = 0$. The measure of risk aversion is

$$R = \frac{x(m_1 - v)u_{22}}{u_2} < 0$$

(assuming positive investment). Then, in view of the above and Eqs. (7.27) and (7.28), we have:

PROPOSITION 7.7. *If* $u_{21} \geq 0$ *and* $R < -1$, *then an FSD shift in the distribution of the rate of return will induce the consumer to increase his consumption in the first period (and hence decrease his investment).*

For an SSD shift we invoke Eqs. (7.28) and (7.17), which yield the following:

PROPOSITION 7.8. *If* $u_{212} \leq 0$, $R < -1$, *and* $R_x > 0$, *then an SSD shift in the distribution of the return will induce the consumer to increase his consumption in the first period (and hence decrease his investment).*

7.1.5 Conclusion

The main purpose of this section was to generalize the analysis of the effects of changes in uncertainty in the context of certain optimization models. In most existing works, changes in uncertainty are effected either by horizontal shifts in the probability distribution, or by stretching the distribution in a particular fashion. In effect, these types of changes are equivalent to defining a new random variable that is a linear function of the original random variable. In this analysis, the distribution function is allowed to shift in a more general fashion; specifically, we considered both general FSD and SSD shifts. As in previous works on comparative statics of uncertainty, the effects of shifts in the distribution function depend on the signs of second-order and third-order derivatives of the objective function. The signs of these derivatives, in turn, were shown to be related to properties of a generalized measure of risk aversion.

The significance of these results for applied problems is somewhat difficult to predict. A great deal of the formal analysis in the general area of decision-making under uncertainty has been carried out only recently, and so far the gap between the generation of theoretical conclusions and empirical testing has not been bridged. The question to which comparative static analysis is addressed does have empirical relevance since it is concerned with decision-makers' responses to changes in the probability distributions of random variables entering into the decision-making process. And while there is little doubt that probability distributions do shift from time to time due to a variety of economic forces as well as government policies and acts of nature, it is obvious that the difficulties of estimating probability distributions and tracing their shifts through time are quite formidable. Among others, one of the difficulties arises from the fact that decision-makers may employ subjective probabilities, so that a particular random phenomenon may very well be perceived differently by different decision-makers. In the absence of knowledge of these subjective probabilities, and the subjectively perceived changes in these probabilities, prediction concerning the behavior of decision-makers is virtually impossible. The situation is perhaps not quite so hopeless in those cases in which probabilities are accepted as "objective" by a decision-maker as, for example, in the case of actuarial statistics and the like. But the main hazard one encounters in attempting an assessment of the potentials of theoretical models of behavior under uncertainty is not unlike the problem of insufficient observations in the context of econometric testing or inference. Since this entire line of research is still in its infancy, the available sample of results is too small for any meaningful extrapolation. It is simply too early to say where all this is going.

7.2 Portfolio Diversification

The notion that the risk of investing in uncertain prospects can be mitigated by spreading the investible fund among several prospects not only has a sound theoretical foundation but is widely practised by investors in the real world. In this section we formalize the concept of diversification and introduce several sets of conditions under which diversification is an optimal strategy. Throughout the discussion it will be assumed that an uncertain prospect is a random variable with a positive variance to distinguish such a prospect from a sure prospect.

For the sake of simplification we exclude borrowing and short sales, so that the amount available for investment is some given positive number. Without loss of generality (since the choice of unit of account is arbitrary), we let this amount be unity. Thus if the entire fund is invested in one prospect, the final wealth at the end of the relevant period is given by a nonnegative random variable X. If, on the other hand, a proportion k is put in one prospect and the remainder is put in another prospect, final wealth is given by $kX^1 + (1 - k)X^2$, where X^1 and X^2 are nonnegative random variables. And similarly for a portfolio consisting of n distinct prospects. Since the investor is assumed to maximize expected utility of final wealth, it is convenient to define a portfolio as the final wealth associated with the prospects in the portfolio.

7.2.1 Basic Definitions and Properties

DEFINITION 7.1. *Let* X^i, $i = 1,2,\ldots,n$, *be* n *nonnegative random variables, and* k^i, $i = 1,2,\ldots,n$, *be* n *scalars satisfying* $k^i \geq 0$, *and* $\Sigma_{i=1}^n k^i = 1$. *Then a portfolio is defined as the random variable* $P(k) = \Sigma_{i=1}^n k^i X^i$, *where* k *denotes the vector of the* n *mixture coefficients* k^i.

It may be useful to point out that one need not necessarily think of a portfolio as the return from a collection of financial assets, which is the more popular meaning of the term. The X^i can be thought of as the returns from any kind of investment project whatsoever (financial or otherwise), so that a portfolio may be thought of more generally as the return from any program that allocates a given fund (or resource) among various available projects.

In some of the results presented below we distinguish between different degrees of diversification, as well as absence of diversification. These will now be defined.

DEFINITION 7.2. *A portfolio is said to be "specialized" (nondiversified) if and only if* $k^i = 1$ *for some* i. *It will be denoted by* X^i.

DEFINITION 7.3. *A portfolio is said to be "partially diversified" if and only if* $k^i = 0$ *for at least one* i, *and* $k^i \neq 0$ *for at least two* i.

It will usually be denoted by P(k).

DEFINITION 7.4. *A portfolio is said to be "completely diversified" if and only if* $k^i \neq 0$ *for all* i. *It will usually be denoted by* P(k).

DEFINITION 7.5. *A portfolio is said to be "equally diversified" if and only if* $k^i = 1/n$ *for all* i, *where* n *is the number of available prospects. It will be denoted by* P(1/n).

When we refer to a portfolio as being "diversified," we mean that it satisfies one of Definitions 7.3-7.5.

Before presenting the results on diversification obtained from the stochastic dominance approach, we briefly mention the mean-variance approach developed by Markowitz (see Section 2.5 in Chapter 2). Under the latter approach, uncertain prospects are ranked according to their means and variances, and the criterion for ordering prospects is as follows: If two prospects have the same variance, the one that has a higher mean is preferred; and if two prospects have the same mean, then the one that has a smaller variance is preferred.

We shall illustrate the mean-variance approach to the problem of diversification with the case of portfolios that are constructed from two uncertain prospects with equal means. Since a portfolio is a linear function of its prospects, changing the proportions of the different prospects will not change the mean of the portfolio so long as all the prospects have equal means. In that case the problem of finding the optimal portfolio is reduced to minimizing the portfolio variance.

We consider portfolios of the form $kX^1 + (1 - k)X^2$ for different values of the mixture coefficient k. The variance of X^i is denoted by v^i, the covariance between X^1 and X^2 by c, and the portfolio variance by v(k). Then we have

$$v(k) = k^2v^1 + (1 - k)^2v^2 + 2k(1 - k)c. \qquad (7.29)$$

Differentiating the above equation gives

$$v'(k) = 2(v^1 + v^2 - 2c)k - 2(v^2 - c), \tag{7.30}$$

and differentiating again yields

$$v''(k) = 2(v^1 + v^2 - 2c). \tag{7.31}$$

Now the optimal portfolio will be a diversified portfolio only if v(k) attains its global minimum at some point in the interior of the unit interval. This implies, for example, that if v(k) is strictly concave, then the minimum point cannot occur in the interior of the domain, and the optimal portfolio is specialized. Thus in view of (7.31), the condition $v^1 + v^2 - 2c < 0$ is a sufficient condition for specialization. In this case the optimal portfolio consists of the prospect that has the lower variance.

It follows, of course, from the above discussion that the condition $v^1 + v^2 - 2c \geq 0$ is necessary for diversification to be optimal. A sufficient condition for diversification is $v^1 > c$ and $v^2 > c$. First, this condition implies that v(k) is strictly convex. Second, from Eq. (7.30) we see that $v'(0) = -2(v^2 - c) < 0$, and $v'(1) = 2(v^1 - c) > 0$. These two inequalities then imply that $v'(k) = 0$ at some point in the interior of the unit interval, and the latter point furnishes a global minimum. The optimal value of k can then be found by solving the equation $v'(k) = 0$. This yields

$$k = \frac{v^2 - c}{v^1 + v^2 - 2c}.$$

In the special case in which the two prospects are identically distributed, i.e., $v^1 = v^2$, one gets $k = 1/2$.

We now leave the mean-variance approach and turn to decision problems based on the maximization of expected utility. First, we need to define optimality of diversification for this approach. Informally, diversification is an optimal policy if, given some set of uncertain prospects, every risk-averter chooses a diversified portfolio. To formalize this definition, we consider the set U_2 consisting of all strictly increasing and concave utility functions. A member of

U_2 is denoted by u^j, and the expected value of the jth utility function is denoted by $E\{u^j[\ ]\}$, where the symbol inside the brackets will indicate the random variable with respect to which the expectation is taken.

DEFINITION 7.6. *Consider a set of* n *uncertain prospects (nonnegative random variables) and the set of all possible portfolios of these prospects. Let* ${}^jk$ *denote a vector of mixture coefficients associated with the portfolio of the* j*th individual (utility function) such that no element of* ${}^jk$ *is equal to one. Then diversification is said to be optimal if and only if for each* $u^j \in U_2$, *there exists* ${}^jk$ *such that* $E\{u^j[P({}^jk)]\} > E\{u^j[X^i]\}$ *for* $i = 1,2,\ldots,n$.

From the above definition it is clear that optimality of diversification need not imply the existence of stochastic dominance between any pair of portfolios. The latter implication would hold, for example, if every risk-averter preferred the same diversified portfolio over a particular specialized portfolio. The definition of optimality of diversification, however, requires only that each risk-averter should prefer *some* diversified portfolio over all specialized portfolios, where these preferred portfolios may differ from individual to individual (hence the superscript j on the vector k).

One case for diversification, in fact, complete diversification, has been demonstrated by Samuelson (1967a). The conditions of this theorem (stated below) do not imply the existence of stochastic dominance.

THEOREM 7.1. *Suppose there are* n *independently distributed uncertain prospects, each of which has the same mean. Then every risk-averter will invest some positive amount in each of the* n *prospects*.

In most of what follows, we shall deal with cases in which diversified portfolios dominate specialized (and other) portfolios in the sense of SSD. This latter condition is, of course, stronger than optimality of diversification as is shown in the following theorem:

THEOREM 7.2. Consider the uncertain prospects X^i, $i = 1,2,\ldots,n$. If there exists a vector k of mixture coefficients such that the distribution of the diversified portfolio $P(k)$ of the above prospects dominates that of each X^i in the sense of SSD, then diversification is optimal.

Proof: We prove the theorem by contradiction. Suppose that for some risk-averter the most preferred portfolio is one of the specialized portfolios, say, X^i. (The existence of a most preferred portfolio is guaranteed by the compactness of the set of mixture coefficients, and the continuity of the utility function.) But the SSD condition of the theorem implies that every risk-averter prefers $P(k)$ over each X^i, and that therefore X^i cannot be the most preferred portfolio of any risk-averter. This implies the existence of ${}^jk$, satisfying Definition 7.6.

Since many of the results presented below derive from certain properties of the integral of the distribution function of a two-prospect portfolio, we first establish these properties formally. In the analysis that follows, the adding-up restriction on the mixture coefficients is taken explicitly into account, and consequently a two-prospect portfolio is written as $kX^1 + (1 - k)X^2$. Its distribution function is denoted by $G(z;k)$, and the integral of the latter function is given by

$$G^*(y;k) = \int_0^y G(z;k)dz.$$

PROPERTY 7.1. The function $G^*(y;k)$ is a strictly convex function of k for all positive y.

Proof: Convexity is established by showing that the second derivative of G^* with respect to k is positive. First we express $G(z;k)$ in terms of the joint density function $h(x^1,x^2)$. This relationship is given by

$$G(z;k) = \int_0^{z/1-k} \int_0^s h(x^1,x^2)dx^1\,dx^2 , \qquad (7.32)$$

where $c = [z - (1 - k)x^2]/k$. Changing variables by means of the transformation $w = z - (1 - k)x^2$, we get

$$G(z;k) = \frac{1}{1 - k} \int_0^z \int_0^{w/k} h(x^1, \frac{z - w}{1 - k})\, dx^1\, dw. \tag{7.33}$$

Integrating the above with respect to z yields

$$\begin{aligned} G^*(y;k) &= \int_0^y G(z;k)dz \\ &= \frac{1}{1 - k} \int_0^y \int_0^z \int_0^{w/k} h(x^1, \frac{z - w}{1 - k})\, dx^1\, dw\, dz. \end{aligned} \tag{7.34}$$

Finally, changing the order of integration in the above triple integral gives

$$\begin{aligned} G^*(y;k) &= \frac{1}{1 - k} \int_0^y \int_w^y \int_0^{w/k} h(x^1, \frac{z - w}{1 - k})\, dx^1\, dz\, dw \\ &= \int_0^y H(\frac{w}{k}, \frac{y - w}{1 - k})\, dw\ , \end{aligned} \tag{7.35}$$

where H is the joint distribution function of X^1 and X^2. Differentiating the above equation with respect to k yields

$$\begin{aligned} G_k^*(y;k) = &\underbrace{- \frac{1}{k^2} \int_0^y H_1(\frac{w}{k}, \frac{y - w}{1 - k})\, w\, dw}_{I_1} \\ &\underbrace{+ \frac{1}{(1 - k)^2} \int_0^y H_2(\frac{w}{k}, \frac{y - w}{1 - k})(y - w)dw,}_{I_2} \end{aligned} \tag{7.36}$$

where subscripts on functional symbols denote partial differentiation with respect to the argument indicated. The integrals I_1 and I_2 are now rewritten by using the transformation $v = w/k$ in

I_1, and $v = (y - w)/(1 - k)$ in I_2. Then we get

$$I_1 = -\int_0^{y/k} H_1\left(v, \frac{y - kv}{1 - k}\right) v\, dv, \qquad (7.37)$$

$$I_2 = \int_0^{y/1-k} H_2\left[\frac{y - (1 - k)v}{k}, v\right] v\, dv. \qquad (7.38)$$

Differentiating each of the above equations with respect to k yields

$$\frac{dI_1}{dk} = -\frac{1}{(1 - k)^2} \int_0^{y/k} H_{12}\left(v, \frac{y - kv}{1 - k}\right)(y - v) v\, dv, \qquad (7.39)$$

$$\frac{dI_2}{dk} = \frac{1}{k^2} \int_0^{y/1-k} H_{21}\left[\frac{y - (1 - k)v}{k}, v\right](v - y) v\, dv. \qquad (7.40)$$

Finally, we change variables in the integral in Eq. (7.40) with the transformation

$$w = \frac{y - (1 - k)v}{k},$$

so that

$$\frac{dI_2}{dk} = \frac{1}{(1 - k)^3} \int_0^{y/k} H_{21}\left(w, \frac{y - kw}{1 - k}\right)(y - w)(y - kw)\, dw. \qquad (7.41)$$

But since $H_{12} = H_{21}$, the integrals in Eqs. (7.39) and (7.41) can be combined to give

$$\frac{dI_1}{dk} + \frac{dI_2}{dk} = \frac{1}{(1 - k)^3} \int_0^{y/k} H_{12}\left(v, \frac{y - kv}{1 - k}\right)(y - v)^2 dv > 0. \qquad (7.42)$$

Thus, since

$$G_{kk}^*(y,k) \quad \frac{dI_1}{dk} + \frac{dI_2}{dk},$$

the convexity property is established.

COROLLARY 7.1. <u>The value of the function</u> $G^*(y;k)$ <u>never exceeds that of the weighted sum of the integrals of the distribution functions of the two prospects, the weights being the corresponding mixture coefficients; that is</u>,

$$G^*(y;k) \leq k \int_0^y F^1(x)dx + (1 - k) \int_0^y F^2(x)dx,$$

<u>where</u> F^1 <u>and</u> F^2 <u>are the marginal distribution functions</u> of X^1 <u>and</u> X^2, <u>respectively</u>.

<u>Proof</u>: Eq. (7.35) implies that $G^*(y;k)$, considered as a function of k, is defined only on the interior of the unit interval. We now extend this function over the entire interval by defining the following new function:

$$\hat{G}(y;k) = G^*(y;k) \quad \text{for } 0 < k < 1,$$

$$\hat{G}(y;0) = \lim_{k \to 0} G^*(y;k) = \int_0^y F^2(x)dx,$$

$$\hat{G}(y;1) = \lim_{k \to 1} G^*(y;k) = \int_0^y F^1(x)dx.$$

Since $\hat{G}$ is continuous, it follows that $\hat{G}$ is a strictly convex function of k. Then for any k satisfying $0 < k < 1$, we have

$$G^*(y;k) = \hat{G}(y;k) < k \int_0^y F^1(x)dx + (1 - k) \int_0^y F^2(x)dx \quad \text{for all positive } y, \tag{7.43}$$

thus proving the corollary.

The above corollary implies another intuitive corollary; it asserts that if one prospect (in a two-prospect portfolio) dominates the other in the sense of SSD, then the distribution of the portfolio dominates the inferior prospect in the sense of SSD.

COROLLARY 7.2. *If* $F^1(x) >_2 F^2(x)$, *then* $G(x;k) >_2 F^2(x)$ *for* $0 < k < 1$.

Proof: Replacing $F^1(x)$ by $F^2(x)$ in (7.43) gives

$$G^*(y;k) < k \int_0^y F^2(x)dx + (1 - k) \int_0^y F^2(x)dx = \int_0^y F^2(x)dx$$

for all positive y.

PROPERTY 7.2. *If the joint distribution function of the two prospects is symmetric in its arguments, then the function* $G^*(y;k)$ *is symmetric around* $k = 1/2$ *for all* y; *that is, if* $H(x^1,x^2) = H(x^2,x^1)$ *for all non-negative* x^1 *and* x^2, *then* $G^*(y;k) = G^*(y;1 - k)$ *for all nonnegative* y *and all* k *in the unit interval*.

Proof: Changing variables in the integral given in Eq. (7.35), using the transformation $v = y - w$, proves the result.

7.2.2 Two-Prospect Portfolios

We first focus attention on the case in which the number of available prospects is two. For one thing, it gives rise to some results that do not extend to the case of n prospects. Furthermore, some theorems for two-prospect portfolios can be used in the proofs of theorems involving more than two prospects.

A basic result is that diversification is always optimal so long as the two prospects are identically distributed, regardless of the interdependence between them. This is established by showing that the distribution of any diversified portfolio dominates that of the specialized portfolio in the sense of SSD. Optimality of diversification then follows from Theorem 7.2.

THEOREM 7.3. Let $G(x;k)$ denote the distribution function of the portfolio $kX^1 + (1 - k)X^2$, and let $F^1(x)$ and $F^2(x)$ denote the distribution functions of X^1 and X^2, respectively. If $F^1(x) = F^2(x) = F(x)$ for all nonnegative x, then $G(x;k) \geq_2 F(x)$ for all k.

Proof: Substituting $F(x)$ for $F^1(x)$ and $F^2(x)$ in the inequality in (7.43) gives

$$G^*(y;k) \leq \int_0^y F(x)dx \quad \text{for all } y \text{ and } k,$$

which proves the dominance of G over F (see the definition of SSD in Section 2.14).

A stronger result obtains if the joint distribution function of the two prospects is symmetric in its arguments. In that case the function $G^*(y;k)$ has Properties 7.1 and 7.2, which means that for every positive y, the function $G^*(y;k)$ is a U-shaped function of k, attaining a unique minimum at $k = k/2$. This in turn implies that for any two portfolios constructed from the above two prospects, the portfolio whose mixture coefficient k is closer to 1/2 dominates the other in the sense of SSD, and vice versa.

THEOREM 7.4. Let $G(x;k)$ denote the distribution function of a two-prospect portfolio. If the joint distribution function of the two prospects is symmetric in its arguments, then $G(x;k) >_2 G(x;k')$ if and only if

$$(\tfrac{1}{2} - k)^2 < (\tfrac{1}{2} - k')^2.$$

Proof: The result is an immediate implication of Property 7.2.

What the above theorem says in effect is that, under the symmetry condition, two-prospect portfolios can be completely ordered according to the distance between the mixture coefficient k and the point 1/2 as well as according to the SSD condition. It also follows, of course, that the best portfolio is that for which $k = 1/2$. [The optimality of equal diversification in the case of symmetry is well known. An alternative proof is in Samuelson (1967a).]

A slightly different representation of this result is obtained by multiplying both sides of the inequality in the conclusion of the theorem by 2. But

$$2(\tfrac{1}{2} - k)^2 = (\tfrac{1}{2} - k)^2 + [\tfrac{1}{2} - (1 - k)]^2,$$

which is the square of the Euclidean distance between the vectors $(1/2,1/2)$ and $(k,1 - k)$. Therefore under the symmetry condition, the SSD condition and the Euclidean distance (or its square) induce the same ordering.

A still different (but equivalent) ordering can be constructed by considering the variance of a two-prospect portfolio. Since the symmetry condition implies that the two prospects are identically distributed, they have the same variance. If the common variance is denoted by v, the covariance of the two prospects by c, and the variance of the portfolio $kX^1 + (1 - k)X^2$ by $v(k)$, then it can be shown that

$$v(k) = (v - c)[k^2 + (1 - k)^2] + c. \tag{7.44}$$

We do exclude the case of perfect correlation between the two prospects, so that $v - c > 0$. Now since

$$\left(\frac{1}{2} - k\right)^2 + \left[\frac{1}{2} - (1 - k)\right]^2 = k^2 + (1 - k)^2 - \frac{1}{2},$$

we see from Eq. (7.44) that the portfolio variance is a linear (positive) transformation of the square of the Euclidean distance. Consequently, we obtain the following equivalent inequalities for pairs of mixture coefficients:

$$u(k) > u(k') \iff \left(\frac{1}{2} - k\right)^2 + \left[\frac{1}{2} - (1 - k)\right]^2$$

$$< \left(\frac{1}{2} - k'\right)^2 + \left[\frac{1}{2} - (1 - k')\right]^2 \qquad (7.45)$$

Thus when the symmetry condition holds, the preference ordering of an arbitrary risk-averter over all two-prospect portfolios can be constructed by ordering all such portfolios by their variances. Formally, the variance inequality stated in (7.45) can be substituted for the inequality given at the end of Theorem 7.4. What is of some interest in this conclusion is that under the conditions of the present case, the mean-variance criterion yields a correct ordering for all utility functions in the set U_2. [For discussions on the theoretical shortcomings of the mean-variance criterion see, for example, Quirk and Saposnik (1962), Hanoch and Levy (1969), and Feldstein (1969). A debate on this issue was conducted by Bierwag (1974), Borch (1974), Levy (1974), and Tsiang (1974).]

7.2.3 n-Prospect Portfolios

A natural way of looking at this general case is by asking whether the results obtained above for the case of n = 2 also hold for n > 2. The answer to this question is that they do not, and in the following discussion we shall point out some of the reasons for this situation and provide additional restrictions that enable us to prove quite similar theorems for n-prospect portfolios.

First we discuss one result that does carry over from the case of n = 2: the inferiority of the strategy of specialization when the marginal distributions of the prospects are identical. What is meant by this is that every specialized portfolio is dominated by some diversified portfolio. Of course, in Theorem 7.3 it has already been shown that under the condition of identical marginal distributions, any mixture of two prospects is always preferable to any of the specialized portfolios. But it is possible to show that, in fact, any mixture of s prospects, $2 \leq s \leq n$, dominates each of the specialized portfolios.

THEOREM 7.5. *Let* $F^i(x)$ *denote the distribution function of prospect* X^i, $i = 1,2,\ldots,n$, *and let* $G^s(x;k)$ *denote the distribution function of a portfolio* $P(k)$ *with* s *prospects*, $2 \leq s \leq n$, *where* k *is the vector of* s *mixture coefficients*. *If* $F^i(x) = F(x)$ *for all nonnegative* x, *and* $i = 1,2,\ldots,n$, *then* $G^s(x;k) >_2 F^i(x)$ *for* $i = 1,2,\ldots,n$, *and* $2 \leq s \leq n$.

Proof: The proof is by induction. First it is shown that if all portfolios with r prospects dominate each of the given n prospects in the sense of SSD, then all portfolios with r + 1 prospects dominate each of the n prospects in the sense of SSD, where $2 \leq r \leq n - 1$.

Let

$$P(k) = \sum_{i=1}^{r+1} k^i X^i$$

be any portfolio of any r + 1 prospects taken from the given set of n prospects, $2 \leq r \leq n - 1$. Consider a portfolio with any r of the above r + 1 prospects, say,

$$P^{-j}(c) = \sum_{\substack{i=1 \\ i \neq j}}^{r+1} c^i X^i,$$

where $1 \leq j \leq r + 1$, and $c^i = k^i/1 - k^j$. Since the assumption is that any r-prospect portfolio dominates each X^i in the sense of SSD, it follows from Corollary 7.2 that any mixture of $P^{-j}(c)$ and any X^i dominates X^i in the sense of SSD for $j = 1,2,\ldots,r + 1$ and $i = 1,2,\ldots,n$. If we let $q = 1 - k^j$, then the mixture $qP^{-j}(c) + (1 - q)X^j$ is given by

$$\sum_{\substack{i=1 \\ i \neq j}}^{r} qc^i X^i + (1 - q)X^j = \sum_{i=1}^{r+1} k^i X^i = P(k)$$

for $j = 1,2,\ldots,r + 1$.

Therefore the portfolio P(k) dominates each X^i in the sense of

SSD.

It remains to show that the dominance condition assumed in the proof holds for some r. By Theorem 7.3 it holds for $r = 2$, thus completing the proof.

Essentially, Theorem 7.5 says that when the marginal distributions are identical, any diversified portfolio, whether partially or completely diversified, dominates each specialized portfolio. But this implies that no risk-averter will choose a specialized portfolio, which is of course equivalent to saying that each risk-averter will choose a diversified portfolio. Consequently, diversification is optimal. We summarize this result in the form of a theorem:

THEOREM 7.6. _If the marginal distributions of all available prospects are identical, then diversification is optimal_.

Comparing briefly Theorems 7.1 and 7.6 we see that Theorem 7.6 dispenses with the independence assumption, and instead it replaces the condition of equal means by the stronger condition of identical marginal distributions. As for the conclusions, while Theorem 7.1 proves optimality of complete diversification, Theorem 7.6 demonstrates only the optimality of diversification. Of course, when $n = 2$, the conclusions of both theorems are the same.

It would be possible to prove optimality of complete diversification if it were true that for any partially diversified portfolio there existed at least one completely diversified portfolio that dominated the former portfolio in the sense of SSD. In general, however, the condition of equal marginal distributions is not sufficient to obtain such a result because the case of $n > 2$ admits of a pattern of correlations among the prospects which is much more complex than that in the case of $n = 2$. To see this in a more concrete fashion, we may recall that when two distributions have the same mean, a necessary condition for one distribution to dominate the other in the sense of SSD is that the dominating distribution should have a smaller variance [see Theorem 3 in Hadar and Russell (1971)]. This condition is relevant since all the portfolios under consideration have the same mean (because the marginal distributions are identical). Since under the present conditions all prospects also have the same variance, it can be shown that for some appropriate choice of values for the covariances, the portfolio variance attains a global minimum at some point on the boundary of the set of mixture coefficients. This means that some partially diversified portfolios cannot be dominated by any completely diversified portfolio in the sense of SSD, and hence it is not possible to deduce the optimality of complete diversification. In other words, under the condition of identical marginal distributions we can say only that each risk-averter will choose some diversified portfolio.

Optimality of complete diversification can be demonstrated if all joint distribution functions of dimension $n - 1$ are identical. This condition is, of course, stronger than the identity of the marginal distributions since it implies the latter condition. Obviously, when $n = 2$ the two conditions are the same. Optimality of complete diversification under these stronger conditions follows directly from the following theorem:

THEOREM 7.7. *Let* $H(x^1,x^2,\ldots,x^s)$ *denote the joint distribution function of the nonnegative random variables* X^i, $i = 1,2,\ldots,s$, *and let* $H^{-r}(x^1,x^2,\ldots,x^{r-1},x^{r+1},\ldots,x^s)$ *denote a joint distribution function of the* $s - 1$ *variables* X^i, $i = 1,2,\ldots,s$, $i \neq r$. *Consider any partially diversified portfolio with* $s - 1$ *prospects, say,*

$$P(k) = \sum_{\substack{i=1 \\ i\neq j}}^{s} k^i X^i$$

If $H^{-r} = H^{-t}$ *for all nonnegative values of the respective arguments, and* $r,t = 1,2,\ldots,s$, *then there exists a vector* k' *with s mixture coefficients such that the distribution of* $P(k')$ *dominates that of* $P(k)$ *in the sense of SSD*.

Proof: Consider the $(s - 1)$-prospect portfolio

$$V = \sum_{\substack{i=1 \\ i \neq j \\ i \neq t}}^{s} k^i X^i + k^t X^j .$$

From the assumption concerning the joint distribution functions of dimension $s - 1$ it follows that $P(k)$ and V are identically distributed. Then the distribution of the mixture $W = qP(k) + (1 - q)V$, $0 < q < 1$, dominates that of $P(k)$ in the sense of SSD by virtue of Theorem 7.3. But

$$W = \sum_{\substack{i=1 \\ i \neq j \\ i \neq t}}^{s} k^i X^i + qk^t X^t + (1 - q)k^t X^j$$

is an s-prospect portfolio $P(c)$ where $c^i = k^i$, $i = 1,2,\ldots,s$, $i \neq j$, $i \neq t$, $c^j = (1 - q)k^t$, and $c^t = qk^t$. Therefore the theorem holds for $k' = c$.

Now if the condition of the theorem holds for $s = n$, then the joint distribution functions of any dimension less than n are identical. Then by induction on s, and by virtue of the transitivity of the SSD relation, it immediately follows that choosing a completely diversified portfolio is superior to choosing any partially diversified portfolio, making complete diversification optimal.

For the case of $n = 2$ we also saw that when the joint distribution function of the given two prospects is symmetric in its arguments, then there exist (at least) two complete orderings that are the same as the ordering by SSD: one ordering is by the distance of the mixture coefficient from the point 1/2, and the other is by the portfolio variance. As it turns out, the equivalence between the inequalities given in (7.45) still holds, provided of course that the distance function is defined for the n-dimensional vector k. This distance function is given by

$$D(k) = \sum_{i=1}^{n} (k^i - \frac{1}{n})^2 = \sum_{i=1}^{n} (k^i)^2 - \frac{1}{n} . \tag{7.46}$$

The portfolio variance, on the other hand, is given by a straightforward generalization of Eq. (7.44), namely,

$$v(k) = (v - c) \sum_{i=1}^{n} (k^i)^2 + c, \tag{7.47}$$

where the symbols are defined as in Eq. (7.44). Hence, as in the case of $n = 2$, we see that $v(k)$ is a linear and increasing function of $D(k)$, so that for any vectors k and k' we have

$$v(k) < v(k') \Longleftrightarrow D(k) < D(k'). \tag{7.48}$$

The generalization of Theorem 7.4 to $n > 2$ breaks down, however, since the orderings by the SSD relation on the one hand and the distance of k from the center point on the other, are no longer equivalent. In other words, greater proximity to the center point is no longer a sufficient condition for dominance in the sense of SSD. But it is still possible to obtain partial orderings of portfolios; specifically, given any portfolio located at any point other than the center of the set of feasible mixture coefficients, one can generate sequences of portfolios in such a way that each portfolio in such a sequence dominates its predecessor in the sense of SSD. And within each sequence the portfolios are completely ordered by the SSD relation as well as by the distance function $D(k)$ and the portfolio variance.

If a typical portfolio is given by

$$Y_t = \sum_{i=1}^{n} k_t^i X^i,$$

not all k_t^i equal to $1/n$, let

$$Y'_t = \sum_{i=1}^{n-1} k_t^{i+1} X^i + k_t^1 X^n$$

be called a <u>rearrangement</u> of Y_t. It is clear from the symmetry condition that Y_t and Y'_t are identically distributed. Then it follows from Theorem 7.3 that any mixture of Y_t and Y'_t dominates Y_t in the sense of SSD. Thus for any c satisfying $0 < c < 1$, the portfolio $Y_{t+1} = cY_t + (1 - c)Y'_t$ dominates Y_t in the sense of SSD. Similarly, mixing Y_{t+1} and its rearrangement yields the portfolio $Y_{t+2} = cY_{t+1} + (1 - c)Y'_{t+1}$, which dominates Y_{t+1}, and so on. Thus each successive portfolio generated by the above mixing procedure dominates its predecessor in the sense of SSD.

With each portfolio Y_t in the above sequence, we associate the distance $D(k_t)$ as defined in Eq. (7.46) with k_t being the vector of mixture coefficients of Y_t. Then given $D(k_t)$ for the portfolio Y_t, we can show that

$$D(k_{t+1}) = [1 - 2c(1 - c)] \sum_{i=1}^{n} (k_t^i)^2 + 2c(1 - c) \sum_{i=1}^{n} k_t^i k_t^{k+1} - \frac{1}{n}. \tag{7.49}$$

where $k_t^{n+1} = k_t^1$. But

$$\sum_{i=1}^{n} k_t^i k_t^{i+1} < \frac{1}{n}$$

for all k_t^i, hence

$$\begin{aligned} D(k_{t+1}) &\leq [1 - 2c(1 - c)] \sum_{i=1}^{n} (k^i)^2 - \frac{1}{n}[1 - 2c(1 - c)] \\ &= [1 - 2c(1 - c)]\, D(k_t). \end{aligned} \tag{7.50}$$

Since $0 < 1 - 2c(1 - c) < 1$, it follows that the sequence $D(k_t)$ converges to zero. But $D(k) = 0$ if and only if $k^i = 1/n$ for all i, therefore each sequence of portfolios converges to the equally diversified portfolio P(1/n), regardless of the initial portfolio, and the value of c.

As in the case of n = 2, the equally diversified portfolio dominates all other portfolios in the sense of SSD. For the proof we shall adopt a slightly different notational scheme. Thus if Y_t is any portfolio, its rearrangement (as defined above) is denoted by Y_{t+1}. The rearrangement of the latter portfolio is denoted by Y_{t+2}, and so on.

THEOREM 7.8. _Suppose there are_ n _nonnegative uncertain prospects. If the joint distribution function of the above prospects is symmetric in its arguments, then equal diversification is optimal._

Proof: The theorem is proved by showing that the distribution of the portfolio P(1/n) dominates that of the portfolio P(k) in the sense of SSD for all vectors k whose elements are not all equal to 1/n. Let Y_1 denote an arbitrary (but not equally diversified) portfolio P(k). Consider the rearrangements Y_t, $t = 2,3,\ldots,n$. The symmetry condition implies that all the portfolios Y_t are identically distributed. Then it follows from Theorem 7.5 that any mixture of the above n portfolios dominates Y_1 in the sense of SSD. In particular, choose the mixture

$$\frac{1}{n}\sum_{i=1}^{n} Y_t \, .$$

But the latter mixture is the portfolio P(1/n), thus proving the theorem. [This proof was suggested by Ayala Cohen.]

7.2.4 Nonidentically Distributed Prospects

In all the preceding results (except Theorem 7.1) the various conditions for diversification required, among other things, that the prospects under consideration should be identically distributed. When this is not the case, and if in addition the distributions of the prospects are not independent, diversification is less likely to be an optimal strategy.

One result on diversification of prospects that are not identically distributed is provided by Samuelson (1967a, Theorem IV). In this theorem (no proof given) the basic assumption is that each conditional distribution function should be an increasing function of each conditioning variable. [In Samuelson's paper the theorem erroneously states that small increases in the conditioning variables should reduce the conditional distribution functions.] This condition implies that the covariance between any two prospects should be negative.

Another approach to this problem is by means of stochastic dominance, although the solution presented here is for the case of two-prospect portfolios only. In this approach, the concept of FSD is extended to joint distribution functions. We shall denote a joint distribution function by notation such as $H(x) = H(x^1, x^2, \ldots, x^n)$.

DEFINITION 7.7. _For any two joint distribution functions_ $H(x)$ _and_ $H^*(x)$, $H(x) >_1 H^*(x)$ _if and only if_ $H(x) \leq H^*(x)$ _for all_ x _in the domain, the strict inequality holding for some_ x _in the domain_.

The utility of individual j associated with a two-prospect portfolio $P(k) = kX^1 + (1 - k)X^2$ is denoted by $u^j[P(k)]$, and the expected value of this utility function under the joint distribution function $H(x^1, x^2)$ is written as $E\{u^j[P(k), H]\}$. Suppose now that two prospects X^1 and X^2 may be statistically interrelated in either one of two ways: one form of interdependence is given by the joint distribution function $H(x^1, x^2)$, and the other by $H^*(x^1, x^2)$. In other words, H and H* are two bivariate distribution functions whose respective marginal distributions are identical. Then the following can be shown [See Theorem 3 in Hadar and Russell (1974a)]:

$$E\{u^j[P(k),H]\} - E\{u^j[P(k),H^*]\}$$

$$= k(1-k)\int^{\infty}\int^{\infty} u_2{}^j[H(x^1,x^2) - H^*(x^1,x^2)]dx^1\, dx^2, \tag{7.51}$$

where $u_2{}^j$ denotes the second derivative of u^j. From this equation one immediately obtains the following theorem:

THEOREM 7.9. _For any risk-averter with utility function_ u^j, _if_

$$H(x^1,x^2) >_1 H^*(x^1,x^2),$$

then

$$E\{u^j[P(k),H]\} > E\{u^j[P(k),H^*]\}.$$

This theorem is not about preference between two different portfolios, but about the expected utility associated with a given portfolio under two different joint distribution functions. It says, in effect, that if the individual (that is, any risk-averter) could select the joint distribution function that is to govern the interdependence between the two prospects, he would choose the distribution that dominates the other in the sense of FSD.

The result embodied in the above theorem can now be applied to the question of diversification under conditions in which the two prospects are not identically distributed but are still required to have equal means.

THEOREM 7.10. _Let_ $F^1(x^1)$ _and_ $F^2(x^2)$ _denote the marginal distribution functions of two nonnegative prospects_ X^1 _and_ X^2, _and let_ $H(x^1,x^2)$ _denote the joint distribution function of these prospects. Assume that both prospects have the same mean. Then_ $H(x^1,x^2) >_1 F^1(x^1)F^2(x^2)$ _implies that diversification is optimal._

Proof: Theorem 7.1 states that when two prospects have the same mean and are independently distributed (i.e., the joint distribution function is given by the product of the marginal distributions), then diversification is optimal. In symbols, for each individual j there exists a vector of mixture coefficients ${}^{j}k$ (all the coefficients being positive) such that

$$E\{u^{j}[P({}^{j}k),F^{1}F^{2}]\} > E\{u^{j}[X^{i},F^{i}]\}, \quad i = 1,2.$$

But Theorem 7.9 implies that

$$E\{u^{j}[P(k),H]\} > E\{u^{j}[P(k),F^{1}F^{2}]\}$$

so that

$$E\{u^{j}[P({}^{j}k),H]\} > E\{u^{j}[X^{i},F^{i}]\}, \quad i = 1,2.$$

It therefore follows that each expected-utility-maximizing risk-averter will choose a diversified portfolio.

It may be pointed out that as in Samuelson's theorem for non-identically distributed prospects, the above theorem implies that the covariance between the two prospects is negative.

7.2.5 Conclusion

We summarize briefly the main results on diversification. One basic conclusion is that diversification is always optimal when the available prospects are identically distributed, regardless of the nature of the interdependence among the prospects. While in the special case of n = 2 this means that complete diversification is optimal, in the more general case of n > 2 one can conclude only that every risk-averter will choose some diversified portfolio, but not necessarily one that contains all the n prospects. Complete diversification is optimal under two different sets of conditions. One of these requires that all prospects should have the same mean and should be independent of each other. In the other case the independence assumption is not required, but the nature of the interdependence among the prospects is restricted in that the joint distribution functions of any dimension less than n should be identical. When the joint distribution function of the n prospects is symmetric in its arguments, then every risk-averter should allocate an equal amount to each prospect.

When the prospects are not identically distributed, diversification is less likely to be optimal. In the case of two-prospect portfolios, diversification is optimal if the prospects have equal means, and if their joint distribution function dominates the product of the marginal distributions in the sense of FSD.

Introduction to Chapter 8
Additional Topics and Conclusions

There are many areas of inquiry in which stochastic dominance methodology has a role to play, but they have been barely touched by it and hence do not have an extensive literature. This chapter begins with two sections on topics that are not in the mainstream of stochastic dominance research as defined by the work reported in earlier chapters. Nevertheless, they are representative of the diverse directions in which the frontiers of this field are moving.

In Section 8.1, Peter C. Fishburn discusses convex stochastic dominance (CSD), a type of dominance produced when convex linear mixtures (i.e., mixed strategies) of probability distributions are considered. He reviews some key theorems and shows their relevance to several new fields, among them game theory and group choices among risky alternatives.

In Section 8.2, G. A. Whitmore considers the problem of inferring the presence or absence of stochastic dominance between a pair of prospects on the basis of sample data. As noted in earlier chapters, there is a need for better statistical procedures in empirical SD research (for example, in SD tests of capital market efficiency). As he points out, adequate statistical procedures do not exist for the more complicated (and some might say, the more common) cases. For instance, there does not exist a distribution-free statistical test for FSD based on dependent random samples. In spite of the difficulty of proceeding very far with the subject, Whitmore does present a couple of tests that will add to the statistical tools presently available to those interested in SD inferences.

Section 8.3 contains concluding remarks prepared by the coeditors. Needless to say, the section speaks for itself.

8 Additional Topics and Conclusions

8.1 Convex Stochastic Dominance

Peter C. Fishburn

The purpose of this section is to discuss the notion of stochastic dominance as it applies to simple mixtures or convex linear combinations of probability distributions. This type of dominance will be called "convex stochastic dominance" (CSD). Following a general discussion of CSD, we will describe some corollaries of the main theorems and note potential areas of application. The final part of the section details one application that involves the question of transitivity of simple majorities in votes between risky decision alternatives.

8.1.1 Introduction to CSD and Its Applications

To motivate our discussion, let F, G, and H be three distribution functions defined on an interval of the real line, and suppose that the individual's utility function u is in U_1 as defined by (2.17). As pictured in Figure 8-1, each pair of distributions from {F,G,H} has a crossing point so that FSD does not hold for any pair. However, consider the even-chance mixture of G and H defined by $\frac{1}{2}$ G + $\frac{1}{2}$ H. Formally, this convex combination is a distribution function that assigns the value $\frac{1}{2}$ G(x) + $\frac{1}{2}$ H(x) to each real number x. Operationally $\frac{1}{2}$ G + $\frac{1}{2}$ H can be thought of as a strategic mixture of two risky alternatives that, if "chosen," would be implemented by first flipping a fair coin and then implementing the alternative with distribution function G if a "head" occurs or implementing the alternative with

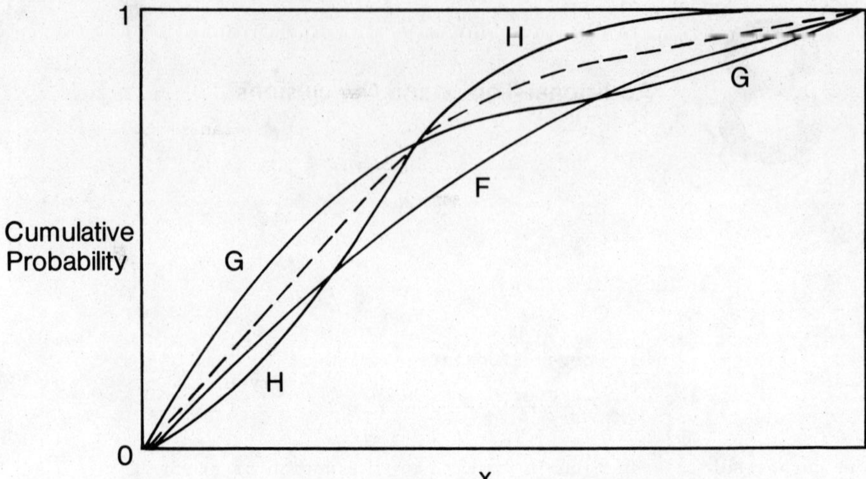

Figure 8-1. F First-degree Stochastically Dominates an Even-chance Mixture of G and H

distribution function H if a "tail" occurs. There may or may not be a basic (nonmixed) alternative with the distribution function $\frac{1}{2}$ G + $\frac{1}{2}$ H. In this connection, it is important to note that if X and Y are respectively the random variables corresponding to G and H, then even when X and Y are independent, it will not generally be true that $\frac{1}{2}$ G + $\frac{1}{2}$ H is the distribution function of the portfolio $\frac{1}{2}$ X + $\frac{1}{2}$ Y.

Returning to Figure 8-1 we see that $\frac{1}{2}$ G + $\frac{1}{2}$ H, which is pictured by the dashed curve, lies above F. That is,

$$\frac{1}{2} G(x) + \frac{1}{2} H(x) \geq F(x) \quad \text{for all } x,$$

with the strict inequality holding in the interval except at the end-points. Therefore by Theorem 2.1, $F >_1 \frac{1}{2} G + \frac{1}{2} H$, so that F dominates $\frac{1}{2}$ G + $\frac{1}{2}$ H by FSD. In terms of utility functions $u \in U_1$, this says that

$$E(u,F) > E(u,\frac{1}{2} G + \frac{1}{2} H) = \frac{1}{2} E(u,G) + \frac{1}{2} E(u,H).$$

Hence for every $u \in U_1$, either $E(u,F) > E(u,G)$ or $E(u,F) > E(u,H)$. Because FSD does not hold between F and G or between F and H, there will be some $u \in U_1$ that have $E(u,H) > E(u,F) > E(u,G)$ and others that have $E(u,G) > E(u,F) > E(u,H)$. There will also be $u \in U_1$ for which $E(u,F)$ exceeds both $E(u,G)$ and $E(u,H)$, but as noted above, it will never be true that both $E(u,G)$ and $E(u,H)$ are larger than $E(u,F)$.

Generalizing the analysis of the preceding paragraph, it can be stated that if F dominates by FSD some convex combination $\alpha G + (1 - \alpha)H$ of G and H, with α between 0 and 1, then since $E(u,F) > E[u,\alpha G + (1 - \alpha)H] = \alpha E(u,G) + (1 - \alpha)E(u,H)$, either $E(u,F) > E(u,G)$ or $E(u,F) > E(u,H)$ for every $u \in U_1$. The main thrust of Theorem 8.2 (presented later) says that the converse of this statement holds. That is, when $E(u,F) > E(u,G)$ or $E(u,F) > E(u,H)$ for every $u \in U_1$, then there must be an α between 0 and 1 such that $F >_1 \alpha G + (1 - \alpha)H$. The key to the proof of this fact is the linearity property of mixtures, namely, $E[u,\alpha G + (1 - \alpha)H] = \alpha E(u,G) + (1 - \alpha)E(u,H)$, which says that the expected utility of a convex combination of distribution functions equals the convex combination of their expected utilities.

Before developing formal statements of the CSD theorems, we mention some ways in which convex stochastic dominance can be used in decision analysis. These will be discussed in greater detail in Section 8.1.3.

First, within the context of a specified class U of utility functions, CSD can be used to determine whether some mixture of one set of probability distributions dominates a mixture of a second set of distributions. If such dominance does not hold, then there is a utility function in U such that the expected utility of every distribution in the second set is greater than the expected utility of every distribution in the first set. This result can be used to examine mixed strategies in statistical decision theory and game theory.

Second, CSD can be applied to determine whether stated or revealed preferences between risky decision alternatives are consistent with the assumption that the decision-maker's utility function lies within a specified class U of utility functions. This may be important in deciding whether a particular U set is applicable in a given context.

Third, CSD can be used to eliminate from further consideration alternatives that are SD-efficient in the usual sense but that are not efficient in the sense of CSD, being dominated by a mixture of other alternatives. This approach may complicate the analysis, however, since it requires the efficient set to be composed of strategic mixtures of alternatives along with basic alternatives.

Convex stochastic dominance can also be used in portfolio analysis to examine diversification questions. For example, CSD applies directly to the question of whether diversification might be advantageous in a given situation.

Finally, we note that CSD has relevance in contexts where a group of individuals, such as the members of an investment club or the investment decision group of a pension fund, make decisions between risky prospects by simple majority voting. Among other things, CSD can be used to determine whether simple majorities within a set of risky prospects must be transitive. As is well known, the final result of a sequence of simple majority votes within a fixed set of alternatives can depend on the order in which alternatives are voted on when simple majorities are not transitive. For example, if A has a simple majority over B, B has a simple majority over C, and C has a simple majority over A, then the outcome of a voting process in which the simple-majority winner of a vote between two of the three alternatives is pitted against the third alternative to determine an overall winner will depend on which two alternatives are voted on first.

8.1.2 Basic CSD Theorems

The discussion now turns to a general presentation of convex stochastic dominance. It is no longer required that the consequences of decisions be real numbers or vectors of real numbers, and the class U of utility functions under consideration is allowed to be quite general. As in Section 2.21, we let C denote the set of consequences. The set C can be finite or infinite. Risky decision alternatives will be characterized by finitely-additive probability measures p,q,... defined on a Boolean algebra $\mathcal{A}$ of subsets of C.

In general, we shall suppose that the set P of all finitely additive probability measures on $\mathcal{A}$ under consideration is a convex set, so that $\alpha p + (1 - \alpha)q$ is in P whenever $p,q \in P$ and $0 \leq \alpha \leq 1$. The measure $\alpha p + (1 - \alpha)q$ assigns probability $\alpha p(A) + (1 - \alpha)q(A)$ to each event A in $\mathcal{A}$. Moreover, it will be assumed that P contains every measure that assigns probability 1 to a single element of C, i.e., the "sure-thing" alternatives. The smallest P set that satisfies the conditions of this paragraph is the set P_s of all simple gambles on C (i.e., the set of all probability measures that assign probability 1 to a finite subset of C). If C itself is finite, then $P = P_s$.

The only things that will be required of the class U of utility functions on C under consideration are that U be convex, so that $\alpha u + (1 - \alpha)v$ is in U whenever $u,v \in U$ and $0 \leq \alpha \leq 1$, that every $u \in U$ be bounded, and that for every interval I of real numbers and every $u \in U$, the set $\{c:u(c) \in I\}$ of consequences whose utility values are in I be an event in $\mathcal{A}$. The sets U_1, U_2, U_3, and U_d used in Chapter 2 satisfy these requirements. Under these requirements the expected utility $E(u,p)$ of measure p, defined by

$$E(u,p) = \int_C u(c)dp(c),$$

exists and is finite for every $p \in P$ and every $u \in U$.

Within this formulation we first consider a nonstrict version of stochastic dominance, defining the relation $\geq_U$ on P by

$$p \geq_U q \text{ if and only if } E(u,p) \geq E(u,q) \text{ for all } u \in U. \quad (8.1)$$

The subscript U is used on $\geq$ rather than i or d, as in Chapter 2, to denote that U might be any one of a number of different classes of utility functions. In the following theorem, n can be any positive integer, Λ_n is the set of all n-dimensional real vectors with non-negative components that add to 1:

$$\Lambda_n = \{\lambda = (\lambda_1,\ldots,\lambda_n): \lambda_i \geq 0 \text{ for all } i, \text{ and } \Sigma\lambda_i = 1\},$$

and $\Sigma\lambda_i p_i$ is the measure in P that assigns probability $\Sigma\lambda_i p_i(A)$ to each event A in $\mathcal{A}$. With $\lambda \in \Lambda_n$ and $p_i \in P$ for each i, $\Sigma\lambda_i p_i$ can be thought of as the strategic mixture of n risky alternatives described by the

p_i measures. If implemented, it will result in the selection of the alternative corresponding to p_i with probability λ_i.

THEOREM 8.1. *Suppose* $p_1,\ldots,p_n$, $q_1,\ldots,q_n$ *are in* P. *Then there is a* $\lambda \in \Lambda_n$ *such that*

$$\sum_{i=1}^{n} \lambda_i p_i \geq_U \sum_{i=1}^{n} \lambda_i q_i \tag{8.2}$$

if and only if for every $u \in U$ *there is an* $i \in \{1,\ldots,n\}$ *such that* $E(u,p_i) \geq E(u,q_i)$.

Note that by definition (8.1) and the linearity of expected utility for mixtures of probability measures, (8.2) is equivalent to

$$\sum_{i=1}^{n} \lambda_i E(u,p_i) \geq \sum_{i=1}^{n} \lambda_i E(u,q_i) \quad \text{for every } u \in U. \tag{8.3}$$

Thus Theorem 8.1 says that (8.3) holds for some λ in Λ_n if and only if

$$E(u,p_1) \geq E(u,q_1) \text{ or } E(u,p_2) \geq E(u,q_2) \text{ or} \ldots \text{or } E(u,p_n) \geq E(u,q_n) \tag{8.4}$$

for every $u \in U$. Therefore the test of whether some mixture of the p_i stochastically dominates a similar mixture of the q_i can be conducted solely on the basis of (8.4) without any direct reference to the λ vectors. A short proof of Theorem 8.1 is given in Fishburn (1974b).

To touch base with our prior developments in Chapter 2, consider the case where P corresponds to the set of all right-continuous distribution functions having total probability 1 on an interval I = [a,b] of Re, and U is the set U_2 of risk-averse utility functions on I. Theorem 8.1 then says that with $F_1,\ldots,F_n$, $G_1,\ldots,G_n$ distribution functions of the presumed type, there is a $\lambda = (\lambda_1,\ldots,\lambda_n)$ in Λ_n such that $\Sigma\lambda_i F_i \geq_2 \Sigma\lambda_i G_i$ if and only if for every $u \in U_2$ there is an $i \in \{1,\ldots,n\}$ for which $E(u,F_i) \geq E(u,G_i)$. With

$$F_i^2(x) = \int_a^x F_i(y)dy,$$

as in Eqs. (2.31), it then follows from $\int[\Sigma\lambda_i F_i(x)]dx = \Sigma\lambda_i \int F_i(x)dx = \Sigma\lambda_i F_i^2(x)$ that there is a $\lambda \in \Lambda$ such that

$$\sum_{i=1}^{n} \lambda_i G_i^2(x) \geq \sum_{i=1}^{n} \lambda_i F_i^2(x) \quad \text{for all } x \in I,$$

if and only if at least one of $E(u,F_1) \geq E(u,G_1)$, $E(u,F_2) \geq E(u,G_2), \ldots$ and $E(u,F_n) \geq E(u,G_n)$ holds for every $u \in U_2$. Unlike the notation of Sections 2.6 and 2.20, the F_i and G_i used here and later are not marginal distributions.

We now turn to strict versions of stochastic dominance, defining $>_U$ and $>>_U$ on P by

$$p >_U q \text{ if and only if } p \gtrsim_U q \text{ and } E(u,p) > E(u,q) \text{ for some } u \in U, \tag{8.5}$$

$$p >>_U q \text{ if and only if } E(u,p) > E(u,q) \text{ for all } u \in U. \tag{8.6}$$

Examples in Fishburn (1974b) show that when C is infinite, the strict partial orders $>_U$ and $>>_U$ need not be equal, and when this is the case the "obvious" correspondents of Theorem 8.1 can be false. However, $>_U$ will equal $>>_U$ in many important contexts, as when U equals one of the U_i of Chapter 2, and we shall therefore state a strict version of Theorem 8.1 for such contexts.

THEOREM 8.2. *Suppose* $>_U$ *equals* $>>_U$ *and* $p_1,\ldots,p_n$, $q_1,\ldots,q_n$ *are in* P. *Then there is a* $\lambda \in \Lambda_n$ *such that*

$$\sum_{i=1}^{n} \lambda_i p_i >_U \sum_{i=1}^{n} \lambda_i q_i \tag{8.7}$$

if and only if for every $u \in U$ *there is an* $i \in \{1,\ldots,n\}$ *such that*

$E(u,p_i) > E(u,q_i)$.

The remarks following Theorem 8.1 apply also to Theorem 8.2 with the obvious change from $\geq$ to $>$. A proof of Theorem 8.2 is given in Fishburn (1974b).

We conclude this section by returning to the earlier example for Figure 8-1 where $F >_1 \frac{1}{2} G + \frac{1}{2} H$. To apply Theorem 8.2 to a comparison between F and mixtures $\alpha G + (1 - \alpha)H$ of G and H, take $F_1 = F_2 = F$, $G_1 = G$, $G_2 = H$ and $(\alpha, 1 - \alpha) = (\lambda_1, \lambda_2)$. Then with $U = U_1$, $F >_1 \alpha G + (1 - \alpha)H$ if and only if $\lambda_1 F + \lambda_2 F >_1 \lambda_1 G + \lambda_2 H$. Hence by Theorem 8.2, $F >_1 \alpha G + (1 - \alpha)H$ for some α between 0 and 1 if and only if either $E(u,F) > E(u,G)$ or $E(u,F) > E(u,H)$ for every $u \in U_1$.

8.1.3 Applications of the CSD Theorems

Comparisons of mixed acts. Our first corollary of Theorem 8.1 considers different mixtures of finite sets of probability measures, as follows.

COROLLARY 8.1. *Suppose* $p_1,\ldots,p_n$, $q_1,\ldots,q_m$ *are in* P. *Then there is a* $\lambda \in \Lambda_n$ *and a* $\mu \in \Lambda_m$ *such that*

$$\sum_{i=1}^{n} \lambda_i p_i \geq_U \sum_{j=1}^{m} \mu_j q_j \tag{8.8}$$

if and only if for every $u \in U$ *there is an* $i \in \{1,\ldots,n\}$ *and a* $j \in \{1,\ldots,m\}$ *such that* $E(u,p_i) \geq E(u,q_j)$.

This follows from Theorem 8.1 by replacing $\Sigma_i \lambda_i p_i$ and $\Sigma_j \mu_j q_j$ in (8.8) by $\Sigma_i \Sigma_j \rho_{ij} p_i$ and $\Sigma_j \Sigma_i \rho_{ij} q_j$ respectively with $\rho_{ij} = \lambda_i \mu_j$ for all i and j. Corollary 8.1 says that if no convex combination of the p_i stochastically dominates a convex combination of the q_j, then there must be a $u \in U$ for which the expected utility for every q_j exceeds the expected utility for every p_i.

For an illustration of the corollary, consider a situation in which there are n basic acts, labeled 1,2,...,n, and a set of states of nature (or states of the world) over which a probability measure is defined. Each act-state pair yields a consequence in C and, associated with act i, there will be a probability measure p_i over the consequences that might arise under act i. Partition the set of acts $\{1,2,\ldots,n\}$ into two nonempty subsets J and K. Corollary 8.1 then says that some strategic mixture of the acts in J stochastically dominates a strategic mixture of the acts in K if and only if for every $u \in U$ there is a $j \in J$ and a $k \in K$ such that $E(u,p_j) \geq E(u,p_k)$. Hence, if no J mixture dominates a K mixture, then there must be a utility function in U that makes the expected utility of every act in K greater than the expected utility of every act in J.

An interesting twist to this example comes about by letting m pure strategies be available to an opponent in a game situation, and associating λ_j $(j = 1,\ldots,m)$ with the probability that the opponent will use his pure strategy j. Consider two mixed strategies $\alpha = (\alpha_1,\ldots,\alpha_n)$ and $\beta = (\beta_1,\ldots,\beta_n)$ defined over the basic acts available to the primary decision-maker. With c_{ij} the consequence that occurs when the decision-maker uses act i and his opponent uses the jth act in his set, α and β induce probability measures over C for each j with expected utilities $\Sigma_i\alpha_i u(c_{ij})$ and $\Sigma_i\beta_i u(c_{ij})$. According to Theorem 8.1 there is a $\lambda \in \Lambda_m$ such that

$$\sum_{j=1}^{m} \lambda_j \sum_{i=1}^{n} \alpha_i u(c_{ij}) \geq \sum_{j=1}^{m} \lambda_j \sum_{i=1}^{n} \beta_i u(c_{ij}) \quad \text{for all } u \in U \qquad (8.9)$$

if and only if for every $u \in U$ there is a state $j \in \{1,\ldots,m\}$ for which $\Sigma_i\alpha_i u(c_{ij}) \geq \Sigma_i\beta_i u(c_{ij})$. In other words, there is a probability distribution over the opponent's strategies such that β does no better than α, regardless of which u in U might in fact be the decision-maker's utility function, if and only if for every $u \in U$ there is a state j under which the decision-maker's expected utility with β is no greater than his expected utility with α. If there is no λ that satisfies (8.9), then and only then there is a utility function $u \in U$ such that $\Sigma_i\beta_i u(c_{ij}) > \Sigma_i\alpha_i u(c_{ij})$ for every j. In this same setting, Theorem 8.2 says that there is no λ that satisfies (8.9) with strict inequality if and only if there is a $u \in U$ for which $\Sigma_i \beta_i u(c_{ij}) \geq \Sigma_i \alpha_i u(c_{ij})$ for all j.

Consistency of stated or revealed preferences. Theorem 8.1 can be used to test whether a finite set of preference judgments between measures in P is consistent with the assumption that the decision-maker's utility function is in a specified class U. In particular, suppose that the decision-maker says (or otherwise reveals) that he prefers p_i to q_i for $i = 1,\ldots,n$. Then these judgments are consistent with $u \in U$ if and only if there is a $u \in U$ such that $E(u,p_i) > E(u,q_i)$ for $i = 1,\ldots,n$ and, by Theorem 8.1, this is true if and only if there is no convex combination of the q_i that stochastically dominates a similar convex combination of the p_i. For example, if F_i is preferred to G_i when $U = U_2$ for $i = 1,\ldots,n$, then this set of preference statements is consistent with the assumption that $u \in U_2$ if and only if there is no $\lambda \in \Lambda_n$ for which $\Sigma_i \lambda_i F_i^2(x) \geq \Sigma_i \lambda_i G_i^2(x)$ for all $x \in I$.

Eliminating alternatives by CSD. Convex stochastic dominance can also be used to eliminate basic alternatives from a finite set of available basic alternatives. For example, suppose in the context of distribution functions on an interval of real numbers with $U = U_2$ that there are n basic alternatives with distribution functions $F_1, F_2, \ldots, F_n$. With $\lambda \in \Lambda_n$, $\Sigma \lambda_j F_j$ is the distribution function of the mixed strategy λ over the basic alternatives. Now suppose that F_1 is not dominated by any other F_j so that $F_j >_2 F_1$ is false for every $j \in \{2,\ldots,n\}$. Then F_1 is SSD efficient in the usual sense. It can still be true, however, that $\Sigma \lambda_j F_j >_2 F_1$ for some $\lambda \in \Lambda_n$ and, if so, then $\Sigma \lambda_j F_j >_2 F_1$ for some $\lambda \in \Lambda_n$ that has $\lambda_1 = 0$. In this case there is a mixed strategy not involving F_1 that has greater expected utility than does F_1 for every $u \in U_2$. Hence F_1 can be eliminated from further consideration since the decision-maker can do something else that makes him better off in the expected utility sense than he would be with F, regardless of which risk-averse utility function actually applies. (If the distribution function F in Figure 8-1 is placed above the dashed curve so it intersects both G and H, then F is FSD efficient in the usual sense, but it is not FSD efficient in the sense of convex stochastic dominance.)

According to Theorem 8.2, $\Sigma\lambda_j F_j >_2 F_1$ will be false for every $\lambda \in \Lambda_n$ if and only if some $u \in U_2$ has $E(u,F_1) \geq E(u,F_j)$ for $j = 2,\ldots,n$. In other words, F_1 is efficient in the sense of convex SSD when some utility function in U_2 gives F_1 as large an expected utility as every other basic distribution.

<u>Using additional information</u>. Even when basic alternatives cannot be eliminated by CSD analysis, it may be possible to make such eliminations when CSD is coupled with preference judgments obtained from the decision-maker. To illustrate this, consider the following "payoff" matrix:

		Probabilities			
		1/4	1/4	1/4	1/4
Acts	1	0	5	20	30
	2	0	0	30	30
	3	0	12	12	30
	4	5	5	20	20

Supposing that $u \in U_2$, the criterion of the preceding paragraph shows that no one act is inefficient in the sense of convex SSD. Suppose, however, that the decision-maker offers the judgment that he prefers act 3 to act 4. Then his utility function must satisfy

$$u(0) + 2u(12) + u(30) > 2u(5) + 2u(20),$$

and when this holds, it follows that an even-chance mixture of acts 2 and 3 dominates act 1. This can be computed directly from acts 1, 2, and 3, or else by noting that act 1 is probabilistically equivalent to an even-chance mixture of acts 2 and 4, so that $E(u,\text{act } 3) > E(u,\text{act } 4)$ implies

$$\frac{1}{2} E(u,\text{act } 3) + \frac{1}{2} E(u,\text{act } 2) > \frac{1}{2} E(u,\text{act } 4) + \frac{1}{2} E(u,\text{act } 2) = E(u,\text{act } 1).$$

Portfolio diversification. Convex stochastic dominance may also be useful in examining certain questions about diversification in portfolio analysis. Suppose, for example, that there are n basic securities. With Λ_n* the subset of Λ_n in which at least two λ_i are positive, let $\lambda \in \Lambda_n$* denote the diversified portfolio in which 100λ_i percent of total capital is invested in security i. Moreover, let F_λ be the probability distribution of gross returns for portfolio λ. It may then be said that diversification is never optimal for class U if and only if for every $\lambda \in \Lambda_n$* and every $u \in U$ there is a nondiversified portfolio with distribution function F_i (for one of the basic securities) such that $E(u,F_i) > E(u,F_\lambda)$. Applying Theorem 8.2, it follows that diversification is never optimal for class U if and only if for every $\lambda \in \Lambda_n$* there is a $\mu \in \Lambda_n$ such that

$$\sum_{i=1}^{n} \mu_i F_i >_U F_\lambda .$$

The next section comments briefly on one more area of potential application for CSD involving majority votes between risky decision alternatives.

Majority voting on risky alternatives. Continuing in the general context of Theorems 8.1 and 8.2, with $>>_U \, = \, >_U$ presumed for the latter, we consider situations in which m voters are to make pairwise decisions between risky decision alternatives on the basis of simple-majority voting. The set of all voting groups with utility functions in U will be represented by the set $\mathcal{V}$ of all nonempty finite sequences of functions in U, so that

$$\mathcal{V} = \{(u_1,\ldots,u_m)\colon \text{m is a positive integer and } u_k \in U \text{ for } k = 1,\ldots,m\}. \tag{8.10}$$

A typical voting group in $\mathcal{V}$ is $V = (u_1,\ldots,u_m)$ with m voters whose utility functions on C are respectively $u_1,u_2,\ldots,u_m$. Assuming that voters vote to maximize individual expected utility and abstain when their expected utilities for the two risky alternatives under consideration are equal, we define the following simple-majority relations on P for each $V \in \mathcal{V}$ with $V = (u_1,\ldots,u_m)$:

$$p \gtrsim_V q \text{ if and only if the number of } k \text{ in } \{1,\ldots,m\} \text{ for which } E(u_k,p) > E(u_k,q) \text{ is as great as the number of } k \text{ for which } E(u_k,q) > E(u_k,p); \quad (8.11)$$

$$p >_V q \text{ if and only if } p \gtrsim_V q \text{ and not } q \gtrsim_V p; \quad (8.12)$$

$$p =_V q \text{ if and only if } p \gtrsim_V q \text{ and } q \gtrsim_V p. \quad (8.13)$$

Thus a simple-majority relation $\gtrsim_V$, a strict simple-majority relation $>_V$, and a simple-majority tie relation $=_V$ are defined for each voting group $V \in \mathcal{V}$.

Within this setting we first consider the question of what must be true of probability measures $p_1,\ldots,p_n$, $q_1,\ldots,q_n$ in P so that $p_i \gtrsim_V q_i$ or $p_i >_V q_i$ for some $i \in \{1,\ldots,n\}$ for each voting group $V \in \mathcal{V}$. Since there appears to be no simple expression for this in terms of convex stochastic dominance based on U, except for smaller values of n, we focus on $n \in \{1,2,3\}$.

COROLLARY 8.2. *Suppose that* $p_1,p_2,p_3,q_1,q_2,q_3 \in P$ *with* P *and* U *satisfying the conditions set forth prior to* (8.1), *and let* $\mathcal{V}$ *be defined by* (8.10). *Then:*

$(1,\gtrsim_V)$. $p_1 \gtrsim_V q_1$ *for all* $V \in \mathcal{V}$ *if and only if* $p_1 \gtrsim_U q_1$;

$(1,>_V)$. $p_1 >_V q_1$ *for all* $V \in \mathcal{V}$ *if and only if* $p_1 >_U q_1$;

$(2,\gtrsim_V)$. *For every* $V \in \mathcal{V}$ *either* $p_1 \gtrsim_V q_1$ *or* $p_2 \gtrsim_V q_2$ *if and only if* $\alpha p_1 + (1-\alpha)p_2 \gtrsim_U \alpha q_1 + (1-\alpha)q_2$ *for some* $\alpha \in [0,1]$;

$(2,>_V)$. *For every* $V \in \mathcal{V}$ *either* $p_1 >_V q_1$ *or* $p_2 >_V q_2$ *if and only if either* $p_1 >_U q_1$ *or* $p_2 >_U q_2$;

$(3,\gtrsim_V)$. *For every* $V \in \mathcal{V}$ *either* $p_1 \gtrsim_V q_1$ *or* $p_2 \gtrsim_V q_2$ *or* $p_3 \gtrsim_V q_3$ *if and only if either* $\alpha p_1 + (1-\alpha)p_2 \gtrsim_U \alpha q_1 + (1-\alpha)q_2$ *for some* $\alpha \in [0,1]$ *or* $\beta p_1 + (1-\beta)p_3 \gtrsim_U \beta q_1 + (1-\beta)q_3$ *for some* $\beta \in [0,1]$ *or* $\gamma p_2 + (1-\gamma)p_3 \gtrsim_U \gamma q_2 + (1-\gamma)q_3$ *for some* $\gamma \in [0,1]$;

$(3, >_V)$. <u>For every</u> $V \in \mathcal{V}$ <u>either</u> $p_1 >_V q_1$ <u>or</u> $p_2 >_V q_2$ <u>or</u> $p_3 >_V q_3$ <u>if and only if either</u>

(a) $p_1 >_U q_1$ <u>or</u> $p_2 >_U q_2$ <u>or</u> $p_3 >_U q_3$,

<u>or</u>

(b) $\alpha p_1 + (1 - \alpha)p_2 >_U \alpha q_1 + (1 - \alpha)q_2$ <u>and</u> $\beta p_1 + (1 - \beta)p_3 >_U \beta q_1 + (1 - \beta)q_3$ <u>and</u> $\gamma p_2 + (1 - \gamma)p_3 >_U \gamma q_2 + (1 - \gamma)q_3$ <u>for some</u> $\alpha, \beta, \gamma \in [0,1]$.

Parts $(1, \geq_V)$ and $(1, >_V)$ follow immediately from Theorems 8.1 and 8.2, respectively, with $n = 1$, and like part $(2, >_V)$ of the corollary, they do not use the notion of <u>convex</u> stochastic dominance except in a degenerate form. The other three parts of Corollary 8.2 employ convex combinations of pairs of probability measures. Proofs of the several parts of the corollary are given for restricted versions of P and U in Fishburn (1974a), but these proofs apply also to the general context adopted in Section 8.1.1.

We now turn to the question of transitive simple majorities. Since $\geq_V$ or $>_V$ will be transitive on a subset Q of measures in P if and only if it is transitive on each three-element subset of Q, we shall confine our attention to an arbitrary subset $\{p,q,r\}$ of three probability measures in P.

THEOREM 8.3. <u>The simple-majority relation</u> $\geq_V$ <u>is transitive on</u> $\{p,q,r\}$ <u>for every</u> $V \in \mathcal{V}$ <u>if and only if either</u>

(a) <u>two of the three measures both strictly stochastically dominate</u> $(>_U)$ <u>the third</u> (<u>e.g.</u>, $p >_U r$ <u>and</u> $q >_U r$); <u>or</u>

(b) <u>two of the three measures are both strictly stochastically dominated by the third</u> (<u>e.g.</u>, $p >_U r$ <u>and</u> $p >_U q$); <u>or</u>

(c) <u>one of the measures equals a convex combination of the other two</u> (<u>e.g.</u>, $r = \alpha p + (1 - \alpha)q$ <u>for some</u> $\alpha \in [0,1]$).

Transitivity of $\geq_V$ on $\{p,q,r\}$ is equivalent to the transitivity of both $>_V$ and $=_V$ on $\{p,q,r\}$. The sufficiency of condition (a), (b), or (c) for transitivity of $\geq_V$ on $\{p,q,r\}$ follows easily from part $(1, >_V)$ of Corollary 8.2 and the fact that, for example, $E(u,r) = \alpha E(u,p) + (1 - \alpha)E(u,q)$ when $r = \alpha p + (1 - \alpha)q$. The necessity of condition (a), (b), or (c) for the transitivity of $\succsim_V$ for all $V \in \mathcal{V}$ is established by showing that $=_V$ is not transitive for some $V \in \mathcal{V}$ when none of (a), (b) or (c) holds, as is done in Fishburn (1974a:96-97).

Conditions on p, q, and r that are necessary and sufficient for the transitivity of $>_V$ on $\{p,q,r\}$ for all $V \in \mathcal{V}$ involve CSD in a non-degenerate way and are not so restrictive as the conditions of Theorem 8.3, because $>_V$ can be transitive when $\succsim_V$ is not transitive. The proof of the following theorem that is given in Fishburn (1974a) is based on part $(3,\succsim_V)$ of Corollary 8.2.

THEOREM 8.4. *The strict simple-majority relation* $>_V$ *is transitive on* $\{p,q,r\}$ *for every* $V \in \mathcal{V}$ *if and only if either a convex combination of two of the three measures stochastically dominates the third* [*e.g.*, $\alpha p + (1 - \alpha)q \succsim_U r$] *or a convex combination of two of the three measures is stochastically dominated by the third* [*e.g.*, $r \succsim_U \alpha p + (1 - \alpha)q$].

To illustrate Theorems 8.3 and 8.4, suppose F, G, and H are distribution functions on a real interval as illustrated in Figure 8-1. Then since $F >_1 \frac{1}{2} G + \frac{1}{2} H$, every voting group whose members have utility functions in U_1 must have transitive strict simple majorities on $\{F,G,H\}$ according to Theorem 8.4. In particular, since $F >_1 \frac{1}{2} G + \frac{1}{2} H$ implies $E(u,F) > \frac{1}{2} E(u,G) + \frac{1}{2} E(u,H)$, every voter who likes G as much as F must prefer F to H and hence must prefer G to H, so that $G >_V H$ whenever $G >_V F$. Similarly, $H >_V G$ whenever $H >_V F$. Therefore it is impossible to have a $>_V$ cycle such as $F >_V G >_V H >_V F$ or $F >_V H >_V G >_V F$. Moreover, if there were a voting group that had a non-transitive $>_V$, such as $F >_V H$, $H >_V G$, and $F =_V G$, then there would be another voting group W for which $>_W$ is cyclic in the form $F >_W H >_W G >_W F$, and a contradiction is obtained. Therefore $>_V$ must be transitive for every $V \in \mathcal{V}$.

Given $F >_1 \frac{1}{2} G + \frac{1}{2} H$ as in Figure 8-1, however, none of the conditions in Theorem 8.3 hold and therefore $=_V$ will be intransitive for some $V \in \mathcal{V}$. For example, a two-voter V in which one voter prefers F to G to H and the other prefers H to F to G (which are possible for utility functions in U_1) gives $F =_V H$, $H =_V G$, and $F >_V G$.

8.2 Statistical Tests for Stochastic Dominance

G. A. Whitmore

Earlier chapters referred to the difficulty of deciding on the basis of sample evidence whether one uncertain prospect dominates another. This section discusses tests of significance for the presence of stochastic dominance. Although the testing procedures are reasonably straightforward, in all but the simplest case the sampling distributions of the relevant test statistics are unknown. Remedial procedures for circumventing this deficiency are discussed. These are not wholly satisfactory, however, so statistical testing remains one of the important unsolved problems of stochastic dominance methodology.

8.2.1 Applications Requiring Statistical Tests

There are numerous applied contexts in which one may be interested in SD inferences; I will describe two typical contexts here.

Market efficiency. Suppose a financial market offers investors a choice between two prospects, $F(x)$ and $G(x)$. If investors with positive marginal utility for wealth have access to the market, prospects F and G should be mutually efficient in the FSD sense, i.e., neither $F >_1 G$ nor $G >_1 F$. An investigator who is interested in whether this efficiency requirement holds for the prospects might accumulate historical evidence in the form of sample distribution functions $\overline{F}(x)$ and $\overline{G}(x)$, respectively. He would then test whether one dominates the other by FSD. Similarly, the investigation of market efficiency might also look for evidence of second- or third-degree stochastic dominance by studying relevant historical evidence.

Decision simulation. Suppose an economic or financial model has been built of some investment decision problem in which the investment return distribution is a function of a decision variable d. It is desired to compare two decisions d_F and d_G by studying their respective return distributions $F(x)$ and $G(x)$. If the decisions are to be compared by means of a simulation of the investment model, then of necessity the comparison will be based on the sample distribution functions of the two decisions $\overline{F}(x)$ and $\overline{G}(x)$, respectively. One objective of the simulation might be to establish if one decision stochastically dominates the other (at the first-, second-, or third-degree levels).

8.2.2 Types of Inferential Error

As the foregoing applications illustrate, the statistical test of interest relates to the following set of alternative hypotheses about the population distribution functions F and G:

C_1: F dominates G (at the specified degree)
C_2: G dominates F (at the specified degree) (8.14)
C_3: Neither F nor G is dominant (at the specified degree)

Depending on the application, it may be desired to exercise control over various types of inferential error. In the market-efficiency application described above, for instance, the investigator may wish to conclude that the financial market offers a dominated prospect (i.e., the market is inefficient) only if strong evidence exists to support this conclusion. In this case he would want to control the probability of concluding C_1 or C_2 when in fact C_3 is true at a reasonably low level. On the other hand, in the simulation application, or in any setting where a decision-maker must make an investment choice, the approach might be one of establishing dominance in whatever direction the evidence lies. In this case the desire is to reduce the efficient set to as small a collection of prospects as possible. This would be done by keeping the probability of concluding C_3 when either C_1 or C_2 is true at quite a low level.

8.2.3 Distribution-free Test for FSD with Two Independent Samples

When testing a pair of sample distributions for the presence of dominance, the sample data generally are available in one of two forms. In one case the two sample distributions are based on independent random samples (possibly of different sizes). This might be the situation, for instance, in the simulation example mentioned earlier. In the second case the two sample distributions are based on statistically independent matched pairs of observations. An example of matched samples is the historical observation of rates of return from two securities. Under the random-walk hypothesis, it might be accepted that returns in different periods are independent, but in each period the returns for the two securities are matched (i.e., are statistically dependent) to the extent that common economic and social forces determine them.

Testing for FSD in the case of two independent samples is the only test situation for which there is adequate statistical theory. Since it may form a model for test procedures developed for other cases, it is presented here in full. The test is based on Kolmogorov-type statistics and has the following form.

Test procedure. Let $\overline{F}(x)$ and $\overline{G}(x)$ be two sample distributions based on independent random samples of sizes m and n from unknown population distributions F(x) and G(x), respectively. It is assumed that the underlying random variables are continuous. Define:

$$\begin{aligned} &\text{(a)} \quad T_{FG} = \sup_x[\overline{F}(x) - \overline{G}(x)] \\ &\text{(b)} \quad T_{GF} = \sup_x[\overline{G}(x) - \overline{F}(x)] \end{aligned} \qquad (8.15)$$

Note that T_{FG} and T_{GF} are simply the largest negative and positive vertical differences between the sample distribution functions of F and G.

The test statistics T_{FG} and T_{GF} may be used to test hypotheses C_1, C_2 and C_3 in the case of FSD by means of the following decision rule:

$$\begin{aligned} &\text{If } T_{FG} \leq A < T_{GF}, \text{ conclude } C_1 \\ &\text{If } T_{GF} \leq A < T_{FG}, \text{ conclude } C_2 \\ &\text{Otherwise, conclude } C_3 \end{aligned} \qquad (8.16)$$

Here A is a nonnegative action limit selected to control the probability of concluding C_1 or C_2 when C_3 is true. Specifically, A is selected so P(concluding $C_3 | F \equiv G) = 1 - \alpha$. When A is selected in this manner, the probability of concluding C_1 or C_2 when C_3 is true cannot exceed α. Note, of course, that C_3 is considered to be true if F and G are identical distributions, i.e., $F \equiv G$. Figure 8-2 displays decision rule (8.16) graphically. From the probability specification above it follows that P(concluding $C_1 | F \equiv G)$ = P(concluding $C_2 | F \equiv G)$ $= \alpha/2$.

Letting P(A) denote the probability of concluding C_3 when $F \equiv G$ with action limit A, it is easily seen that

$$P(A) = 1 + 2P(\max[T_{FG}, T_{GF}] \leq A) - P(T_{FG} \leq A) - P(T_{GF} \leq A) \quad (8.17)$$

For small values of m and n, a variety of tables are available from which the exact probability in (8.17) may be obtained. Note that T_{FG}, T_{GF}, and $\max[T_{FG}, T_{GF}]$ are the familiar two-sample Kolmogorov statistics. Owen (1962:431-436), for instance, gives probabilities for these statistics for equal sample sizes (n = m) up to 40. For large m and n, the following asymptotic approximation to P(A) is available [see Johnson and Kotz (1970:257) for the derivative asymptotic distributions].

$$P(A) \simeq -1 + 2 \exp[-2\left(\frac{mn}{m + n}\right)A^2] + 2 \sum_{j=-\infty}^{\infty} (-1)^j \exp[-2j^2\left(\frac{mn}{m + n}\right)A^2] \quad (8.18)$$

The rightmost term on the right-hand side of (8.18) is a widely tabulated sum [cf. Owen (1962:440)]. Table 8-1 contains values of P(A) for selected values of $[mn/(m + n)]^{\frac{1}{2}}A$ based on the asymptotic approximation.

Generally, two distinct values of A satisfy $P(A) = 1 - \alpha$. For this test procedure, the larger value of A is selected. (This will be demonstrated in the numerical example that follows shortly.) It should also be noted that if α is too large, no value of A can be

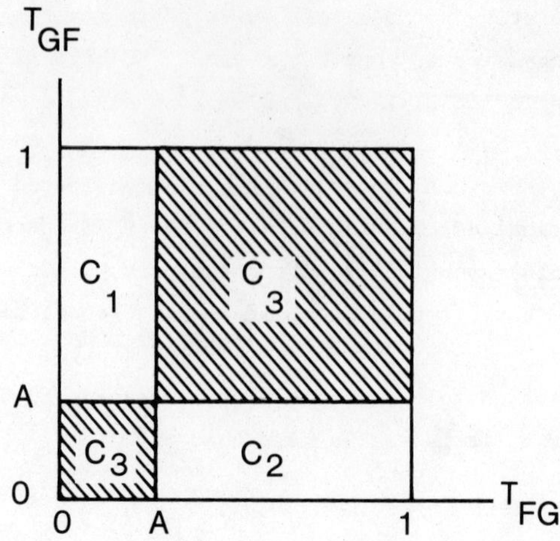

Figure 8-2. Decision Rule for Dominance Based on Maximum Differences T_{FG}, T_{GF}

found that will provide error control at this probability level. For large sample sizes, the asymptotic probabilities in Table 8-1 show that an action limit cannot be found for $\alpha > .7587$.

Decision rule (8.16) is not consistent against all alternatives satisfying hypotheses C_1 and C_2. For instance, for a test situation in which C_1 is true and α is fixed, it only can be guaranteed that

$$\lim_{n,m\to\infty} P(T_{FG} \leq A < T_{GF}) \geq 1 - .673\alpha. \qquad (8.19)$$

[Shown here is the best lower bound that is linear in α.]

<u>Numerical example</u>. Table 8-2 shows the computation of the test statistics T_{FG} and T_{GF} for two hypothetical independent random samples of size 15. In the table, X_i and Y_i denote the ordered sample observations from F and G, respectively. Values of $T_{FG} = 3/15$ and $T_{GF} = 2/15$ are obtained (see the asterisks in the table).

For small sample sizes, the error probability α cannot be controlled exactly at any specified level. Using Owen's Tables 15.3 and 15.4 for $n = m = 15$ and the probability relation (8.17), it is easily

Table 8-1
Values of P(A) for Selected Values of $[mn/(m+n)]^{1/2}A$ Based on Asymptotic Approximation (8.18).

$\left(\frac{mn}{m+n}\right)^{1/2} A$	.00	.01	.02	.03	.04	.05	.06	.07	.08	.09
0.5									.2413	.2425
0.6	.2449	.2487	.2536	.2598	.2669	.2751	.2842	.2941	.3048	.3162
0.7	.3282	.3407	.3537	.3671	.3809	.3950	.4093	.4237	.4384	.4531
0.8	.4678	.4825	.4972	.5119	.5264	.5409	.5551	.5692	.5832	.5969
0.9	.6103	.6236	.6366	.6493	.6618	.6740	.6859	.6975	.7089	.7199
1.0	.7307	.7411	.7513	.7612	.7708	.7801	.7891	.7978	.8063	.8145
1.1	.8224	.8301	.8374	.8446	.8515	.8581	.8645	.8706	.8766	.8823
1.2	.8878	.8930	.8981	.9030	.9077	.9121	.9164	.9206	.9245	.9283
1.3	.9319	.9354	.9387	.9418	.9449	.9478	.9505	.9531	.9557	.9580
1.4	.9603	.9625	.9646	.9665	.9684	.9702	.9718	.9734	.9750	.9764
1.5	.9778	.9791	.9803	.9815	.9826	.9836	.9846	.9855	.9864	.9873
1.6	.9880	.9888	.9895	.9902	.9908	.9914	.9919	.9924	.9929	.9934
1.7	.9938	.9942	.9946	.9950	.9953	.9956	.9959	.9962	.9965	.9967
1.8	.9969	.9971	.9973	.9975	.9977	.9979	.9980	.9982	.9983	.9984
1.9	.9985	.9986	.9987	.9988	.9989	.9990	.9991	.9991	.9992	.9993

shown that P(.4) = .924. Hence for $\alpha = .076$, A = .4. Since $T_{FG} = 3/15$ and $T_{GF} = 2/15$, it follows from decision rule (8.16) in this case that hypothesis C_3 should be accepted, i.e., that neither distribution dominates the other by FSD. If A were obtained from the asymptotic approximation for $\alpha = .076$, the value A = .467 would be obtained, which also leads to conclusion C_3.

<u>Test for unidirectional shift in probability mass</u>. Interestingly, the test described above for FSD is a distribution-free test for a unidirectional shift in the probability mass of a continuous random variable, where the shift may be of <u>any</u> form. For this reason the test may be useful in a number of contexts in which stochastic

Table 8-2
Numerical Example for Case of Two Independent Random Samples (First-Degree Stochastic Dominance)

X_i	Y_i	$15[\overline{F}(x) - \overline{G}(x)]$	X_i	Y_i	$15[\overline{F}(x) - \overline{G}(x)]$
-4.9		1 - 0 = 1	6.9		9 - 7 = 2
-4.7		2 - 0 = 2		7.0	9 - 8 = 1
	-4.2	2 - 1 = 1		7.7	9 - 9 = 0
-3.7		3 - 1 = 2	8.2		10 - 9 = 1
	-0.7	3 - 2 = 1		8.7	10 - 10 = 0
1.3		4 - 2 = 2	9.2		11 - 10 = 1
1.4		5 - 2 = 3*		9.6	11 - 11 = 0
	2.5	5 - 3 = 2		10.2	11 - 12 = -1
	3.0	5 - 4 = 1		10.7	11 - 13 = -2*
	4.7	5 - 5 = 0	11.8		12 - 13 = -1
5.7		6 - 5 = 1		12.4	12 - 14 = -2*
	6.4	6 - 6 = 0	12.9		13 - 14 = -1
6.6		7 - 6 = 1	13.3		14 - 14 = 0
	6.7	7 - 7 = 0		14.3	14 - 15 = -1
6.9		8 - 7 = 1	14.6		15 - 15 = 0

dominance (in a decision-theoretic sense) is of little or no direct interest but a test for a distribution shift is. For instance, in an analysis of experimental data, interest may lie in whether the response to one treatment tends to be stochastically larger than it is for another.

8.2.4 Other Distribution-free Two-sample Tests

As stated earlier, the test for FSD with two independent random samples is the only case for which complete statistical theory exists. Where interest lies in FSD but the two samples are matched, the test statistics and decision rule defined in (8.15) and (8.16), respectively, form the basis of an appropriate distribution-free test. Unfortunately the joint sampling distribution of the test statistics T_{FG} and T_{GF} is not known in this case. Certainly, the functional form of the sampling distribution, at least for small sample sizes, will be related to the type of statistical dependence that exists between the samples. Little else can be said on the matter at this time.

No distribution-free test for SSD exists presently for either the independent- or matched-samples cases. By analogy with the FSD case, it would appear that the relevant test statistics for such a distribution-free test are:

$$T_{FG} = \sup_x [\bar{F}^2(x) - \bar{G}^2(x)]$$

$$T_{GF} = \sup_x [\bar{G}^2(x) - \bar{F}^2(x)] \qquad (8.20)$$

Here $\bar{F}^2(x)$ and $\bar{G}^2(x)$ denote areas to the left of x under the sample distribution functions $\bar{F}$ and $\bar{G}$. A decision rule of the same form as (8.16) would be used to make an inference about SSD dominance.

As was the case for SSD, distribution-free tests for TSD do not now exist for either the independent- or matched-samples situations. A test procedure based on deviations such as those in (8.20), defined for $\bar{F}^3(x)$ and $\bar{G}^3(x)$ instead of $\bar{F}^2(x)$ and $\bar{G}^2(x)$, would be appropriate. [$\bar{F}^3(x)$ and $\bar{G}^3(x)$ denote areas to the left of x under the functions $\bar{F}^2(x)$ and $\bar{G}^2(x)$, respectively.] In the case of TSD, however, a complicating factor is the need to make a simultaneous inference about the relative magnitudes of the means of distributions F and G (see Theorem 2.3).

8.2.5 Test for SSD in Single-crossing Distribution Families

Although no distribution-free test procedures are yet available for SSD and TSD in the case of two independent random samples, it is possible to derive some test procedures for dominance in cases where both distributions are known to be from a common family. In Chapter 2, for instance, it was noted that SSD can be established by a simple procedure when the distributions are from a single-crossing family, i.e., a family in which any distinct pair of distributions coincide at most once in the interior of the joint sample space. Most of the important two-parameter families have this property including, inter alia, the normal, lognormal, gamma, and rectangular families. In the case of a single-crossing family, $F >_2 G$ if and only if (1) $\mu_F \geq \mu_G$ and (2) there exists x_0 in the joint sample space such that $G(x) \geq F(x)$ for all $x < x_0$. Hence the test for SSD reduces to a joint test on the means and lower tails of the candidate distributions.

Test procedure. Consider the case of two independent random samples of sizes m and n from distributions F(x) and G(x), respectively. F and G are assumed to be from the same single-crossing family of distributions. For m and n both reasonably large and distributions with finite variance, it is known that

$$T_1 = \frac{\bar{X} - \bar{Y}}{s(\bar{X} - \bar{Y})} \tag{8.21}$$

has an approximate normal distribution. Here $\bar{X}$ and $\bar{Y}$ denote the sample means for F and G, respectively, and $s(\bar{X} - \bar{Y})$ denotes the standard error of their difference. Therefore T_1 is a natural statistic for testing the difference $\mu_F - \mu_G$.

For the lower-tail condition, consider the following test statistic:

$$T_2 = \begin{cases} +t & \text{if } Y_t \leq X_1 < Y_{t+1} \\ -t & \text{if } X_t \leq Y_1 < X_{t+1} \end{cases} \tag{8.22}$$

where X_i and Y_i denote the ith order statistics of the samples from F and G, respectively. T_2 is simply a count of the number of sample values of one sample that do not exceed the first-order statistic of the other sample. (Since X and Y have been assumed to be continuous, tied values should not occur in the samples. If ties occur nevertheless, it is assumed here that they are broken randomly.)

For these two test statistics, the following decision rule can be employed to test the alternative hypotheses given in (8.14).

$$\text{If } T_1 > A \text{ and } T_2 > B_1, \text{ conclude } C_1.$$
$$\text{If } T_1 < -A \text{ and } T_2 < -B_2, \text{ conclude } C_2. \qquad (8.23)$$
$$\text{Otherwise, conclude } C_3.$$

Figure 8-3 contains a graphical display of the decision rule.

The action limits A, B_1, and B_2 in decision rule (8.23) are selected to control the probability of concluding C_1 or C_2 when C_3 is true. Specifically, the action limits are selected so P(concluding C_3 $|F \equiv G) = 1 - \alpha$. Clearly, if the action limits are selected in this manner, the probability of concluding C_1 or C_2 when C_3 is true cannot exceed α.

The joint sampling distribution of T_1 and T_2 for $F \equiv G$ depends on the specific single-crossing family under consideration. For reasonably large m and n, however, it is known that T_1 has an approximate standard normal distribution. Furthermore, T_1 and T_2 will be approximately independent for large m and n. Finally, the exact probabilities for T_2 (under the assumption that $F \equiv G$) are

$$P(T_2 \geq k) = \frac{\binom{m+n-k}{n-k}}{\binom{n+m}{n}} \text{ for } k = 1,2,\ldots,n \quad \text{and} \quad P(T_2 \leq -k) = \frac{\binom{m+n-k}{m-k}}{\binom{n+m}{n}} \text{ for } k = 1,2,\ldots,m \qquad (8.24)$$

The validity of (8.24) is shown by the following reasoning.[a] To begin, let the m + n observations be ranked in ascending order with each being identified as coming from the F distribution (the sample of size m) or the G distribution (the sample of size n). Under the assumption that $F \equiv G$, every permutation of the ordered m + n observations (identified as to parent population) is equally probable. Therefore if all k of the smallest observations are to be from distribution G (the sample of size n), then the probability $P(T_2 \geq k)$ is equivalent

---

[a] I thank J. K. Ord for his assistance in constructing this simple demonstration of (8.24), but responsibility for any error or ambiguity is mine alone.

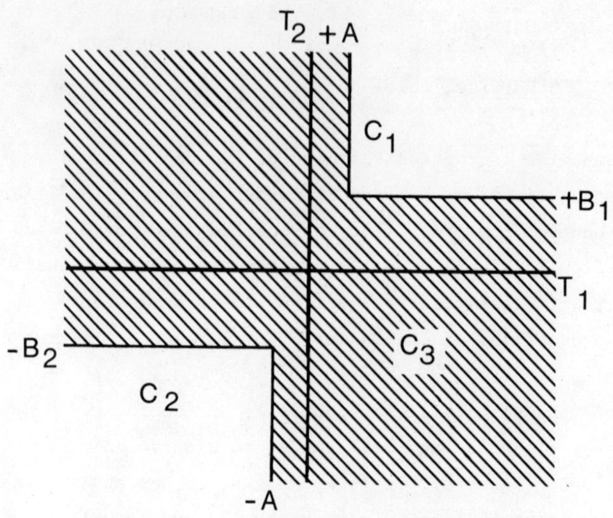

Figure 8-3. Decision Rule for Dominance in Single-crossing Distribution Families. T_1 denotes sample mean difference; T_2 denotes count of excess number of smallest observations

to the following hypergeometric probability:

$$\frac{\binom{n}{k}\binom{m}{0}}{\binom{n+m}{k}},$$

which when rearranged gives the first expression in (8.24). A similar argument gives the second expression in (8.24).

Values of $P(T_2 \geq k)$ for selected values of n, for the common case in which n = m, are given in Table 8-3. The asymptotic distribution of T_2 when n = m is given in (8.25) and is also tabulated in Table 8-3.

$$\lim_{n\to\infty} P(T_2 \geq k) = \left(\frac{1}{2}\right)^k \tag{8.25}$$

<u>Numerical example</u>. To illustrate decision rule (8.23), consider again the numerical example in Table 8-2. Let α = .20. By setting A = .22 and $B_1 = B_2 = 1$, it is seen that α is controlled at the desired level.

Table 8-3
Values of $P(T_2 \geq k)$ for Selected Values of n = m

	n					
k	5	10	15	20	30	∞
1	.5000	.5000	.5000	.5000	.5000	.5000
2	.2222	.2368	.2414	.2436	.2458	.2500
3	.0833	.1053	.1121	.1154	.1186	.1250
4	.0238	.0433	.0498	.0530	.0562	.0625
5	.0040	.0163	.0211	.0236	.0261	.0312
6		.0054	.0084	.0101	.0119	.0156
7		.0015	.0032	.0042	.0053	.0078
8		.0004	.0011	.0016	.0023	.0039
9		.0001	.0003	.0006	.0009	.0020
10			.0001	.0002	.0004	.0010

From the table, m = n = 15, $\overline{X} = 5.70$, $\overline{Y} = 6.60$, and $s(\overline{X} - \overline{Y}) = 2.11$, so $T_1 = -.43$. Also, $T_2 = -2$. Hence the decision rule leads to conclusion C_2, i.e., that G dominates F by SSD. Note that the sample size is actually quite small in this example, so the test should be viewed as only approximate.

8.3 Conclusion

G. A. Whitmore and M. C. Findlay

It is perhaps a contradiction in terms to write a conclusion to a book about stochastic dominance, since the theory and applications of this decision methodology are growing daily. However, this section gives us, the coeditors, an opportunity to reflect overtly on what has been done in this book and, more important, on what has not been done. It also gives us a chance to anticipate the nature of new developments that are almost certainly going to make stochastic dominance a subject of continuing interest to scholars and practitioners alike. It is convenient and we hope sensible to have our concluding remarks follow the basic organization of the book. Therefore we turn first to the theoretical foundations of stochastic dominance methodology.

8.3.1 Theoretical Foundations

Although it is altogether too easy to lose sight of the fact, the strength of SD methodology lies in the following construct. If in any decision making framework one has reason to restrict the set of applicable utility functions to some class U, then a rule exists (albeit perhaps a complex one) that divides available courses of action or prospects into two groups: those dominated by others and those not dominated by others (i.e., those that are efficient). The rule in such a situation has been called a "stochastic dominance rule" for utility class U.

The extreme simplicity of this theoretical construct is the source of both its strength and its weakness. It does require an acceptance of (1) the validity of a utility-theoretic approach to decision analysis and (2) the conditions that define U as the utility class of interest. The first requirement, although not universally accepted as an accurate description of real decision behavior, has been widely adopted as a model for decision analysis. The second requirement is the one that gives difficulty with the SD approach. If the utility class U is not defined with considerable care, then the corresponding stochastic dominance rule will be unsuitable in some respect. Either it will be too complex to operationalize or it will yield an efficient set that is too large or that has the wrong membership.

This latter difficulty has manifested itself in the cases of the SD rules for decreasing absolute risk-averse (DARA) utility functions and multivariate utility functions. The DSD rule for the DARA case, as noted in Chapter 2, can be implemented only by means of algorithmic procedures. Further progress with this rule would appear to require basic discoveries in mathematics itself. As Fishburn and Vickson point out in Appendix 2A, the class U_d of DARA utility functions is a convex cone in the space of real-valued functions and "appropriate integral representation theory for such cones appears to be undiscovered." Thus one development we may see emerge from foundational research in SD is a discovery in mathematical analysis that will provide applied researchers with a completely operational DSD rule. As Fishburn and Vickson also note, the same difficulty exists with representing the convex cone in the multivariate case. From an applied point of view, both in finance and economics, SD methodology will make a quantum leap forward when the DARA and multivariate SD rules are developed to the point where they can be used as standard tools in theoretical and empirical research.

Possibly the other great need in the foundations of SD methodology is the development of SD rules for other classes of utility functions. With respect to the utility function for wealth, none of the current strong SD rules (SSD, TSD, and DSD) accommodate the Friedman-Savage utility function that was postulated in their classic 1948 article. For this case U would have to contain increasing utility functions with both concave and convex sections (as well as others perhaps). A complaint frequently registered against the same strong SD rules is that their corresponding utility classes include members that exhibit "ludicrous" risk aversion. These members give rise to the "left-tail" problem in SD analysis because they invariably focus on the worst possible outcome of each prospect (see Section 2.14). Whether or not decision-makers with these utility functions actually exist, there is a need to translate this complaint into a precise analytical form and to develop the corresponding SD rule.

Utility analysis is used in many fields outside economics and business where attention focuses on nonmonetary decision consequences. Even in the areas of economics and business, many decision problems are formulated in nonmonetary terms. SD rules for nonmonetary decision problems are likely to be of theoretical and practical interest, and we can expect many such rules to appear in the not too distant future. In the health field, for instance, consequences defined in terms of length of hospital stay, duration of remaining life, and similar health variables are common. Research is required on the class U of utility functions that are relevant to risky decision problems involving such variables. To name other fields where decision problems are often posed in nonmonetary terms, consider geography (e.g., location preference), sociology of employment (e.g., job satisfaction), and education (e.g., educational achievement). One can speculate that SD methodology incorporating new concepts and rules will find numerous applications in these diverse fields.

8.3.2 Portfolio Selection and Financial Management

As the content of this book makes clear, portfolio selection and financial management problems have seen the greatest number of SD applications, perhaps because of uneven research interests but also because decision problems in this area lend themselves to the risk analysis that is basic to SD methodology. What has been especially attractive about the SD rules presently in use is their validity in terms of the expected utility principle and the fact that they require few assumptions about utility functions and, basically, no assumptions about outcome probability distributions. Hence SD is especially attractive if little is known about the beneficiary's utility function (a point we return to later) or if outcome distributions are not from one of the more mathematically tractable families (e.g., the normal family). Almost by definition, the SD rules represent the most general criteria of choice and include all others (such as the EV rule) as special cases.

SD methodology has a glaring weakness with respect to its use as an operational portfolio selection approach. At present, there does not exist an algorithm for the selection of SD efficient portfolio mixes. On the surface, this deficiency would appear to preclude the development of SD-based asset pricing and market efficiency theories. This latter aspect may be more apparent than real, however, since a capital market equilibrium model worked out on SD principles may not require an explicit portfolio selection algorithm. In essence, state preference constructs are weak-form dominance arguments. Therefore, if Jacob and Sharpe [cf. Sharpe (1970:Chapter 10)] can provide a market theory (i.e., their market similarity model) based on Arrow-Debreu state preference principles, it is not unreasonable to expect that a richer theory might emerge with the use of stronger SD concepts.

Returning to the algorithm problem itself, several theoretical and empirical studies reported in this book indicate that the mean-semivariance (ES_h) criterion may represent a partial solution to the problem. In the ES_h plane, the ES_h efficient set (for fixed h) is a subset of the TSD-efficient set and, consequently, is also a subset of the SSD efficient set. Furthermore, an algorithm for finding ES_h-efficient portfolios exists (see Burgess's discussion in Section 4.1 on this point). Future research on this topic is likely to provide interesting and useful results. One important issue that surely must be considered is whether the ES_h portfolio selection procedure can be extended to generate the actual SD-efficient sets, perhaps by computing the ES_h efficient sets for different values of h.

It has been claimed that an SD approach to portfolio selection requires exorbitant amounts of data for implementation, i.e., that the specification of complete joint probability distributions requires more inputs than the specification of, say, key parameters of these distributions. This concern is little more than a red herring. The data requirements of the SD approach are inherent to any formal analytical approach to decision-making and not the SD methodology itself. The data requirements differ between decision criteria only to the extent that some criteria employ more simplifying assumptions than others. In spite of this observation, it is still important to recognize that the data problem is real even if it is not unique to SD analysis. Future research is sure to be concerned with the problem of describing a decision-maker's expectations and constructing subjective outcome probability distributions. The difficulty of using ex post data as surrogates for ex ante data is central to this problem. The statistical inference problems that arise in working with SD data will receive our attention subsequently.

Aside from the portfolio problem (in its traditional setting), SD methodology is certain to find increased use in the area of financial management. Standard theoretical results probably can be extended or sharpened using SD concepts [cf. Baron's study of the Modigliani-Miller theorem (1974) as an example of what is possible]. No doubt theoretical insights into the pricing of financial instruments (such as warrants, options, leases, convertible securities, and debt obligations) will result from applications of SD methodology. Progress is also likely with the problem of selecting an optimal capital budget and financing program under conditions of risk. In Section 6.1 Bey and

Porter described the strong appeal that the SSD rule will have to managers responsible for selecting the optimal combination of real assets for the firm. They have noted also that the lack of an SD selection algorithm is likely to be less of a handicap in this problem setting than it is in the security portfolio setting. Brooks (1975) describes an application of SD methodology to selection of a debt issuance strategy.

Viewing the field of financial management more broadly, one can expect some exciting SD applications to such problems as selecting an optimum insurance program, incorporating the human wealth component into personal financial decision-making, and investigating group decision making under risk. The latter topic already has received the attention of Fishburn in Section 8.1, where the concept of convex stochastic dominance (CSD) is used to study a group choice among investment alternatives with simple majority voting. The phrase "remote client problem" has been used to describe the problem of decisions being taken by an individual or organization on behalf of another (the client). [The term "remote client" was borrowed from Hildreth (1963) where it is used to describe the user of a statistical report.] The word "remote" is appended to the phrase to stress the fact that the decision-maker may know very little about his client (specifically, about his utility function). The problem is pervasive in financial and investment management, where presumably firm managers make decisions for owners, investment fund operators make decisions for participating investors, etc. Research into the remote client problem is certain to draw on SD methodology and concepts, since by definition the SD efficient set represents the subset of best available prospects for all decision-makers in a given class.

8.3.3 Economic Theory and Analysis

There is a fine distinction between economic and finance applications of SD, so topics discussed in this and the foregoing sections could have been rearranged without much loss of coherence. This is particularly true of the topic of capital market efficiency, which interests both finance and economic scholars. Stochastic dominance methodology has already found application in the measurement of efficiency in various segments of the capital market (cf. Section 6.3) and applications along these and related lines are likely to be numerous in the future. Stated crudely, one might say that a market is inefficient if it offers two prospects, one of which dominates the other for all decision-makers in a particular class who have access to the market. Following Findlay's idea, which he presents in Section 6.3, the larger the class of utility functions for which the inefficiency exists, the greater the "degree" of inefficiency in the market. The SD rule corresponding to the class of utility functions is therefore the correct criterion to employ in judging whether that degree of inefficiency is present. Notwithstanding the theoretical appeal of this concept of market efficiency, a number of statistical and conceptual hurdles must be overcome. Section 8.2 has discussed some aspects of the statistical problem. One major conceptual problem is that of identifying a prospect that is offered by the market. Since nonmarketable components are not observed directly (the most elusive of these being human capital), one is left drawing conclusions about market inefficiency based on observations of isolated investment opportunities. Of course, this is not the only conceptual problem, so it is clear that SD methodology will encounter some difficult (but healthy) challenges in this area of inquiry.

Turning now to comparative statics (under conditions of risk), we recall the interesting sample of SD applications given by Hadar and Russell in Section 7.1. Stochastic dominance methodology seems ideally suited to analyzing the response of economic units to risk shifts in their environment. Further, because of the broad applicability of SD criteria, they should prove useful in constructing testable economic hypotheses.

To the list of economic applications considered in Chapter 7, one can add SD analyses of multiperiod consumption and investment, competitive bidding situations, the impact of tax policy on risk-taking [cf. Russell and Smith (1970)], the economics of search and information processing, and mixed strategies in economic games. To expand briefly on one of these topics, consider the problem of an individual searching for the lowest-priced item, highest-paid occupation, etc., in a marketplace. If F(x) is the probability distribution of values in the marketplace and a random sample of n of these values is selected in the search, then the probability distribution of, say, the largest value in the sample is $F(x)^n$. Obviously, adjustments must be made for the cost of search (i.e., of sampling) and other factors, but the problem reduces to one of choosing among prospects of the type $F(x)^n$ for various values of n [cf. Paroush (1974)]. It will be surprising if SD concepts cannot contribute to our general understanding of the search behavior of individuals under such conditions.

8.3.4 Statistical Theory and Analysis

Under this topic, concluding remarks fall into two natural categories: (1) remarks on the need to develop statistical procedures to cope with the new problems of inference that SD analysis (based on sample data) creates; and (2) remarks on the role that SD concepts can play within statistical decision theory itself.

As Whitmore stated in Section 8.2, a great deal of research must be devoted to the SD area by statisticians before empirical SD analysis will be on a solid statistical footing. The complicating features are: (1) the frequent presence of statistical dependence between samples and (2) the lack of distribution-free tests for shifts in distribution functions and integrals of distribution functions. Furthermore, because of the decision-theoretic approach implicit in SD analysis, it may make more sense to shift from a classical to a Bayesian framework when one wishes to consider ex ante beliefs of decision-makers that incorporate prior and random sample information.

In statistical decision theory, SD concepts would appear to have considerable potential for application. Although standard presentations of statistical decision theory acknowledge the importance of utility considerations, they rarely work with utility concepts explicitly. For instance, a Bayes strategy may be viewed as a maximum expected utility strategy, but the cost of sampling is usually incorporated in the analysis in a way that implies that utility is synonymous with a monetary outcome of the same magnitude. Consider the increased insight that would be obtained by embedding SD principles in a standard decision tree analysis, for instance, or in a determination of optimal sample size. To illustrate the potential of such research, consider the following.

The basic problem of point estimation is to decide which sample statistic S is the best estimator of a parameter θ. If $L(s,\theta)$ is the absolute monetary loss experienced when S = s and the parameter value is θ, then the distribution function defined by $P(-L(S,\theta) \leq x) = F_S(x)$ characterizes the goodness of estimator S. Obviously, an estimator S is better than an estimator T if $F_S(x)$ dominates $F_T(x)$ for an appropriate class of utility functions. Hence it is meaningful to speak of SD efficient estimators and it is of more than passing interest to see which estimators in standard problem settings are efficient in an SD sense [cf. Baron (1973)].

8.3.5 Closing Remarks

Imagination, time, and space limitations force us to close our discussion of stochastic dominance methodology, but in spite of this, in our opinion, it is a methodology with a potential to make substantial contributions to diverse fields of inquiry concerned with people as decision-makers. Whether one's interests lie in creating new knowledge or in applying existing knowledge, stochastic dominance appears to offer something for everybody. The developments to date in this subject have been ably chronicled by our coauthors in the preceding pages. Deficiencies have also been noted throughout. We hope that reading about the developments will induce some of our readers to join the hunt to eradicate the deficiencies.

Bibliography

Ali, Mukhtar M. 1974a. "Stochastic Dominance and Portfolio Analysis." Working paper, University of Kentucky, Lexington, Kentucky.

Ali, Mukhtar M. 1974b. "Stochastic Ordering and Kurtosis Measure." Journal of American Statistical Association, 69:543-545.

Arditti, F.D. 1971. "Another Look at Mutual Fund Performance." Journal of Financial and Quantitative Analysis, 6:909-912.

Arrow, K.J. 1965. Aspects of the Theory of Risk Bearing. Helsinki: Yrjo Jahssonin Saatio.

Arrow, K.J. 1971. Essays in the Theory of Risk Bearing. Chicago: Markham.

Arrow, K.J. 1974. "The Use of Unbounded Utility Functions in Expected Utility Maximization: Response." Quarterly Journal of Economics, 88:136-138.

Atkinson, A.B. 1970. "On the Measurement of Inequality." Journal of Economic Theory, 2:244-263.

Baron, David P. 1970. "Price Uncertainty, Utility, and Industry Equilibrium in Pure Competition." International Economic Review, 11:463-480.

Baron, David P. 1973. "Point Estimation and Risk Preferences." Journal of American Statistical Association, 68:944-950.

Baron, David P. 1974. "Default Risk, Homemade Leverage, and the Modigliani-Miller Theorem." American Economic Review, 64:176-182.

Baron, David P. 1976. "Probabilistic Expectations and Bidding Behaviour," in Bidding and Auctioning for Procurement and Allocation, ed. Yakov Amihud, New York: New York University Press, pp. 65-85.

Batra, R. and A. Ullah. 1974. "Competitive Firm and the Theory of Input Demand Under Uncertainty." Journal of Political Economy, 82:537-548.

Baumol, W.J. 1963. "An Expected Gain--Confidence Limit Criterion for Portfolio Selection." Management Science, 10:174-182.

Bawa, V.S. 1975. "Optimal Rules for Ordering Uncertain Prospects." Journal of Financial Economics, 2:95-121.

Bawa, V.S. and R.D. Willig. n.d. "Safety First and Stochastic Dominance." Working Paper, Bell Laboratories, Holmdel, N.J.

Bergstrom, H. 1952. "On Some Expansions of Stable Distributions." Arkiv. fur Matematik, 2:375-378.

Bernoulli, D. 1954. "Exposition of a New Theory of the Measurement of Risk." Econometrica, 22:23-36. Translation of a paper originally published in Latin in St. Petersburg in 1738.

Bertsekas, D.P. 1974. "Necessary and Sufficient Conditions for Existence of an Optimal Portfolio." Journal of Economic Theory, 8:235-247.

Bessler, S.A., and A.F. Veinott. 1966. "Optimal Policy for Dynamic Multi-Echelon Inventory Models." Naval Research Logistics Quarterly, 13:355-389.

Bey, Roger P. and R. Burr Porter. 1974. "A Test of Capital Budgeting Rules for Handling Risk." Paper presented at the Financial Management Association Meeting.

Bey, Roger P. 1976. "The Application of Stochastic Dominance and Mean-Semivariance to a Public Utility's Cost of Equity." Paper presented at the Financial Management Association Meeting.

Bierwag, G.O. 1974. "The Rationale of the Mean-Standard Deviation Analysis: Comment." American Economic Review, 64:431-433.

Blackwell, D. and M.A. Girshick. 1954. Theory of Games and Statistical Decisions. New York: Wiley.

Blattberg, R.C., and N.J. Gonedes. 1974. "A Comparison of the Stable Paretian and Student Distributions as Statistical Models for Stock Prices." Journal of Business, 47:244-280.

Booth, G.G. 1972. "Programming Bank Portfolios Under Uncertainty: An Extension." Journal of Bank Research, 2:28-40.

Borch, K. 1969. "A Note on Uncertainty and Indifference Curves." Review of Economic Studies, 36:1-4.

Borch, K. 1974. "The Rationale of the Mean-Standard Deviation Analysis: Comment." American Economic Review, 64:428-430.

Bradley, S.P. n.d. "Computing Optimal Portfolios Using Risk-Expected Return Efficient Points." Mimeographed, Graduate School of Business, Harvard University.

Bradley, S.P., and S.C. Frey, Jr. 1974. "Fractional Programming With Homogeneous Functions." Operations Research, 22:350-357.

Breen, W. 1968. "Homogeneous Risk Measures and the Construction of Composite Assets." Journal of Financial and Quantitative Analysis, 3:405-413.

Breiman, L. 1964. "Stopping-Rule Problems," in Applied Combinatorial Mathematics, ed. E.F. Beckenbach. New York: Wiley, 284-319.

Breiman, L. 1968. Probability. Reading, Mass.: Addison-Wesley.

Brooks, L.D. 1975. "Stochastic Dominance Tests for Selecting Acceptable Debt Issuance Strategies." Management Science, 22: 477-486.

Brumelle, S.L., and R.G. Vickson. 1975. "A Unified Approach to Stochastic Dominance," in Stochastic Optimization Models in Finance, ed. W.T. Ziemba and R.G. Vickson. New York: Academic Press, 101-113.

Burgess, Richard C. 1974. Alternative Measures of Risk and Ex Post Portfolio Performance. Unpublished doctoral dissertation, University of Kentucky.

Burgess, Richard C., and K.H. Johnson. 1976. "The Effects of Sampling Fluctuations on the Required Inputs of Security Analysis." Journal of Financial and Quantitative Analysis, 11:847-854.

Butterworth, J.E. 1972. "On the Comparative Value of Information Systems." Working Paper 152, Faculty of Commerce, University of British Columbia.

Cass, D., and J.E. Stiglitz. 1970. "The Structure of Investor Preferences and Asset Returns and Separability in Portfolio Allocation: A Contribution to the Pure Theory of Mutual Funds." Journal of Economic Theory, 2:122-160.

Charnes, A., and S.C. Littlechild. 1968. "Intertemporal Bank Asset Choice with Stochastic Dependence." System Research Memorandum 188, Technological Institute, Northwestern University.

Chipman, J. 1973. "On the Ordering of Portfolios in Terms of Mean and Variance." Review of Economic Studies, 40:167-190.

Cohen, K.J., and F.S. Hammer. 1966. Analytical Methods in Banking. Homewood, Ill.: Irwin.

Crane, D.B. 1971. "A Stochastic Programming Model for Commercial Bank Bond Portfolio Management." Journal of Financial and Quantitative Analysis, 6:955-975.

Dantzig, G.B. 1963. Linear Programming and Extensions. Princeton, N.J.: Princeton University Press.

Dantzig, G.B., and A. Madansky. 1961. "On the Solution of Two-Stage Linear Programs Under Uncertainty." Proceedings of the Fourth Berkeley Symposium on Mathematical Statistics and Probability, vol. I, ed. J. Neyman. Berkeley: University of California Press.

Davis, P.J., and P. Rabinowitz. 1967. Numerical Integration. Waltham, Mass.: Blaisdell.

de Beco, Jean Paul. 1973. "Effect of Diversification on Portfolio Risk Levels and Management Costs." Unpublished M.B.A. thesis, Faculty of Management, McGill University.

Diamond, P.A., and J.E. Stiglitz. 1974. "Increases in Risk and in Risk Aversion." Journal of Economic Theory, 8:337-360.

Drion, E.F. 1952. "Some Distribution-Free Tests for the Difference Between Two Empirical Cumulative Distribution Functions." Annals of Mathematical Statistics, 23:563-574.

El-Agizy, M. 1967. "Two Stage Programming Under Uncertainty with Discrete Distribution Functions." Operations Research, 15: 270-294.

Evans, John L., and S.H. Archer. 1968. "Diversification and the Reduction of Dispersion: An Empirical Analysis." Journal of Finance, 23, 761-769.

Fama, E.F. 1965a. "The Behavior of Stock Market Prices." Journal of Business, 38:34-105.

Fama, E.F. 1965b. "Portfolio Analysis in a Stable Paretian Market." Management Science, 11:404-419.

Fama, E.F. 1970a. "Efficient Capital Markets: A Review of Theory and Empirical Work." Journal of Finance, 25:383-417.

Fama, E.F. 1970b. "Multiperiod Consumption-Investment Decisions." American Economic Review, 60:163-174.

Fama, E.F., and R. Roll. 1968. "Some Properties of Symmetric Stable Distributions." Journal of the American Statistical Association, 63:817-836.

Fama, E.F., and R. Roll. 1971. "Paremeter Estimates for Symmetric Stable Distributions." Journal of the American Statistical Association, 66:331-338.

Feldstein, M.S. 1969. "Mean-Variance Analysis in the Theory of Liquidity Preference and Portfolio Selection." Review of Economic Studies, 36:5-12.

Feller, W. 1962. An Introduction to Probability Theory and Its Applications, vol. I. New York: Wiley.

Feller, W. 1966. An Introduction to Probability Theory and Its Applications, vol. II. New York: Wiley.

Feller, W. 1968. An Introduction to Probability Theory and Its Applications, vol. I, 3d ed. New York: Wiley.

Ferguson, T. 1955. "On the Existence of Linear Regression in Linear Structural Relations." University of California Publications in Statistics, 2:143-166.

Fiacco, A.V., and G.P. McCormick. 1968. Non-linear Programming: Sequential Unconstrained Minimization Techniques. New York: Wiley.

Findlay, M. Chapman III, and Alain A. Danan. 1975. "A Free Lunch on the Toronto Stock Exchange." Journal of Business Administration, 6:31-40.

Fishburn, Peter C. 1964. Decision and Value Theory. New York: Wiley.

Fishburn, Peter C. 1973. "Stochastic Dominance: Theory and Applications." Nato Conference Proceedings, Luxembourg.

Fishburn, Peter C. 1974a. "Majority Voting on Risky Investments." Journal of Economic Theory, 8:85-99.

Fishburn, Peter C. 1974b. "Separation Theorems and Expected Utilities." Utilities." Unpublished manuscript, the Pennsylvania State University.

Fishburn, Peter C. 1974c. "Convex Stochastic Dominance with Continuous Distribution Functions." Journal of Economic Theory, 7:143-158.

Fishburn, Peter C. 1974d. "Convex Stochastic Dominance with Finite Consequence Sets." Theory and Decision, 5:119-137.

Fishburn, Peter C., and R. Burr Porter. 1976. "Optimal Portfolios with One Safe and One Risky Asset: Effects of Changes in Rate of Return and Risk." Management Science, 22:1064-1073.

Fleming, W.H. 1964. Functions of Several Variables. Reading, Mass: Addison-Wesley.

Fletcher, R. 1969. Optimization. London: Academic Press.

Francis, Jack Clark, and Stephen H. Archer. 1971. Portfolio Analysis. Englewood Cliffs, N.J.: Prentice-Hall.

Frank, M., and P. Wolfe. 1956. "An Algorithm for Quadratic Programming." Naval Research Logistics Quarterly, 3:95-110.

Frankfurter, George M., and Herbert E. Phillips. 1975. "Efficient Algorithms for Conducting Stochastic Dominance Tests on Large Numbers of Portfolios: A Comment." Journal of Financial and Quantitative Analysis, 10:177-179.

Freund, R.J. 1956. "The Introduction of Risk into a Programming Model." Econometrica, 24:253-263.

Fried, J. 1970. "Bank Portfolio Selection." Journal of Financial and Quantitative Analysis, 5:203-227.

Friedman, M., and L.J. Savage. 1948. "The Utility Analysis of Choices Involving Risk." Journal of Political Economy, 56:279-304.

Gentry, James A., and K. Kim Moon. 1972. "Semi-Variance: A Risk Measure for Portfolio Manager of Insurance Companies." C.P.C.U. Annals, 319-337.

Glass, Gene V., and Julian C. Stanley. 1970. Statistical Methods in Education and Psychology. Englewood Cliffs, N.J.: Prentice-Hall.

Gnedenko, B.V., and A.N. Kolmogorov. 1954. Limit Distributions for Sums of Independent Random Variables. Reading, Mass.: Addison-

Wesley.

Gould, John P. 1974. "Risk, Stochastic Preference, and the Value of Information." Journal of Economic Theory, 8:64-84.

Hadar, J., and W.R. Russell. 1969. "Rules for Ordering Uncertain Prospects." American Economic Review, 59:25-34.

Hadar, J., and W.R. Russell. 1971. "Stochastic Dominance and Diversification." Journal of Economic Theory, 3:288-305.

Hadar, J., and W.R. Russell. 1972. "Optimal Portfolios Under Conditions of Interdependence." Working paper 5, Department of Economics, Southern Methodist University, Dallas, Texas.

Hadar, J., and W.R. Russell. 1974a. "Diversification of Interdependent Prospects." Journal of Economic Theory, 7:231-240.

Hadar, J., and W.R. Russell. 1974b. "Decision Making with Stochastic Dominance: An Expository Review." OMEGA, 2:365-377.

Hadar, J., and W.R. Russell. 1974c. "Stochastic Dominance in Choice Under Uncertainty," in Essays on Economic Behavior Under Uncertainty, ed. M. Balch, D. McFadden, and S. Wu. Amsterdam: North-Holland, pp. 133-150. Discussion by K. Hamada and G. Nordquist, pp. 150-156.

Hakansson, N.H. 1969. "Risk Disposition and the Separation Property in Portfolio Selection." Journal of Financial and Quantitative Analysis, 4:401-416.

Hakansson, N.H. 1970. "Optimal Investment and Consumption Strategies Under Risk for a Class of Utility Functions." Econometrica, 38: 587-607.

Hammond, John S. III. 1974. "Simplifying the Choice Between Uncertain Prospects Where Preference is Nonlinear." Management Science, 20:1047-1072.

Hanoch, G., and H. Levy. 1969. "The Efficiency Analysis of Choices Involving Risk." Review of Economic Studies, 36:335-346.

Hardy, G.H., J.E. Littlewood, and G. Polya. 1967. Inequalities, 2d ed. Cambridge, England: Cambridge University Press.

Hart, O.D., and D.M. Jaffee. 1974. "On the Application of Portfolio Theory to Depository Financial Intermediaries." Review of Economic Studies, 41:129-147.

Hewitt, E., and K. Stromberg. 1965. Real and Abstract Analysis. Berlin: Springer-Verlag.

Hicks, J. 1962. "Liquidity." Economic Journal, 72:787-802.

Hildreth, Clifford. 1963. "Bayesian Statisticians and Remote Clients." Econometrica, 31:422-438.

Hildreth, Clifford. 1974. "Expected Utility of Uncertain Ventures." Journal of the American Statistical Association, 69:9-17.

Hildreth, Clifford, and Leigh Tesfatson. 1974. "A Model of Choice with Uncertain Initial Prospect." Discussion Paper no. 74-38, Center for Economic Research, Department of Economics, University of Minnesota.

Hillier, F.S. 1969. The Evaluation of Risky Interrelated Investments. Amsterdam: North-Holland.

Hogan, William W., and James M. Warren. 1972. "Computation of the Efficient Boundary in the E-S Portfolio Selection Model." Journal of Financial and Quantitative Analysis, 7:1881-1896.

Hogan, William W., and James M. Warren. 1974. "Toward the Development of an Equilibrium Capital-Market Model Based on Semivariance." Journal of Financial and Quantitative Analysis, 9:1-11.

Hommes, Rudolf. n.d. "Partial Variance: Formulation of an Alternative Measure of Downward Risk in Relation to the Portfolio Selection Problem." Uncirculated working paper, University of Massachusetts, Amherst.

Huang, C.C., D.A. Wehrung and W.T. Ziemba. 1976. "A Homogeneous Distribution Problem with Applications to Finance." Management Science, 23:297-304.

Ilano, A.R. 1969. "Alternative Approaches to Risk in Portfolio Analysis." Unpublished doctoral dissertation, University of California, Berkeley.

Jean, William H. 1975a. "Comparison of Moment and Stochastic Dominance Ranking Methods." Journal of Financial and Quantitative Analysis, 10:151-161.

Jean, William H. 1975b. "A General Class of Three-Parameter Risk Measures: Comment." Journal of Finance, 30:224-225.

Jean, William H., and Billy P. Helms. 1974. "Mutual Fund Performance 1966-1972." Working paper, University of Alabama.

Jensen, Michael C., ed. 1972a. Studies in the Theory of Capital Markets. New York: Praeger.

Jensen, Michael C. 1972b. "Capital Markets: Theory and Evidence." Bell Journal of Economics and Management Science, 3:357-398.

Johnson, Keith H., and Richard C. Burgess. 1974. "The Effects of Sample Sizes on the Accuracy of EV and SSD Efficiency Criteria." Working paper, University of Kentucky, Lexington.

Johnson, Norman I., and Samuel Kotz. 1970. Distributions in Statistics: Continuous Univariate Distribution, vol. II. Boston: Houghton Mifflin.

Joy, O. Maurice, and R. Burr Porter. 1974. "Stochastic Dominance and Mutual Fund Performance." Journal of Financial and Quantitative Analysis, 9:25-31.

Karlin, S. 1960. "Dynamic Inventory Policy with Varying Stochastic Demands." Management Science, 6:231-258.

Kuhn, H.W., and A.W. Tucker. 1951. "Nonlinear Programming," in Proceedings of the Second Berkeley Symposium on Mathematical Statistics and Probability, ed. J. Neyman. Berkeley: University of California Press, pp. 481-492.

La Cava, Gerald J. 1974. "Improving the Mean-Variance Criterion Using Stochastic Dominance." Working paper, Georgia State University.

Lehmann, E.L. 1955. "Ordered Families of Distributions." Annals of Mathematical Statistics, 26:399-419.

Leland, H.E. 1968. "Saving and Uncertainty: The Precautionary Demand for Saving." Quarterly Journal of Economics, 82:465-473.

Leland, H.E. 1972. "On the Existence of Optimal Policies Under Uncertainty." Journal of Economic Theory, 4:35-44.

Levari, D., J. Paroush and B. Peleg. 1975. "Efficiency Analysis for Multivariate Distributions." Review of Economic Studies, 42: 87-91.

Levy, Haim. 1973a. "Stochastic Dominance Among Log-Normal Prospects." International Economic Review, 14:601-614.

Levy, Haim. 1973b. "Stochastic Dominance, Efficiency Criteria, and Efficient Portfolios: The Multi-Period Case." American Economic Review, 63:986-994.

Levy, Haim. 1974. "The Rationale of the Mean-Standard Deviation Analysis: Comment." American Economic Review, 64:434-441.

Levy, Haim. 1976. "Multi-period Consumption Decision Under Conditions of Uncertainty." Management Science, 22:1258-1267.

Levy, Haim, and Giora Hanoch. 1970. "Relative Effectiveness of Efficiency Criteria for Portfolio Selection." Journal of Financial and Quantitative Analysis, 5:63-76.

Levy, Haim, and Yoram Kroll. 1976. "Stochastic Dominance with Riskless Assets." Journal of Financial and Quantitative Analysis, 11:743-777.

Levy, Haim, and Jacob Paroush. 1974a. "Multi-period Stochastic Dominance." Management Science, 21:428-435.

Levy, Haim, and Jacob Paroush. 1974b. "Toward Multivariate Efficiency Criteria." Journal of Economic Theory, 7:129-142.

Levy, Haim, and Marshall Sarnat. 1970. "Alternative Efficiency Criteria: An Empirical Analysis." Journal of Finance, 25:1153-1158.

Levy, Haim, and Marshall Sarnat. 1971a. "Two-period Portfolio Selection and Investors' Discount Rates." Journal of Finance, 26:757-761. 761.

Levy, Haim, and Marshall Sarnat. 1971b. "A Note on Portfolio Selection and Investors' Wealth." Journal of Financial and Quantitative Analysis, 6:639-642.

Levy, Haim, and Marshall Sarnat. 1972. Investment and Portfolio Analysis. New York: Wiley.

Levy, P. 1954. Theorie de l'Addition des Variables Aleataires, 2d ed. Paris: Gauthier Villurs.

Lintner, J. 1965. "The Valuation of Risk Assets and the Selection of Risky Investments in Stock Portfolios and Capital Budgets." Review of Economics and Statistics, 47:13-37.

Lippman, Steven A. 1972. "Optimal Reinsurance." Journal of Financial and Quantitative Analysis, 7:2151-2155.

Loeve, M. 1963. Probability Theory, 3d ed. Princeton, N.J.: Van Nostrand.

Lorie, James H. 1966. "Some Comments on Recent Quantitative and Formal Research on the Stock Market." The Journal of Business, 39:107-110.

Mandelbrot, B. 1963a. "The Variation of Certain Speculative Prices." Journal of Business, 36:394-419.

Mandelbrot, B. 1963b. "New Methods of Statistical Economics." Journal of Political Economy, 61:421-440.

Mandelbrot, B., and H.M. Taylor. 1967. "On the Distribution of Stock Price Differences." Operations Research, 15:1057-1062.

Mangasarian, O.L. 1969. Nonlinear Programming. New York: McGraw-Hill.

Mantell, Edmund H. 1974. "A Statistical Estimator in a Problem of Stochastic Dominance." Management Science, 21:326-329.

Mao, James C.T. 1970a. "Survey of Capital Budgeting: Theory and Practice." Journal of Finance, 25:349-360.

Mao, James C.T. 1970b. "Models of Capital Budgeting, E-V vs. E-S." Journal of Financial and Quantitative Analysis, 4:657-675.

Mao, James C.T., and John F. Brewster. 1970c. "An ES_h Model of Capital Budgeting." Engineering Economist, 15:103-121.

Markowitz, Harry M. 1952. "Portfolio Selection." Journal of Finance, 7:77-91.

Markowitz, Harry M. 1959. Portfolio Selection: Efficient Diversification of Investments. New York: Wiley.

Marschak, J. 1950. "Rational Behavior, Uncertain Prospects and Measurable Utility." Econometrica, 18:111-141.

Martin, John D., and Robert C. Klemkosky. 1974. "Stochastic Dominance and Mutual Fund Performance: Some Additional Evidence." Working paper, Virginia Polytechnic Institute and State University.

Masse, Pierre. 1962. Optimal Investment Decisions: Rules for Action and Criteria for Choice. Englewood Cliffs, N.J.: Prentice-Hall.

Menezes, C.F., and D.L. Hanson. 1970. "On the Theory of Risk Aversion." International Economic Review, 11:481-487.

Merton, R.C. 1972. "An Analytic Derivation of the Efficient Portfolio Frontier." Journal of Financial and Quantitative Analysis, 7:1851-1872.

Meyer, J. 1975. "Increasing Risk." Journal of Economic Theory, 11:119-132.

Miller, M., and M. Scholes. 1972. "Rates of Return in Relation to Risk: A Re-examination of Some Recent Findings," in Studies in the Theory of Capital Markets, ed. M. Jensen. New York: Praeger, pp. 47-78.

Nantell, T.J., and James B. Greene. 1974. "Semivariance Portfolio Theory and Capital Market Theory." Paper presented at the Western Finance Meetings, Las Vegas, Nev.

Neumann, J. von, and O. Morgenstern. 1947. Theory of Games and Economic Behavior, 2d ed. Princeton, N.J.: Princeton University Press.

Norgaard, Richard L. 1974. "An Examination of the Yields of Corporate Bonds and Stocks." Journal of Finance, 29:1275-1286.

Owen, D.B. 1962. Handbook of Statistical Tables. Reading, Mass.: Addison-Wesley.

Paroush, Jacob. 1974. "Investment Policy Under Uncertainty: The Case of Search in a Multimarket Situation." Southern Economic Journal, 41:397-403.

Pearson, E.S., and H.O. Hartley. 1954. Biometrika Tables for Statisticians, vol. I. Cambridge, Mass.: Harvard University Press.

Petty, William J., David F. Scott, and Monroe M. Bird. 1975. "The Capital Expenditure Decision-Making Process of Large Corporations." Engineering Economist, 20:159-172.

Philippatos, George C., and Nicolas Gressis. 1975. "Conditions of Equivalence Among E-V, SSD, and E-H Portfolio Selection Criteria: The Case for Uniform, Normal and Lognormal Distributions." Management Science, Applications Series, 21: 617-625.

Phillips, Herbert E. 1974. "Stochastic Dominance Efficiency Criteria: A Theory in Search of Methodology," Working paper, Temple University, Philadelphia.

Porter, R. Burr. 1971. "A Comparison of Stochastic Dominance and Mean Variance Portfolio Models." Paper presented at the Financial

Management Association Meeting.

Porter, R. Burr. 1973a. "An Empirical Comparison of Stochastic Dominance and Mean-Variance Portfolio Selection Criteria." Journal of Financial and Quantitative Analysis, 8:587-608.

Porter, R. Burr. 1973b. "Capital Budgeting." Unpublished manuscript, the Pennsylvania State University.

Porter, R. Burr. 1974a. "Semivariance and Stochastic Dominance: A Comparison." American Economic Review, 64:200-204.

Porter, R. Burr. 1974b. "A Comparison of Stochastic Dominance and Stochastic Programming." OMEGA, 2:105-117.

Porter, R. Burr, and Roger P. Bey. 1974. "An Evaluation of the Empirical Significance of Optimal Seeking Algorithms in Portfolio Selection." Journal of Finance, 29:1479-1490.

Porter, R. Burr, and Kenneth Carey. 1974. "Stochastic Dominance as a Risk Analysis Criterion." Decision Sciences, 5:10-21.

Porter, R. Burr, and Jack E. Gaumnitz. 1972. "Stochastic Dominance vs. Mean-Variance Portfolio Analysis: An Empirical Evaluation." American Economic Review, 62:438-446.

Porter R. Burr, and Roger C. Pfaffenberger. 1975. "Efficient Algorithms for Conducting Stochastic Dominance Tests on Large Numbers of Portfolios: Reply." Journal of Financial and Quantitative Analysis, 10:181-185.

Porter, R. Burr, James R. Wart, and Donald L. Ferguson. 1973. "Efficient Algorithms for Conducting Stochastic Dominance Tests on Large Numbers of Portfolios." Journal of Financial and Quantitative Analysis, 8:71-81.

Praetz, P.D. 1972. "The Distributions of Share Price Changes." Journal of Business, 45:49-55.

Pratt, J.W. 1964. "Risk Aversion in the Small and in the Large." Econometrica, 32:122-136.

Press, S.J. 1967. "A Compound Events Model for Security Prices." Journal of Business, 40:317-335.

Press, S.J. 1968. "A Modified Compound Poisson Process with Normal Compounding." Journal of the American Statistical Association, 63:607-613.

Press, S.J. 1970. "A Compound Poisson Process for Multiple Security Analysis," in Random Counts in Scientific Work, ed. G. Patil. University Park: Pennsylvania State University Press.

Press, S.J. 1972a. Applied Multivariate Analysis. New York: Wiley.

Press, S.J. 1972b. "Multivariate Stable Distributions." Journals of Multivariate Analysis, 2:444-463.

Press, S.J. 1972c. "Estimation in Univariate and Multivariate Stable Distributions." Journal of the American Statistical Association, 67:842-846.

Press, S.J. n.d. "Stable Distributions: Probability, Inference and Applications in Finance--A Survey, and a Review of Recent Results." Proceedings of the NATO Advanced Study Institute on Statistical Distributions. Boston, Mass.: D. Reidel (forthcoming).

Pye, G. 1966. "The Value of the Call Option on a Bond." Journal of Political Economy, 84:200-205.

Pye, G. 1967. "Portfolio Selection and Security Prices." Review of Economics and Statistics, 49:111-115.

Quirk, J.P., and R. Saposnik. 1962. "Admissibility and Measurable Utility Functions." Review of Economic Studies, 29:140-146.

Ramsey, F.P. 1931. "Truth and Probability," in The Foundations of Mathematics and Other Logical Essays. London: Kegan Paul.

Rao, C.R. 1965. Linear Statistical Inference and Its Applications. New York: Wiley.

Rentz, William F., and Richard B. Westin. 1973. "Comparative Statics for Portfolios with No Safe Asset." Working paper no. 73-34, Graduate School of Business, University of Texas, Austin.

Rentz, William F. and Richard B. Westin. 1975. "A Note on First-Degree Stochastic Dominance and Portfolio Composition." Management Science, 22:501-504.

Richter, M.K. 1959. "Cardinal Utility, Portfolio Selection and Taxation." Review of Economic Studies, 27:152-166.

Rockafellar, R.T. 1970. Convex Analysis. Princeton, N.J.: Princeton University Press.

Ross, S.M. 1970. Applied Probability Models with Optimization Applications. San Francisco: Holden-Day.

Rothschild, Michael, and Joseph E. Stiglitz. 1970. "Increasing Risk I: A Definition." Journal of Economic Theory, 2:225-243.

Rothschild, Michael, and Joseph E. Stiglitz. 1971. "Increasing Risk II: Its Economic Consequences." Journal of Economic Theory, 3: 66-84.

Rothschild, Michael, and Joseph E. Stiglitz. 1973. "Some Further Results on the Measurement of Inequality." Journal of Economic Theory, 6:188-204.

Rubinstein, M. 1973. "The Fundamental Theorem of Parameter-Preference Security Valuation." Journal of Financial and Quantitative Analysis, 8:61-69.

Russell, William R., and Paul E. Smith. 1970. "Taxation, Risk-Taking, and Stochastic Dominance." Southern Economic Journal, 36:425-433.

Ryan, T.M. 1974. "Unbounded Utility Functions in Expected Utility Maximization: Comment." Quarterly Journal of Economics, 88: 133-135.

Samuelson, P.A. 1967a. "General Proof That Diversification Pays." Journal of Financial and Quantitative Analysis, 2:1-13.

Samuelson, P.A. 1967b. "Efficient Portfolio Selection for Pareto-Levy Investments." Journal of Financial and Quantitative Analysis, 2: 107-122.

Sandmo, A. 1969. "Capital Risk, Consumption, and Portfolio Choice." Econometrica, 37:586-599.

Sandmo, A. 1971. "On the Theory of the Competitive Firm Under Price Uncertainty." American Economic Review, 61:65-73.

Sarnat, Marshall. 1972a. "The Gains from Risk Diversification on the London Stock Exchange." Journal of Business Finance, 4:54-63.

Sarnat, Marshall. 1972b. "A Note on the Prediction of Portfolio Performance from Ex Post Data." Journal of Finance, 27:903-906.

Sarnat, Marshall. 1974. "Capital Market Imperfections and the Composition of Optimal Portfolios." Journal of Finance, 29: 1241-1253.

Schneeweiss, H. 1968. "Note on Two Dominance Principles in Decision Theory." Unternehmensforschung, 12:213-216.

Sharpe, William F. 1963. "A Simplified Model for Portfolio Analysis." Management Science, 9:277-293.

Sharpe, William F. 1964. "Capital Asset Prices: A Theory of Market Equilibrium Under Conditions of Risk." Journal of Finance, 19: 425-442.

Sharpe, William F. 1966. "Mutual Fund Performance." Journal of Business, 39:119-138.

Sharpe, William F. 1970. Portfolio Theory and Capital Markets. New York: McGraw-Hill.

Sherman, S. 1951. "On a Theorem of Hardy, Littlewood, Polya, and Blackwell." Proceedings of the National Academy of Sciences, 37: 826-831.

Stapleton, R. 1971. "Portfolio Analysis, Stock Valuation and Capital Budgeting Decision Rules for Risky Projects." Journal of Finance, 26:95-117.

Stiglitz, J.E. 1969. "Book review of: Aspects of the Theory of Risk Bearing by Kenneth J. Arrow." Econometrica, 37:742-743.

Stone, B.K. 1970. Risk, Return and Equilibrium. Cambridge, Mass.: MIT Press.

Stone, M.H. 1948. "The Generalized Weirstrass Approximation Theorem." Mathematics Magazine, 21:167-184.

Strassen, V. 1965. "The Existence of Probability Measures With Given Marginals." Annals of Mathematical Statistics, 36:423-439.

Swalm, Ralph O. 1966. "Utility Theory--Insights into Risk Taking." Harvard Business Review, 54:123-136.

Tesfatsion, Leigh. 1974. "Stochastic Dominance and the Maximization of Expected Utility." Discussion Paper no. 74-37, Center for Economic Research, Department of Economics, University of Minnesota, Minneapolis.

Tilley, R.P.R., and Samuel Eilon. 1975. "Stochastic Dominance for Ranking Ventures." OMEGA, 3:177-184.

Tobin, J. 1958. "Liquidity Preference as Behavior Towards Risk." Review of Economic Studies, 25:65-86.

Tobin, J. 1965. "The Theory of Portfolio Selection," in The Theory of Interest Rates, ed. F.H. Hahn and F.P.R. Brechling. London: Macmillan.

Topkis, D.M., and A.F. Veinott, Jr. 1967. "On the Convergence of Some Feasible Direction Algorithms for Nonlinear Programming." Journal of the Society for Industrial and Applied Mathematics: Control, 5:268-279.

Tsiang, S.C. 1974. "The Rationale of the Mean-Standard Deviation Analysis: Reply and Errata for Original Article." American Economic Review, 64:442-450.

Vickson, R.G. 1975a. "Stochastic Dominance Tests for Decreasing Absolute Risk Aversion I: Discrete Random Variables." Management Science, Application Series, 21:1438-1446.

Vickson, R.G. 1975b. "Separation in Portfolio Analysis," in Stochastic Optimization Models in Finance, ed. W.T. Ziemba and R.G. Vickson. New York: Academic Press, pp. 157-170.

Vickson, R.G. 1977. "Stochastic Dominance Tests for Decreasing Absolute Risk Aversion II: General Random Variables." Management Science, Application and Theory Series, 23:478-489.

Wagner, H.M. 1969. Fundamentals of Operations Research. Englewood Cliffs, N.J.: Prentice-Hall.

Weingartner, H. Martin. 1963. Mathematical Programming and the Analysis of Capital Budgeting Problems. Englewood Cliffs, N.J.: Prentice-Hall.

Weingartner, H. Martin. 1966. "Capital Budgeting of Interrelated Projects: Survey and Synthesis." Management Science (Series A), 12:485-516.

Whitmore, G.A. 1970. "Third-Degree Stochastic Dominance." American Economic Review, 60:457-459.

Whitmore, G.A. 1975. "The Theory of Skewness Preference." Journal of Business Administration, 6:13-20.

Whitmore, G.A. 1976. "The Mortality Component of Health Status Indexes." Health Services Research, 11:370-390.

Williams, Edward E., and M. Chapman Findlay III. 1974. Investment Analysis. Englewood Cliffs, N.J.: Prentice-Hall.

Winer, B.J. 1971. Statistical Principles in Experimental Design, 2d ed. New York: McGraw-Hill.

Wolfe, Philip. 1959. "The Simplex Method for Quadratic Programming." Econometrica, 27:382-398.

Zangwill, W.J. 1969. Nonlinear Programming: A Unified Approach. Englewood Cliffs, N.J.: Prentice-Hall.

Zeckhauser, R., and E. Keeler. 1970. "Another Type of Risk Aversion." Econometrica, 38:661-665.

Ziemba, William T. 1970. "On the Computation of Optimal Portfolios." Working Paper 52, University of British Columbia, Vancouver.

Ziemba, William T. 1972. "Solving Nonlinear Programming Problems with Stochastic Objective Functions." Journal of Financial and Quantitative Analysis, 7:1809-1827.

Ziemba, William T. 1974a. "Choosing Investments When the Returns Have Stable Distributions," in Mathematical Programming in Theory and Practice, ed. P.L. Hammer and G. Zoutendijk, Amsterdam: North-Holland, pp. 443-482.

Ziemba, William T. 1974b. "Stochastic Programs with Simple Recourse," in Mathematical Programming in Theory and Practice, ed. P.L. Hammer and G. Zoutendijk. Amsterdam: North-Holland, pp. 213-273.

Ziemba, William T., and J.E. Butterworth. 1975. "Bounds on the Value of Information in Uncertain Decision Problems." Stochastics, 1:361-378.

Ziemba, William T., C. Parkan, and F.J. Brooks-Hill. 1974. "Calculation of Investment Portfolios with Riskfree Borrowing and Lending." Management Science, 21:209-222.

Ziemba, William T., and R.G. Vickson. 1975. Stochastic Optimization Models in Finance. New York: Academic Press.

Zoutendijk, G. 1960. Methods of Feasible Directions. Amsterdam: Elsevier.

Zoutendijk, G. 1970. "Nonlinear Programming Computation Methods," in *Integer and Nonlinear Programming*, ed. J. Abadie. Amsterdam: North-Holland.

Index

Index

List of Contributors

Roger P. Bey, Department of Finance, College of Business and Public Administration, University of Missouri

Richard C. Burgess, Graduate School of Business Administration, Washington University

Peter C. Fishburn, School of Business Administration, The Pennsylvania State University

Josef Hadar, Department of Economics, Southern Methodist University

R. Burr Porter, School of Business Administration, Southern Methodist University

William R. Russell, Department of Economics, Southern Methodist University

Raymond G. Vickson, Department of Management Sciences, Faculty of Engineering, University of Waterloo

W.T. Ziemba, Faculty of Commerce and Business Administration, University of British Columbia

About The Editors

G.A. Whitmore is professor in the Faculty of Management, McGill University. He received the B.Sc. at the University of Manitoba and the M.S. and Ph.D. from the University of Minnesota. Professor Whitmore's interests are concentrated primarily in applied statistics and decision analysis, and he is the author of a number of articles and books on these subjects, with particular interest in applications in finance, economics and health care.

M.C. Findlay, III received the Ph.D. from the University of Texas at Austin and has taught at the Universities of Houston, Connecticut, and McGill. He is currently professor of finance and chairman, Department of Finance and Business Economics at the University of Southern California. He was coauthor, with E.E. Williams, of *An Integrated Analysis for Managerial Finance* (1970) and *Investment Analysis* (1974), and has published numerous articles in journals including the *Journal of Finance* and the *Journal of Finance and Quantitative Analysis.* He is also an associate editor of *Financial Management.*